THE WAY OF SYMBOL DICTIONARY

2017 EDITION

COLETTE TOACH

www.ami-bookshop.com

The Way of Dreams and Visions Symbol Dictionary 2017 Edition

ISBN-10: 1-62664-149-8
ISBN-13: 978-1-62664-149-5

5663 Balboa Ave #416,
San Diego,
California 92111,
United States of America

3rd Edition August 2016
2nd Edition June 2013
1st Printing July 2011

Published by **Apostolic Movement International, LLC**
E-mail Address: admin@ami-bookshop.com
Web Address: www.ami-bookshop.com

Colette Thanks...

The Lord Jesus Christ

His tender love, infinite patience and overwhelming Grace continues to get me up each morning. He never ceases to remind me of how special I am to Him as well as how dependent I am on Him. Lord, when people see me, may they see you.

My Wonderful Husband, Craig Toach

In the midst of my rebellion, it was Craig who got born again and ran full steam ahead for God – dragging me along with him at first. Had it not been for his inspiration and continued support, I would not have the strength to climb each mountain God led me to overcome. Together we continue to take the land for the Lord.

Craig, I suspect the next mountain is just up ahead. Ready for another adventure?

My Unwavering Team and Spiritual Children

If it was not for my team and spiritual kids, you would not be holding this book in your hands right now. Not only did they continue to nag me to put these symbols to print, but they were the first to use them, promote them and then ask for more.

There is no greater honor for a leader than to have such powerful men and women by your side who are not only committed to you 100% but to the Lord Jesus 110%.

My heart belongs to each one of you. Nothing matters more than seeing you rise up and take your place. I challenge you to outdo me!

Word of Caution:

One of the reasons it took me so long to publish this book is a concern that the symbols in it would replace your hunger to seek the truth for yourself.

This book is not the Bible. It is simply an interpretation according to what God has shown me. Weigh each symbol and compare it to your own revelation of the Lord Jesus.

Let my illustrations and explanations spark off ideas and further revelation in your life. Above all, may each symbol draw you closer to your loving Savior, Jesus Christ.

He is speaking to you right now, can you hear His whisper in your heart? Whether in your dreams or in your visions, He is talking to you.

He is drawing you closer to Him. May each page in this book be another step closer into His presence and perfect will for your life.

Colette Toach

Apostle and CEO
Apostolic Movement International

www.apostolic-movement.com

Please note: All reference of AMI throughout this book refers to Apostolic Movement International.

CONTENTS

INTRODUCTION

DREAM INTERPRETATION MADE SIMPLE

Introduction – Dream Interpretation Made Simple

I was an unusual kid. I was the only one on the block who had the ability to interpret dreams. No, I was not super spiritual, I was just blessed enough to be born into the right home. From a young age I understood the basics of dream interpretation as my father taught them to me.

Every day friends would come to me with their dreams. I could easily explain what they meant or if they had no meaning at all.

I guess what I am trying to say here is that learning to interpret dreams is easy enough even for a child to master. It does not take years of study or deep psychological training. In fact, with a few simple principles, you will be well on your way to interpreting dreams for yourself and for others.

No one is just born knowing how to interpret dreams. It is something that is taught and anyone can learn it. In this book, I am going to get you started and by the end, you will have in your hands the tools you need to interpret dreams starting the next time you wake up with a dream that you remember!

The Basics

Everyone dreams. Both Christians and unbelievers dream. So what makes the difference between the dream of a believer and of an unbeliever? The difference lies in the indwelling of the Holy Spirit. While everyone dreams, not everyone receives messages from the Lord like we can as believers.

So the first building block of understanding dream interpretation is to understand that dreams are a natural function of the human soul. There are dreams where we are expressing our desires or living out the conflicts we have faced during the day.

These are a natural function of the soul that lets out all of the tensions and pent up emotions that we have held back. Even an animal has dreams like this. Just watch a puppy sleeping and you can only imagine what he must be dreaming. Twitching and making sucking sounds, you can imagine that he is dreaming of fighting with his brothers and sisters for a chance to make it to mom!

The Purging Dream

Well humans experience the same sort of thing. When you have dreams of accomplishing magnificent things or living out your fantasies you are experiencing what is called a purging or cleansing dream. Everyone has them and they are by far the most common.

In these dreams you will have intense emotions and can even wake up crying or laughing. These dreams do not have an interpretation. They are just an expression of your feelings and desires.

The Garbage Dream

Not all of our dreams are purging though. It is a fact that in today's society we are confronted with more input than any of our ancestors. Daily we are being bombarded from all sides. From TV, news media and radio to what you hear from the pulpit enter your mind at an alarming rate. With so many voices shouting at you all of the time, if we did not dream, I can imagine that we would have an input overload!

Garbage dreams take care of that. They work through everything you have been putting into your mind. In many ways it is a way of your mind sorting through the "junk." Everyone has these kinds of dreams; however, as believers you will find that if you start getting into the Word, you will have more of these dreams.

This is a good sign! It means that your mind is throwing out the junk and making space for the Word of God that you are now putting into your spirit.

These dreams are quite simple to identify. They have lots and lots of scene changes and are quite confusing. They do not have a single message and can contain many different characters and symbols. They can also include real situations and things that you are experiencing right now. They will reflect the circumstances that are surrounding you, the things you have been reading and the conversations you have had.

These dreams have no meaning. Just think of them as a "sorting pool" for your mind.

The Internal Dream

This is the first category of dream that starts to bring a message. Both believers and unbelievers can have them. These dreams are conditioned by your life experience, culture and gender. Because of this, not every symbol means the same thing to everyone.

Internal dreams are fairly short, have a single message and you are the star character in the dream.

So when a friend came to me and shared a dream, just by using the principles below, I could give a pretty good interpretation. It was literally, child's play.

Let me share it with you. So are you ready for it?

INTERPRETATION IN 4 EASY STEPS

In my book *The Way of Dreams and Visions* I give a full teaching on each step you need to take. (Visit www.ami-bookshop.com to get your hands on it.)

However, over here I am just going to give you a quick summary. This should be enough to whet your appetite and give you what you need to interpret your dreams right away!

1. DISCERN THE SPIRIT

Before you can even begin digging into the symbols of your dream, you need to discern if your dream or vision is positive or negative. You will notice that in this dictionary, that I make it even easier for you by separating the positive and negative interpretations for each symbol.

Only you would be qualified to determine if the object or person in your dream is a positive influence or a negative one. Consider your emotions and how you felt waking up from the dream.

Discerning this single difference will change the entire outcome of your interpretation. Say for example you dream of getting married. If in the dream it is a positive experience and you wake up feeling good, then this could indicate that the Lord is drawing you into a new relationship.

However, if you have a dream of being married and in the dream you feel afraid, negative or things turn out badly, the interpretation is completely different! The interpretation would be that you are joining yourself to something that is not of the Lord.

2. GOOD IS GREAT. BAD IS, WELL... BAD.

This alone can turn your interpretation right around. If I dream that my house is being torn down, it can be positive or negative. If your house is being torn down so that something bigger can be built, it means that you are in a process of growing spiritually and mentally in your life right now.

However, if your house is being bombed by terrorists or torn down by a storm, it means that you are facing some severe attack in your life right now and that you are falling apart.

Do you see what I mean? In both cases the house is a symbol of your life. It does not speak of your actual house and you do not need to fear a sudden invasion of terrorists, okay?

So pick up your pen and paper and before even delving into the symbols, ask yourself this simple question and remember:

1. Are the symbols in this dream positive or negative?
2. Everything is Symbolic

Every character, object and building in your dream is symbolic of a part of yourself and your life. This one principle alone will change your entire view of dream interpretation.

It is a common mistake for people to misinterpret the people and objects in their dreams as the real thing. This is a big mistake! If I dream of Aunty Pat throwing a cream pie in my face, I certainly do not have to fear visiting her for Thanksgiving!

It is symbolic and Aunty Pat is a picture of a part of me. If Aunty pat is an aggressive woman that tends to dominate others, then she could represent my will in this dream. Identifying the characters in your dream is the very first step to gaining an understanding of what your dreams are saying.

In fact, just by identifying the dream category and then identifying the symbols, you will already have an idea of what your dream is speaking about.

This goes for buildings, animals or any kind of object in your dream. If you dream that your house is being broken into, you do not need to rush out and buy more insurance. Your house is simply a picture of your life.

This opens up a whole new world to you! There are many common symbols that crop up in our dreams, and I will give you some interpretations for them later on. In fact, in this DAV Symbol Dictionary, I supply a comprehensive list of all the characters and scenarios, and their interpretations.

3. Everything is About You

It's your dream. It's your life. It's about YOU! Another big mistake that people make is that they think if they dream of someone else that the dream is for that person. It's a bit ridiculous actually. If you dream that your co-worker falls pregnant, I would certainly not rush to them and announce the good news!

Not only will you be wrong, but every time you head for the coffee machine the other co-workers might suddenly find a reason to be somewhere else...

Hmmm, I get the feeling that some folks reading this might have made this mistake a few times. Not to worry though! There is hope.

Keep in mind that because the characters in your dream are a picture of yourself, that the dream is a message for you. These dreams are a depiction of what is going on inside of you right now and often also refer to events that have happened in the past.

Either way, you are the star of this show and it's all about YOU!

4. Identifying the Message

It is important to remember that an internal dream has a single message. If your dream has lots of characters and scene changes, then it is a garbage dream and does not have an interpretation. By identifying the symbols in your dreams and determining whether they are given in a positive or negative context, you are armed with everything you need to identify the message.

For more training, you are welcome to sign up at our Fivefold Ministry School (http://www.fivefold-school.com/)

I will be using the entries from this dictionary so that you can see exactly how to use it correctly.

BEYOND THE BASICS

I have only covered the dream categories that apply to everyone. Believers experience way more than this because of the Holy Spirit within them. They can also experience internal prophetic dreams and also external prophetic dreams.

These dreams are a direct message from the Lord where the characters and objects in their dreams are symbolic of something in the Word!

For example, very often your father in such a dream is a picture of God the Father. Your mother could be a picture of the Church and your spouse could represent your recreated spirit in Christ or your relationship with the Lord Jesus.

HOW TO USE THIS BOOK

You will notice that I have divided each symbol under two headings: Character Specific and Universal Symbol.

The reason for this is, that in your dreams your symbols will be mixed with the Word, your real life and what God is telling you right now.

However, when it comes to visions, the message becomes a lot clearer and precise according to the Word. Everyone dreams, even unbelievers, but unbelievers are not given visions from the Lord for the purpose of ministry!

I have further divided the symbols into positive and negative. Once you have discerned the spirit of your dream or vision, the interpretation will become clearer.

When I do not give individual headings for dreams and visions separately, then the definition is meant for both.

CHARACTER SPECIFIC AND UNIVERSAL SYMBOLS

There are so many symbols to interpret that it would take another hundred books to list them all. Instead, what I am going to do in this chapter, is pick out ten of the most popular symbols that I come across all of the time.

These symbols are ones that I find coming up in my own dreams or in the dreams of others I minister to.

Jesus used parables to illustrate spiritual principles to the people of His day. He used pictures that were common to them. In the same way, the Lord will still use symbols in our dreams that are common to us. The Lord still speaks to us in parables, even in our dreams.

These symbols are also ones that span across cultures and denominations. So by arming yourself with some good knowledge here, you will also start picking up the wisdom you need to minister effectively.

It is good to know that each of these symbols can have double meanings, just like I shared in the previous chapter. They can have an internal and a prophetic interpretation, depending on their context.

THE CHARACTER SPECIFIC SYMBOL

There are symbols in your dream that are specific to you. These are symbols such as your pet cat "Fluffy," your mother, father, and eldest child.

These symbols have a specific meaning to you and will change for someone else. This is true even in a family. In your dreams, your father could speak of the Lord, while for your sister, he could speak of the flesh – it all really depends on your relationship with your father.

An internal dream is full of character specific symbols. It might interest you to know that you can even have "internal visions." In other words, visions that are specific just to you.

KEY PRINCIPLE

A character specific symbol can only be applied to you, because the interpretation is based on your personal convictions and not on those of the Word.

The interpretation of these symbols change depending on your gender, culture, upbringing and personal emotions.

THE UNIVERSAL SYMBOL

In contrast, universal symbols can be applied to every believer, because these can be found in the Word.

KEY PRINCIPLE

Universal dream and vision symbols can be applied to every gender, culture and denomination, because their source is the Word of God. The Word never changes.

It might interest you to know that many of them have the same meaning even in visions. For now, determine what they mean to you and also make a note of what their universal meaning is (based on the Word).

A GOOD GUIDELINE TO FOLLOW

When a symbol from your dream can be traced to something directly from the Word, then it is a universal symbol that can be used for any culture or denomination.

If the symbol in your dream can only be found in your life, it relates to you and your present prayer burdens. So for example, if you dream of your father, the interpretation cannot be used in the life of another believer!

The dream relates to what you are going through right now. That symbol is yours personally. To dream of a key, giving birth, or of a cross, is different. These symbols come directly from the Word and they will have the same meaning for every believer.

These universal symbols will also have the same interpretation in visions.

Using the Index

Although I have given main headings for each symbol, I cover a variety of aspects to that single symbol. I suggest using the Index at the back of this book to search for your symbol.

Interpretation is a very exciting realm and one I cover in detail in *The Way of Dreams and Visions* book. Although you can use this dictionary independently, I often assume you have read *The Way of Dreams and Visions* and are familiar with its principles. If you want to not only understand the symbols in this book, but move onto interpreting the dreams of others, as well. I suggest you get your hands on it.

PART 1

SYMBOLS STARTING IN A

PART 1

SYMBOLS STARTING IN A

AIRPLANE

The vehicle for your ministry. It will be fast, effective and will reach new heights.

CHARACTER SPECIFIC SYMBOL

POSITIVE
As with visions, dreaming of a large jumbo jet could speak of a public ministry or, certainly an expansion into something more public. If you are dreaming of flying the plane, this could speak of a promotion.

NEGATIVE
If you have a fear of flying, then dreaming of being in a plane could represent having to face your fears.

Also if you dream that you are flying this plane but that you are not meant to, that someone else should be flying it, this could indicate that you are taking charge of things that are not yours to take charge of.

In a spiritual context it could speak of you taking things out of the Lord's hands. The solution of course is to let go and put God back in control of your life.

UNIVERSAL SYMBOL

POSITIVE
I have come to see airplanes in dreams and visions as a representation of ministry. The larger the plane, the larger the ministry. The larger the plane, the more members and helpers are needed on board to aid the ministry.

At one time the Lord kept showing each of the AMI (Apostolic Movement International) team as fighter planes flying in formation.

A fighter plane is a weapon of war. It is fast and effective, and if you want to find a good comparison for it in Scripture, you would use the eagle or the bird of prey as an example.

The fighter plane speaks of a ministry of intercession and warfare. It speaks of surveying the land on behalf of the body of Christ and overcoming the enemy in it - of going ahead and scouting the area for any attacks.

This speaks of a very aggressive ministry that is more personal in nature and will cripple the kingdom of darkness! Consider this passage:

Speaking of war:

Jeremiah 49:22 Behold, He shall come up and fly like the eagle, and spread His wings over Bozrah; the heart of the mighty men of Edom in that day shall be like the heart of a woman in birth pangs.

See also: Car, Vehicles

ALIEN

1. *People that are strange or foreign to you.*
2. *When you are foreign or on the outside looking in.*
3. *Monsters or creatures that are demonic in nature.*

Positive: To be set apart
Negative: To feel like you are on the outside looking in

CHARACTER SPECIFIC SYMBOL

POSITIVE
If you are the alien in your dreams, or if you feel on the outside looking in, then the Lord has separated you from others. You will not be like them for you are called out, "separated" and set apart for His work.

If you dream that you are overcoming monsters or aliens, then it indicates that you are gaining a victory in your life. If the alien is a childhood fear, then it indicates that you have overcome that fear.

1 John 4:4 You are of God, little children, and have overcome them, because He who is in you is greater than he who is in the world.

NEGATIVE
Speaks of the works of the enemy, of deception - of things appearing different to what they really are.

If you keep dreaming of monsters, aliens or other strange creatures, consider what you are feeding into your spirit.

If you keep watching movies with this content, then your spirit is only throwing out what you keep feeding into your mind.

If these dreams are coming out of nowhere, then consider that you are experiencing demonic attack in your life.

Check your bedroom for any contaminated objects or reading materials that you have brought in lately. Also look at any new relationships or reading materials that you got into at the time the dreams began.

Internal prophetic dream:

*Psalms 69:8 I have become a **stranger** to my brothers, and an alien to my mother's children.*

You are feeling an outcast. Alienated from others in your family, your church or your surroundings.

Universal Symbol

POSITIVE
Anyone who is called to the fivefold ministry is separated just as Apostle Paul was. To see someone set apart is an indication of a ministry calling.

Jesus Himself was sent alone to the wilderness to face pressures for his call. The Church is in the world, but not of it. We are a peculiar people and separated onto God.

NEGATIVE
If you see someone alone and upset at a certain age, this could indicate a hurt that occurred to them in the past. They require inner healing.

See also: Demons

Alligator / Crocodile

A spirit of destruction.

Character Specific Symbol

POSITIVE AND NEGATIVE
You would need to determine your view on alligators. For many people they will speak of fear, however in regions where these animals are common, they could easily represent a part of a person's life.

For example, an alligator in your dream could represent a region that is famous for having alligators. What is the first thing you think of when you see an alligator? For must of us, it would represent caution, the enemy or fear.

However, if you run an alligator farm, it would speak of your business or workplace!

Universal Symbol

NEGATIVE
It's not often that I interpret a vision where an alligator is seen as a positive picture. In most cases it is seen as an agent of destruction and theft.

It resembles the work of the enemy, and if I see it the spirit in vision I class it as a power demon. (See *Demons*, for levels of demonic power).

The teeth of the animal represent a tearing and a violent attack. Daniel describes a creature with many teeth. This is what he had to say:

> *Daniel 7:19 Then I wished to know the truth about the fourth beast, which was different from all the others, exceedingly dreadful, with its teeth of iron and its nails of bronze, which devoured, broke in pieces, and trampled the residue with its feet;*

See also: Animal, Bear, Demons

ALOES

Aloes were used as a perfume in bible times. Woman used it to perfume themselves, but it was also used for the embalming of the dead, as in the case of Jesus.

Aloes also have a healing quality so can also represent a season of rest and healing.

Positive: A season of rest and healing
Negative: Seduction and distraction

POSITIVE

> *Song of Songs 4:14 Spikenard and saffron, calamus and cinnamon, with all trees of frankincense, myrrh and **aloes**, with all the chief spices: 16...Let my beloved come to his garden and eat its pleasant fruits.*

This speaks of the love of romance and the intimate relationship the bride has with the groom. It refers to the Lord Jesus and our relationship with Him as His bride.

NEGATIVE

> *Proverbs 7:17 I have perfumed my bed with myrrh, **aloes**, and cinnamon*

This speaks of seduction of the world. To trust more in the medical systems of the world than you do in the Lord to heal you.

See also: Balm, Perfume, Plants

ALTAR

To pay the price for the call of God on your life.

Positive: To "burn your bridges"
Negative: Idolatry

Character Specific Symbol

POSITIVE
It could be that the Lord is asking you to give something up. The point of a sacrifice is to yield something up that is valuable to you. The most famous example of this in the Word is Abraham and Isaac.

If you feel that the Lord has been asking you to give something up and then you dream of an altar, it is a confirmation of what He is telling you. It is time to give that thing up to Him and let go.

> *Philippians 4:18 Indeed I have all and abound. I am full, having received from Epaphroditus the things sent from you, a sweet- smelling aroma, an acceptable* ***sacrifice****, well pleasing to God.*

NEGATIVE
If you are having nightmares or negative dreams of ritual sacrifice, then there is an indication that something is wrong in your spiritual life.

Has there been a history of witchcraft or false religion in your family generations? If so, then the Lord is exposing a generational curse that needs to be dealt with.

If you wake from your dreams in fear, then this dream has no interpretation. It is a demonic attack.

Universal Symbol

POSITIVE
Used as a prophetic symbol:

> *Exodus 20:24 An* ***altar*** *of earth you shall make for Me, and you shall sacrifice on it your burnt offerings and your peace offerings, your sheep and your oxen. In every place where I record My name I will come to you, and I will bless you.*

This speaks of death to the flesh. It speaks of giving up those things that hinder you in your work; of laying on the altar your sins and iniquity.

It also speaks of "burning your bridges," as Elisha did when he burned his cattle and the plow upon the altar.

I often see the altar of God when I enter the Throne Room in praise and worship. It is golden, and I imagine it is a duplicate of what Moses built in the ark of the covenant.

At one time I saw upon it a small lamb that had been slaughtered. The Lord placed the broken and bleeding lamb from that altar and placed it in my hands.

He said very clearly to me, "Take my blood and give it to my people. Go heal my people!"

At other times when I have seen an altar the Lord has said to me, "I need you to sacrifice those things that are important to you, so that I might take you to the next level." I have often been asked to "sacrifice my Isaac" on the altar of God.

NEGATIVE
May speak of idol worship and demonic rituals that were also prevalent in that time. To burn something on an altar that you should not be, speaks of "giving up" things that the Lord never asked of you in the first place. Determine if it is the Lord calling you to let something go, or if your flesh just wants to "be rid of something" and you are forcing His hand.

See also: Baptism, Bath, Blood, Death

AMBUSH

To be surrounded and overcome.

Positive: To engage in counter insurgence warfare
Negative: To be trapped by a lie

POSITIVE
If you are the one setting up an ambush, then the picture would be a positive one. It would indicate that you are in control and that the Lord is setting up a plan to thwart the work of the enemy in your life.

It is a fantastic picture of COIN (counter insurgence) warfare. To dream or have a vision of setting up an ambush means the Lord wants you to attack the enemy in a specific way – it means engaging in "undercover" spiritual warfare and not attacking him openly where you are obvious. (I recommend the book *Prophetic Counter Insurgence* for more teaching on COIN warfare)

> *Jeremiah 51:12 Lift up a banner against the walls of Babylon! Reinforce the guard, station the watchmen,* ***prepare an ambush****! The LORD will carry out his purpose, his decree against the people of Babylon. (NIV)*

NEGATIVE
If it is another group setting up an ambush against you, this would indicate that there is deception in the camp and that you must be careful of what lies ahead.

Such a dream or vision would be a warning vision to make you aware of the enemy that lies in wait to kill and destroy.

See also: Army, Attacked, Chasing, Trap, War

Ancestor

The generations that have gone before you.

Positive: Blessings passed down
Negative: Curses passed down

Character Specific Symbol

POSITIVE
If the ancestor you dream of is someone you knew personally and had a good influence in your life, then they would represent something positive concerning yourself.

A man whose dream I interpreted dreamed of his grandmother (now deceased) in which she was telling him that he needed to go out and face his fears.

In reality, this same relative brought him to the Lord and was a good influence in his life. In his dream, she represented the Holy Spirit, leading him to a place of victory in his life.

NEGATIVE
If you dream of deceased ancestors whom you knew "visiting" you in your dreams, then there is likely some demonic bondage you are still under.

The Word is very clear on communicating with the dead, and unfortunately many still receive "spirits" who come in the name of their long-lost dead ones.

If you dream of ancestors that you had never met, they could represent things of the past that you are still holding on to and need to let go of.

Perhaps you had sin or bad experiences in your past and you cannot let them go. Dreaming of past family could indicate to you that there are sins, hurt or guilt, in your past that are still part of your present.

Ancestors could also speak of generational traditions and morals that control you. As you have come to the Lord, perhaps you are struggling to break free of the sinful habits of your old life.

Dreaming of interacting with ancestors could mean that you need to move on in your new life with Christ.

Universal Symbol

POSITIVE
If seen in vision, it can represent past generations that walked in the power and blessing of the Lord.

The blessing of the parents is passed on to the children! I have often seen how children will carry on the spiritual blessing of their parents.

I knew one person whose father was a Christian minister, but he died while she was young. Even though she was brought up in a non-Christian home, there was still a draw to the Lord she could not understand. Later in life she was born again and Spirit-filled in the privacy of her own home.

Now with a powerful calling on her life, it is clear to see that the generational blessing and calling that was on her father, is now prevalent in her life also.

Blessings can also be carried down the generations. The good news is that while curses are passed to the third and fourth generations, blessings carry to a thousand!

> *Psalms 105:8 He remembers His covenant forever, the word which He commanded, for a thousand* ***generations****.*

NEGATIVE
It is most likely however, that if the Lord reveals past ancestors to you in a prophetic dream or vision that the revelation speaks of generational curses.

When I minister with a person, particularly if I am counseling them, I will often see a cord or chains that string from them to the number of generations back the curse extends.

I remember one incident in ministry, where the person in question was demonized and had demonic experiences from youth. As I prayed I saw a chain from this person, to his father and then his grandfather.

As I shared this revelation, it turned out that both his father and grandfather had delved into the occult and considered themselves "medicine men."

Upon breaking this link and resisting the enemy, the person was set free from the demonic manifestations in his life!

Here is a supporting Scripture:

> *Exodus 20:5 ...visiting the iniquity of the fathers upon the children to the third and fourth* ***generations*** *of those who hate Me.*

See also: Cursing, Family, Father, Mother, Siblings

ANCHOR

An anchor could represent the Lord, a person or a teaching.

It is a picture of security, steadfastness and hope. It can also be a picture of a season of being settled in your life.

> *Hebrews 6:19 This hope we have as an* ***anchor*** *of the soul, both sure and steadfast, and which enters the Presence behind the veil.*

Positive: To reach a place of security
Negative: To be hindered from moving forward

POSITIVE
If you have been moving from one thing to the next and then dream of dropping anchor, it means that a season is coming of rest and of being settled for a while.

When seen in a positive light, an anchor could represent the security you have in the Lord.

As in the passage above, hope is our anchor! It keeps our eyes set on the goal ahead of us, and we are then secure in our vision and in the Lord. It speaks of a season where you will remain in one place for a while – much like when the cloud rested on the tabernacle in the Old Testament and the people set up camp... time to drop anchor for a while!

If the symbol is positive, it also means to be in a place of safety. An anchor prevents a ship from drifting off course. On the one hand you might feel "stuck" but the purpose of this situation, is to keep you in a season of safety until you are ready, once again, for open seas. This scripture paints the picture beautifully:

> *Acts 27:29 Then, fearing lest we should run aground on the rocks, they* ***dropped four anchors*** *from the stern, and prayed for day to come*

NEGATIVE
Sometimes when I see an anchor in the spirit, it has a negative connotation. In other words, the anchor is holding you back! An anchor is meant to keep a ship stationary, which is great when coming to shore, but not when you are trying to catch the wind!

Now if you look at the ship as a form of ministry, there will be times for rest and "dropping anchor." But when the Lord wants you to move on to the next phase, you need to hoist that anchor and move on.

At such times we release the ministry in the spirit, hoist those sails, and move full steam ahead!

See also: Root, Ship, Vehicle

ANGELS

Strong's 32: aggelos- a messenger, an envoy, one who was sent, an angel, a messenger from God.

UNIVERSAL SYMBOL

POSITIVE
There are various types of angels that fall into the categories below. Note that the following interpretations relate to visions or prophetic dreams only.

It is also worthwhile to note that if you often see angels and demons in the spirit that you function in the gift of discerning of spirits. I cover this gift in detail in the *Way of Dreams and Visions* and *Prophetic Essentials*.

Guardian angels:

> *Psalms 91:11 For He shall give His angels charge over you, to keep you in all your ways.*

These angels are issued to you at birth, namely they are your guardian angels. In personal experience, such angels are larger than life and look very powerful in the spirit.

We often see them dressed in various gear, and they often carry swords and wear sashes.

Worship angels:

> *Psalms 148:2 Praise Him, all His **angels**; praise Him, all His hosts.*

This speaks of the worship angels who worship the Lord in the Throne Room. They are present during praise and worship.

In personal revelation and experience, such angels usually have wings and sing with the loveliest of voices. They often carry instruments such as harps, tambourines, trumpets, and various stringed instruments.

Messenger angels:

> *Luke 1:30 Then the **angel** said to her, "Do not be afraid, Mary, for you have found favor with God.*

Here is a reference to a messenger angel. He is the one who brings messages from the Lord.

In personal experience, such angels are plain looking, in flowing robes, often bearing a scroll or ram's horn.

Warrior angels:

> *Revelation 12:7 And war broke out in heaven: Michael and his **angels** fought with the dragon; and the dragon and his **angels** fought.*

Here is a reference to Michael, the leader of the warrior angels. In personal experience, such angels carry swords, have eyes of fire and look very foreboding.

NEGATIVE

> *2 Corinthians 11:14 And no wonder! For Satan himself transforms himself into an **angel of light**.*

This speaks of the enemy who appears as an angel of light - a deception. In personal experience, such angels do not reveal their faces and are very bright. They are accompanied by intense emotion and are very forceful.

Such an angel would try to get you to receive from them or open your heart to them. Doing so would open your heart wide to the enemy, giving him license in your life.

It is not common for a believer to have experiences with angels, unless they are operating in the gift of discerning of spirits. I have also noted that these kinds of experiences usually happen to those with an evangelistic calling.

Check all revelations of angels that you receive with someone who is more mature in Christ and will be able to judge the spirit for you. Also consider the following verse that warns against the worship of angels:

> *Colossians 2:18 Let no one cheat you of your reward, taking delight in false humility and worship of* ***angels****, intruding into those things which he has not seen, vainly puffed up by his fleshly mind,*

Although seeing angels in vision can give tremendous direction, it is not something that you should go looking for.

New Age cults emphasize angelic experiences, and you should be cautious of receiving from anyone that emphasizes their experiences with angels and does not share their relationship with the Lord Jesus.

See also: Demons, Light

ANIMALS

Depending on the animal, the interpretation for your dream will change. In a dream it is important to identify your view or relationship with the animal. If the animal is a pet, then it could speak of your responsibilities.

In visions or prophetic dreams, animals have quite clear interpretations in the Scriptures. Some are a source of blessing, and others, a picture of the attack of the enemy. Browse the various animals I have listed below.

See also: Alligator, Badger, Bat, Bear, Calf, Camel, Horse, Lamb, Lion, Pet

ANKLE

A sensitive area or a point of weakness in your life.

Positive: To overcome a weakness
Negative: To be tripped up by an insecurity or weakness

POSITIVE
If you dream of your ankle being healed or getting stronger, this refers to a weakness that has been made strong.

> *Acts 3:7 And he took him by the right hand and lifted him up, and immediately his feet and* ***ankle*** *bones received strength.*

This is likely to refer to a natural weakness in your life. Consider any character flaws or weaknesses that you have faced and overcome lately.

NEGATIVE
Your ankle is often a point of weakness. If you injure your foot, it is likely to occur at the ankle. If you dream of hurting your ankle or twisting it, it is referring to a weakness in your life that is tripping you up.

Although you might be strong in other areas, this single weakness has the power to trip you. It might be referring to a character flaw or even a spiritual weakness that you have.

See also: Barefoot, Legs, Feet

ANT

A hard worker.

Positive: To push through without wavering
Negative: A spirit of infirmity

POSITIVE

> *Proverbs 6:6 Go to the* ***ant****, you sluggard! Consider her ways and be wise*

The ant is hard-working, positive, building up.

This passage gives a full interpretation of what an ant could speak of in a positive context. It speaks of working hard and planning ahead.

NEGATIVE
In personal experience, we have often seen ants and such insects as spirits of infirmity. Although spirits do not have any shape or form, these symbols stand as a guide to us as to what the Holy Spirit is saying. Ants then speak of infirmity that is irritating.

Flies are often spoken negatively of in Scripture. The connotation of such insects is one of contamination and uncleanliness. This can be interpreted as a standard negative interpretation.

See also: Demons, Insect, Flies

APPLE

A fruit common to most people. It has both a negative and positive connotation.

Positive: Speaks of favor
Negative: Speaks of temptation

CHARACTER SPECIFIC SYMBOL

POSITIVE

> *Acts 14:17 Nevertheless He did not leave Himself without witness, in that He did good, gave us rain from heaven and **fruitful** seasons, filling our hearts with food and gladness.*

An apple in an internal dream can speak of favor or a gift. It also speaks of being fruitful and of something that has reached maturity. As in the Scripture above, it speaks of spiritual maturity.

NEGATIVE
A rotten apple in an internal dream can speak of poison, deception, sin or hidden evil within.

UNIVERSAL SYMBOL

POSITIVE

> *Psalms 17:8 Keep me as the **apple** of Your eye; hide me under the shadow of Your wings.*

The apple in this case speaks of favor and a position of importance, as we are the apple of God's eye. We are also to keep His teaching as the apple of our eyes (Proverbs 7:2). This means to esteem the Word as of great importance.

NEGATIVE

> *Genesis 3:6 So when the woman saw that the tree was good for food, that it was pleasant to the eyes, and a tree desirable to make one wise, she took of its **fruit** and ate. She also gave to her husband with her, and he ate.*

This speaks of temptation and the fruits of the flesh. Often referred to as "the forbidden fruit."

You need to discern if the fruit you are seeing in your vision has a positive or negative connotation.

If you have a vision that someone is eating fruit that looks good on the outside, but is bad on the inside, this could definitely speak of temptation - to not give into those things just because they look good, but also to discern the spirit.

See also: Fruit

ARK

Symbolic of salvation and the process we undergo when entering into the body of Christ through baptism. It is a picture of the baptism unto death to resurrect in new life.

Positive:

- A season of change is ahead
- Now is your kairos time

Negative: Your time of visitation is over

Noah's ark: A season of change where we go through a process of death to the flesh to allow the Lord to lead us to a new level of growth and promotion. Because of this, it is also a place of safety in the midst of the storm.

POSITIVE
In personal experience, the Lord showed us Noah's ark as a team and indicated that change was coming.

Sure enough the Lord led us through a season of death and tremendous change. It did not stay this way however, and the death and the struggle led to a resurrection and many new doors opened up. The Lord kept us safe in the storm until the heavens opened to show a new world!

So if you are in this situation and things seem to be closing down around you, do not be discouraged. The Lord is doing something new in your life, but before it can manifest you have to go through a phase of "incubation."

Just like Noah and his family were shut away in the ark for a season, so you too might feel shut away. Hang in there though, because soon your feet will land on a new land with lots of new promises!

> *1 Peter 3:20 who formerly were disobedient, when once the Divine longsuffering waited in the days of Noah, while the* ***ark*** *was being prepared, in which a few, that is, eight souls, were saved through water. 21 There is also an antitype which now saves us - baptism (not the removal of the filth of the flesh...*

NEGATIVE
The Lord gave me a vision once where I saw the door of Noah's ark closing. He told me that the new promise and season ahead was for those who passed through the tests and entered the ark. Those who refused to go through the process would have to stay behind. Do not be surprised then after getting such a revelation if relationships are suddenly severed and those that were with you for a while suddenly leave or are removed from your ministry or life.

The Ark of the Covenant: The Ark of the Covenant has a twofold meaning.

The first speaks of walking in obedience to the Lord and as a result, in His abundant blessing.

The second speaks of the manifest power and anointing of God.

POSITIVE
See also *Altar* in reference to the ark of the covenant.

The Ark of the Covenant is where God's glory rested in the Old Testament. It is a type and shadow of the anointing that we now have as New Testament believers.

When you got born again, the Holy Spirit came to dwell inside of you. You now have the Ark right in your spirit. The Lord no longer needs a temple made by man, because we are the temples of the Holy Ghost. The Ark also speaks of protection and the power of God. When the manna was put inside the Ark, it did not spoil.

The Lord gave us a revelation once of putting our finances "in the Ark" and dedicating it to Him before making all decisions. He said, when we do that, we give Him authority over it and allow Him to bless it. The gold that overlaid the Ark is a picture of the anointing and God's power to keep us.

> *Numbers 7:89 Now when Moses went into the tabernacle of meeting to speak with Him, he heard the voice of One speaking to him from above the mercy seat that was on the* ***ark of the Testimony****, from between the two cherubim; thus He spoke to him*

NEGATIVE
Because the Ark held the glory of God in the Old Testament, it has, in many ways, become an idol to many. Instead of walking the the power we have within, many seek the actual Ark, as if the object itself could bring power.

This has lead to some heretical doctrines and if you see a vision or have a dream where the Ark seems to be negative, then it speaks of idolatry, a counterfeit spirit, or a religious doctrinal mindset.

See also: Altar, Baptism, Cursing, Gold, Idol, Rainbow, Tabernacle

ARM

A picture of security, strength and favor.

Positive: Ability and strength
Negative: Using your natural strength instead of the Lord's

Character Specific Symbol

POSITIVE

An arm speaks of your abilities and strengths. Your arm is something you use all of the time, and you would be greatly hindered without it. In referring to the position of "the right hand," this speaks of a position of authority. See *Hand* for more on this.

To be surrounded by strong arms also speaks of protection and security. If you dream of being held securely, then the Lord is reassuring you that He is taking care of you.

NEGATIVE:

In an internal dream, if an arm is causing damage and is associated with a negative emotion, it could speak of those things that hinder or block you in your spiritual life.

If you have a dream of your arm being weak, it could indicate that a weakness is being exposed in you, but that it needs to become strong again.

If you dream that you try to use your arm, but you are not able to do the task, it could be that the Lord is trying to tell you that you keep trying to do things in your own strength instead of trusting Him.

If your arm is being damaged, it could speak of an attack that is causing you to become weak and to lose favor.

Universal Symbol

POSITIVE

> *Deuteronomy 9:29 Yet they are Your people and Your inheritance, whom You brought out by Your mighty power and by Your outstretched **arm**.*

In this case, the arm of the Lord is seen as a tower of strength and deliverance. In a prophetic dream, an arm would symbolize the protection, deliverance, and strength of the Lord.

An embrace from the Lord speaks of acceptance regardless of what you have done. It is a picture of the Lord taking on your cares and giving you a hiding place of security.

NEGATIVE

> *2 Chronicles 32:8 With him is an **arm** of flesh; but with us is the Lord our God, to help us and to fight our battles." And the people were strengthened by the words of Hezekiah king of Judah.*

If an arm is seen in a negative light in a prophetic dream or vision, it would represent fleshly strength.

This strength is human and not at all comparable to the strength of God. It would mean that you are trying to do something in your own strength that God can do better in His!

See also: Hand, Back, Body

ARMOR

The embodiment of protection for your body and heart. The condition of your spiritual strength for the purpose of spiritual warfare.

It is also representation of your position in the Kingdom.

CHARACTER SPECIFIC SYMBOL

If the armor you are wearing in your dream is something that you have had in real life, then you need to discern what part of your life it represents.

If the armor dates back to a specific era of your life, then it could well be that something from that era is being exposed in your life right now. For example, if you were in the military and begin dreaming of the armor you had back then, your dream is speaking about something from the past that is surfacing. It is referring to something that you are "guarding" or perhaps even that you feel emotionally "guarded" because of something that might have happened back then.

UNIVERSAL SYMBOL

POSITIVE

When you see either yourself or another person dressed in armor, this without a doubt refers to the armor of God! We are to gird ourselves with this armor for war. This is a source of protection, defense, and offense. It is the suit every believer should have.

From personal experience, depending on the grandeur of the armor, this indicates the level of ministry and authority the person you are praying for has.

Armor that is gold could indicate that this person is called to one of the fivefold ministry offices. It is common to see Roman or ancient style armor in vision to indicate the armor of God.

I have also on occasion noticed that the warrior angels are usually dressed in armor when I see them in the spirit.

Various forms of armor also represent specific nations or tasks that you need to do. If you are wearing armor designed for stealth, you know the spiritual warfare you are engaging in needs to be counter insurgence. If your armor is ceremonial, then the Lord is speaking about a new position He wants to give you.

If your armor is gritty and designed for hand-to-hand combat, the Lord is saying that it is time to engage in spiritual warfare and to take back the land that the enemy has stolen from you!

Paul speaks of our armor here:

> *Ephesians 6:11 Put on the whole* ***armor*** *of God, that you may be able to stand against the wiles of the devil.*

NEGATIVE

If the armor you see is the armor of man, or if the armor is too big, this would have a negative picture. This would indicate that the person in question is trying to do things in their own strength.

Perhaps they are trying to attain something in their ministry or spiritual life using natural means. In this case, they are headed for disappointment, because look at what Jesus says about the man who wears the armor he has fashioned for himself:

> *Luke 11:22 But when a stronger than he comes upon him and overcomes him, he takes from him all his* ***armor*** *in which he trusted, and divides his spoils.*

In a ministry sense, this can also speak of being more like Saul than like King David. (1 Samuel 17:39)

This passage is a picture of those that try to put on a "big and bold" image but inside are simple shepherd boys.

I have often seen a vision like this in the spirit when ministering to individuals. They look around and feel insecure next to other great men and women, and try to imitate them instead of just being their weak selves.

The Lord called King David when he was nothing but a shepherd boy. He was not called because of his great skill and strength, but because of his humility and his warrior's heart. The answer is to let go of the status quo images and all the false pretenses and just to be what God has called you to be.

Rusted or damaged armor: There are two reasons why you might see a vision of rusted or dented armor. The first is that the person is using strengths and anointing from the past that have long since become irrelevant to their current mission.

The second speaks of contamination and indicates that either they have been under tremendous spiritual attack, or that they have allowed the enemy to wear them down and contaminate the weapons of their spiritual warfare. Although this scripture speaks of a weapon, it is relevant to armor as well.

> *Ecclesiastes 10:10 If the ax is dull, And one does not sharpen the edge, Then he must use more strength; But wisdom brings success*

See also: Arrow, Axe, Bow, Clothing, Rust, Sword, Shield

ARMY

The collective work of the enemy or the Lord in your life. Can also represent a season of training for the work God has called you to for the purpose of participating in a ministry function that involves working with others.

Positive: The call to engage in spiritual warfare
Negative: A warning of the attack of the enemy

CHARACTER SPECIFIC SYMBOL

POSITIVE
Dreaming of an army in a positive light could indicate that you have been strengthened. Perhaps you dreamed of being enlisted in an army. This would mean that you have been going through spiritual training to equip you to take your place in a team (ministry or business).

The army speaks of training, being equipped, and a force of strength, unity, and protection. Keep in mind though, it is training that equips you in a team or in the body of Christ. An army is not made up of a single person, but is a collective of mighty warriors.

NEGATIVE
If you dream negatively of an army, i.e. being captured, chased, or oppressed, this would indicate that you are captive to desires and works of the flesh that are not of the Lord.

It could also indicate oppression in your life that is controlling you. In another context it could also mean that you are controlling and dominating others to your own will.

If you keep having garbage or purging dreams of being captured or of being a prisoner and you are trying to fight your way out, this could indicate that you are under spiritual attack at the moment, or in spiritual conflict. In a situation like this, your solution is to rise up in the name of Jesus and to overcome the enemy.

If this dream is recurring and you wake up tired, then the solution is next time you have this dream, you make a choice to stop running and make the choice to rest, give in, and to let God take control.

This dream is just a picture of the conflict inside of you right now. You are trying so hard to get away and win the war by yourself, that you have forgotten that Jesus has already won the battle!

UNIVERSAL SYMBOL

The struggle between the Kingdom of God and of the enemy is very real. We call this spiritual warfare and depending on which army you are in determines whose side you are fighting for. In my book the *Prophetic Warrior,* I share how when we fulfill the enemy's will, we fight on his behalf instead of the Lord's! It is for us to use our weapons of warfare and to walk in obedience on the right side of the line!

> *Revelation 19:19 And I saw the beast, the kings of the earth, and their* ***armies****, gathered together to make war against Him who sat on the horse and against His* ***army***

POSITIVE

> *Joel 2:11 The Lord gives voice before His* ***army****, for His camp is very great; for strong is the One who executes His word. For the day of the Lord is great and very terrible; who can endure it?*

The body of Christ is known as the army of God. In a positive light, this army is seen as powerful, enabled of the Lord, and able to overcome any obstacle.

It is God's hand extended into the earth. This image speaks of the body of Christ as a whole and the part you are being called to play.

Angels: I often see armies of angels set in array in the spirit. When in intercession for the nations, I will see platoons of angels all dressed in various armor – each representing a nation or specific task. I know that as I speak, they will go and do spiritual warfare on our behalf.

In the trenches: A prophetic dream or vision of "being in the trenches" speaks of getting personally involved in spiritual warfare and in the problems of others. It means going beyond just praying and helping out by ministering to the person in a practical way. This is pretty much what David did in this passage. He got his hands dirty!

> *1 Samuel 17:48 So it was, when the Philistine arose and came and drew near to meet David, that David hurried and ran toward the* ***army*** *to meet the Philistine*

The fivefold ministry: In relation to the fivefold ministry, we have often seen the apostle pictured as a "General" in God's army. Also I have seen the prophet as a watchman on the wall, and also as a warrior.

NEGATIVE

A dark army, speaks of the forces of satan. His mission is one of destruction, fear, theft, and strife. Such an army indicates an attack and curse in the life of the believer.

If you were to dream of the Lord's army that was in disarray, this would speak of disunity in the body.

To dream of wounded soldiers speaks of those who have been attacked from the enemy in their Christian walk.

If you have a vision that you are fighting in the wrong army, the Lord is indicating that you are being obedient to what the enemy wants you to do and not obedient to the instruction He has given to you.

You will find all the teaching you need concerning spiritual warfare in my books *Prophetic Warrior* and *The Strategies of War*.

See also: Ambush, Chasing, War

ARROW

Arrows speak of spiritual warfare as words are sent forth into the earth.

Positive: The word of God going forth
Negative: Negative words sent against you in the spirit

POSITIVE
Referring to deliverance and decree:

> *2 Kings 13:17 ... Then Elisha said, "Shoot"; and he shot. And he said, "The arrow of the Lord's deliverance and the arrow of deliverance from Syria;*

The arrow of the Lord speaks of deliverance and the Lord working on our behalf.

I have often seen a fiery arrow in the spirit, which indicates the word of the Lord going forth like lightening and accomplishing the work for which it was sent.

Seeing an arrow going out in the spirit also refers to speaking forth decrees like fire into the night sky.

Referring to children:

> *Psalms 127:4 Like* ***arrows*** *in the hand of a warrior, so are the children of one's youth.*

Arrows are also a picture of children, both natural and spiritual. Just like an arrow in the natural is prepared and then fired into a target, so also is it our job as parents to prepare and then send our children into the world.

When my parents were facing a divorce, the Lord showed my father how each of us were as arrows that were still newly cut from a green branch. The Lord said to him, that it was up to him to "keep the arrows straight" until the time came for us to be sent out.

NEGATIVE
The dark arrow in dreams and visions always speaks of the weapons of the enemy. They seek to destroy and cast down the righteous.

In the spirit I have often seen negative words and curses spoken over God's people as black arrows that pierce and cause theft, strife, destruction, and fear. To back up this revelation by the Word:

Proverbs 25:18 A man who bears false witness against his neighbor is like a club, a sword, and a sharp ***arrow****.*

See also: Armor, Bow, Cursing, Shield, Sword

ATTIC (UPPER ROOM)

The upper room is an invitation to separate yourself from the noise to enter into a new relationship with the Lord. You will leave this season changed.

Positive: Separation unto God for a season
Negative: A cluttered spiritual life

CHARACTER SPECIFIC SYMBOL

POSITIVE
An attic is famous for keeping treasures that you have long forgotten about. If you dream of going into an attic and find something of value, then the Lord is telling you that He is bringing things back to you that you have forgotten about.

NEGATIVE
Because what we store in our attic is usually junk, to dream of visiting it and experiencing something negative there, the Lord is saying clearly, "Your life is cluttered! There is some junk that you need to get rid of."

If you dream of an attic from the past, then the Lord is pointing to that specific time in your life.

UNIVERSAL SYMBOL

In the time of Christ, the Upper Room was used as a gathering place, away from the noise. The Lord had His final supper in the Upper Room. The disciples gathered in the Upper Room after Jesus ascended while waiting for the baptism of the Holy Spirit.

Being called away to the Upper Room is an invitation from the Lord to enter into a new relationship with Him. In both instances of the Upper Room, the disciples had an encounter with God. The first was with Jesus and their first communion. The second was when tongues of fire fell from heaven!

If you see the Upper Room in a vision or prophetic dream, then the Lord is calling you aside from the noise to draw you into a new relationship and to give you an experience in the Spirit.

Acts 1:13-14 And when they had entered, they went up into the upper room where they were staying: Peter, James, John, and Andrew; Philip and Thomas; ... These all continued with one accord in prayer and supplication,

See also: Buildings, House

AUDIENCE

Your performance in life and how others perceive you.

Positive: The call to stand up in front of others.
Negative: Performing to get attention

CHARACTER SPECIFIC SYMBOL

POSITIVE
If you dream of standing in front of an audience and you are bold and confident, this could indicate a healing dream and the fact that you have risen up.

Perhaps you were never confident as such, in which case such a dream would indicate that you had overcome this fear.

NEGATIVE
If you are "playing" to an audience in your dream, this would mean that you are putting on a performance.

I interpreted a dream once where the lady in question had an audience waiting, to do a show. Yet before she went on stage she had to find the correct clothing to wear. She kept changing outfit after outfit, but none were suitable.

The interpretation was very clear: She was concentrating on externals to try and get others to accept her. She thought that if she could put on a good enough "show" then she would not be rejected any more.

UNIVERSAL SYMBOL

POSITIVE
A call to preach! If you have a vision of standing in front of an audience preaching, the interpretation is clear. The Lord is calling you to stand up and minister His word like Paul did. (Acts 17:22)

NEGATIVE
If you are seeing a person striving in front of an audience putting on a "show" this would have the same interpretation as the internal dream.

It would mean that the person in question is more interested on pleasing the crowds, than on promoting the Lord and the truth of His Word.

See also: Crowd, Stage

AUTHORITIES

These are those people who are senior to you and have authority over you.

They may be represented by your parents, boss, pastor, or any other figure who is set over you in an administrative or spiritual position.

CHARACTER SPECIFIC SYMBOL

POSITIVE

If you dream of an authority in a positive light, then it could indicate that your leadership is being accepted and that you are growing in that area.

It could mean that you are attaining to that level of leadership and authority in your spiritual walk.

If they are authorities from worldly circles, they could speak of archetypes and mindsets that control your thinking.

NEGATIVE

Dreaming of being in bondage to an authority would mean that you are under some form of oppression or attack.

Perhaps you are being controlled by influences that are not of God and have been brought under the domination of something that is against the Word. It may also indicate that you are trying to dominate and impose your own will on others.

UNIVERSAL SYMBOL

POSITIVE

> *Romans 13:1 Let every soul be subject to the governing **authorities**. For there is no authority except from God, and the authorities that exist are appointed by God.*

The highest authority is naturally the Lord Himself.

I will often see this depicted as an umbrella in the spirit. I will see someone with an umbrella above them with holes in it. Or I will perhaps see that they are not standing under the umbrella away from the storm.

When I see this I know that the Lord is saying that this person's authority is not covering them correctly. Secondly they are not under cover at all and are under attack.

As the Scripture says, all authority ultimately comes from the Lord.

NEGATIVE

To rebel against an authority that you personally know God has told you to be under, is tantamount to rebelling against the Lord Himself.

See also: Father, Man, Woman

AUNT

In a dream, your aunt would represent a specific part of yourself. However, in a vision, it could represent the actual woman or speak of someone that is a distant part of your life and is not something that is close to you.

CHARACTER SPECIFIC SYMBOL

Consider the main qualities of your aunt. When she comes to mind, what is the first thing that comes to you? This will give you an indication of what she represents in your dream.

Once you know what she represents, the circumstances surrounding your dream will tell you clearly what is going on in your life right now.

UNIVERSAL SYMBOL

POSITIVE
If you see your aunt in your vision, the Lord could be telling you to pray for her. If you function in the ministry of intercession, then the Lord is bringing her to your mind for the purpose of prayer into her life.

NEGATIVE
Often the Lord will show you someone in vision to bring healing to a specific event or even to break spiritual ties. If you have been seeking God regarding a curse or a blockage in your life, and he brings your aunt to your mind, it could be that you received something from her that was not of Him.

The Lord could also be exposing a generational curse. Consider the life of your aunt and see what it is the Lord is trying to expose.

See also: Uncle, Ancestor

AXE

A weapon of spiritual warfare.

Positive: Completely destroying the work of the enemy
Negative: Refers to destruction or humiliation.

POSITIVE

> *Jeremiah 51:20 You are My battle-**ax** and weapons of war: for with you I will break the nation in pieces; with you I will destroy kingdoms;*

Seen in a positive light, we as the Church are an axe in the hand of the Lord. We are His weapon against the enemy. This represents strength and destruction against the works of satan.

It is a powerful, but crude, instrument and refers more to brute strength than precision. It not only tears down, but brings permanent damage. When a tree is cut off at the roots, it is completely destroyed! An axe is an aggressive weapon and denotes spiritual warfare that is going to be difficult and requires you to follow through for complete victory. A long journey is ahead of you – fight and do not give up!

NEGATIVE

> *Matthew 3:10 And even now the* ***ax*** *is laid to the root of the trees. Therefore, every tree which does not bear good fruit is cut down and thrown into the fire.*

The axe seen in a negative light speaks of separation and destruction. It separates the good fruit from the bad.

When I see an axe bringing a division in the Spirit, I know that the Lord is speaking of bringing a division between those who mean business with God, and those who do not.

In a situation where the axe is being brought to the root of a tree as in the Scripture above, I know that the Lord is speaking of removing an aspect from a person's life entirely. This can speak of bringing the flesh to death.

This vision taken literally, speaks of the Lord removing a ministry, position, or person that is standing in the way of His will. For God to accomplish this sort of division, he will use a prophet to send out a decree.

See also: Armor, Sword, Trees

Symbols Starting in B

SYMBOLS STARTING IN B

BABEL

Strong's Definition: 894 Babel-

Babel or Babylon = "confusion (by mixing)"

CHARACTER SPECIFIC AND UNIVERSAL SYMBOLS

Babel has no positive connotation. It is known as the tower of confusion. In the spirit when I see the tower of babel, it resembles the "status quo" Church or those ministries that are trying to make a name for themselves using external strength, but not the spirit of God.

It is a perfect picture of a ministry that has risen up using natural strength and the spirit of the world.

See also: City

BABY

Babies have a twofold meaning. They represent being given a new ministry responsibility. Secondly they speak of having trust, vulnerability, and innocence.

In a negative light, they speak of immaturity.

CHARACTER SPECIFIC SYMBOL

POSITIVE
A baby speaks of a new life and a new aspect in your life and ministry. A baby boy often speaks of a teaching and leadership type of ministry, whereas a baby girl speaks of a more prophetic or creative emphasis in your ministry.

If you dream of a baby that suddenly matures beyond its age (for example it is a newborn that can walk already) this indicates that the new thing that has taken place in your life is going to mature fast.

If you dream of having twins, this speaks of having either a ministry or gaining a responsibility that is twofold or that has two different aspects to it.

The dream is indicating that you should nurture both aspects and not take one or the other.

If you dream that someone else you know hands you their baby, this could speak of that person giving you either their responsibility or ministry mandate.

This depends, of course, on what this person would represent in your dream. If they are an image to you of a ministry type, then it would speak of the Lord giving you this kind of ministry also.

If the person giving you the baby is a spiritual parent, then this would speak of them handing their mandate over to you.

If the person handing you the baby is someone that has a negative connotation in your life, then this would be negative and speak of you being put under pressure to take something you do not want or something that is not of the Lord.

NEGATIVE

If you dream that you lose your child or baby, it means that you have neglected and lost the promotion in the spiritual realm that God was giving you.

If you have been trusting God for something specific and dream that you lose a baby, it could mean that you have lost your faith or that a curse is causing that blessing to be lost.

If you dream of neglecting your baby, it means you have not been using your spiritual gifts.

If you dream that you are taking another person's baby, it means that you have taken on responsibilities that are not your own.

A baby and child also indicate that this spiritual gift is yet young in you. It means that you are yet immature in that calling.

UNIVERSAL SYMBOL

POSITIVE

Babies speak of a new life and also of trust. They speak of innocence and purity. They are not yet corrupted and have strong faith. This is why Jesus told us to be like little children. Children also speak of the blessing of the Lord.

If you see someone in the spirit with many children around them, it could be that the Lord is calling them to become spiritual parents. It can also indicate that the Lord has many blessings in store for them.

> *1 Peter 2:2 as newborn* ***babes****, desire the pure milk of the word, that you may grow thereby,*

Babies receive with innocence what they are fed and hunger for it. To see someone as a baby would indicate that the Lord wants them to receive without asking questions. To trust the Lord completely as Jesus explains in this passage:

> *Matthew 11:25 At that time Jesus answered and said, "I thank You, Father, Lord of heaven and earth, that You have hidden these things from the wise and prudent and have revealed them to* ***babes****.*

If you see someone you are ministering to as a baby in the arms of the Lord, the message is that the Lord wants them to rest in Him, to be a baby and to trust that He will care for them.

NEGATIVE
If you see a baby in the spirit, it could mean that the person you are ministering to is still a baby in their spiritual walk. If I am counseling a person and see them as a baby, this could also indicate hurts from the past that started at that age that need inner healing.

If you have a vision that is negative then it could also speak of birthing things that were not conceived by the Lord, but rather by the flesh or from the enemy.

Inner healing: If you are prophetic and you are ministering inner healing and see a baby that is hurt or upset, the Lord is showing you where the hurts for this person began. Ask them if anything traumatic happened at the age you see the baby as in your vision.

Actual events: In some instances, if you see a baby, the Lord could be showing you a real baby that this person had. Always share your vision with the person you are ministering to and ask them to clarify. Especially when you feel that the baby you are seeing in the spirit is not symbolic, but a revelation of actual events.

It could well be that the person is struggling over guilt from an abortion or was adopted as a baby.

See also: Birth, Child, Miscarriage, Pregnant

BACK

To have a strong backbone in humanistic terms means to be confident and strong. It also indicates your level of conviction.

A weak back indicates a lack of conviction or confidence.

In the realm of visions and prophetic dreams, the back is a good picture of the strength and structure of the Church.

CHARACTER SPECIFIC SYMBOL

POSITIVE
To dream that your back is strengthened is an indication that you have begun to get a strong conviction.

If in the natural you have serious back problems and then you dream that they suddenly leave, this means that there is a weakness in you that has become strengthened.

NEGATIVE
If you dream that you hurt your back or that it is broken, it indicates that strength has been taken from you. Consider what has been happening in your life lately. Have you lacked strong conviction?

Have you failed to stand up for what you believe in? If so, then dreaming of a broken or weak back is a confirmation that you have let go of your conviction and it is time to stand in them once again.

Universal Symbol

POSITIVE
The back or backbone, speaks of strength and the center of the human body. The back is what holds up the body, without it the body is useless. It also holds up the head.

If we compare the back to the body of Christ, it would represent the strength and structure of the Church. As all the bones and flesh are held up by the backbone, if you had to dream of your back being broken, this indicates that your strengths are being broken.

If you are in prophetic training this is commonplace. You need to discern in the dream whether this "backbreaking" is something positive or negative.

Carrying a burden on your back: The back is also a picture of carrying a burden. Consider this passage:

> *1 Peter 2:24 who Himself* ***bore*** *our sins in His own body on the tree, that we, having died to sins, might live for righteousness - by whose stripes you were healed.*

Because of the burden Jesus carried on our behalf, we are set free. He took the load for us.

If you dream that you are carrying a load and it is taken from your back, then it means that the Lord is going to remove this pressure or that he desires to take your load from you.

The Word says that the Lord's yoke is light and His burden is easy, if you have a vision of exchanging your heavy load for His light load, it means you are putting God in control of your life and circumstances.

NEGATIVE
To have something put behind your back, means to be rejected. It can also refer to words being spoken behind your back.

To break your back, indicates that your strength has been broken. To break the back of the body would mean disabling the entire body.

To turn your back in battle speaks of fear and cowardice.

To see someone's back may indicate that they have turned their back on the Lord and are refusing to hear His word. It would indicate rebellion and deception.

Seeing a stiff back can also refer to being stubborn or "stiff-necked" as the Scriptures call it.

> *Jeremiah 17:23 But they did not obey nor incline their ear, but made their* ***neck*** *stiff, that they might not hear nor receive instruction.*

This speaks of being stubborn and refusing to receive God's word or the direction He is giving.

See also: Ankle, Arm, Body, Hand, Skeleton, Skull

BADGER

A badger in the biblical era was used for its skin. It was used to make the tent for the tabernacle in the wilderness as well as covering within the tabernacle. It speaks of wealth and prosperity.

> *Ezekiel 16:10 I clothed you in embroidered cloth and gave you sandals of* ***badger*** *skin; I clothed you with fine linen and covered you with silk.*

BAG

A bag often represents finance and provision in Scripture.

Positive: To be generous
Negative: To horde

CHARACTER SPECIFIC AND UNIVERSAL SYMBOLS

POSITIVE

Bags were used for money and the shepherd had a shepherd's bag. In a positive light, it speaks of "storing up" blessings for a time when you will need them most.

This was the kind of bag David used to put his stones into when confronting Goliath.

> *Proverbs 7:20 He has taken a bag of money with him, and will come home on the appointed day.*

NEGATIVE

A bag with holes has a very bad connotation. It refers to financial loss and theft. This would indicate that a curse is prevalent in your life.

It means that no matter how hard your work or how much you earn, it seems to slip through your fingers. Such a curse is often generational or a result of direct sin in your life, which has opened the door to the enemy.

> *Haggai 1:6 ... You clothe yourselves, but no one is warm; and he who earns wages, earns wages to put into a **bag with holes**.*

Transparent bag: If you see someone or something caught in a bag that is transparent, it means that they are bound by religious thinking. The bag is transparent, because although there is a blockage, it is deceptive. It appears to be white and clear, when it in fact, is restrictive.

See also: Baggage/Luggage, Briefcase, Gold, Journey, Silver, Money, Traveling

BAGGAGE/LUGGAGE

A collection of your knowledge and experience in life.

Positive: A new adventure awaits!
Negative: There are some things of your past you need to let go of

CHARACTER SPECIFIC SYMBOL

POSITIVE
To dream of being given new luggage means that the Lord wants to take you on a journey, to have new experiences and also to gain new knowledge. It can also mean that the Lord is about to do something completely new in your life that you have never experienced before.

To get rid of old luggage is also good, because it means that you are getting rid of the old to make way for the new.

To pack new luggage that is a mix of something old and new can also be positive. It means that the Lord is taking you through a sorting process and that He is picking out the best from what you lived through and what you know now to bring you to a new level of maturity. The best scripture for this is:

> *Matthew 13:52 Then He said to them, "Therefore every scribe instructed concerning the kingdom of heaven is like a householder who **brings out of his treasure** things new and old.*

NEGATIVE
To dream of being weighed down means that you are allowing the "baggage" of the past to hinder your future. The perfect solution is this scripture:

> *Hebrews 12:1 Therefore we also, since we are surrounded by so great a cloud of witnesses, let us **lay aside every weight**, and the sin which so easily ensnares us, and let us run with endurance the race that is set before us*

To dream of losing your luggage or getting rid of it means that the Lord wants you to put the past and its hurts behind you so that you can move forward.

Universal Symbol

POSITIVE AND NEGATIVE
While ministering, I have seen someone holding onto old luggage. This had the same interpretation as above. It spoke of things from the past that they were unwilling to let go of. This can speak of old teachings, hurts, or experiences that they keep using as an excuse for not moving forward in their lives.

See also: Bag, Briefcase, Traveling

Balances

Balances were used for weighing produce and money in biblical times. They also speak of justice or judgment.

Positive: To have something swung in your favor
Negative: To be cheated or stolen from

POSITIVE
We often see balances in the spirit which have swung to our favor. Often as we have trusted the Lord for a miracle, we will see the balances swung in our favor, indicating that our answer is on its way!

To be judged correctly is to see the balances at equilibrium. To have the balance swing in your favor is positive and indicates that your answer is on the way.

NEGATIVE
To see a balance means you are to be judged. In the case of Belshazzar, his judgment was not so positive:

> *Daniel 5:27 Tekel: You have been weighed in the balances, and found wanting.*

Balances swung against you do not have a negative connotation and either represent sin in your life or indicate that you have great odds going against you.

If you dream or have a dream that the balances are being cheated, it means that there is a spirit of theft operational in your life that is stealing your financial provision.

See also: Money, Weights

BALDNESS

To be bald is seldom positive. It speaks of humiliation and of being exposed.

A bald woman speaks of not being under covering.

POSITIVE
If you are a man and you are happy in the dream, waking up feeling positive, then it can speak of a change in your image as the condition of your hair is very much part of your "face to the world."

NEGATIVE
Baldness has a negative connotation and speaks of shame, being uncovered, and exposed.

In the Old Testament, to make one's head bald was a sign of mourning. The priests of Baal also shaved their heads as part of their cult.

If you are a woman and you dream of being bald, it could mean that you are not under covering as in the following passage:

> *1 Corinthians 11:15 But if a woman has* ***long hair****, it is a glory to her; for her hair is given to her for a covering.*

If you are a man and dream that you go bald it speaks of being exposed and being made vulnerable.

For the opposite of baldness, see *Hair*.

A bald leader: If you dream that your leader or husband goes bald, the Lord is warning you that your covering is under attack. This is a call to pray and also to be cautious as you are not being fully covered spiritually at the moment. Determine the area where you feel that you are either not under covering, or where the covering you are under is going astray.

If you are in a team, this dream does not just speak about the actual leader in your group, but what he or she represents. It also speaks of the organization or denomination that they are under.

See also: Beard, Face, Hair

BALL

A representation of childlike desires.

Positive: A return to the simplicity of childhood
Negative: Immaturity and being tossed around

POSITIVE
A ball is a childhood toy. In a positive context, it represents childhood joys and fun. It would represent something from your childhood that brought pleasure and peace.

NEGATIVE
In an internal dream, seeing a ball in a negative context, it would mean that you are being tossed from here to there and are not on a solid foundation.

UNIVERSAL SYMBOL

If seen in a vision, a ball represents someone who is being tossed to and fro by the enemy.

Perhaps the person in question has been in confusion or has been doing too many things at one time.

Balls are easily tossed and it would also mean that you are not secure in your position in Christ, because the enemy is able to buffet you easily.

> *Isaiah 22:18 He will surely turn violently and toss you like a* ***ball*** *into a large country; there you shall die, and there your glorious chariots shall be the shame of your master's house.*

See also: Toy

BALM

An ointment used to bring healing and peace. If spoiled, it represents contamination and a curse.

Positive: The ministry of inner healing
Negative: Contamination in someone's spirit

UNIVERSAL SYMBOL

POSITIVE
Balm: To see the healing balm in vision means that the Holy Spirit is bringing healing to hurts. Often when I have ministered inner healing I have seen the Lord rub a healing balm on a heart that is cut and torn. As the balm is rubbed in, the wounds and cuts are healed.

> *Jeremiah 51:8 Babylon has suddenly fallen and been destroyed. Wail for her! Take* ***balm*** *for her pain; perhaps she may be healed.*

Ointment: An ointment is slightly different in that it speaks not only of healing, but of being perfumed as well. The difference is slight, but worth mentioning. It is what the priests used according to Exodus 30:25 to use as anointing oil.

Ointment in scriptures speaks not only of healing, but of diffusing the fragrance of Christ.

A blend, if you will of both healing and then walking out that healing in such a way that others can see and smell the change in you! This kind of healing is one that will not be done in private, but will likely occur where others are involved and likely to see the process you go through.

NEGATIVE
To have a fly in the balm means that the medicine is ruined and brings harm instead of good. The smell is unpleasant and instead of bringing healing, it brings harm instead.

This speaks of being contaminated either through receiving ministry from someone whose spirit is not right before God, or through your own sin.

> *Ecclesiastes 10:1 Dead flies putrefy the perfumer's **ointment**, and cause it to give off a foul odor; so does a little folly to one respected for wisdom and honor.*

To refuse the ointment: This speaks of refusing the healing of the Lord. This might be because you refuse to look at the sin or hurt involved. If you are ministering and see a vision of someone wiping away or refusing the ointment, then they are drawing back from the healing hand of God or do not want to push through with the process.

See also: Anoint, Oil, Perfume

BAND – MUSIC/IRON

MUSIC: CHARACTER SPECIFIC AND UNIVERSAL SYMBOLS

A Music Band

Representation of musical archetype, style, and ministry.

POSITIVE
If you dream or have a vision of a particular band that you would say represents a specific style or culture, it could well be that the Lord wants you to minister or adapt to this particular group. If it is a band that it completely out of what you find comfortable, the Lord is saying that He is stretching you and taking you into areas you have never developed before.

If you always dreamed of being in a music band, but never made it, then the dream is speaking about desires of the past that are unfulfilled.

If you dream about a band you were part of in the past, the dream is speaking of that era in your life, as well as the archetype that the band represents.

NEGATIVE
If the band you are dreaming about is negative, it speaks of allowing the spirit of the world to contaminate your Christian walk. Because music is such a powerful tool for praise and worship, dreaming of musicians and worldly bands is a picture of things that are influencing you negatively.

Iron: Character Specific and Universal Symbols

A Band of Iron

A band of Iron and brass put around the stump of a tree speaks of restricted growth. Of being stifled and held back.

POSITIVE
It is not often that this is positive. The only time that having a band restricting you could be positive is if the Lord is saying that you need to step back for a season until the time is right.

In most cases though, it speaks of being hindered from moving forward.

NEGATIVE
To put a band around the stump of a tree means to stunt and prevent further growth. It speaks of a spiritual lack of growth.

It speaks of being held back and being prevented from progressing in what the Lord has for you.

To place a band on a person or ministry, would mean to curse it and prevent it from further progress. Nebuchadnezzar was hindered and cursed in this way (Daniel 4:15)

See also: Axe, Music, Rope, Trees

Banquet

A place of blessing, abundance and unmerited favor in both natural and spiritual things.

In a negative light, it represents gluttony.

Positive: Favor and provision for your desires
Negative: Getting into the flesh

POSITIVE
A banquet in vision speaks of the Lord's favor. It speaks of a place of blessing, abundance and royalty. Not just providing a need, but rather providing the desire of the heart in access of any need. David says here in Psalms 23:5:

> *You prepare a table before me in the presence of my enemies; You anoint my head with oil; my cup runs over.*

If you have a vision that you are invited to the Lord's banqueting table, He could be telling you that He has only blessings for you and wants you to take hold of them. Perhaps you have been happy to live off the little scraps you have or feel that God does not want to bless you.

To have such a vision would confirm the Word where God says:

> *Song of Songs 2:4 He escorts me to the* ***banquet*** *hall; it's obvious how much he loves me.*

To be seated at the head of a table also refers to be giving a seat of honor as in the case of Benjamin when Joseph gave him the larger portion when his brothers visited him in Egypt.

NEGATIVE

If seen in a vulgar sense, a banquet can be seen as gluttony, excess and evil intentions.

> *1 Peter 4:3 For we have spent enough of our past lifetime in doing the will of the Gentiles—when we walked in lewdness, lusts,* ***drunkenness, revelries, drinking parties****, and abominable idolatries*

See also: Barn, Basket, Food, Table

BAPTISM

To start a new life. To put the old behind you and to step forward in something new.

Strong's Definition: baptizo (bap-tid'-zo);

from a derivative of 911; to immerse, submerge; to make overwhelmed (i.e. fully wet); used only (in the N. T.) of ceremonial ablution, especially (technically) of the ordinance of Christian baptism:

KJV-Baptist, baptize, wash.

POSITIVE

Baptism speaks of leaving the old behind and then being raised up in new life. It means to put away the old and to walk in the resurrection life of Jesus Christ.

> *Romans 6:4 Therefore we were buried with Him through* ***baptism*** *into death, that just as Christ was raised from the dead by the glory of the Father, even so we also should walk in newness of life. 5 For if we have been united together in the likeness of His death, certainly we also shall be in the likeness of His resurrection,*

If you have a vision of being baptized and have not in reality been baptized yet, then the Lord is telling you that you need to fulfill this covenant act in your Christian walk.

If you have a vision of someone else being baptized, ask them if they have been baptized yet as the Lord is telling them that now is the time.

If you have already been baptized, then the vision is indicating that you must leave the old you behind and press on. Jesus has covered your sin with His blood and as you chose to come and be part of His Kingdom, you do not need to keep looking to the past any longer. Press on now to resurrection!

NEGATIVE
Paul makes us aware also of the baptism unto death. Death to the flesh is painful and is brought about by means of the cross and by fire.

> *Romans 6:4 Therefore we were buried with Him through* ***baptism*** *into death, that just as Christ was raised from the dead by the glory of the Father, even so we also should walk in newness of life.*

See also: Altar, Ark, Coffin, Cross, Death, Fire

Barefoot

A picture of vulnerability and servanthood. In a negative light, it speaks of being ill-equipped in your spiritual walk with the Lord.

Positive: You are fearless in showing what is in your heart
Negative: To be unprotected in the case of spiritual warfare

POSITIVE
To be barefoot, or to see someone barefoot, speaks of humility and transparency. It means to be a servant. It also means that the person in question has nothing to hide. It is a beautiful picture of how we should come into the presence of the Lord, just like the Lord said to Moses

> *Acts 7:33 'Then the Lord said to him,* ***"Take your sandals off your feet,*** *for the place where you stand is holy ground*

NEGATIVE
In a negative light, to be barefoot means to be exposed and unprotected. It also speaks of mourning and vulnerability.

> *2 Samuel 15:30 So David went up by the Ascent of the Mount of Olives, and wept as he went up; and he had his head covered and went* ***barefoot****:*

The Word tells us to "shod our feet" with the gospel of peace. If you dream that you are barefoot and it feels negative, it means that you are not wearing all of your spiritual armor.

> *Ephesians 6:15 and having shod your* ***feet*** *with the preparation of the gospel of peace;*

See also: Ankle, Armor, Feet, Leg

BARLEY

Your basic needs, also referred to as your "daily bread" in scripture. Barley was the food of the people in the Old Testament. Although wheat was a higher class of grain, barley tolerated poor soil and drought better. It was also cheaper than wheat and more available.

Positive: Provision for your daily needs
Negative: A curse stealing God's blessing in your life

CHARACTER SPECIFIC SYMBOL

In an internal dream, barley would need to have a meaning to you to make sense. For example, if you are allergic to barley, to dream of eating it could indicate that you are consuming something that is poison to your spirit.

CHARACTER SPECIFIC AND UNIVERSAL SYMBOLS

POSITIVE
To receive barley speaks of having your daily needs met. This does not refer to your desires, but your basic living expenses and what you need to survive.

> *Ruth 3:17 And she said, "These six ephahs of* ***barley*** *he gave me; for he said to me, 'Do not go empty-handed to your mother-in law.'"*

NEGATIVE
To have spoiled or stolen barley speaks of a curse regarding your daily needs and finances.

> *Exodus 9:31 Now the flax and the* ***barley*** *were struck, for the barley was in the head and the flax was in bud.*

See also: Bake, Bread, Wheat

BARN/STOREHOUSE

A good picture of the blessing of the Lord. A barn speaks of provision for both your needs and desires coming from God's storehouse.

Positive: The accumulation of wealth
Negative: All that the enemy has stolen from you

CHARACTER SPECIFIC AND UNIVERSAL SYMBOLS

POSITIVE
A full barn or storehouse always speaks of blessing and prosperity in accordance with the promises of the Lord.

*Deuteronomy 28:8 The Lord will command the blessing on you in your **storehouses** and in all to which you set your hand, and He will bless you in the land which the Lord your God is giving you.*

*Luke 12:24 Consider the ravens, for they neither sow nor reap, which have neither **storehouse** nor **barn**; and God feeds them. Of how much more value are you than the birds?*

We have often seen the storehouse of the Lord in the spirit and it is overflowing with every good thing and the fulfillment of every need known to man.

There is no lack in the Kingdom of Heaven and when we have seen His heavenly storehouse, it contains gold, gems and every other treasure you can think of!

There is a lovely description of such a vision in my book, *The Journey of Tamar*.

To see a barn filling up is a picture of the accumulation of wealth:

*Proverbs 3:10 So your **barns** will be filled with plenty, and your vats will overflow with new wine.*

NEGATIVE

The enemy also steals from the believer and often in the spirit I have seen myself go into satan's kingdom and take back what he has stolen. I have seen his storehouse also in the spirit and two doorkeepers on either side of the entrance usually guard it.

At the name of Jesus, the thief that is found will return sevenfold. What satan has stolen and what the enemy's children earn, is to be put in the hands of the righteous i.e. in the hands of every believer.

*Job 27:16 Though he **heaps up** silver like dust, and piles up clothing like clay - 17 He may pile it up, but the just will wear it, and the innocent will divide the silver.*

To see a barn being robbed or sitting empty speaks of theft and a curse in your life.

*Joel 1:17 The seed shrivels under the clods, storehouses are in shambles; **barns** are broken down, for the grain has withered.*

See also: Banquet, Basket, Food

BARNABAS

Barnabas was the one who introduced Paul to the disciples when they were doubted his salvation. He is known as:

*Acts 4:36 And Joses, who was also named **Barnabas** by the apostles (which is translated Son of Encouragement), a Levite of the country of Cyprus,*

Barnabas was an encourager and once he had mentored Paul, he took Mark under his wing when Paul and he separated.

To be a "Barnabas" means to be an encourager and a motivator.

BARREL

A barrel has the same meaning as *Barn* or Storehouse, but simply contains a smaller measure of blessing.

> *1 Kings 17:16 And the **barrel** of meal wasted not, neither did the cruse of oil fail, according to the word of the Lord, which he spake by Elijah. (KJV)*

See also: Barn/Storehouse

BARS

The meaning changes depending on the kind of bar you see in your dream or vision.

A prison bar(s) speaks of restriction and being bound. A gold bar is positive and speaks of the anointing and provision.

A metal rod or bar used as a weapon, speaks of destruction.

A bar is the sense of a place where they serve alcoholic beverages can represent either being filled with the "new wine" (the anointing) or of walking in sinful drunkenness (the flesh). See *Pub* for more on this.

CHARACTER SPECIFIC SYMBOL

POSITIVE

The only time that a bar or bars (as in prison bars) can be seen as positive, is when the enemy is behind it. In other words, to dream of a vicious animal that is behind bars would be good. It indicates that the enemy cannot touch you. Sure, he can make a loud noise, but he cannot bring you any harm.

NEGATIVE

Bars of a prison always have a negative connotation. It speaks of bondage, loss of freedom, and being trapped. Often someone places themselves behind bars for protection from rejection.

By putting up these bars or "walls" they feel secure. I have not seen a positive image for a bar or prison, for Christ came to set us free and not to keep us in bondage. We are bond-slaves, slaves willing to remain. We are not forced to remain.

Universal Symbol

A prison or bars speak of captivity by sin, oppression from the enemy, or by personal choice. As Christians, we are to speak the good news to free those in bondage. This bondage may be to sin, past hurts, demonic oppression, or fear.

Often in counseling someone who is under bondage from past hurts, I see them as that hurt child, having shut themselves up in a prison or cave to defend themselves from further hurt.

Unfortunately, by hiding in this way, they prevent the Lord from reaching in and so they need to be healed and led out from those walls. As I lead that person out in the spirit, the Lord leads them to an open meadow where He holds and lifts them into His arms. This is our mandate as believers: Isaiah 61:1

> *The Spirit of the Lord God is upon Me, because the Lord has anointed Me to preach good tidings to the poor; He has sent Me to heal the brokenhearted, to proclaim liberty to the captives, and the opening of the prison to those who are bound.*

See also: Cage, Gold, Prison, Pub, Rod, Wine

Basement

Being a lower division of a home or building, it speaks of demotion or a season of lying low. It also represents a starting point that is humbling right now, but will lead to promotion later.

Positive: The starting place of all promotion
Negative: Hindered from rising up

POSITIVE
When dreaming of a basement, it usually represents a "going down" or a time of humbling. The saying "promotion begins in the basement" is still very prevalent in the spiritual life today.

Paul called himself "the scum of the earth" and if you are looking to the Lord for promotion or to move on to the next phase in your spiritual life, be sure that the promotion begins in the basement!

I remember one case where I was giving direction to someone with regards to their ministry. I saw them standing proud. Then by the floor, I saw this small door that led to their promotion.

The message was very clear - before they could enter into the next phase of their ministry, they would be humbled first. True enough, not long after that revelation, the person in question had to humble themselves to people they had left behind on bad terms with, along with being ostracized in their current ministry position.

The good news however, is that this person did indeed rise up into that promotion!

NEGATIVE
If you dream of being trapped in a basement, it indicates that you are being hindered from rising up. You are in bondage and the enemy has you bound.

Now is the time to use your authority in the name of Jesus and to rise up.

If you dream of being in a basement that is cluttered and unclean, the Lord is saying that there are hidden parts of your life that need to be cleaned out! This can speak of sins that you have not repented of, curses that need to be dealt with, or even anger and fear that you have "pushed down" and refused to look at.

It also speaks of a place of hiding:

> *2 Chronicles 18:24 And Micaiah said, "Indeed you shall see on that day when you go into an* ***inner chamber*** *to hide.*

See also: Elevator

BASKET

A bowl or basket speaks of financial blessing and provision for your physical needs.

Positive: Financial blessing
Negative: A curse on your finances because of sin

POSITIVE
A basket filled with fruit or bread speaks of good things. It speaks of blessing and provision.

> *Deuteronomy 28:5 Blessed shall be your* ***basket*** *and your kneading bowl.*

I have often seen the Lord give someone a basket of fruit in the spirit, speaking of abundance and of His blessings. Because baskets are more often used to hold food, it is a picture of financial and natural provision.

If you dream or see a vision of receiving a basket full of food, then the Lord is making you a wonderful promise. He is saying:

> *Philippians 4:19 And my God shall supply all your need according to His riches in glory by Christ Jesus.*

> *Mark 8:8 So they ate and were filled, and they took up seven large* ***baskets*** *of leftover fragments.*

NEGATIVE
An empty basket speaks of lack and a curse. A good example of this contrast is found in:

> *Deuteronomy 28:17 Cursed shall be your* ***basket*** *and your kneading bowl.*

The only time such a vision would be negative is if the food inside the basket was rotten or if the basket is empty. In such a case it could mean that you either have not invested into the Kingdom of God financially or that your faith is low and that you do not trust God to meet your financial needs.

See also: Barn/Storehouse, Banquet, Barrel, Bread, Food

BASIN

A symbol of a particular aspect of your life being purified or cleansed.

Positive: A cleansing process to wash the past away (dealing with a very specific aspect of your past)
Negative: To revel in the dirt of the past

UNIVERSAL SYMBOL

A basin used for washing speaks of cleansing and purifying. A basin is not like a bath or baptism where the entire body is immersed, but rather just the feet are washed. The prime example used in Scripture is:

> *John 13:5 After that, He poured water into a* ***basin*** *and began to wash the disciples' feet, and to wipe them with the towel with which He was girded.*

As we walk through the world we become contaminated with its ways and its curses. To "wash your feet" means to cleanse yourself of the curses and sin you passed through for that day. This should be a daily activity for a Christian.

To Be Free of Guilt: To "wash your hands clean" of a situation means to relinquish your responsibility for the outcome of the events that follow your decision. This is the kind of act that Pilate took when claiming innocence of Christ's death.

> *Matthew 27:24 When Pilate saw that he could not prevail at all, but rather that a tumult was rising, he took water and* ***washed his hands*** *before the multitude, saying, "I am innocent of the blood of this just Person. You see to it*

So if you have a vision or prophetic dream of washing your hands, the Lord is saying that you are free of guilt and should relinquish the responsibility for the circumstances surrounding your vision.

NEGATIVE
Now in a negative light, if you dream of a basin being dirty or of trying to wash your hands and they never get clean, this means that you are struggling with false guilt.

A dirty basin also indicates that the pressures that you are going through right now are not of the Lord to purify you, but from the enemy to bring you under condemnation.

Wallowing in dirty water? You are wallowing in the sins and failures of the past. It is time to move on and put these things behind you.

See also: Baptism, Bath, Water

BATH

A process of cleansing that deals with your life as a whole.

Positive: The promise of complete deliverance
Negative: To wallow in sin and self-pity

CHARACTER SPECIFIC SYMBOL

POSITIVE
Dreaming of a bath often speaks of a complete cleansing. While cleansing with water from a basin simply washes the feet, to immerse oneself in a bath speaks of a total cleansing.

This is much like water baptism where the old is left behind and the new brought to life.

NEGATIVE
I was given a dream to interpret once where a lady dreamed that she was made to bathe in a bathtub of dirty water. She shared that as a child she was made to wash the bathtub of her father, who due to his illness did not bath often, so when he did, it left the most vile water and ring around the tub.

This dream indicated that there were things in her past that she was not free from. The rejection and hurts from the past (the filth) was still with her and she was not free to move on now in a new cleansed life.

This led to a ministry time of inner healing and the Lord raising her up into a new confidence in herself in Christ.

Always remember that in an internal dream, the object in the dream will have a different interpretation depending on the person. Perhaps for you or me, a bath might have a wonderful connotation, but for this woman, it was not good at all.

For someone who has good connotations to bathing, it might speak of a season of being cleansed of the sins of the past. It can also speak of simply being immersed in the peace of the Lord and letting go of all striving.

To enter into a time of rest and to let Him finish the work.

Universal Symbol

POSITIVE

> *2 Kings 5:10 And Elisha sent a messenger to him, saying, "Go and **wash in the Jordan seven times**, and your flesh shall be restored to you, and you shall be clean."*

You will see a few instances in the Scripture where someone was told to go and wash. In this passage Elisha told Naaman to wash in the Jordan. And Jesus told the blind man to wash his eyes. (John 9:6-7)

However, the best two passages on this subject are:

> *Ezekiel 16:9 Then I **washed** you in water; yes, I thoroughly washed off your blood, and I anointed you with oil.*

> *Acts 22:16 And now why are you waiting? Arise and be baptized, and **wash** away your sins, calling on the name of the Lord.*

This is a wonderful picture of the work of the Holy Spirit. As you come to Christ, you are washed clean of all your sin and you are made whole again.

If you have a vision of someone being washed or bathed, then the interpretation is very clear. The Lord is forgiving them of their sins and in His sight they are pure. This is a wonderful message and you should encourage the person to take hold of the Lord's love and grace.

If you had a dream where you were being washed, then this speaks of a process that is about to take place in your life. The Lord is about to remove all the things you have been struggling with.

This picture is in stark contrast to being "baptized with fire" where the process indicates a season of death to the flesh.

A washing with water speaks more of a replacement of dirt. This will take place in two ways:

1. Through being cleaned by the Word
The Scriptures speak of the "washing of the Word." This is a wonderful process and is not painful. Rather it builds you up and changes you from the inside out.

2. Experiencing the presence of the Lord and His external anointing
This is where you experience the Lord for yourself in a powerful way either through ministry or in your private time. By being in His presence, you are continually soaked in His love and it will displace the struggles that you have in your life.

NEGATIVE
To dream of a bath that is dirty or of bathing in dirty water is very negative. This means that firstly, the enemy is the one exposing all your sin and secondly, you are allowing yourself to wallow in self pity because of it!

Consider this passage:

> *2 Corinthians 7:10 For godly sorrow produces repentance leading to salvation, not to be regretted; but the sorrow of the world produces death*

When the Lord takes you through a bathing process, you repent and feel alive. When the enemy does it, you end up coming under condemnation and self pity (sorrow) that leads to depression (death). A good picture of what this looks like is found in Psalms 69:2 – the perfect Psalm of what wallowing in self-pity looks like!

See also: Baptism, Basin, Death, Wash, Water

BATHROOM/TOILET

A private cleansing process indicating disposal of spiritual contaminants – an indication of walking in the flesh or the spirit.

Dreaming of going to the toilet is a common one amongst many people and has a variety of meanings. See which one applies to you most.

Positive: Proof that you have undergone a cleansing process
Negative: To struggle with sin – your sin or the sins of others

CHARACTER SPECIFIC AND UNIVERSAL SYMBOLS

The most common dream and one that does not have an interpretation is when you need to use the bathroom and aren't able to find one. You wake up needing the toilet! This is just a classic purging dream and a reflection of what is really happening to you. This dream has no meaning.

POSITIVE
If you dream of cleaning the toilet or somehow getting rid of waste and the dream is positive, then this is an indication that you have dealt with impurities in your life that had the potential to cause you harm.

Just like getting rid of natural impurities is a sign of good natural health, dreaming of this indicates good spiritual health! It means that you are getting rid of all the junk that you have accumulated in your spirit. There is so much input you take in through your day - conflicts at work, movies you watch, and things you read. They are an accumulation of contamination in your spirit.

As you process these things and then "throw them out," it means that the Word of God that is inside of you is winning the battle. You have decided to walk in the spirit rather than hold onto the things of the flesh. It is like Jesus said:

> *Matthew 15:17 Do you not yet understand that whatever enters the mouth goes into the stomach and* ***is eliminated****? 18 But those things which proceed out of the mouth come from the heart, and they defile a man.*

Going to the bathroom publically: Depending on what you are going through in your life, this can be negative or positive. If you are a private person that seldom likes others to see your struggles, then it could well be that the Lord is telling you that He is going to bring you to a place of being able to share your struggles with others.

If you dream of using the toilet where everyone can see and you do not feel ashamed, then the Lord is saying that He is bringing you to the place where you will no longer be afraid to share your inner conflicts and even sins with others. You are coming to a place of being vulnerable. It is also an indication that although there is some "junk" to get rid of in your life that you do not have to be ashamed and struggle alone. God intends for you to lean on others to help you get through.

NEGATIVE

Feces and urine: If you dream of not going to the toilet successfully or somehow being covered by your own feces or urine when going to the bathroom, it is an indication of the flesh taking a hold in your life. By holding onto some things that are not of the Lord, the flesh is contaminating you and causing you to come under attack.

This uncleanness could refer to personal sin or a grudge you are holding against someone. It could also indicate something you keep feeding on spiritually. If you are in the habit of always watching worldly things and allowing your emotions to control you instead of the Lord, then this dream would confirm that you are walking in the flesh.

The solution is simple!

> *Galatians 5:16 I say then: Walk in the Spirit, and you shall not fulfill the lust of the flesh.*

Get your spiritual life healthy once again by getting back into the Word and obeying the Spirit of God rather than your own fleshly struggles.

Feces and urine of others: If you dream of being covered in feces and urine from someone else, then you are experiencing what I call a spiritual backlash. (I suggest the *Strategies of War* book for help on this one). Essentially, this means that someone just dumped all of their sin all over you! This is not uncommon when ministering to others. If they did not get a breakthrough and you have this dream, then you know you just got a spiritual backlash.

It could also mean that you have become contaminated with their sin. Either you had overidentified with them and allowed their sin to become your own, or you simply forgot to break spiritual ties after ministering.

Going to the bathroom publically: To dream of having to go to the bathroom publically or being mocked means that your private sins are being exposed in front of others. The Lord is not an accuser and although you might have failed, He does not accuse you. The enemy is the accuser of the brethren.

The solution is to bring your sin to the Lord and to receive His cleansing so that you can let go of the guilt that you are reveling in. If you do not allow the Lord to cleanse you, but you keep hiding the sin, you will continue to struggle with guilt and wallow in the dirt (spiritually speaking) that you are dreaming of.

God does not intend for you to be humiliated publically and even the Old Testament instructed everyone to “cover up their excrement” or to go to a private place outside of town (Deut 23:12-13)

See also: Bath, Farting, Shower

BATS

Creatures of the night that have a negative connotation. They speak of the work of the enemy in the life of a believer.

I have often seen bats in vision and they are usually tied to the occult.

Once in ministry I saw a vision of a certain person encased in the wings of a bat. As it turned out, they had been in contact with someone from a false religion and had been suffering a “backlash” from ministering to them.

There are other animals that have negative connotation, they are listed here in the following passage. Here we see a negative connotation for each of these, declaring them as unclean. If you flow in the gift of discerning of spirits, it is common to see animals such as these as power demons in the spirit. Each having a specific purpose according to its character. Here we see the following birds listed: eagle, vulture, buzzard, kite, falcon, raven, ostrich, owl , sea gull and heron.

> *Leviticus 11:13 And these you shall regard as an abomination among the birds; they shall not be eaten, they are an abomination: the eagle, the vulture, the buzzard,*
>
> *14 the kite, and the falcon after its kind;*
>
> *15 every raven after its kind,*
>
> *16 the ostrich, the short-eared owl, the seagull, and the hawk after its kind;*

> *17 the little owl, the fisher owl, and the screech owl;*
>
> *18 the white owl, the jackdaw, and the carrion vulture;*
>
> *17 the stork, the heron after its kind, the hoopoe, and the* ***bat***

See also: Birds, Eagle, Owl, Raven

BEAR

Generally negative in orientation, the bear indicates a spirit of destruction.

Positive: Aggressive protection
Negative: Spirit of destruction

POSITIVE
If you are fond of bears, then they could speak of something that is important to you. Certainly if you dream of a teddy bear or a stuffed toy bear, it speaks of something relating to your childhood or the "inner child" in you.

In Scripture, a bear is more often seen in a negative light although the one quality it is given is that it protects its young.

The bear is seen as one who protects its young.

Speaking of a desire to protect:

> *2 Samuel 17:8 For, said Hushai, you know your father and his men, that they are mighty men, and they are enraged in their minds, like a bear robbed of her cubs in the field; and your father is a man of war, and will not camp with the people.*

NEGATIVE
The bear almost always speaks of a curse operating with destruction. The bear is known to tear its pray to pieces and is a violent creature.

The bear speaks of an attack of destruction from satan who is known as the devourer. When I see a bear in the spirit I know that the person in question is under a curse and that the enemy is causing things in their life to be destroyed.

> *2 Kings 2:24 So he turned around and looked at them, and pronounced a curse on them in the name of the Lord. And two female* ***bears*** *came out of the woods and mauled forty-two of the youths.*

Cultural: In some cultures, worship the bear or believe in "bear spirits." If you originate from this culture or are ministering to someone from this culture, your vision is negative and is referring to a generational curse – a demonic influence passed from one generation to the next.

See also: Alligator, Lion, Toy

BEARD

A picture of the image you portray to others. The same interpretation applies to a mustache and other facial hair.

CHARACTER SPECIFIC SYMBOL

POSITIVE
When dreaming of a beard it represents the appearance you give others. If an existing beard is shaved, it means then that you will be showing a "new face" to the world.

To remove or grow a beard changes the entire look of a person. The shaving of one's beard could mean putting some things away and facing the world afresh.

NEGATIVE
If a woman dreams of having a beard, this would have a negative connotation as this would be a disgrace to her. It would mean that she is trying to put on the appearance of being a man and perhaps letting go of her femininity.

UNIVERSAL SYMBOL

POSITIVE
A strong beard in Scripture spoke of strength and favor. For a man to have a long beard was considered a sign of favor from the Lord.

NEGATIVE
To have one's beard shaved off was a sign of disgrace and humility. Shaving off your beard was often done in mourning to show extreme grief. David's servants were disgraced when their beards were shaved off:

> *2 Samuel 10:5 When they told David, he sent to meet them, because the men were greatly ashamed. And the king said, "Wait at Jericho until your **beards** have grown, and then return."*

See also: Baldness, Face, Hair

BED/BEDROOM

A bedroom could mean different things to different people. For most it would speak of a place of intimacy and privacy.

Positive: A call to intimacy and to just be "you"
Negative: Entertaining sin through temptation

Character Specific Symbol

In our family it was very common for all of the kids to pile onto my parents' bed every night as our father read us a bible story. Afterwards, we would pray together.

So for me, the bed, or my parents' bedroom would speak of a place of security and a sense of belonging. Depending on what your experiences were in your family, what a bedroom would mean to you will change in your dreams.

In some families, their parents' bedroom is completely off limits and would be a place that feels awkward. Take into account the kind of bed or bedroom in your dream or vision.

In a vision however, the bedroom takes on a very clear interpretation based on types and shadows in the Word.

POSITIVE
Naturally the most common interpretation, especially when dreaming of a marriage bed, speaks of intimacy. It also speaks of being vulnerable and open with the person that you are with. It also speaks of being in a covenant relationship with someone.

Have you ever heard the saying, "He is in bed with the enemy?" It means that he is in league with the enemy. In a positive sense, if you dream of being in a bedroom with someone that represents the Lord in your dreams, then it means that you are entering into intimacy with the Lord.

If you dream of being in bed with an unknown female character, it could mean that you are embracing your creative side or have a prophetic orientation.

Alternately, if you are in bed with a strange man and you feel positive in the dream, this speaks of entering into a more teaching orientation or perhaps getting more intellectual or logical in your thinking.

NEGATIVE
If you keep reliving past bad sexual experiences or have frightening dreams relating to being in bed with someone, this could indicate a hurt from the past that has not been dealt with or perhaps a fear you have.

Having a dream like this does not indicate that something like this will happen to you.

You need to discern if what you are dreaming stems from a past hurt, a current fear, or if it is simply a demonic attack from the enemy.

In each case, you can overcome and I teach you clear steps to working through this in *The Way of Dreams and Visions* book in the chapter on "Nightmares, Deception and Demonic Dreams."

UNIVERSAL SYMBOL

POSITIVE
In a vision or prophetic dream, being in bed with someone can be very positive. I have often dreamed that I was trying to be intimate with my husband in a dream, but we kept being interrupted. The message was clear... something in my life was interfering with my relationship with the Lord Jesus.

The bed and bedroom in Scriptures speaks of a place of intimacy, vulnerability, and submission to the Lord. Consider this passage:

> *Song of Songs 1:4 Draw me away! The king has brought me into his **chambers**. We will be glad and rejoice in you. We will remember your **love** more than wine. Rightly do they love you...*

NEGATIVE
Dreaming of being in bed with someone that is negative in your life is not a good picture. It means that you are in a relationship that is not of the Lord and that you are going the wrong way.

It also speaks of prostitution in Scripture and the prophets used this illustration often to show Israel how much they had turned their backs on God.

If you have a dream of adultery, it means that you have allowed the flesh to take control of your life and have left the Lord out.

It could also mean that you have allowed other things and other people in your life to take the place of the Lord. The Lord is the only one in the world who should be meeting your needs.

In a business sense, if you have a negative dream of getting into bed with a business partner, it could be that the step you are about to take is not of the Lord and you should be cautious.

> *Isaiah 57:8 Also behind the doors and their posts You have set up your remembrance; for you have uncovered yourself to those other than Me, and have gone up to them; you have enlarged your **bed** and made a covenant with them; you have loved their **bed**, where you saw their nudity.*

See also: Adultery, Arousal, Incest

BEELZEBUB

Beelzebub in Scriptures is called the "lord of the flies" or "the prince of demons."

If you have read the *Prophetic Warrior* book, you will know that Beelzebub is a prince demon. In our personal experience we have seen this demon as a very large and ugly mixture between a man and a fly.

We have also come to note that each time we have confronted this demon in the spirit that it has been linked to the New Age movement. If you are a prophet or evangelist and have been coming into confrontation with this particular prince demon, then it is likely that you have been either confronting people who have been involved in the New Age cult, or have yourself unwittingly embraced some of these false teachings yourself.

See also: Demons, Flies

BEES

As a positive symbol, bees speak of provision through hard work. Negatively they speak of physical attack.

UNIVERSAL SYMBOL

POSITIVE

In a positive sense they speak of blessing and of provision. Honey has very good connotations in the Scripture and you can see more of that under the symbol *Honey*.

> *Judges 14:8 Then he went down and talked with the woman; and she pleased Samson well. 8 After some time, when he returned to get her, he turned aside to see the carcass of the lion. And behold, a swarm of **bees** and honey were in the carcass of the lion.*

NEGATIVE

A swarm of bees do not have a good connotation and in Scriptures they spoke of attack and of pain.

> *Psalms 118:12 They surrounded me like **bees**; they were quenched like a fire of thorns; for in the name of the Lord I will destroy them.*

The psalmist here speaks of them as a fire of thorns. This is a good picture of an attack of the enemy in your life where he is bringing you pain from all directions. This can refer to physical attacks in the way of sickness or attacks from others whose words caused you pain.

Although bees do not kill you, they do cause a lot of pain, so if you dream or have a vision of being attacked by bees, this is a clear picture of demonic attack. The enemy seeks to hurt you and discourage you and to dissuade you from the direction or the blessing that God has for you.

> *Deuteronomy 1:44 And the Amorites who dwelt in that mountain came out against you and chased you as bees do, and drove you back from Seir to Hormah.*

See also: Insects, Wasp/Hornet

BEVERAGES/DRINKS

To get spiritually and physically charged to face the pressures of life

CHARACTER SPECIFIC SYMBOL

Before interpreting your dream, determine what this beverage means to you. If you are a tea drinker and then dream of drinking coffee, the interpretation will vary greatly to someone that is an avid coffee lover!

Alcohol: Consumption of alcohol to get drunk is called sin in the Word. Do you have a problem with alcohol? If so, then drinking it in a dream or vision is an indication that you are walking in disobedience and walking in sin.

Now on the other extreme if abstinence of all wine has become a religious bondage the interpretation will differ. There was someone whose greatest boast was "I have never touched a drop of alcohol in my life." The Lord challenged him and said, "So then your boast is in yourself? What if I told you to drink wine? Would you do it?"

So for him, this meant breaking out of a religious bondage.

Coffee: If you do not like coffee, then drinking it means learning to explore new things and being open to enjoying things you did not before.

Most coffee drinkers do it for the caffeine boost though, and drinking it means that you need to add something to your life right now. You need a spiritual boost! You are weary and just need a bit of encouragement to press on.

Soda: Everyone loves a sugar boost! If you are drinking your favorite soda, the Lord is saying that He delights in giving you the desires of your heart!

If you are drinking a soda that tastes bad, the Lord is saying that what you are feeding yourself right now might seem like a good idea, but it is going to leave a bitter aftertaste in your spirit! Stop doing it!

An abundance of soda is great for a season, but you cannot live on them. They are meant for a short boost, but can never replace true water. If your dream or vision is negative, then the Lord is saying that you keep seeking out things that make you feel good, but give no depth to your spirit.

Tea: Is tea drinking a part of your culture? Because of its nature, seeping tea is a lot like "boiling" and refers to a slow process that will eventually lead to perfection.

Do not rush the blessings of the Lord. Wait on Him. Allow Him to take you through the process, until it is perfected.

See also: Boil (Cooking), Thirst, Milk, Poison, Wine

BIBLE

A representation of both the Covenant and Word of God in our lives.

Positive: The Word of God to you right now
Negative: To be bound by tradition and the book of the Law

POSITIVE
The Scriptures speak a lot of the book of the Law. I had a vision once where the Lord gave me a scroll to eat and He said that this was His Word. The interpretation was pretty clear. I needed to get the Word into me!

The Bible is also a picture of the covenant we have with the Lord. It is the foundation of our Christian walk. To see a bible as the foundation of a house, speaks about making the Word a foundation.

Also to dream of a bible or see one in the spirit, it is possible to take the interpretation literally. Perhaps the Lord is saying quite clearly... pick up the bible and read it sometime!

NEGATIVE
It is hard to imagine a vision of a bible having a negative connotation, but it is indeed possible. Some families have a big old family bible. Often in the spirit I have seen something like that and then I know that the Lord is speaking of a generational curse in this person's life.

Perhaps even teaching or traditions that they received from their parents that seemed innocent, but were not based in Scripture at all.

The Lord is indicating that even though their motivations seem to indicate that they are doing things for the Lord, they are operating under an ungodly religious spirit that will bring division to the Church and not healing.

> *Galatians 3:10 For as many as are of the works of the law are under the curse; for it is written, "Cursed is everyone who does not continue in all things which are written in the* ***book of the law****, to do them'"*

See also: Scroll

BIRDS

Birds symbolize joy, freedom, and a new season in your life.

In a negative context they speak of demonic attack and the things that wear you down.

Positive: The joy associated with a change in seasons
Negative: Small attacks meant to wear you down

Character Specific Symbol

If you had a pet bird, then dreaming of this bird would mean something in your life. It could speak of a responsibility or of a joy in your life. Depending on the context of this dream, the interpretation would be different. First identify what this bird means to you. Is it something you love or is it someone else's bird that you hated?

If you loved it, then certainly it speaks of the Lord's blessing or a responsibility you have that you enjoy. However, if it is a bird you hate, then your dream is telling you that there is something in your life that is causing you irritation. The enemy is wearing you down with small irritations that are discouraging you.

Universal Symbol

POSITIVE

Birds can speak of joy and are the sign of spring when things are blooming. If you see a vision where spring has come and there are lots of birds in the air, then it is an indication that something new is about to come into your life.

It is a change of season and the tough time of winter is about to give way to springtime! Your lack is about to be turned into prosperity, just like the Lord promises you in Matthew 6:26

> *Song of Songs 2:12 The flowers appear on the earth; the time of singing has come, and the voice of the turtledove is heard in our land;*

> *Matthew 6:26 Look at the **birds** of the air, for they neither sow nor reap nor gather into barns; yet your heavenly Father feeds them. Are you not of more value than they?*

Eagle: The eagle is also a picture of the Holy Spirit. I know that it is a common picture of prophetic ministry, but this is inaccurate if you research the Scriptures. The Lord tells us that He will lift us up on eagle's wings!

In my book, *The Journey of Tamar,* I picture the Holy Spirit as the mighty eagle who is the one who takes Tamar on her journey. Representing his raw power, courage, and grace, the eagle is a powerful image of the Holy Spirit and it is such stark contrast to the dove.

However, both symbols together indicate his loving gentleness towards us and his fierce power to save us.

> *Exodus 19:4 You have seen what I did to the Egyptians, and how I bore you on **eagles'** wings and brought you to Myself.*

Then finally an eagle is a picture of strength stamina and power as in this famous passage:

*Isaiah 40:31 But those who wait on the Lord shall renew their strength; they shall mount up with wings like **eagles**, they shall run and not be weary, they shall walk and not faint.*

NEGATIVE
Birds are also a very strong negative picture in the Scriptures. You will see that they are often used as an illustration for attack or of the enemy destroying you. The prophets spoke often about the birds that would "eat the flesh" of those that were slain.

And so in the spirit when we see birds of prey, the message is very clear. This speaks of demonic attack. The kind of attack that tries to pick at you and pull you apart a piece at a time. It is not just one large attack, but many small things that are coming at you from all directions.

If you have a vision of being surrounded by black birds, it means that the enemy is trying to destroy you a bit at a time and to wear you down. You can overcome though in the name of Jesus!

*Ezekiel 39:4 You shall fall upon the mountains of Israel, you and all your troops and the peoples who are with you; I will give you to **birds** of prey of every sort and to the beasts of the field to be devoured.*

All carnivorous birds: These birds, in Scripture were called "unclean" and were always depicted as attack, destruction, sorrow, lack, and being devoured. It is common for the phrase "birds of the air" to refer to the demonic realm.

Matthew 24:28 For wherever the carcass is, there the eagles will be gathered together.

See also: Dove, Eagle, Seasons, Swan

BIRTH

If you are dreaming of giving birth, it means that there is something new that you are busy entering into in the spiritual realm.

POSITIVE
To dream of giving birth means that the season of preparation that you have been in has come to an end and that you are now ready to walk in what God has conceived in you.

If you have a ministry calling and dreamed previously that you were pregnant and then later dream that you are giving birth, this means that your season of training for that call is coming to an end.

*Galatians 4:19 My little children, for whom I labor in **birth** again until Christ is formed in you,*

If you dream that you give birth and it is painless, this is positive and means that whatever it is that God is giving you right now, you will enter into it easily.

If you dream that the labor is difficult, this means that whatever new thing that is coming into your life – you will need to work at it.

To dream that you did not know you were pregnant, but now are suddenly giving birth, also has a good interpretation.

It means that although you did not know it, the Lord had been doing a work in you behind the scenes and now you are ready to walk into it. Expect something new to open up in your life at the Lord's hand.

NEGATIVE
To dream that you give birth to a baby that is deformed, is negative. This also goes for giving birth to anything that is unclean or not human.

This means that you have conceived something in your heart that is not of the Lord and has its roots in sin.

> *Psalms 7:14 Behold, the wicked brings forth iniquity; yes, he* ***conceives*** *trouble and brings forth falsehood.*
>
> *James 1:15 Then, when desire has* ***conceived****, it gives* ***birth*** *to sin; and sin, when it is full- grown, brings forth death.*

To dream of giving birth prematurely and the baby dies is also negative. This means that you ran ahead of the Lord and did not wait until you had reached maturity.

See also: Baby, Child, Miscarriage, Pregnant

BLACK

Mostly negative in connotation, black refers to oppression, disease, contamination, ignorance and deception.

Relating to skin color: While dreaming of being in a black room or being surrounded by the color black would have a negative connotation, you might dream of a black person. If you feel comfortable around black people or are black yourself, then that person would mean something good in your dreams.

When dreaming about a black person, the first thing you must do is identify how you feel about this race in the natural.

I do remember one time though, when a black man I knew, had grown up feeling uncomfortable around other blacks (not having been exposed to other blacks when growing up) so when he dreamed of a black person, it had a negative connotation to him.

Being black also speaks of being different or standing out - but in a positive sense. Consider the following passages:

> *Song of Songs 1:5 I am **black**, but comely, O ye daughters of Jerusalem, as the tents of Kedar, as the curtains of Solomon. (KJV)*
>
> *Song of Songs 1:6 Look not upon me, because I am **black**, because the sun hath looked upon me: my mother's children were angry with me; they made me the keeper of the vineyards; but mine own vineyard have I not kept. (KJV)*

Relating to hair color: Now to dream that you were grey and your hair turned back to its original black, means that the Lord desire to "restore to you that which the locust has stolen." (Joel 2:25) In other words, what you have lost through time, He will restore to you.

Relating to the actual color: The only time seeing the color black in the Scripture would be positive is if it referring to a valuable resource such as oil or coal. Rich, black coal indicates the materials that are good for starting a fire! This indicates a promise of abundance from the Lord. A blessing that has been there all along, but that you have just not seen it before.

Rich, black coal means that you have within you the potential to be a raging inferno for the Lord! All that is left now, is for you to light it and move forward.

NEGATIVE

For the most part though the color black is very seldom positive in a vision.

Unless referring to a specific person of culture or race, the color black almost always speaks of darkness and the work of the enemy.

You might see a person bound by black chains. Perhaps you will see a person in a dark room. All of these are negative.

When ministering personally, I have often seen a person covered by a black, death shroud in the spirit. When I see this, I know they are under demonic attack.

I have also seen cities with a dark cloud over them. When I see this, I know I am seeing the work of the enemy in that area.

The color black will more likely be negative than positive in a dream or vision.

When I pray for someone for healing, the Lord will often show me the area that is infected as black in the spirit. This speaks of disease and sickness. When praying for healing of a specific injury or infirmity, I will often see the person's organ or infected area in the spirit. The parts that are diseased, will appear black in my vision. I will continue to pray the healing through until I see the color of that organ change from black to its original state.

Here are some Scriptures to consider:

Speaking of oppression and physical attack:

> *Job 30:30 My skin grows **black** and falls from me; my bones burn with fever.*

Speaking of mourning:

> *Jeremiah 4:28 For this shall the earth mourn, and the heavens above be **black**, because I have spoken. I have purposed and will not relent, nor will I turn back from it.*

Speaking of sin:

> *Luke 11:34 The lamp of the body is the eye. Therefore, when your eye is good, your whole body also is full of light. But when your eye is bad, your body also is full of **darkness**. 35 Therefore take heed that the light which is in you is not **darkness**.*

Speaking of the work of the enemy:

> *Ephesians 6:12 For we do not wrestle against flesh and blood, but against principalities, against powers, against the rulers of the **darkness** of this age, against spiritual hosts of wickedness in the heavenly places.*

See also: Hair

BLIND

The inability to see what is going on around you in the natural and spiritual realm.

Positive: To be made to stop and wait on God for the next step
Negative: Hindered from seeing the truth

POSITIVE
Being blind is negative for the most part, however there is an exception and it is when your enemy is blinded! The Lord has often told me to pray that the eyes of the enemy are made blind to His plans in our life. To have a vision that the enemy is blinded is good. It means that God is going to move forward with His plan, but you will not experience spiritual warfare. Isn't this what Paul did in the following passage?

> *Acts 13:11 And now, indeed, the hand of the Lord is upon you, and you shall be **blind**, not seeing the sun for a time."*
>
> *And immediately a dark mist fell on him, and he went around seeking someone to lead him by the hand*

I am reminded of Paul's own experience with blindness when he was surrounded by a bright light on the way to Damascus. Blindness in this context has a clear message: It is time to stop being bullheaded in the direction you are going and to hear what God has to say! You are trying hard in the flesh to do what you think is God's will, but going in the wrong direction. To have a prophetic dream or vision of being made blind, it is time to consider your current actions.

This will likely accompany a "spiritual blindness" that you are currently experiencing. The Lord will not give you the next step in your walk, until you take time to remain quietly in His presence and hear what He has to say.

NEGATIVE
To be blind is always negative and means to be unable to see the truth and to walk in darkness.

In both dreams and visions, to be blind means to be unable to see the truth. It denotes confusion and conflict. Consider these passages:

> *1 John 2:11 But he who hates his brother is in darkness and walks in darkness, and does not know where he is going, because the darkness has **blinded** his eyes.*

Here the blindness refers to bitterness in your heart. Bitterness causes your heart to become hard and to not see the truth even when it is in front of you.

> *2 Corinthians 4:4 Whose minds the god of this age has **blinded**, who do not believe, lest the light of the gospel of the glory of Christ, who is the image of God, should shine on them.*

To be blind also means that you do not understand the Word of God.

There have been many times that I have seen someone blindfolded in the spirit. When I see this, then I know that the enemy is preventing them from seeing the truth. They are stumbling around in darkness.

See also: Darkness, Eyes

BLOOD

The blood of Christ refers to our salvation, however menstrual blood or blood from being hurt are both negative and indicate spiritual attack, walking in the flesh, or bitterness in your heart.

Positive: Life and salvation
Negative: Hurt and attack

CHARACTER SPECIFIC SYMBOL

Regular blood:

POSITIVE
When a wound bleeds, although it is painful, it can sometimes refer to a season of cleansing. In most cases though if you dream of blood or of bleeding, it is negative.

NEGATIVE
To dream of blood being on your hands refers to being responsible for the lives of others.

In a natural sense, to bleed indicates pain, hurt, and destruction.

So if you dream of being cut and of bleeding, then it is means that you are under attack.

Certainly to dream of someone else's blood on your hands means taking responsibility for them, but also an indication of being the reason for their hurt.

Universal Symbol

POSITIVE
The blood of Jesus Christ is the most positive picture you can get. It was His blood that washed us clean and allows us to enter into a covenant with God, being only man.

The crucifixion of Christ is a picture of the blood covenant God made with man.

> *1 Corinthians 11:25 In the same manner He also took the cup after supper, saying, "This cup is the new covenant in My **blood**. This do, as often as you drink it, in remembrance of Me."*

> *1 John 1:7 But if we walk in the light as He is in the light, we have fellowship with one another, and the **blood** of Jesus Christ His Son cleanses us from all sin.*

NEGATIVE
In the spirit I have often seen a bleeding heart when praying for someone. The interpretation is clear. They have had many hurts in life and still carry these hurts with them.

The Lord always desires to heal these hurts, and if you are a prophet, you will be used of the Lord to speak healing to these hurts. This process is called inner healing and is part and parcel of prophetic ministry.

Menstrual blood: In Scriptures, menstrual blood was considered a time when a woman was unclean. If you are a woman and you dream of being on your period, it speaks of being in the flesh or of allowing sin into your life. This is a warning dream.

> *Leviticus 15:19 "If a woman has a discharge, and the discharge from her body is **blood**, she shall be set apart seven days; and whoever touches her shall be unclean until evening.*

The same thing applies to any man who has an "issue from his flesh" according to Scripture:

> *Leviticus 15:2 Speak unto the children of Israel, and say unto them, When any man hath a running* ***issue out of his flesh****, because of his issue he is unclean. (KJV)*

See also: Altar, Wound

BLUE

Blue is almost always a positive picture in dreams and visions, representing the Kingdom of Heaven.

Positive: A call to ministry
Negative: Bruising – a hurt from the past that continues to bring discomfort

POSITIVE

Blue is a royal color in the Scriptures and you will find it mentioned many times in the tabernacle of Moses. Blue linen, lace, and cloths were used to cover the many instruments in the tabernacle and this color represents the Kingdom of Heaven.

It speaks of the Throne Room of the Lord. If you were to see a vehicle in blue, it would mean that your ministry has been given to you by the Lord.

It is a representation of the Kingdom of God. Blue clothing also speaks of representing the Kingdom of God. If you saw someone dressed in blue it would mean that they have been sent by the Lord as a representative of the Kingdom of God. In other words, they are called to the ministry.

Some Scriptures to meditate on:

> *Exodus 26:1 Moreover you shall make the tabernacle with ten curtains of fine woven linen and* ***blue****, purple, and scarlet thread; with artistic designs of cherubim you shall weave them.*

Being called to ministry:

> *Exodus 28:31 You shall make a veil woven of* ***blue****...*

NEGATIVE
The only time you might see the color blue in a negative light is when it refers to bruising, as in wounds and pain. Yet even in this, a bruise in the natural indicates a healing that is taking place beneath the skin. So while the bruise indicates a past hurt, it also represents a healing process.

Speaking of hurt and healing:

*Proverbs 20:30 The **blueness** of a wound cleanseth away evil: so do stripes the inward parts of the belly. (KJV)*

See also: Bruise, Colors

BOAT

Vehicles always represent the tool or "vehicle" for your ministry. Depending on the kind of vehicle indicates different ministry types. A boat also speaks of the ministry you are currently involved with. It does not refer to your personal ministry.

When I see a boat or ship in vision, it represents our ministry as a whole. I seldom see it as relating to my personal ministry, but rather to my corporate ministry involving my ministry team members.

So if you see a ship in dry docks, it means that things have dried up and that the Holy Spirit has not been given license in this ministry.

A small sailing ship represents your personal ministry, unlike a passenger ship that would represent an organization as a whole.

Battleship: A large battleship represents a ministry involved in spiritual warfare and defense.

I remember once the Lord showing us that our "ship" had been transformed into a battleship. The message was clear. We were being led into circumstances that required continual warfare and battle against the enemy.

This did come to pass and we faced a season of continual warfare.

Yet again, we saw that same ship being transformed to a cruise ship. The Lord let us know that a new season of rest and peace was coming. This also came to pass.

There have been other times when we saw the ship in harbor taking on supplies. The Lord told us that this would be a season of not making any major moves, but of waiting in His presence to be filled up and prepared.

A cargo ship: A cargo ship or a ship of Tarshish refers to trade and industry. See more about this under *Ship.*

Depending on the size of the boat, its surroundings and its condition, it will give you a good idea of what the Lord is saying to you at this time with regards to the size, function, and season of your ministry.

It could also be that the boat you keep seeing refers to Noah's ark.

The Lord also gave me a vision once of a fleet of ships sailing together and indicated that He would be bringing many ministries to "sail alongside" us as we fulfilled the mandate He had given to us for ministry.

See also: Airplane, Anchor, Ark, Car, Ship, Train, Vehicles

BODY

The most obvious translation for a body is a picture of the body of Christ. To see a dead body can also speak of death to your flesh.

Positive: The unity and health of the Church
Negative: The disunity and failure in the Church

I have often seen the Church as a body in the Spirit. Depending on the state of the body, the Lord will show me different things.

At one time I saw the Church as a mighty giant, but unarmed. He said that it was time for the fivefold ministry to rise up and equip the Church.

Another time, I saw a part of the Body that was diseased. He showed me that this was an aspect of heretical teaching that was a disease to His Church.

If you see this while in intercession, then the Lord is calling you to pray for His Church.

> *1 Corinthians 12:27 Now you are the* ***body*** *of Christ, and members individually.*

Although it might seem strange that a vision or dream of a dead body could be positive, it truly is! It indicates that there is an aspect of your life that the Lord is calling to death. I cover this concept in my description of *Death* so please go there for a full understanding.

See also: Arm, Back, Chest, Feet, Hand, Skeleton, Skull

BOILS (SKIN INFECTION)

A painful exposure of sins that are hindering your spiritual life

Positive: Forgiveness and healing
Negative:

- A curse because of disobedience
- Sin being exposed

Character Specific Symbol

Did you suffer with boils as a child? If you dream of these, then it could well be that your dream is referring to hurts of the past you have not dealt with. It might even be speaking of generational sins that are starting to "break out" in your life.

Universal Symbol

POSITIVE
Although it is hard to imagine a good interpretation for a "boil" there is one! A boil that is healed in your dream means that the Lord has brought healing to the effects of your sin. Hezekiah had fallen ill and was about to die, as he pleaded to God, this is what happened:

> *Isaiah 38:21 Now Isaiah had said, "Let them take a lump of figs, and apply it as a poultice on the boil, and he shall recover."*

NEGATIVE
A boil is the manifest proof of impurities in the blood. This applies to both the natural and spiritual realm. God caused the Egyptians to break out in boils because Pharaoh would not let His people go. (Exodus 9:10)

To dream of boils breaking out means that the Lord is about to "bring out" (expose) the underlying contamination in your spirit. There is something within that is unclean and it needs to be exposed and dealt with!

There is good news! In the moment the sins of your heart are exposed, you have a choice to make. You can repent and go through a healing process, or your sin can turn "leprous." You can receive healing and promotion or make the situation worse.

> *Leviticus 13:23 But if the bright spot stays in one place, and has not spread, it is the scar of the boil; and the priest shall pronounce him clean.*

See also: Wound

Book

A precedent set in stone and a memorial to the events of your life and ministry.

Positive: The beginning of a new spiritual journey
Negative: The end of a chapter in your life – you cannot go back

Character Specific Symbol

To come to "the end of a chapter" speaks about a season in your life coming to an end. This can be both a good and a negative thing. Whatever the season is, this one message is clear: It is over and you can never return to it. Let it go with its joys and its disappointments.

POSITIVE
"Do not judge a book by its cover" is a common expression. It means that you should not come to conclusions about anyone until you get to know them.

A book is a perfect picture of the life and actions of a person. A book cover then would be the image that you use to portray yourself.

If you dream of a new book cover, then the Lord is saying that the way you present yourself is about to change!

A textbook or a clearly labeled study book speaks of education and learning. If it is positive in your dream, then perhaps the Lord is saying that it is time to increase your knowledge.

NEGATIVE
If the dream is negative, then the Lord is saying that you are putting too much emphasis on intellect and learning. It is time to get into the spirit and to move into action!

To dream of having a book cover ripped off speaks of being made vulnerable and of being exposed. This is negative though because it is speaking of tearing you down in the sight of others.

Universal Symbol

POSITIVE
The moment you put pen to paper what is written is something that is "carved in stone" so to speak. It is something that will remain for generations. It is not simply a passing thought but it is a precedent that will remain.

This is why when I see a book in the spirit, I know that the Lord is saying that what I am about to do is something that will remain.

There have been times when I have seen a book with blank pages. The message is clear: I am about to start over again. Whatever direction that the Lord is sending me into, it is something I have not done before.

If you have a dream or vision that pages of a book are wiped clean, it means that what you have done up until now is over and it is time to start afresh.

To dream of having pages added to a book, then the Lord is saying that there is more that He wants you to accomplish and learn.

> *Job 19:23 Oh, that my words were written! Oh, that they were inscribed in a **book**! 24 That they were engraved on a rock with an iron pen and lead, forever!*

A memorial: A book is also a memorial of the things that have taken place in your life. It is a memorial of the works you have done for the Lord and the accomplishments in your life.

> *Exodus 17:14 Then the Lord said to Moses, "Write this for a memorial in the **book** and recount it in the hearing of Joshua, that I will utterly blot out the remembrance of Amalek from under heaven."*

NEGATIVE

Because books contain the words of the author, it means that they also contain the spirit. Not all books contain the spirit of Christ and it is common for the Lord to use a book in a negative sense.

If you have been praying to the Lord about things going wrong in your life and see a book in the spirit, then the Lord is saying that there are some things you have read and believe that have contaminated your spiritual walk.

He might also be speaking of an actual book that you bought and have in your house. It could even be that the teachings of the author of that book have something wrong with them.

> *Isaiah 10:1 Woe to those who decree unrighteous decrees, who **write** misfortune, which they have prescribed;*

See also: Letter, Pen, Scroll

Boss

An image of authority in your life. Consider your boss and the kind of relationship you have with him. In a negative sense he could represent the system of the world or as a spiritual Pharaoh.

If he is positive in your life, then it is a good indication that he is a picture of your success in the workplace and in the world.

See also: Authorities

Bow

The call to a higher level of spiritual warfare that will require precision and counter insurgence warfare.

Positive: Strength and precision in spiritual warfare
Negative: To be under spiritual attack from a source you cannot see

Universal Symbol

A bow is a weapon of warfare and has many positive connotations in Scripture.

POSITIVE
To see a bow in the spirit speaks of strength in spiritual warfare. It is not easy to draw back a bow in the natural! It takes skill. It is also a weapon that is used from afar – much like a sniper in our modern day.

This speaks of spiritual warfare that is not done face to face, but rather in intercession and under the radar.

> *Genesis 49:23-24*
> *The archers have bitterly grieved him, Shot at him and hated him. But his bow remained in strength, And the arms of his hands were made strong by the hands of the Mighty God of Jacob (From there is the Shepherd, the Stone of Israel*

I recommend the *Prophetic Counter Insurgence* book for more on this subject

Speaking of children: Children are likened to an arrow in the bow of a man. The Scripture also refers to us, God's children as arrows in his quiver!

> *Isaiah 49:2 And He has made My mouth like a sharp sword; in the shadow of His hand He has hidden Me, and made Me a polished shaft; in His quiver He has hidden Me.*

We are the Lord's weapons against the enemy and if we keep straight, He will shoot us into the heart of the world to bring change.

NEGATIVE
To be shot at with a bow and arrow speaks of the attack of the enemy. This may be happening through negative words being spoken over you by others.

To see your bow broken in the spirit means that the enemy has discouraged you and has "broken" your strength and desire to fight. It is time to get up again. Get strengthened in the Lord and take the fight to the enemy once again!

See also: Arrow, Weapons

BRACELET

A bracelet is a picture of favor and blessing.

UNIVERSAL SYMBOL

A bracelet as an item of jewelry has a good connotation. In the Scriptures, the servant gave Rebekah bracelets to show her favor and to indicate that she was special to the Lord.

In Ezekiel, the Lord says how he reached out to Israel and put bracelets on her and gave her honor.

They were also an indication of a person's position and when the foolish Amalekite wanted to convince David that he had killed Saul, he brought him Saul's bracelets as proof.

> *Ezekiel 16:11 I adorned you with ornaments, put **bracelets** on your wrists, and a chain on your neck.*

> *2 Samuel 1:10 So I stood over him and killed him, because I was sure that he could not live after he had fallen. And I took the crown that was on his head and the **bracelet** that was on his arm, and have brought them here to my lord.*

See also: Ring, Gold, Jewelry

BRANCH

A picture of tapping into or being connected to a source of blessing or curses.

POSITIVE

By far the best image we have of branches in Scripture is where Jesus says that He is the vine and we are His branches.

A branch cannot bear fruit by itself, but needs the vine or tree trunk to feed it. It is a lovely picture of how we as believers are "tapped into" the Lord, to receive the power we need to produce fruits of righteousness.

> *John 15:5 I am the vine, you are the **branches**. He who abides in Me, and I in him, bears much fruit; for without Me you can do nothing.*

NEGATIVE

Paul spoke of the gentiles being grafted into the olive tree and how as a result, they tapped into the blessing of the Lord.

> *Romans 11:17 And if some of the **branches** were broken off, and you, being a wild olive tree, were grafted in among them, and with them became a partaker of the root and fatness of the olive tree;*

We have often seen this vision in this ministry. There have been times when the Lord removed some people from us and in the spirit we saw them as branches being cut from a tree.

On the other hand, though, we have also had a vision where we saw the Lord graft a new branch into the tree.

Meaning that He was adding this person to part of this ministry and replacing what was once removed.

I have also seen this in relation to divorce and remarriage. After a divorce, as we have prayed with someone, we will see the Lord cut off the "old branch" and replace it with a new one.

If we see a branch attached someone in the spirit that needs to be removed, this means that they need to go through a season of pruning or that an intimate relationship from the past has to be cut off.

See also: Trees, Vine

BREAD

A picture of the body of Christ and the Word of God. It also speaks of those things that we feed on and that sustain us both spiritually and naturally.

Positive: The Word of God
Negative: Contaminated doctrine

POSITIVE
Bread speaks of the body of Christ in Scripture. Apostle Paul likens the body of Christ to being one loaf of bread all being part of Christ.

It is a lovely picture of the communion service where the bread it broken and each one partakes. This is a covenant ritual and says, "Just as I eat this bread, I declare that I am part of Christ and in so being, I am also part of this Body"

> *1 Corinthians 11:26 For as often as you eat this **bread** and drink this cup, you proclaim the Lord's death till He comes.*
>
> *1 Corinthians 10:17 For we, though many, are one **bread** and one body; for we all partake of that one **bread**.*

Bread also speaks of the Word of God. I had a dream once where I was taken to a table full of bread. It smelled so good and I could eat all I wanted.

The interpretation was clear. The Lord at that time was leading me into the teaching ministry and He was encouraging me to get into the Word and to study and consume as much as I could.

Manna: Manna was referred to in Scriptures as the "food of heaven" It is a lovely picture of God's provision for our needs. Jesus used manna as an illustration of Himself saying:

> *John 6:58 This is the bread which came down from heaven—not as your fathers ate the **manna**, and are dead. He who eats this bread will live forever.*

NEGATIVE
Rotten Manna: The Scriptures say that if the Israelites left their manna until morning, that it got worms and was rotten. This is a picture of disobedience and rebellion. It means that you started out doing what God wanted you to do, but then took matters into your own hands.

A good example of this is King Saul who started out serving God correctly, but then took things into his own hands.

Stale bread: I remember ministering with someone once who was used by the Lord as a teacher in years past. As I was sharing though, I saw stale bread in the spirit. The Lord said that he was trying to minister all his old revelations and knowledge that he got when he first started in ministry.

Years later he had become stagnant. His relationship with the Lord was dead and now he was feeding God's people stale bread.

Sad to say, the man did not receive it. He clung to his old revelations and half-truths instead of taking the risk of letting it all go and getting something fresh from the Lord.

> *1 Corinthians 5:8 Therefore let us keep the feast, not with old leaven, nor with the leaven of malice and wickedness, but with the unleavened* ***bread*** *of sincerity and truth.*

See also: Bake, Barley, Cake, Wheat

BREAST

The breast has two functions. The first is to nourish and the second it is what identifies a woman.

Positive: To have a wealth of love to give
Negative:

- To keep your blessings to yourself
- To be unable to pour out in love

CHARACTER SPECIFIC SYMBOL

A woman's breasts are an image of her femininity. To dream of damaged or missing breasts as a woman indicates a problem with how you view your femininity.

It also is an indication that you have lost the blessing you once had and have nothing more to give out.

UNIVERSAL SYMBOL

For both genders though they are an image in Scriptures of containing milk, which is a picture of the blessings that you have to pour out.

To wean or be weaned refers to a process of individuation and maturity. The Word tells us that a time must come when we leave the milk to move onto the strong meat of the Word. To dream of being weaned or of weaning a baby has a clear message: it is time to grow up!

POSITIVE

Breastfeeding: To dream of breastfeeding a child means that you are giving your blessing and imparting all you have to that child. If it is a child you know, you need to identify what they mean to you.

If that child speaks of your ministry, it means that you are pouring everything you are and have into your ministry.

You are nurturing and causing it to grow. This is a good picture.

To drink off the breast of another means that you will partake of their blessing and abundance.

> *Isaiah 60:16 You shall drink the milk of the Gentiles, and milk the **breast** of kings; you shall know that I, the Lord, am your Savior and your Redeemer, the Mighty One of Jacob.*

NEGATIVE

If you keep dreaming of breastfeeding infants that do not belong to you, it is not a good picture.

It means that you are being "sucked dry" by others who have no intention of returning the favor. You keep giving of yourself to the point where there is nothing left to pour into those that really do matter.

In a ministerial sense, it means that you keep taking care of other people's ministries instead of putting the responsibility back into their own hands.

In a natural sense, it speaks of taking on too many responsibilities at one time that are not actually your concern.

To have dry breasts that do not produce milk speaks of having a curse in your life or of having given out so much, you have nothing left.

See also: Baby, Milk, Pregnant

BRIDE

A call to a season of intimacy and innocence - to be drawn into an intimate relationship with the Lord. It is also a representation of the things that you have joined yourself to.

Positive: An invitation to the secret place

Negative:

- Inability to draw nearer to the Lord
- To "marry" things that pull you away from the Lord

The wedding ceremony is a covenant ritual that symbolizes two people giving themselves completely to one another. In the Old Testament when two people performed a covenant ritual, they were saying, "All my strengths belong to you. All my possessions belong to you. Nothing I own belongs to me alone."

Keep this imagery in mind when considering both the bride and bridegroom as a symbol in your dreams and visions.

Character Specific Symbol

POSITIVE

Relevant for both bride and groom.

The image of a bride is a picture of someone willingly entering into a covenant with someone else. We as the church are called the bride of Christ. It represents purity, belonging and giving everything to the one you love.

> *Ephesians 5:27 that He might present her to Himself a* ***glorious church****, not having spot or wrinkle or any such thing, but that she should be holy and without blemish.*

Bride: If you have a vision of being a bride, the Lord is calling you into an intimate relationship with Him. To put aside all your own striving and works and to let Him lead and be in control.

NEGATIVE

Relevant for both bride and groom.

If you dream of being married to someone that you do not like, it could be an indication that you have "joined yourself" to something that is not of the Lord.

It is worth mentioning that just because you dream of marrying someone is *not* an indication that you will really marry them. Keep in mind that the people and objects in your dreams are symbolic.

Universal Symbol

If you flow in intercession, it is common to see the church as the bride of Christ. We have often see her as a bride that was beaten and dirty. The Lord wanted us to pray that she would rise up and be healed from all the attacks of the enemy.

The Lord is also calling her to rise up and to be beautiful in His sight. For the Church to be without spot or wrinkle means to bring her to a place of being fully in love with her bridegroom. Only once she is perfected in love will she be without any spot.

Here John the Baptist shares how the church will be the bride of Christ, but how he is simply the friend of the bridegroom, not yet having entered into the New Covenant that Jesus brought through His death.

> *John 3:29 He who has the **bride** is the bridegroom; but the friend of the bridegroom, who stands and hears him, rejoices greatly because of the bridegroom's voice. Therefore, this joy of mine is fulfilled.*

See also: Wedding, Woman, Wife

BRIDEGROOM

A picture of the things you are joined to. Christ is the ultimate picture of our bridegroom and represents entering into an intimate relationship with Him.

The bridegroom is a picture of the Lord Jesus. He referred to Himself as the Bridegroom.

Positive:

- To enter into a new intimacy in your relationship with the Lord
- A picture of protection and security
- To be taken care of

Negative: To fear the Lord and distance yourself from Him

CHARACTER SPECIFIC SYMBOL

If you dream of marrying someone you know, this is not an indication that you will marry them in real life. Consider what they represent in your life. If you had a relationship with them in the past, then they could be a picture of your relationship with the Lord Jesus.

Becoming a bridegroom: For a man, this represents a call to maturity. The Lord is calling you to embrace the fullness of your masculinity and to enter into the next season of spiritual maturity. The time is over for you to only care for your needs – He is calling you to care for the needs of others and to be their protector instead of just thinking of your own needs first.

UNIVERSAL SYMBOL

Christ is the ultimate picture for the Bridegroom, speaking of one who paid every price possible for us. He speaks of protection, security, and our ability to rest in His arms. To be "called by the Bridegroom" is not only a picture of intimacy, but also of security. It is a call to rest in His finished work and to allow Him to protect and vindicate you.

> *John 3:29 He who has the bride is the **bridegroom**; but the friend of the bridegroom, who stands and hears him, rejoices greatly because of the bridegroom's voice. Therefore, this joy of mine is fulfilled*

See also: Bride, Wedding

BRIDGE

A transitional phase in your life leading you into something new. It is also a picture of connecting two aspects of your life with regards to circumstances and relationships.

Positive: A passage is going to be established that was not there before
Negative: Failure to step out in faith

CHARACTER SPECIFIC SYMBOL

POSITIVE
To dream of finding a bridge indicates a transition into something new. It comes with some risk though and just as you cannot keep walking on the old road when you cross a bridge in the natural, you also cannot take the old stuff with you as you move into this new phase that God is leading you into.

To coin a phrase, "With everything that God gives you, you will be required to give something up." It is very similar to a "mountain climbing experience" where you cannot take all the baggage with you that you would like. It involves leaving something old behind and taking hold of something new.

In a positive context, this also means that you are making progress in your spiritual walk. If you have been asking God regarding your circumstances and you dream of crossing a bridge, this means that you are in a phase of transition now and to keep moving forward! You will soon enter your Promised Land.

NEGATIVE
To dream of falling off a bridge, a bridge being broken, or not being able to find one, is an indication that something is holding you back right now. There is something in your life that is preventing you from moving forward. You are "stuck" in your spiritual life and circumstances.

You are much like the children of Israel stranded on the wrong side of the river Jordan. The Lord is able to make a way where there is no way! Identify what is holding you back and put your faith in the Lord!

UNIVERSAL SYMBOL

POSITIVE
To dream of a bridge means that the Lord is opening the way to something new in your life. Just like He opened the Red Sea and stopped the river Jordan a bridge is a picture of being given passageway across something you could not have done on your own.

It means that the Lord will move His hand and make a way where there was none before.

> *Isaiah 43:19 Behold, I will do a new thing, now it shall spring forth; shall you not know it? I will even make a road in the wilderness and rivers in the desert.*

Whatever your struggle has been, seeing a new bridge means that God is about to make a new way for you. This way will be unexpected and it will not be something you could have done by yourself. You could not have made this with your own hands. It will be miraculous and what you need to do is stand in faith and trust God completely.

Connecting two aspects: I have often seen a bridge between two pieces of land or even between two warships. The Lord indicated that He would be adding a completely new aspect to my ministry. In the case of the two warships, He was telling me that I would be connected to another ministry and that we would work together.

If you see a bridge being built between two ministries or organizations, then the Lord is indicating a new relationship or "connection" with them.

Rope bridge: A bridge that looks shaky and insecure indicates a transition that will be difficult and will test your faith. There is no need to be afraid. The message is to press on forward regardless of what you see or feel right now – you will surely reach the other side!

Bridge falling away: If you cross a bridge in the spirit (or in a dream) and then you turn to see it fall away afterwards, the message if very clear. The Lord is "burning your bridges." The circumstances, relationships, and strengths you had in the previous season will pass away and there will be no way for you to go back to it.

Jesus our bridge: The greatest example of a bridge in our lives is the Lord Jesus! He is the one that bridged the gap between God and man. To see a bridge while witnessing means that Jesus is the way! The Lord intends for you to introduce this person to Jesus and to give them a bridge to cross.

The Holy Spirit bridge: When you are baptized in the Holy Spirit, a bridge is created in the spirit. From the time of salvation, you have the Holy Spirit dwelling inside of you, however, when you get baptized into the spirit, you enter into a relationship with the Holy Spirit. From that time, you will operate in the gifts of the Spirit. If you are praying for a believer and see a bridge, either it refers to moving into a new season. If they have not been spirit-filled, then it means that the Holy Spirit wants to baptize them.

NEGATIVE

If a bridge is in front of you in the spirit, God means for you to walk over it! If you see yourself faltering or afraid to cross the bridge, it means that you do not have faith in the Lord. It means that you would rather lean on your own understanding than trust that He will get you through this circumstance.

To see a broken bridge in a vision is a clear picture of an attack. You will need to determine if that attack has come from the enemy or if you have "broken the bridge" yourself through unbelief or fear.

See also: River, Road

BRIDLE

To be lead or forced into a particular direction by external pressures.

Positive: God changing your direction
Negative: Fighting against God's direction for your life

POSITIVE
Because it is used as a device to change the direction of a horse, having a bridle refers to having your direction changed for you.

You do not have a choice in the direction you would like to go, but have to simply follow:

> *2 Kings 19:28 Because your rage against Me and your tumult have come up to My ears, therefore I will put My hook in your nose and My* ***bridle*** *in your lips, and I will turn you back by the way which you came.*

If it is the Lord in charge of the bridle, then it means you must surrender your will and what you want to let Him have his way.

NEGATIVE
If the enemy is in charge of the bridle, then it means you are being led astray and are going in the wrong direction. It also means that you are allowing the pressures around you to hinder your own convictions.

See also: Horse

BRIEFCASE

A symbol of commerce and well-kept principles. It is also a picture of personal strengths, talents, and abilities.

CHARACTER SPECIFIC AND UNIVERSAL SYMBOLS

POSITIVE
Depending on the context of your dream, a briefcase can mean many things. If the briefcase is one you use for work, then it is a picture of your own workplace or the natural qualities that you have right now. If the briefcase belongs to someone else that you know, then it speaks of their position or the qualities that they possess.

Because a briefcase is used mostly in a business context, it carries the connotation of wealth and commerce. To dream of receiving a new briefcase is a good picture of promotion and being given new natural abilities.

A briefcase full of money is a picture of being given the ability to create finance. It means that the Lord wants to provide, but that He will do it through your work and natural strengths.

Depending on what is in the suitcase, the contents will indicate the new strength or area of your life that God wants to strengthen.

If I see an angel in the spirit, delivering a new briefcase, then I know that the Lord wants to do something new in the business aspect of my life. It requires change and also adding something new that I did not have before.

NEGATIVE
To dream of stealing someone else's briefcase means that you wish you had someone else's position or strengths, however, they are not your own. You should be content with what you do have and then the Lord can prosper you further. Envy will not help you attain your desire, rather it will leave you discouraged.

If you dream that you are forced to take a briefcase or that you have to carry one that is heavy and you feel very frustrated, it means that you are concentrating too much on natural/money matters instead of the things of God.

If you are in active ministry and have a similar dream, it means that you are being sidetracked by things of the world instead of focusing on the work of the ministry. This is what happened in Nehemiah 13:10 when the Levites went out to work in the fields instead of doing their ministry. They were corrected and called back to order.

Carrying someone else's briefcase: This means that you are taking on a load that is not your own to carry. In the end, you will not benefit from all the effort because you are investing into someone else's position and not your own. You need to discern if God has led you to take on this load or if you are allowing the enemy to weigh you down with obligation.

See also: Bag, Baggage, Gold, Money

Bronze/Brass

A picture of prosperity relating specifically to ministry (Finances used towards establishing ministry). Utensils in the tabernacle were overlaid with bronze. It is also a picture of beauty and strength.

Character Specific and Universal Symbols

POSITIVE

To dream of being given a bronze/brass object speaks of receiving resources to do the work of the ministry. Has the Lord laid it on your heart to provide for others who are doing the work of the ministry? To dream of giving away bronze suggests that the Lord wants you to provide the resources needed towards His work.

To see bronze armor is a promise that not only will the Lord establish you in ministry, but He will also provide from His storehouse so that you can do the work.

Not only is bronze armor a picture of strength, but it is also a picture of financial favor to "get the job done."

Mountains of bronze are pictures of prosperous, established ministries. Because bronze is a picture of wealth as well as beauty and strength, you can combine all three of these aspects for a full interpretation.

Notice in the passage below that Hiram (a picture of business) provided the utensils (speaking of ministry) for the temple.

> *1 Kings 7:45 And the pots, and the shovels, and the basons: and all these vessels, which Hiram made to king Solomon for the house of the Lord, were of bright* ***brass****. (KJV)*

NEGATIVE

To have bronze stolen or destroyed would be a picture of the enemy stealing finances that are being used for the work of God. The enemy is only too happy to attack the Church in this way! When the temples were ransacked, the bronze was always torn off the doors. When repairs were needed, they needed laborers using both iron and bronze.

Below is a picture of the enemy stealing resources from the work of God. (Babylon being a picture of the world)

> *2 Kings 25:13 The bronze pillars that were in the house of the Lord, and the carts and the* ***bronze*** *Sea that were in the house of the Lord, the Chaldeans broke in pieces, and carried their bronze to Babylon.*

See also: Altar, Colors, Gold, Iron

Brown

Positive: potential for blessing. Negatively it speaks of contamination and impurity.

POSITIVE
Brown is the color of earth and can speak of promise and blessing, especially if you are seeing an open fertile field ready for planting. This would indicate that the Lord desires you to sow so that He can bless and prosper you.

NEGATIVE
However more often than not, it speaks of being soiled or impure.

Consider this passage:

> *Genesis 30:32 Let me pass through all your flock today, removing from there all the speckled and spotted sheep, and all the **brown** ones among the lambs, and the spotted and speckled among the goats; and these shall be my wages.*

Jacob took all the animals that were considered of less worth than the rest. The Lord still blessed him though and he ended up having more than Laban.

If you see a garment that is stained brown, this speaks of being unclean and relates to sin. Water that is brown speaks of a spiritual contamination. Just as you would think twice about drinking brown water in the natural, so also is it a sign of a contaminated anointing in the spirit.

See also: Colors, Dress, Cloak

BRUISE

Refers to hurts of the past.

Positive: The promise of healing that will soon be yours
Negative: A hurt of the past that you have failed to look at and receive healing for

POSITIVE
To be bruised means to be crushed. Not just cast down, but beaten down. The Word promises us that the enemy will be bruised under our feet!

> *Romans 16:20 And the God of peace shall bruise Satan under your feet shortly. The grace of our Lord Jesus Christ be with you. Amen. (KJV)*

Although a bruise is a sign of a hurt, it can also mean that a hurt is being healed. If you dreamed of an open wound and then later on dreamed that the wound had turned into a bruise, this is an indication that you are in a phase of healing.

NEGATIVE
Bruises speak of a hurt that is not obvious, but very painful. When ministering inner healing, in the spirit, it is common for me to see bruises on a person.

When I see this, I know that the Lord is showing me that this person has many hidden hurts from the past that they still struggle with.

If something is bruised it is also ruined. The Lord required that the Israelites did not offer anything bruised to him. It was viewed as defective.

It is important to realize that the Lord is never the author of bruising. It is the enemy that bruises or seeks to destroy you. Isaiah says that a "bruised reed he will not break."

The Word says that Jesus was bruised for us, so that we do not have to suffer. If you dream or have a vision of being bruised, it means that the Lord desires to heal the brokenness in your heart and in your body.

He died so that you could be healed. He was bruised so that you could be made whole.

> *Isaiah 53:5 But He was wounded for our transgressions, He was* ***bruised*** *for our iniquities; the chastisement for our peace was upon Him, and by His stripes we are healed.*

See also: Wound

BUD

A promise of blessing and beauty soon to be revealed.

POSITIVE

The bud of a flower or fruit is a picture of promise and blessing, just like spring is the promise of coming abundance. It speaks of something that is still delicate and can easily be broken, but holds the potential for great things.

If you have recently been led into a new ministry or direction, seeing a bud in the spirit will represent this new thing. It requires protection and nurturing.

> *Isaiah 27:6 Those who come He shall cause to take root in Jacob; Israel shall blossom and* ***bud****, and fill the face of the world with fruit.*

The Lord is the author of blessing and a bud indicates that He desires to bless you naturally as well as spiritually. It is common for us to see financial provision that we have believed for as small seeds that are budding in the ground. As we press on with faith, hope, and love, those buds will bring fruit and we then see the provision in the natural.

> *Isaiah 61:11 For as the earth brings forth its* ***bud****, as the garden causes the things that are sown in it to spring forth, so the Lord God will cause righteousness and praise to spring forth before all the nations.*

NEGATIVE

Because a bud is so delicate in the natural, it is also an indication of something that is new and starting out. If you see that bud being crushed or destroyed, it speaks of loss and destruction in your life.

If you see the bud of a weed, this is negative and speaks of a contamination in your spirit. This could have happened through receiving teaching that was not Word based, or you have been filling your spirit too much with influences from the world.

See also: Flowers, Weeds

BUILDINGS

Established works or visions in your life. Different buildings will represent different visions or ministries.

If you are dreaming of being in a building from your past, it is possible that hurts or what happened back there is being stirred up once again in your life. If you dream of the house you grew up in, it could indicate that you are either facing conflicts from the past or perhaps putting things from the past to rest.

Look up the subject of healing dreams in the *Way of Dreams and Visions* for more on this.

Office buildings: An office building is where you work and speaks of your life in the workplace and world.

It is also a good picture of business and wealth. In the Old Testament, such business was conducted at the city gate.

POSITIVE

We have often seen a ribbon cutting ceremony in front a new building.

This is a picture of a new ministry or division of the ministry that the Lord has established in the spirit. If you are in intercession and see something like this, then the Lord is calling you to birth the new vision in the spirit and to release it through decree.

NEGATIVE

If you see a building being demolished, you need to decide of this is a good or a bad thing. At times a prophet will be called of the Lord to speak destruction on a work that is not of Him.

If you are a prophet, you might see a building being built or torn down in the spirit. It is for you to speak that forth in the spirit.

> *Jeremiah 1:10 See, I have this day set you over the nations and over the kingdoms, to root out and to pull down, to destroy and to throw down, to* ***build*** *and to plant.*

See also: Church, House

BULL

A picture of business that is progressive and sometimes aggressive in nature. A picture of financial provision that has the ability to reproduce itself.

Positive: To be bold in commerce
Negative: Being attacked by the world system

CHARACTER SPECIFIC SYMBOL

POSITIVE

To dream of receiving a bull or of a bull gaining in strength is a picture of an increase in your business or workplace. Because of the aggressive nature of the bull often mentioned in the Old Testament, the nature of this business is not passive.

It means that you will need to be offensive in your attitude towards this business opportunity and put some effort into it. You will need to "go out and get it."

NEGATIVE

To dream of being attacked or gored by a bull is very negative and speaks of spiritual attack on your natural life. It is a good picture of the enemy destroying you using either finances or the world's system.

The Lord had some strong rules regarding bulls that attacked people and it is a good picture of the enemy that often attacks finances to destroy God's people.

> *Exodus 21:29 If, however, the **bull** has had the habit of goring and the owner has been warned but has not kept it penned up and it kills a man or woman, the **bull** must be stoned and the owner also must be put to death. (NIV)*

UNIVERSAL SYMBOL

POSITIVE

If the Lord shows you a bull in the spirit that you need to sacrifice, He is asking you to offer up the best you have. He is asking you to give Him your abilities to make finances. This includes all your strengths and boasts.

To be given a bull or to see a strong bull is an indication that the Lord wants you to engage in business more aggressively. If you are involved with marketing, then the message is to become more aggressive in your marketing and not to be afraid to announce who you are.

A bull was an expensive commodity in the Old Testament and though it was a great source of reproduction it could also be quite aggressive. It is the perfect picture of walking in blessing and being bold about it as well!

It was also used in the most important sacrifices. A bull was sacrificed when Aaron and his sons were ordained to the work of the ministry. It speaks of something that should "cost you." It speaks of a position that "does not come cheap" but will involve a price to walk in.

Whether this position is in the workplace or ministry, it will bring blessing, but it will also carry a heavy responsibility. (Exodus 29:10)

NEGATIVE
Just like in a dream, a bull attacking or being destroyed is not positive. Either you are being attacked by the world system or the enemy is stealing God's blessing from you. If you have a vision of a bull being captured or taken away, this would indicate a spirit of theft.

Keep in mind that a young bull was used for the purpose of a sin sacrifice. If you dream or have a vision of being attacked by a young bull, this could be an indication that you are suffering a backlash. Have you ministered to someone recently? It could be that as you tried to help them break free of their sin, that they did not break free and you are now under the same attack.

Speaking of dealing with sin:

> *Ezekiel 43:21 Then you shall also take the **bull of the sin** offering, and burn it in the appointed place of the temple, outside the sanctuary*

See also: Cattle, Horse

BUTCHER

Mostly negative in connotation, speaking of heartless destruction.

Positive: Preparation of the Word
Negative:

- A false shepherd
- A spirit of death and destruction
- Utter destruction

CHARACTER SPECIFIC SYMBOL

POSITIVE
Are you a butcher by trade? Then your dream is referring to your workplace. Did you dream of an actual butcher? Then that person would represent a part of yourself.

If the person is unfamiliar to you, then move on to the universal symbol for your dream.

NEGATIVE
Because the nature of a butcher, in most cultures he would speak of death and destruction. To dream of an animal being butchered, there could be various interpretations.

Animal sacrifice: Is animal sacrifice common in your culture? Dreaming of sacrifice or butchery is talking about a generational bondage prevalent in your life.

Random butchery: Because of the utter destruction to whatever is butchered, a dream filled with butchery is speaking of a spirit of death and destruction.

Butcher chasing you: If you are being chased by a butcher or are being butchered in your dream and you are gripped with fear, realize that you are under demonic attack! Especially if your dream is complex with many scene changes, then it does not have an interpretation. Rather you are experiencing a nightmare (demonic attack in your dream.)

Universal Symbol

POSITIVE
The writer of Hebrews told his readers that they should be ready to eat the meat of the Word. To have a vision or prophetic dream about butchering meat means that the Lord needs you to take time to prepare the Word. You cannot serve anyone an entire cow! It needs to be cut down into smaller pieces.

This is a fantastic picture of the job of a pastor teacher. He will take the meatier aspects of the Word and then break it down into bite-sized pieces for everyone to eat. I talk about this in the *Today's Pastor* book.

NEGATIVE
A shepherd is meant to feed the sheep, but for a shepherd to be a butcher speaks of a leader that is failing in his position. He is indeed a false shepherd. A true shepherd leads and feeds. A butcher chases the sheep from behind to lead them to slaughter.

> *Ezekiel 34:2-4 "Woe to the shepherds of Israel who feed themselves! Should not the shepherds feed the flocks? You eat the fat and clothe yourselves with the wool; you slaughter the fatlings, but you do not feed the flock.*

Above all, seeing a "butcher" in the spirit speaks of a spirit of death and destruction. If the vision is negative, the Lord is showing you how to pray. You need to stand against this attack from the enemy, because he not only determines to hurt the work of God, but to destroy it completely.

See also: Altar, Demons, Kitchen, Meat, Shepherd

BUTTERFLY

A picture of maturity and beauty. Represents the end of a season of being hidden and of now being released into the world

Positive: A call to let the world see your potential
Negative: A beauty that will soon fade

POSITIVE
Through my various phases of ministry training by the Holy Spirit I often saw myself in a chrysalis indicating that God had set me apart for a season.

In the same way when I saw a butterfly in the spirit, I knew that this season of being hidden was over and that it was time now to be revealed to the world.

Seeing a butterfly indicates the end of a season of being hidden and the start of a season where God will reveal you to the world and open new doors to walk in the work He did inside of you in private.

NEGATIVE
Because the lifespan of a butterfly is so short, it is also a picture of beauty that is short-lived. To see a butterfly in a negative light is a picture of an outward beauty that will wane quickly. In other words – this is not a blessing or a beauty that will last. Consider this passage

> *Psalm 39:11 When with rebukes You correct man for iniquity, you make his beauty melt away like a* ***moth****; Surely every man is vapor*

See also: Caterpillar, Moth

Symbols Starting in C

SYMBOLS STARTING IN C

CAGE

To have your freedom taken away. A place of restriction and oppression.

Positive: To ensnare the enemy in his own plans
Negative: To be caught unawares and held captive by circumstances

CHARACTER SPECIFIC SYMBOL

In interpreting a cage in an internal dream, I would not see a positive connotation to it unless your enemies were in that cage! In dreaming that you are in a cage or being held captive, it would represent your lack of freedom.

This would indicate that you are bound either by your circumstance, by your past, or by some form of oppression. The enemy keeps you in bondage while the Lord gives freedom.

The mind can often be a cage in that it restricts you. Your analytical mind could be stopping your progress. A cage also represents fear, which could indicate being bound by a fear of the past that has been exposed in your life.

In personal experience I have seen people in cages and the Lord has told me that they have put themselves in the cage. One such case was a woman who had a fear of opening her heart to the Lord. I saw her in a cage and the Lord was only able to pass small objects through it to her. The interpretation was that because she had closed off her heart to the Lord out of fear, He could only give her small blessings because of her restriction.

UNIVERSAL SYMBOL

I could not find a positive connotation for a cage in Scripture, either. A cage in an external dream or vision speaks of the deceit and devices of the enemy. It is a warning of a trap that has been set, or it is a word of knowledge that the person you are ministering to is in bondage.

> *Jeremiah 5:26 For among My people are found wicked men; they lie in wait as one who sets snares; they set a* ***trap****; they catch men.*

Birds in a cage: Birds caught in a cage is also negative – especially if those birds are restless. The scripture here tells us that just as a cage is full of birds, so also are the houses of sinners full of deceit. In other words, that sin might seem restricted, but it is still very much present.

This also indicates a work of the enemy that is currently restricted. Just because he is restricted in a cage though, does not mean that he is gone – it simply means that he is being held back for the time being.

> *27 As a **cage** is full of birds, so their houses are full of deceit. Therefore, they have become great and grown rich.*

It is a place of evil and a place where the enemy and his evil works abound

> *Revelation 18:2 ...and the hold of every foul spirit, and a cage of every unclean and hateful bird*

To see a dove in a cage is also negative. It means that the Holy Spirit is bound in your life right now. He is being restricted from doing His work.

See also: Bars, Birds, Prison

CAKE

Provision for your desires and not only your needs.

Positive: The unmerited blessing of the Lord
Negative: Overindulgence

CHARACTER SPECIFIC SYMBOL

POSITIVE
A cake speaks of fun, enjoyment, and blessing. It speaks of receiving a gift and something that is enjoyable.

I remember once dreaming of walking into my home and my father had bought me a whole load of different cakes from a bakery. I can smell them now just thinking about it! It was a good dream and it spoke of the blessings and the gifts the Lord was giving me.

The different types of cakes, spoke of the different ways I would minister and the different blessings the Lord would give me. Not long after this dream the Lord moved me into the teaching ministry.

NEGATIVE
"To have your cake and eat it" is a negative saying that means you are trying to impose yourself and also be one better above your fellow brother or sister. This speaks of strife, contention, and vainglory.

Dreaming of a cake that is not fully baked speaks of being "half-baked" meaning that your commitment is lacking.

UNIVERSAL SYMBOL

POSITIVE
Cake in a vision or external dream speaks of provision. In the case of this passage, by giving of her last cake, the widow woman had provision for the rest of the drought. Perhaps the Lord has led you to give the little "cake" or blessing

you have away. If this be the case, rejoice, because it means that the Lord means to prosper you in return!

> *1 Kings 17:13 And Elijah said to her, "Do not fear; go and do as you have said, but make me a small* ***cake*** *from it first, and bring it to me; and afterward make some for yourself and your son.*

NEGATIVE
To see a cake that is burned or gone hard on one side, due to not being turned has a bad connotation. It speaks of being having the life taken out of you. It also speaks of compromise as in the passage in Hosea. It speaks of mixing yourself with those things that are not of the Lord and because of it, your blessing has now become a curse.

> *Hosea 7:8 Ephraim has mixed himself among the peoples; Ephraim is a* ***cake*** *unturned.*

It is not possible to live on cake! You need the basics of life to be healthy. Always easting sake in a sense of gluttony, speaks of seeking out only the blessings of the Lord, but not being willing to pay the price to walk out the weightier matters of your Christian life that require you to deny your flesh.

See also: Bake, Bread

CALF

A new birth. A new blessing or gift to be given to you. Often relates to business and finances.

Positive: The birth of potential in the business realm
Negative: The onset of a financial attack from the enemy

CHARACTER SPECIFIC SYMBOL

POSITIVE
A calf in a dream in a positive context speaks of a new birth. Some new blessing or new gift that is about to be given to you. It could also speak of a new venture or a new direction you have gone on. Cattle speak of business and of production, so it could very well relate to those things you have worked at and are now sowing as a result.

NEGATIVE
Dreaming of a calf instead of a fully-grown cow could also indicate immaturity. I interpreted a dream once where the gentleman dreamed of a young calf coming from the stall and overtaking the fully-grown calf. The interpretation was that this person had gone ahead of themselves in their immaturity and instead of going at a steady pace to maturity, had run ahead of what the Lord had been doing in their lives.

Universal Symbol

POSITIVE
A calf in a vision could have various interpretations. The first speaks of joy. In Scripture the calf is seen as something joyful and exuberant as in this Psalm:

> *Psalms 29:6 He makes them also skip like a **calf**, Lebanon and Sirion like a young wild ox.*

However, calves were also used in sacrifice and represent the covenant the Lord made with His people. Abraham cut a calf in two and walked between the pieces and in so doing entered into covenant with the Lord.

To dream of sacrificing a calf means that there is something in your life that the Lord is asking you to give up.

Jeremiah speaks of this covenant:

> *Jeremiah 34:19 the princes of Judah, the princes of Jerusalem, the eunuchs, the priests, and all the people of the land who passed between the parts of the **calf**.*

NEGATIVE
A calf as seen as an idol i.e. the golden calf has a very negative connotation. This speaks of idolatry or occultist activities. It could also speak of things in the life of a believer that they have put above the Lord and consider more important than the Lord and due to that, this "calf" has now become their god.

> *Exodus 32:4 And he received the gold from their hand, and he fashioned it with an engraving tool, and made a molded **calf**. Then they said, "This is your god, O Israel, that brought you out of the land of Egypt!".*

See also: Bull, Cattle, Idol

Camel

A carrier of blessing and a picture of wealth.

Universal Symbol

POSITIVE
The camel was responsible for carrying the trade of the merchants. The camel is a carrier of blessing.

I saw once in the spirit, a herd of camels carrying precious cargo and blessing. The Lord indicated that he was sending provision from afar and that His blessing would come from all over the globe. This vision was and still is being fulfilled.

In the Old Testament, the prophets used to wear camel's hair as clothing as mentioned here in Mark. Camel's hair is very uncomfortable and scratchy. Wearing camel's hair is a picture of walking in humility.

> *Mark 1:6 Now John was clothed with* ***camel's*** *hair and with a leather belt around his waist, and he ate locusts and wild honey.*

NEGATIVE
The camel also speaks of a place of stumbling as mentioned here in Luke. Jesus also said to the Pharisees that they strained out a gnat, but swallowed a camel. This speaks of stumbling over insignificant things, but overlooking glaring mistakes in your life.

> *Luke 18:25 For it is easier for a* ***camel*** *to go through the eye of a needle than for a rich man to enter the kingdom of God.*

See also: Donkey

CANDLE

Your testimony before the world as a believer. The passion that you have for life.

Positive: A renewed conviction
Negative: To be demotivated

POSITIVE
A candle speaks of light and the spirit of the Lord within you. It speaks of your testimony before the world. The light from just one candle can displace any darkness. The candle represents overcoming evil and the light of Jesus Christ that shines in each one of us!

Look at the following passages for good examples:

> *Proverbs 20:27 The spirit of man is the* ***candle*** *of the Lord, searching all the inward parts of the belly. (KJV)*

To have someone "light your fire" means to have a renewed passion to do the work of the Lord. There are times when you might feel that you have lost all zeal for serving the Lord. To see a candle being lit means that God is going to restore that passion to you.

> *Psalms 18:28 For thou wilt light my* ***candle****: the Lord my God will enlighten my darkness.*

NEGATIVE
To dream of your candle being blown out is a picture of demotivation and discouragement. It means that you have allowed circumstances and others to hide the spirit of God inside of you.

To hide a candle means you are too afraid to be bold in your convictions.

*Matthew 5:15 Neither do men light a **candle**, and put it under a bushel, but on a **candlestick**; and it giveth light unto all that are in the house. (KJV)*

See also: Fire, Light

CANDY

A treat or small blessing from the Lord. In a negative light it speaks of indulging the flesh.

Positive: A gift from the Lord – a token of His love for you
Negative: To follow after your feelings instead of what you know is right

POSITIVE
Candy or chocolate speaks of something that is a treat and a gift. Many believe that the Lord only provides our needs and not our desires. However how often have you given your own children candy just to delight them? The Lord is the same. If you dream or have a vision of the Lord giving you candy, then He is saying that he wants to delight you.

He does not only want to provide your needs, but your desires as well. If you want a good picture of candy in the Scriptures look up "honey" which was the equivalent in their day.

*Isaiah 7:22 So it shall be, from the abundance of milk they give, that he will eat curds; for curds and **honey** everyone will eat who is left in the land.*

NEGATIVE
Eating candy can also speak of getting into the flesh. This passage describes it wonderfully:

*Revelation 10:9 So I went to the angel and said to him, "Give me the little book." And he said to me, "Take and eat it; and it will make your stomach bitter, but it will be as sweet as **honey** in your mouth."*

It is just like when you try to fulfill the desires of the flesh outside of Christ. For that short moment the taste is sweet, but after you have indulged, the emptiness and bitterness fills your spirit.

If you dream or have a vision of eating something sweet, but feeling sick, then the Lord is showing you that the things you are indulging in are damaging your spiritual life. You are chasing your emotions and what you want, rather than what the Lord has told you to do. It is time, once again, to walk in obedience.

See also: Cake, Honey

CAR

A representation of your ministry.

POSITIVE
Cars are by far the most common vehicle seen in dreams. In an internal dream, you might dream of an old car you once owned, or even of a car you desire to own.

A car from the past could represent the circumstances surrounding that time of your life. It could also refer to the "old ministry functions" that you flowed in during that time of your life.

I remember a lady who shared once how she dreamed that she was trying to drive the car she had when she first got saved. The car was old and broken, but she was being pressured into driving it.

The interpretation was clear. She was being pressured to function in a ministry and spiritual capacity she had functioned in, in the past. But she had moved on since then and it was no longer appropriate. It was time for her to move on.

Dreaming of cars is common. You might dream that you receive a fast sports or racing car.

This means that the Lord is going to lead you into a different type of ministry that has a bigger realm of influence. It also indicates that this will be a fast move for you.

If you dream that someone else is driving your car, depending on the character driving your car, the interpretation could vary.

Your father or husband driving your car could mean that the Lord Jesus is in control of your ministry (depending on your relationship with your father or husband). This would have a good connotation.

Driving the car, yourself could be good. It speaks of being in control and going in the right direction.

NEGATIVE
Someone driving your car that represents the flesh, pride, or the world system would have a negative connotation. This would mean that something other than the Lord is in control of your ministry and spiritual life!

Different cars in your dream could represent different ministries.

Having your car stolen, taken over or stopped, speaks of your ministry being taken from you. This does not have a good connotation.

Now that you have a general idea, allow the Holy Spirit to define your dream or vision for you.

See also: Vehicles

CAT

If the cat is a pet it speaks of responsibility. If negative, it speaks of a sneak attack from the enemy. If positive, it speaks of a surprise blessing that will involve you having a new responsibility.

CHARACTER SPECIFIC AND UNIVERSAL SYMBOLS

POSITIVE
Just like in the symbol for pets, if you own the cat, it speaks of a responsibility. So a healthy cat would mean that you are taking good care of your responsibilities. Taking a cat that belongs to someone else means taking on cares that are not your own.

You need to identify what cats mean to you. If you love them, then dreaming of cats is positive. Identify what cats mean to you in real life and your dream will become clearer.

NEGATIVE
The cat was used as an idol in the early days of Egypt and in a negative light speaks of the subversive work of the enemy - the kind of attack that steals and sneaks in undetected. In a negative light it also speaks of the enemy "spying" on what you are doing.

A black cat is a clear picture of obvious demonic activity, while a white cat is a picture of something that looks innocent, but is not. (Note this refers to cats if you feel negative about them. If you love cats, then the interpretation will change in your dreams)

You do not need to be concerned if you have such a dream or a vision because you have the authority in the name of Jesus to tell the enemy to be gone.

See also: Dog, Lion, Pet

CATERPILLAR

A promise of potential. A picture of immaturity leading to maturity.

Positive: To have a realization of your potential
Negative:

- A spirit of destruction
- To feel insignificant

The caterpillar, although a worm, does not stay that way because it is destined for greatness.

In my description on *Cocoon* you will understand the process of going from caterpillar to butterfly.

Seeing a caterpillar in your dream or in the spirit is an indication that the Lord sees the potential in you and desires to take you through a process of transformation.

NEGATIVE
In a negative context the caterpillar symbolizes a spirit of destruction sent to eat the goodness and blessing that God has given to you.

> *Joel 1:4 That which the palmerworm hath left hath the locust eaten; and that which the locust hath left hath the cankerworm eaten; and that which the cankerworm hath left hath the* ***caterpillar*** *eaten. (KJV)*

See also: Butterfly, Cocoon, Moth, Worm

CATTLE

A picture of business and financial blessing

Positive: Blessing in trade and finances
Negative: Theft in your finances

POSITIVE
Cattle in the Old Testament was a picture of business and trade. Depending on how much cattle you had, determined the level of your wealth.

> *Genesis 13:2 And Abram was very rich in* ***cattle****, in silver, and in gold. (KJV)*

So to dream of being giving cattle or of your cattle reproducing means that your business is going to increase and that the Lord is going to bless the work of your hands.

Jacob is the best illustration of this. He took the worst from Laban and got rich from it! The Lord wants you to prosper in your workplace! It is for you to take what the world gives you and to prosper just as Jacob did.

NEGATIVE
To lose your cattle or to see them struck down means that there is a curse and that the enemy is stealing from you.

If you are a prophet and the Lord gives you a dream or vision of cattle dying it could speak of a season of financial lack.

Fat cattle that become thin also speak of financial lack and a season of economic downturn.

Consider the passage in Genesis 41 where Joseph interprets the King's dream of the seven thin cows consuming the 7 healthy, representing 7 years of famine.

Being attacked by a herd of cattle speaks of a spiritual attack that is likely financial in nature.

See also: Barn, Calf

CAVE

A season of obscurity but also of intimacy with the Lord. In a negative sense, a cave is a picture of trying to escape the pressures of life.

Positive: A call to step down from public ministry
Negative:

- To purposefully hide your heart from others
- To keep yourself bound because of past hurts
- Wrong decisions that keep you in bondage

POSITIVE
Although it might not seem that a cave can be a positive place, it indeed speaks of a place of being protected and hidden away. I remember the Lord giving me a vision once where he drew me to a cave.

The cave was empty except for me and Him. He said that here He would teach me everything that I needed for the next phase of my spiritual walk. For a season, things would quiet down and I would not be involved with a lot of people, but that this was of Him.

It was indeed one of the most precious times of my life where I came to know the Lord Jesus face to face at a new level. It was a time where He brought the Scriptures to life for me and gave me a new impartation of his love.

So if you have a vision or dream of the Lord drawing you aside, this is a good thing. It speaks of a time of seclusion and training that is temporary. However, it will be a time of much growth for you. Even Elijah experienced the still voice of the Lord in the cave. Before David took the throne, he had his time in the cave of Adullam. There he and his mighty men became the unmovable force we see later on.

> *1 Kings 19:9 And there he went into a **cave**, and spent the night in that place; and behold, the word of the Lord came to him, and He said to him, "What are you doing here, Elijah?"*

Prophetic Calling: Being drawn into this relationship with Jesus is an essential phase of prophetic training. If you feel that you are called to be a prophet, this will be the best part of your training. I suggest you get your hands on the *Practical Prophetic Ministry* book at www.ami-bookshop.com for further training.

NEGATIVE
It has been our experience in personal ministry to often see someone we pray for tied to a cave wall. This indicates that they have hidden themselves away from the real world, usually because of hurts in the past. I speak more of this under the symbol *Bars.* In our ministry, we refer to this as "spiritual imprisonment" where someone is unable to move forward because of having spiritually hidden themselves due to hurts of the past.

It also speaks of a place of hiding away from the stress and the pressures that are surrounding you. The only way to overcome is to step out in the name of Jesus, and to overcome.

> *1 Samuel 13:6 When the men of Israel saw that they were in danger (for the people were distressed), then the people hid in* ***caves****, in thickets, in rocks, in holes, and in pits.*

CHAINS

Bondage through association, generational curses or hurts from the past.

Positive: The combined strength of a group of people
Negative: The repeated sin of an individual or generation

POSITIVE
Because a chain is so strong, it is a picture of united strength! This is especially applicable to a group and to marriage. A chain secures the anchor of a boat!

Although it is a picture of strength, its most outstanding characteristic is that it is combined strength that makes it secure. The strength of a single link is nothing. The combined strength of many links is what gives it the edge.

If you are praying for a group or a couple and you see a strong chain, then the Lord is indicating that combined, they are strong, but separately they are weak.

NEGATIVE
A broken link in a chain speaks of someone that has cracked under pressure or that has broken unity and tried to do things on their own.

To dream or see a vision of being bound by gold chains and this means that you are bound by things that you think are good, but are in fact keeping you in bondage.

Black chains represent clear demonic bondage. Chains are something we see often when praying with individuals who have a demonic bondage in their lives. Often we will even see a demon on the other end of the chain.

This can relate to a generational curse or a sin where the person opened the door to the enemy themselves, giving him control in their lives. See more in the symbol *Demons* for more understanding.

> *Jeremiah 39:7 Moreover he put out Zedekiah's eyes, and bound him with chains, to carry him to Babylon. (KJV)*

I have also seen a chain in the spirit when praying about templates and triggers. Each template being a link in the chain and continues to establish the sinful habit and the hurt in the person I am praying for. Please read *Prophetic Boot Camp* for more on templates and triggers.

See also: Demons, Jewelry

CHALKBOARD/BLACKBOARD

A call to either teach others what you know or to take a season of learning.

Positive:

- Imparting your natural strengths to others through instruction
- A call to further education

Negative: Intellectual insecurity

CHARACTER SPECIFIC SYMBOL

POSITIVE

To dream of a chalk or a blackboard is a reference to schooling. If your experiences of the past are positive, then to dream of a chalkboard is a call back to education.

You are in need of some more instruction. It is time to sit down and to learn.

The teacher: If you are the one writing on the blackboard, you need to determine if you should be there or not. If you feel good about it, then it means the Lord is encouraging you to step forward and to teach others what you know.

This does not necessarily denote a call to the teaching ministry, but to the natural function of someone who teaches others. It means imparting the natural strengths you have to others.

Words on a blackboard: Words written on a blackboard are an announcement that God needs you to pay attention to! To use a common expression, "It's time you see the writing on the wall!"

> *Daniel 5:5 In the same hour the fingers of a man's hand appeared and wrote opposite the lampstand on the plaster of the wall of the king's palace; and the king saw the part of the hand that wrote*

That "writing on the wall" is the Lord trying to get your attention. It could be a warning or a set of instructions. I encourage you to journal the message further to get further direction. I teach on journaling in *How to Hear the Voice of God.*

NEGATIVE
Now if your memories of education are negative, a blackboard is going to mean something quite different. It refers to any insecurity you feel regarding your intelligence or education.

Nails against blackboard: A picture of irritation. The attack you are facing is not a bit deal – it only feels that way right now.

See also: Finger, Pen, School

CHEST

Body part: A place of tenderness and intimacy.

Trunk/Chest of goods A container of treasures that are something unknown to you.

POSITIVE
Body Part – Chest: John was known as the disciple who laid on Jesus breast. Because of this in history he is known as the disciple of love. He is the one who was closest to Jesus heart and the only disciple not to be martyred.

> *John 13:25 Then, leaning back on Jesus' breast, he said to Him, "Lord, who is it?"*

John was also the only disciple who stood by the cross as Jesus was crucified. This is a lovely picture of intimacy and someone that will follow through with you until the end. Although all the others scattered, John never left Jesus' side.

If you see a vision of someone lying on your chest, this denotes intimacy and commitment. This is someone that will stick through with you no matter what.

In a literal sense, the chest or ribcage is also the cavity that holds your heart. To dream of your chest being healed speaks of your heart being protected.

In ministry, the Lord will often ask you to reveal your heart to others and to not be afraid. To see your chest opening up means that the Lord is asking you to be vulnerable.

Trunk/Chest of Goods: More often than not, finding goods in a chest that was hidden or put away speaks of resources that you have either forgotten about or that the Lord wants to reveal to you right now.

> *Ezekiel 27:24 These were your merchants in choice items—in purple clothes, in embroidered garments, in* ***chests*** *of multicolored apparel, in sturdy woven cords, which were in your marketplace*

Depending on what is inside the chest you see in your dream or in vision will determine the nature of the blessing, or the nature of the problem if the vision is negative.

NEGATIVE

Body Part – Chest: To dream or have a vision of your chest being ripped open speaks of someone taking advantage of your vulnerability. It speaks of the work of the enemy to expose and to hurt you emotionally.

Trunk/Chest of Goods: If you find a chest full of something foul, then this indicates a hidden evil that is being exposed in your life. It speaks of various works of the enemy that have been given license through the sin that is being brought to life.

It is possible that you have been putting hurts of the past to the side and have tried to bury them. As if "locking them up" in a chest. If you dream of opening a chest that releases things that are unpleasant, the Lord is saying that there is a lot under the surface that needs to be exposed and dealt with correctly.

See also: Heart, Treasure

CHILD

Your responsibilities both in life and in ministry.

a. A depiction of various stages of maturity.

b. A depiction of ministries and visions the Lord desires you to "birth."

CHARACTER SPECIFIC SYMBOL

Children you know: If you have children, each will represent something different to you in each of your dreams. Identify what emotion each child pulls out of you and you will have your interpretation.

When I dream of my youngest daughter I know that the Lord was speaking about my apostolic calling, because I was pregnant with her when I was placed in apostolic office. My eldest has strong faith and represents my faith when I dream of her. My second daughter speaks of my love.

The same applies to any other familiar children you know. Identify what part of yourself your son or daughter could represent in your dreams.

Unfamiliar children/adoption: The apostles always referring to the New Testament believers as "little children." So there are a number of interpretations for your dream.

They could represent the maturity level of the people God has called you to minister to or also your own level of maturity.

If you keep dreaming that you take care over other people's children then it means that you keep taking over responsibilities that are not yours.

If someone gives you a child, it means that you are taking over someone's ministry or "brain child." Depending on how you feel in the dream will indicate how you feel about this whole transition. Dreaming of adopting a child? You are taking on a ministry that you did not originate. Determine if this is a good or bad transition.

Universal Symbol

POSITIVE

Spiritual parenting: I have often seen someone surrounded by children in the spirit and I know that the Lord is telling them that they will have many spiritual children.

Inner healing: Of course if you see a child in the spirit, the Lord could also be showing you that something happened to the person you are praying for when they were around that age that needs healing.

Your fruit: Children in Scripture refer to spiritual maturity, but are also a picture of our "fruit" and those things we have accomplished in this life. To see many children in a vision could very well speak of an expansion in your ministry. The Lord is calling you to be stretched to "fathering" more than just one vision!

It is worth nothing that when it comes to vision interpretation that you will need to determine if the vision you are seeing is symbolic or literal.

NEGATIVE

If your vision or prophetic dream feels negative, then the Lord is saying that you have lost sight of your vision! You have strayed from the original purpose that He has given to you. Your "child" has become corrupt and tainted with the flesh.

Consider the context of the vision. Does the negativity in the vision surround the youth of the child, or the physical state of the child? If the vision is centered around its age, your vision is referring to spiritual maturity. If the vision is centered around its condition, it is referring to the state of your ministry.

> *2 Peter 2:14 having eyes full of adultery, and that cannot cease from sin; enticing unstedfast souls; having a heart exercised in covetousness;* ***children*** *of cursing*

See also: Baby, Umbilical Cord, Mother

Chisel

An instrument used to remove the flaws from something precious.

POSITIVE

Although it is hard to imagine the process of "chiseling" as positive, it is the best description for it.

When a diamond expert prepares a diamond to be set into stone, he has to chisel it on the flaw first. We use this illustration often when it comes to training God's leaders.

They are like diamonds in the rough. Although there is a lot of potential, it has to be uncovered first. This is why the process of mentorship is needed.

It is easy to receive the good things and to learn new things, but it is hard to let go of the things that are not of God. For a leader to truly rise up, they require some chiseling.

A good picture of this is the process of circumcision that Joshua took the Israelites through before they could enter the Promised Land.

If you have a mentor, then God will often use them as a chisel in your life. Someone asked a famous sculptor, "How do you know how to chisel such a beautiful sculpture of an angel out of this marble?" The sculptor said, "It's simple, I just chisel away the parts that are not angel."

This depicts the process of ministry training or anyone wanting to serve God. If you see a chisel in the spirit, then God is about to expose some flaws in your life.

NEGATIVE
When someone does not know how to use a chisel correctly, the diamond can be ruined. This is a heavy responsibility when applied to ministry training. The Lord showed this to me once. He said how important it was that I learned to chisel and correct His way. If I did it in the flesh, I ran the risk of smashing the diamond instead of making it beautiful.

See also: Death, Circumcision, Fire

CHURCH

A picture of the body of Christ or your doctrinal belief system.

CHARACTER SPECIFIC SYMBOL

If the church you dream of is one that is familiar to you, then you need to decide if it is positive of negative. Was this a place where you felt comfortable? What was the doctrine that you were taught here?

If the doctrine is positive, then this could speak of something positive. If this church was negative for you, then it could represent the status quo or the old things in your spiritual life that you have left behind.

If it is a church that you attended in the past, identify what it means to you. Was it a Baptist, Methodist, or Pentecostal Church? If so, then it could represent the entire denomination in the body of Christ, or it can refer to the doctrine of that denomination.

Consider the church and try to think what stands out to you the most about it. If you suffered hurt in that church, then it is a picture of things God wants to heal in your life.

Universal Symbol

Church or Temple: If you see an old style church or temple, this could represent the status quo Church or the religious systems of the world.

Keep in mind though that if you are ministering to someone prophetically and you see a church, that it might speak of an actual church they grew up in or where involved in. Depending on what revelation you get, it could speak of something negative that happened to them during this time of their lives. If this is the case, inner healing is necessary.

See also: Body, Buildings

Circumcision

A process of conviction to do things God's way. To enter into His covenant by faith and without works.

Positive: A call to conviction of sin
Negative: To fight the hand of God

Character Specific Symbol

As a man: If you dream of a foreskin (your own or someone else's) you would need to determine how this relates to you. Are your circumcised in the natural? Then to dream of a foreskin would be unnatural and an indication that there is something that you feel insecure about. Because this is tied so strongly to masculinity, determine if your insecurity lies in your self image as a man.

Did you have personal struggles with your foreskin? Perhaps resulting in circumcision? Then, dreaming of it would refer to a difficult season in your life or a hurt from your childhood that has left an insecurity and emotional scar.

As a woman: If you are a woman, dreaming of a foreskin, you need to determine if you have any personal feelings about it.

Is it something you fear or something you feel unfamiliar with?

There is more that could be said, but I will leave a fuller description on this under the symbol for *Penis*.

Universal Symbol

Although not a very common symbol in internal dreams, the foreskin holds an interesting interpretation in prophetic dreams and visions.

POSITIVE
Probably the best picture I could give you for the foreskin, is when the Lord called Joshua to circumcise the Israelites before they passed over the Jordan and into the Promised Land.

This was a picture of the conviction that the Joshua apostle is called to bring to God's people, before they can enter into the promise that God has for them.

The cutting of the foreskin then speaks of entering into the promises that God has given you via the process of death to the flesh.

It is an indication that there are things in your life right now that are holding you back from receiving those blessings. It is for you to submit to the hand of God and to let go of the sin and hindrances in your life.

Dreaming or having a vision of being circumcised does not indicate that the Lord actually wants you to be physically circumcised. Rather it means that He wants you to be circumcised in heart.

> *Acts 7:51 You stiff- necked and* ***uncircumcised*** *in heart and ears! You always resist the Holy Spirit; as your fathers did, so do you.*

See also: Altar, Death, Penis

City

For visions and prophetic dreams: A community of believers each with distinct functions and talents.

Character Specific Symbol

POSITIVE AND NEGATIVE
If you dream of a city that you are familiar with then you need to determine what it means to you. Ask yourself what happened to you when you lived in this city. What is the first thing that comes to your mind? Either it will represent a certain kind of person or an aspect of your past.

Once you know that, then you know how to proceed with your interpretation. If the city is being destroyed, then it means that whatever it represents is under attack or being removed from your life.

If the city is a picture of a particular church in that city, then to see it under attack is a call to intercession. It is a call to spiritual warfare.

If the city is being added to in your dream, then that aspect of your life or ministry is being expanded. The Lord is about to bring more people into your life and He will bring new opportunities to you as well.

I remember visiting an old style city that had surrounding walls, dreaming of this would represent the Church to me as a "City on a Hill."

Universal Symbol

POSITIVE
Without a doubt, the best picture of a city is a representation of the Church as a whole or even the church in a region. If you see a city on a hill, then it is speaking of the Church universal. If you see a specific city, then it is speaking of the Church (all the believers) in that region.

So if you see the city being added to, this is positive! To see it light up speaks of the anointing of the Lord starting to shine through His people. To see the streets made of gold or anything good happen to the city is a representation of what the Lord wants to do in His Church.

> *Matthew 5:14 You are the light of the world. A **city** that is set on a hill cannot be hidden.*

NEGATIVE
To see a city under siege is negative and speaks of the attack of the enemy. It is a call to spiritual warfare. If you see a vision or have a prophetic dream of cracks being in the city wall, the Lord is warning you that there is sin in your life that is giving the enemy access to your city! Time to seal up the cracks! When there is a curse prevalent in our midst, the Lord will often show me a city wall with cracks in it. He might also show me war machines sending rocks against the wall to weaken it. Both are a picture of spiritual warfare.

See also: Wall, War

Clay

A picture of our humanity. A process of shaping and change.

POSITIVE
Clay is a picture of our humanity in the Scriptures. It is a picture of how we are simply the vessel in God's hand. We are His to shape.

> *Romans 9:21 Does not the potter have power over the **clay**, from the same lump to make one vessel for honor and another for dishonor?*

> *Isaiah 64:8 But now, O Lord, you are our Father; we are the **clay**, and You our potter; and all we are the work of Your hand.*

If you dream of clay being shaped, it means that the Lord is going to take you through a change in image and in your spiritual walk. You will not be the same any longer or fulfill the same tasks.

During my apostolic training I often saw the Lord smash a clay vessel and start to rebuild it. I knew what that meant. It meant that what I was, was not suitable for the task ahead. So I had to be changed to fit in with his plan.

Anyone with a fivefold calling will identify with this process.

See also: Cup, Jar, Potter's Wheel

CLOAK

A picture of covering and an indication of your mandate or position in Christ.

A cloak speaks of a protection as a covering. Depending on the kind of cloak, it can also indicate someone's rank or ministry mandate.

Covering: When you see a cloak as a covering it speaks of being under authority and in submission to those that are under you. To be naked or to have your cloak torn, means that you are not under covering any longer.

Just like Jesus said in John 15:22 because some refused to submit to Him, they had no covering from their sin.

Fortunately, as believers our cloak of covering is the blood of Christ, that covers our sin.

Rank and position: To see a purple robe speaks of a position of favor and honor.

> *John 19:5 Then Jesus came out, wearing the crown of thorns and the purple **robe**. And Pilate said to them, "Behold the Man!"*

It also speaks about receiving favor from the Lord and being raised up in the sight of others. Just as the case of the prodigal son. The father lifted him up in the sight of everyone by putting a robe on him.

It was an indication that this person was favored by the authority. Another example in the Scriptures is where Haman put the king's clothes or Mordecai to show everyone that the King honored him.

> *Luke 15:22 But the father said to his servants, bring out the best **robe** and put it on him, and put a ring on his hand and sandals on his feet.*

To dream or have a vision of receiving a robe speaks of a new position, favor and honor in the Kingdom of God.

Ministry mandate: The most classic example in Scriptures is the one of Elijah and Elisha.

> *2 Kings 2:14 Then he took the **mantle** of Elijah that had fallen from him, and struck the water, and said, "Where is the Lord God of Elijah?" And when he also had struck the water, it was divided this way and that; and Elisha crossed over...*

This is a picture of Elisha receiving not only the anointing that Elijah had, but also his prophetic mandate to finish the work that Elijah had begun. If you see the Lord giving you the mantle of another person, it does not only speak of receiving their anointing, but also the mandate that God has given them.

See also: Clothing, Red

CLOTHING

A representation of the image you show the world.

CHARACTER SPECIFIC SYMBOL

POSITIVE

To dream of getting new clothes where you feel good about yourself, is a picture of God taking you through a transformation. He is about to make the change that He has been doing in your spirit manifest in the natural now.

Clothes are the final step to showing change that has been going on behind closed doors. So new clothes that fit well speak of expressing to the world what the Lord has done inside of you.

As a man, to get new pants means that the Lord is about to establish and confirm your masculinity and leadership. To get a new suit means that He is about to change your image and promote you.

To dream of putting on casual or beach clothes would be an indication that the Lord wants you to relax and learn to take things less seriously.

You might also dream of clothing that you do not feel comfortable in. You need to determine if God is trying to stretch you into a realm that is not familiar to you, or if you are trying to be something that you are not.

NEGATIVE

To dream of wearing clothes that you would never wear (that you do not like) means that what you are showing the world and who you really are, are two separate things. You are not being "real" to those around you.

To be frustrated about your clothing is an indication that you do not know who you are. Have you been struggling to identify your calling or know where you "fit in"? If so, then this dream would be a confirmation of this inner conflict.

To dream of your clothes being stolen means that the enemy is trying to make you feel insecure about yourself.

If you are a woman and put on pants that are clearly meant for a man, this is also negative! It means that you are trying to take on a leadership role that does not fit you.

As a man if you dream of putting on clothing that is feminine in nature, means that you are not fulfilling the true role that God has given to you. You are putting yourself (or being pushed) into a position that does not suit who God has made you to be. This can refer to your calling or a natural position.

Universal Symbol

POSITIVE AND NEGATIVE

When praying for someone regarding their image, I will often see them dressed in a specific way to indicate the new image that God has for them.

On the other hand, if I see a man in women's clothes, then either they are struggling with a spirit of lust, or God is indicating that their masculinity is lacking (the same is true of a woman in men's clothes)

When I see angels, their dress is also very important. It indicates their function. For example, if I see an angel dressed as a warrior, I know it is a warrior angel.

I often see the Church represented as a mighty warrior or as a bride. Depending on the vision I know what God wants me to pray. To see the Church dressed as a warrior, then I know it is a call to take the land. To see the Church dressed as a Bride, I know the Lord is calling her to intimacy.

To see someone in dirty clothes and then being given clean means that the Lord not only forgives their sin, but He will transform them. He will promote them and displace the old with the new.

Sackcloth: To see someone in sackcloth is a picture of mourning and loss.

Bridal gown: A call to intimacy with the Lord (or the lack thereof). (Revelation 21:2)

Veil: Something that is coming in the way of your relationship with the Lord. (2 Cor 3:15)

Priestly robes: A call to the work of the ministry (Exodus 40:13)

Kingly robes: A call to a position of leadership and authority (1 Kings 22:10)

Prostitute's clothing: A picture of compromise and walking in the flesh

Dirty clothes: Contamination from the world and personal sin (Zechariah 3:3)

Animal skins: A confirmation of the covenant that God has given to you (Gen 3:21)

Clean clothes: A picture of being washed clean of your sin

Uniforms: To ally yourself to a particular cause

Underwear: A feeling of being unprepared and vulnerable. (Lacy lingerie/Bra – Speaks of intimacy and femininity)

See also: Bride, Cloak, Dress

CLOUDS

Accumulated blessing or cursing. A process that has taken some time to come about.

Positive: A promise of blessing
Negative: Speaks of the work of the enemy to restrict the blessing of God

POSITIVE
Clouds speak of a promise of blessing. Just like the dry ground waits for the rain to fall to bring it life, so do the clouds speak of the Lord's abundance and prosperity.

Clouds also bring rest and shade from the hot sun, so they speak of taking time to just rest in His presence. If you have been working hard and pressing through, then it is time to put aside the work and just to rest in His presence.

You have done all that you can. Now your job is over and the Lord's can begin.

The Scriptures also speak of the cloud of God as a picture of His anointing and His presence.

> *Exodus 16:10 Now it came to pass, as Aaron spoke to the whole congregation of the children of Israel, that they looked toward the wilderness, and behold, the glory of the Lord appeared in the **cloud**.*

NEGATIVE
Dark storm clouds that block out the sun are a picture of enemy's attack and strife in your life. This is an attack that has been building up for some time now. Perhaps you have been too busy to pray things through or engage in spiritual warfare? Dark clouds in the spirit are an indication that the enemy has been at work and gained license through others.

> *Zephaniah 1:15 That day is a day of wrath, a day of trouble and distress, a day of devastation and desolation, a day of darkness and gloominess, a day of **clouds** and thick darkness,*

See also: Fog/Mist, Rain, Curtain

COALS

A picture of purification and zeal for the things of God.

A picture of the potential you have to flow in the anointing.

A coal burns hot and speaks of being purified. We have often seen this kind of coal in relation to the evangelistic ministry. It is the evangelist who goes through the fire and also to brings that kind of refining fire to God's people.

Conviction: If you see the Lord putting a coal to your lips, then it means that He is going to purge you and take you through a process of refining.

> *Isaiah 6:6 6 Then one of the seraphim flew to me, having in his hand a live **coal** which he had taken with the tongs from the altar. 7 And he touched my mouth with it, and said: "Behold, this has touched your lips; your iniquity is taken away, and your sin purged."*

Spiritual condition: The Lord has often used the vision of burning coals to help me determine the spiritual condition of someone. One that is on fire for God is a white hot coal, while one that has allowed the pressures of life to overwhelm them is cold and has crumbled to ash.

Strife: Now if your vision is negative, then the coals speak of trouble brewing. It speaks of the potential someone has to bring about strife as is laid out in this passage:

> *Proverbs 26:21 As **coals** are to hot embers, and wood to fire, so is a contentious man to inflame strife*

See also: Fire, Baptism, Tongue

COFFIN

Death to the flesh

Dreaming of coffins is an indication that there is something in you that God is calling to death. If the coffin is not buried, it is an indication that you have not completely dealt with these things.

I give a fuller description under the symbol *Death*.

See also: Body, Death, Grave, Tombstone

COCOON

A season of being set apart for the purpose of maturity and transformation.

Positive:

- To submit to a season of positive transformation
- Your willingness to let go of what you have to take hold of something better
- "Putting off" the old man and "putting on" the new

Negative: To be bound by circumstance

POSITIVE
A caterpillar entering a cocoon speaks of a phase of transition from one thing to an entirely different thing. I remember the Lord showing me once being in a cocoon and that I would soon emerge as a butterfly. This was during my prophetic training and is certainly a good illustration of what I went through.

I went from being weak, insecure, and a failure, to being confident and standing in full prophetic authority. Often though people do not want to allow the Lord to take them through the transition, they want the job to be finished already.

However for the butterfly to emerge, the caterpillar and pupae stage are necessary. If you are prepared to be humbled and be that worm, the Lord will raise you up into something beautiful. Right now it might seem that you do not have much to offer. However, wait until the Lord is finished with you! Then you will be something very beautiful.

NEGATIVE
If you feel that you are under demonic attack or in depression and see yourself wrapped in a cocoon, this is not a good picture. This indicates a work of the enemy that is binding you up.

Just as in the case with Delilah and Samson, the enemy seeks to bind you up so that you cannot move and then to destroy you.

All is not lost though because you have the authority in the name of Jesus to break free.

> *Judges 16:6 So Delilah said to Samson, "Please tell me where your great strength lies, and with what you may be bound to afflict you."*

See also: Caterpillar, Worm

COLORS

There are various colors that are relevant in Scripture. I have given a full description of each under their individual characters.

You also need to keep in mind that some colors are quite particular to culture. For example, in some cultures red is a picture of fertility, while in others, green is the picture of fertility. Some colors are universal though, such as the color black.

In all major cultures, black is negative and speaks of darkness and everything opposite to white.

For the understanding of colors to make sense, apply the descriptions I have given to visions and your prophetic dreams.

See also: Black, Blue, Brown, Gold, Gray, Green, Purple, Red, Silver, Yellow

COINS

The currency of the heavenly and earthly realm

Positive: Money and provision
Negative:

- Taxes
- Financial expenses
- Theft

CHARACTER SPECIFIC SYMBOL

Are you a coin collector? If you own certain coins that have value to you, then they speak of your potential to create finances.

Coins are also not worth a lot in today's age. So to dream of losing or gaining coins speaks of either small amounts of wealth or loss. The phrase "penny wise, pound foolish" comes to mind.

Why are you making such a fuss of these coins? They are not of great value and even if you lost a few, it is not the end of the world! To gain a few more is a nice blessing, but a provision for your needs and not your desires.

UNIVERSAL SYMBOL

In the Word, the picture changes a bit. If you are seeking gold or silver coins in the spirit, then the Lord is giving you a message from the Word. This interpretation will match that of *Money*.

POSITIVE
Gold coins (Talents): The ability God gives us to invest in both the natural and spiritual realms.

When the Lord is speaking about finances for our ministry, I usually see gold coins. The reason being that it is not just a case of "receiving funding" but finances that we will take and reinvest into the work of God.

If you keep having dreams and visions about gold coins, then the Lord desires to provide what you need for the work of the ministry. Keep in mind though that these finances are not for personal use, but for reinvestment into the Kingdom of God.

> *Matthew 25:16 Then he who had received the five talents went and traded with them, and made another five talents.*

Silver coins (denarius): Financial currency. Finances for your personal needs.

Jesus called for a silver coin called a denarius in the event below. Silver coins were used to pay tax. They are for you to "pay your dues" to both God and man. Giving away silver coins means that the Lord is telling you to invest into a ministry or fellow believer.

> *Matthew 22:20-21 And He said to them, "Whose image and inscription is this?" They said to Him, "Caesar's." And He said to them, "Render therefore to Caesar the things that are Caesar's, and to God the things that are God's."*

Of course having silver coins stolen means that a spirit of theft is prevalent in your life and the enemy is attacking your finances.

Copper coins: A meagre amount barely enough to live. Your last penny.

This was the mite that the widow woman gave. To give it away means that you are giving the bare minimum. To see it in a vision when praying for someone means that they are either giving the last they have, or that they are giving only the bare minimum. Seek the Lord for clarity in your vision.

> *Luke 21:2-3 and He saw also a certain poor widow putting in two mites. So He said, "Truly I say to you that this poor widow has put in more than all*

See also: Bag, Gold, Money, Silver, Treasure

COMPUTER

A library of information and entertainment

CHARACTER SPECIFIC SYMBOL

What kind of computer are you using right now? Are you comfortable working on the computer? Do you use a computer at your workplace? Each of these questions will help you determine what dreaming of a computer means to you.

Although interpretations will vary – here are some explanations that can help with your interpretation

Email: An expression of the heart and mind. Shares a similar interpretation to *Letter*

Work computer: Your position and status at work. Also speaks of your job responsibilities.

New computer: The Lord wants you to become more efficient

Old computer: You are going backwards! You are trying to use outdated principles that no longer work.

Study computer: What are you studying right now? Dreaming of this computer is a picture of your present journey and where it is about to lead you.

Stolen computer: A theft of your potential, time and money.

Password locked: You are struggling at the moment to "get" what God is trying to teach you.

Pornography: If you keep having sexual dreams and seeing a computer when you pray, it could well be that the person you are praying for is struggling with pornography. Use wisdom in praying this through and get counsel before confronting them.

Note: We have had the Lord show people a computer and tell them to put specific search terms into the search engines, only to come across one of our sites.

See also: Adultery, Letter

CONTRACT

- *A vow*
- *Bound by a promise*
- *A decreed promise or curse*

Positive: A decree sent on your behalf from the Throne Room
Negative: Warning of prayers sent against you

CHARACTER SPECIFIC SYMBOL

To dream of signing a contract is an indication that you have committed to something that you are bound to follow through. Every contract comes with terms to keep and disciplinary actions if the terms are broken.

Ecclesiastes 5:5 Better not to vow than to vow and not pay

I have often ministered to many who made thoughtless vows when they were children that bound them later on in life. Vows such as, "I will never love again!" or "I will never let a man treat me like that!"

What is said in the heat of the moment turned out to be quite binding! When praying for someone and I see a contract like this, I know that they made a vow that they need to let go.

UNIVERSAL SYMBOL

POSITIVE
Contract or a written document: A written document represents a promise and decree sent out on your behalf from the Throne Room.

I have often seen a written contract or document in the spirit, especially when the Lord has given me a promise. The interpretation is clear – the Lord is making a "contract" with me. He is giving me a promise that He is sticking to.

To sign a document means to give authority to its words.

> *Esther 8:8 You yourselves write a decree concerning the Jews, as you please, in the king's name, and seal it with the king's signet ring; for whatever is written in the king's name and sealed with the king's signet ring no one can revoke*

NEGATIVE
Contract: If you see a contract signed by the enemy, the Lord is showing you the enemy's plans for you. I have often seen this in the spirit. I will be in intercession and the Lord will show me a document (decree) that the enemy has sent against me. Fortunately messing with his plans is as simple as standing on the Word! For more on spiritual warfare read Prophetic Warrior.

> *Isaiah 10:1 "Woe to those who decree unrighteous decrees, who write misfortune, which they have prescribed*

See also: Book, Pen, Signature, Scroll

CORDS

Cords are a lot like chains, they speak of bondage and of being restricted. However, they can also refer to the cord or bond of marriage.

I cover this in more detail in the symbol Rope

Positive: To be secure in your relationships
Negative: To feel stifled in your relationships

POSITIVE
When a couple commits themselves to one another they are bound together as one. This speaks of the covenant they are in.

The only time this is negative is of the person is divorced and is still bound to their previous partner in the spirit.

In marriage, the cord that is formed is permanent. In families the cord is temporary. It is also temporary for mentorship relationships. A threefold cord speaks of strength in unity!

Often we have also seen a cord in the spirit attached to a person's first love. Because they did not let that person go fully, it prevented them from uniting completely with their spouse.

NEGATIVE
Very often in life we open our hearts to people we should not or receive teachings we should not. This causes a bond in the spirit. Often when praying for generational curses we will see an umbilical cord. In the case of a past mentor, we might see a cord or chain being attached to that person.

In each case it speaks of a bondage that needs to be broken.

In some cases, to see ropes or cords in the spirit where the person is fighting them, indicates that they feel stifled in a relationship or that they are fighting the bond of that relationship. Is this a marriage relationship? Then this indicates that there is conflict in their marriage and they need counseling.

See also: Chains, Rope, Umbilical Cord

CROSS

The cross speaks of an object that is curse but also speaks of death to the flesh and of redemption.

Positive: To take hold of God's promise
Negative: Idolatry

POSITIVE
The Scriptures tell us to "bear our cross" which means to enter into both the death and resurrection of the Lord Jesus Christ. When we carry the cross we give God control in our lives.

Many believe it to mean that you must suffer and endure to be Jesus' disciple, but it means quite the opposite. It means to walk in His resurrection power, putting aside the things that bind us and keep us down.

> *Luke 14:27 And whoever does not bear his **cross** and come after Me cannot be My disciple.*

For anyone with a ministry calling, the call to the cross will be very real. A call to "die daily" as Apostle Paul said.

> *Hebrews 12:2 looking unto Jesus, the author and finisher of our faith, who for the joy that was set before Him endured the **cross**, despising the shame, and has sat down at the right hand of the throne of God.*

Often I have seen a cross in the spirit and the Lord has invited me to get on the cross and to let Him rule in my life. The message is simple. It means to let go of my own striving and trying and to die to self, so that He can take control.

NEGATIVE
It is important to note that we serve the God upon the cross and not the object itself. A cross as a piece of jewelry is more of an idol than of a picture of redemption. It is much like a "golden calf" that people use as a good luck charm.

A religious cross also represents legalism. If I see a Catholic cross in the spirit when praying for someone either the Lord is telling me that they were once in the Catholic faith or that they are bound by legalism.

See also: Blood, Death

CROWD

A collection of like-minded people for the purpose of good or evil

Positive: Increase of influence
Negative: A massive attack from multiple directions

CHARACTER SPECIFIC SYMBOL

POSITIVE

If you are separated from the crowd, the Lord is saying that it is time to rest a while and come to a place of quiet so that He can speak to you.

Being cheered on by a crowd is a picture of accolades for what you have invested into others.

NEGATIVE

Are you afraid of being in a crowd? Then dreaming of being caught up in a crowd speaks of fear.

Being swept away by the crowd denotes that you lack your own conviction and simply "follow the crowd."

Naked in front of a crowd: An inner fear that others will see your insecurities. If you are naked and do not care, then it means that you are being transparent with others and have nothing to hide.

Naked crowd: Are you in a situation right now that is making you feel uncomfortable? Perhaps there are people around you in the natural that are sharing very personal things with you. This dream indicates that there are some who are being vulnerable with you. Do not be afraid but realize it is a ministry opportunity.

UNIVERSAL SYMBOL

POSITIVE

There is power in unity in Christ. A crowd with a singular purpose has the power of influence. If you see the Lord making you into a crowd or a crowd being added to you, then He is saying that He wants to increase your influence in the world or Church.

> *Revelation 19:6 And I heard, as it were, the voice of a great multitude, as the sound of many waters and as the sound of mighty thunderings, saying, "Alleluia! For the Lord God Omnipotent reigns!*

Against the crowd: To dream of going against the crowd can be positive, meaning that you are sticking to your personal convictions.

NEGATIVE
A crowd attacking you is negative. It speaks of multiple attacks from every direction from people in your life. This will take the form of words being spoken against you. This is certainly what happened to Jesus here:

> *Luke 4:28-29 So all those in the synagogue, when they heard these things, were filled with wrath, ..., that they might throw Him down over the cliff*

In ministry, rejection is common. You will always be the one going against the crowd. However just like Jesus was saved from them, so will you be saved as well.

See also: Audience, Nakedness, Stage

CROWN

Receiving a crown speaks of being given a position of honor and favor. To have run the race faithfully and won.

Positive: To gain a position of honor
Negative:

- Loss of your authority and position
- To take, but force, a position of honor that is not yours

POSITIVE

> *Hebrews 2:9 But we see Jesus, who was made a little lower than the angels, for the suffering of death* ***crowned*** *with glory and honor, that He, by the grace of God, might taste death for everyone.*

Here is the definition for Crown in the Strong's Concordance:

4735 stephanos {stef'-an-os}

AV - crown 18; 18

1) a crown
1a) a mark of royal or (in general) exalted rank
1a1) the wreath or garland which was given as a prize to victors in public games
1b) metaph. the eternal blessedness which will be given as a prize to the genuine servants of God and Christ: the crown (wreath) which is the reward of the righteousness
1c) that which is an ornament and honor to one

If you see the Lord giving you a crown in the spirit, it speaks of being given honor and also authority. Often when we have appointed apostles to apostolic office we have seen the Lord given them a golden crown along with a scepter and a new robe.

Wreath or garland: To receive a laurel wreath or garland indicates that you have run a good race and have won it and received your prize. It means that the Lord is going to honor and reward you for being so faithful.

> *James 1:12 Blessed is the man who endures temptation; for when he has been approved, he will receive the* ***crown*** *of life which the Lord has promised to those who love Him.*

> *1 Corinthians 9:25 And everyone who competes for the prize is temperate in all things. Now they do it to obtain a perishable* ***crown****, but we for an imperishable* ***crown****.*

In the spirit, I have also seen the crown of David which is a picture of the Davidic apostle.

NEGATIVE
To dream of losing your crown or having it stolen speaks of letting go of the authority that God has given to you.

> *Revelation 3:11 Behold, I am coming quickly! Hold fast what you have, that no one may take your* ***crown****.*

To be the one who steals the crown speaks of usurping someone else's position and trying to steal their honor for yourself.

See also: Gold, Hat, Thorns

CUP

The vessel that you are in the Lord. Also representative of the things we are called to endure or take care of for the Lord.

Positive: Your value as a vessel of the Lord
Negative: To feed your spirit with the spirit of the world

A cup is very similar to the picture of a clay vessel. It speaks of us believers very often in Scripture. Even Jesus referred to the wine in the cup as his blood as a picture of the New Covenant.

> *Luke 22:20 Likewise He also took the* ***cup*** *after supper, saying, "This* ***cup*** *is the new covenant in My blood, which is shed for you."*

A cup also represents the things that we endure or have to handle. Sometimes this is good and other times it is not positive.

Consider what Jesus said here to Peter:

> *John 18:11 So Jesus said to Peter, "Put your sword into the sheath. Shall I not drink the* ***cup*** *which My Father has given Me?"*

The cup he had to drink, the trials he had to pass through, were not easy but necessary for our redemption. The same applies to us. Often the cup that we are given to drink means going on a difficult road. However, it will always lead to blessing and walking in God's perfect will.

If you dream of being offered a cup to drink from, the Lord is asking you to partake of the plan He has for your life.

The cup also speaks of partaking of the blessing of the Lord.

> *1 Corinthians 10:16 The **cup** of blessing which we bless, is it not the communion of the blood of Christ? The bread which we break, is it not the communion of the body of Christ?*

It speaks of a celebration and a remembrance of all the good things the Lord has done for you.

NEGATIVE
To drink from a cup that is dirty or defiled means that you are defiling yourself with the spirit of the world. You are doing things the enemy's way instead of God's way.

> *1 Corinthians 10:21 You cannot drink the **cup** of the Lord and the **cup** of demons; you cannot partake of the Lord's table and of the table of demons*

See also: Jar, Silver

CURTAIN

This is the same as the word veil used in Scriptures. A curtain speaks of things that are hidden. Going behind the veil speaks of entering into an intimate relationship with the Lord.

Positive: A call to intimacy
Negative: Hindrances in your relationships with people and the Lord

POSITIVE
Often the Lord hides things from us until we are ready to see them. Often in the spirit as I prayed I saw a curtain in front of a door where the Lord said that He would soon reveal something He has been preparing for me.

This is something to look forward to and a blessing of promise.

The curtains in the Old Testament concealed the glory of the Lord. Going behind a curtain speaks of entering into intimacy with the Lord.

NEGATIVE
Hiding your heart behind a curtain speaks of putting on masks to hide your real self. Often when people have faced difficult things in life, they hide their heart and feelings from others to protect themselves. Unfortunately, these are curtains that prevent them from entering into the presence of God.

They are then stuck on the other side of the curtain and struggle to sense the Lord's presence. The only solution is to allow the Lord to bring healing to the past and to deal with any bitterness that remains.

Often when I have prayed for others, I have seen bitterness in their lives as curtains around their hearts. Before they can be healed or enter into an intimate relationship with the Lord, these curtains/veils need to be lifted.

> *2 Corinthians 3:14 But their minds were blinded. For until this day the same* ***veil*** *remains unlifted in the reading of the Old Testament, because the* ***veil*** *is taken away in Christ.*

See also: Fog/Mist, Veil

SYMBOLS STARTING IN D

Symbols Starting in D

Dagger

A picture of spiritual warfare.

Positive: A call to "get your hands dirty" because prayer is not enough - the Lord is calling you to get involved
Negative: Cruel and underhanded attack from others

POSITIVE
Although not a very powerful weapon, like the sword, the dagger can also speak of a spiritual warfare function. It speaks of spiritual warfare on an intimate level, like helping people break free of bondage - one person at a time. This is not a public ministry but a "one on one" ministry.

If the Lord has been bringing individuals your way, then this is a clear indication that He wants you to use the knowledge and wisdom you already have for Him, to help set them free.

A dagger can also speak of a teaching ministry that is starting out. Perhaps the Lord has been leading you to study more of the Word.

As you learn to use the knowledge you already have, He will increase your ability.

NEGATIVE
The dagger was not by any means an instrument of honor or was ever put on display. Usually it was hidden from sight and was used in close combat. It is a deadly weapon that speaks of destruction and violence. In a negative context, it speaks of a stealth attack from the enemy.

> *Judges 3:21 Then Ehud reached with his left hand, took the **dagger** from his right thigh, and thrust it into his belly...*

Ornate Dagger: Daggers are known to be used in pagan rituals for sacrifice and even in Scripture it is seen as a weapon of violence. If you see a dagger that feels pagan or demonic, it is speaking of attacks by the enemy, through unbelievers or someone that is involved in false religion. If you have recently been involved with people of this nature, the Lord is warning you about a contamination you have picked up through that involvement.

See also: Knife, Sword

DARKNESS

Opposite to everything light. This a picture of sin, deception, confusion and all the works of the enemy.

To walk in darkness means to be led astray or to be confused. As believers we are called to walk in the light.

Positive: A season of rest
Negative:

- Confusion
- The enemy at work

UNIVERSAL SYMBOL

POSITIVE

Sometimes the Lord makes things dark so that the enemy cannot see what is going on! He sent darkness as a plague on the Egyptians! Although we do prefer to walk in the light, sometimes the darkness forces us to rest and to wait on God instead of pushing forward with our own good ideas! A season of darkness has a simple message, "Be still and know that I am God!"

NEGATIVE

For the most part though, darkness does not have a positive picture as it is the opposite of light - which is the very essence of God! The Scriptures tell us that satan and his fallen angels (demons) dwell in darkness. So as light is the epitome of the Lord and His blessing, darkness is the epitome of the enemy and his curses! Jude says it very clearly here:

> *Jude 1:6 And the angels who did not keep their proper domain, but left their own abode, He has reserved in everlasting chains under **darkness** for the judgment of the great day.*

Light vs. Dark: Light, life, and love are used interchangeably in Scripture to often mean the same thing.

Darkness, hate (bitterness) and death are the opposite of these spiritual forces. Darkness also speaks of walking in confusion and being blind. It speaks of being in deception as in this passage:

> *1 John 2:11 But he who hates his brother is in **darkness** and walks in **darkness**, and does not know where he is going, because the **darkness** has blinded his eyes.*

See also: Black, Blind, Death, Night

DAUGHTER

An aspect of your character or something you have birthed in the spirit.

CHARACTER SPECIFIC SYMBOL

In an internal dream, your daughter speaks of the things you have birthed in the spirit. In other words, they can speak of your ministry. They could also speak of the positive forces of the spirit i.e. faith, hope and love.

My daughters have always represented my love and my faith in my dreams. Identify your relationship with your daughter and you will discover what they represent in your dreams. Whether positive, meaning the forces of the spirit, or negative, meaning the works of the flesh, your children will by symbolic of the relationships you have with them in real life.

UNIVERSAL SYMBOL

If you see the daughter of someone you are ministering with in vision, the Lord could be indicating that their daughter needs ministry or that their daughter is directly involved in the problem that you are busy ministering to in them.

If you dream of giving birth to a daughter, then the Lord is saying that He is moving you into a more prophetic orientation.

If you always desired a daughter and then dream of having one, then she represents your hidden desires in that dream.

See also: Birth, Child, Family

DARTS

A picture of spiritual attack usually coming through words spoken against you.

Positive: To strike at the heart of a problem with extreme accuracy
Negative: To be worn down by words or hurts continually sent against you

POSITIVE
To hit a "bull's eye" speaks of being on target. A dart has to be very accurate to have an effect and so to dream or have a vision of being given a dart means that you are being called to focus on the task at hand.

You cannot just head out into nowhere. Rather, your course of action needs to be specific, focused in a single direction, and done with quick force. This is not a weapon that requires a lot of strength, but rather a lot of intellect. To be effective in this kind of spiritual warfare, you will need to have knowledge of the Word combined with the wisdom of the Spirit.

NEGATIVE
The dart is very much like the dagger, in that it speaks of deadly attack. The dart comes from the enemy and it destroys. Darts usually contained poison, so although they were small weapons, the poison on them caused the actual death. Darts to the heart can speak of hurts inflicted by others in your past.

The poison of their rejection remains in that heart and so the hurt remains within, unhealed, still spreading its poison. Here is a passage that confirms that the dart speaks of death:

> *Proverbs 7:23 Till a **dart** strike through his liver; as a bird hasteth to the snare, and knoweth not that it is for his life.*

I often see darts coming at me in the spirit when people have been speaking negative words or praying negative prayers over me. Dealing with them is as simple as standing on this promise:

> *Isaiah 54:17 No **weapon** formed against you shall prosper, and every tongue which rises against you in judgment you shall condemn. This is the heritage of the servants of the Lord, and their righteousness is from Me, Says the Lord.*

See also: Arrow, Bow

DAY

The start of something new. A time of work and activity.

Positive: The onset of a fresh goal
Negative: The end to your time of rest

POSITIVE
To see daybreak or a sunrise is almost always positive. It indicates that a season of hardship and darkness is over and that it is time for resurrection in your life.

To see the sun rise also indicates that the work of the enemy is going to be exposed and destroyed as in this passage:

> *James 1:11 For no sooner has the **sun risen** with a burning heat than it withers the grass; its flower falls, and its beautiful appearance perishes. So the rich man also will fade away in his pursuits.*

Speaking of resurrection: There are times in our spiritual life when we go through seasons of darkness and spiritual death. However, this lasts for only a moment. If you dream or have a vision of it being daylight, then it means that a new season is coming.

It is a season of accomplishing much and of promotion and resurrection.

Remember, weeping may endure for a night, but joy comes in the morning. (Psalms 30:5)

NEGATIVE
The only time daylight would be negative is when it comes to soon and you did not accomplish everything you needed to in the night. Everything has a season and nighttime is a season for rest and taking time to recoup, so be sure to enjoy your seasons of evening as much as your seasons of daytime!

See also: Light, Night

DEATH

A call to spiritual death that will lead to resurrection. Negatively it speaks of the work of the enemy and everything that he has stolen from you.

Positive: Letting go of the old man
Negative: Emotional attack to the point of wanting to give up

CHARACTER SPECIFIC SYMBOL

POSITIVE AND NEGATIVE
Dreaming of dead bodies and coffins often refers to things in your flesh that are being brought to death, spiritually. It is often your first reaction to panic when you dream of someone dying, but this need not be so at all!

There have been times when I have dreamed that dead bodies kept coming out a coffin! While that sounds like a gruesome dream, the interpretation was actually that there were issues I had died to in my life that I was allowing to resurrect again.

It is important to identify the person that is dying in your dream. Identify what part of your life they represent. If it is an unknown male figure, then it seems that your intellect is being brought to death. If an unknown female figure, then your creative side is being brought to death.

UNIVERSAL SYMBOL

POSITIVE
The Scriptures say that there will not be any more death! It also speaks of old things passing away so that the new can be born. It says in:

> *Revelation 21:4 And God will wipe away every tear from their eyes; there shall be no more* ***death****, nor sorrow, nor crying. There shall be no more pain, for the former things have passed away.*

Death of a vision is also a very real experience if you have a ministry calling. This is where the Lord calls you to let your ministry vision die, so that he can give you a new one.

NEGATIVE

There was a time when I saw the angel of death when praying for someone. The message was very clear - her life was about to be taken. As we came against that spirit, she was restored to full health again.

Satan is the author of death and in the spirit, death is epitomized as darkness, black, and evil. David explains this oppression very clearly in:

> *Psalms 143:3 For the enemy has persecuted my soul; he has crushed my life to the ground; he has made me dwell in darkness, like those who have long been* ***dead****.*

In the spirit I have also seen a field of flowers die because of lack of water. This was a picture of the enemy stealing the fruit of our labor.

To dream of someone, that represents your love, dying, means that your love has died.

If you dream of your first love dying, this could mean that you have let go of your first love, Jesus Christ, and that you need to get back into a relationship with him.

Determine what is dying in your vision or prophetic dream – this will tell you whether you are meant to be letting it go, or whether it is time to invest a bit more effort into that area of your life.

See also: Altar, Coffin, Baptism, Blood, Darkness, Grave, Tombstone

DEMONS

It is common to see demons both in dreams and visions. Seeing these beings indicates that you are functioning in the gift of discerning of spirits.

The Lord will reveal these things to you at His bidding, but if you are having demonic manifestations or coming face to face with demonic forces that you cannot control, realize that the enemy has been given license in your life and you need to deal with it accordingly.

CHARACTER SPECIFIC AND UNIVERSAL SYMBOLS

I often see demons in the spirit and I will give you a quick summary here of the different levels of demons. You can then relate this to what you have experienced and seen in the spirit:

> *Ephesians 6:12 For we wrestle not against flesh and blood, but against* ***principalities, against powers, against the rulers of the darkness*** *of this world, against spiritual wickedness in high [places]. (KJV)*

> *1 Corinthians 2:8 Which none of the princes of this world knew: for had they known it, they would not have crucified the Lord of glory. (KJV)*

The following descriptions have been based on *The Prophetic Warrior*. You will find all the Scripture references and full explanations in this book. The following is simply a summary.

Principality demons: These are usually your spirits of infirmities. I see them in the spirit as insects, small crustaceans and so forth. I remember one time really suffering with a pinched sciatic nerve on my left side. The pain was unbearable, shooting from my hip and down my leg, sometimes even making my leg feel lame.

My husband Craig prayed for me and in the spirit he saw what looked like a scorpion on the nerve pinching it. By identifying the spirit of infirmity, he told it to go and I felt an instant relief. The pain and the condition cleared up and by the next day I was walking around as if nothing had happened.

By identifying the spirit of infirmity when praying for someone and telling it to leave will often bring an immediate result.

What I share here is based on my personal experience. You may see these demons in a different way. This is just a guideline for you to follow and help you identify what you may be seeing.

Power demons: These demons are a little stronger and are what are associated to things like depression, discouragement and deception. (See *Snakes* for more on deception)

They are what attacks us in our day-to-day walk. These are the demons that are also given the most license through association with others and by contamination through family generations.

We see these demons often like monkeys or gorillas hanging on and attacking.

Ruler demons: These demons are stronger and look a bit more human in the spirit. The ruler demons are occult in nature and if someone is possessed then there is a ruler demon involved. I often see an occult demon as a broad shouldered, strong-looking demon. Sometime green or grey in color with a bald head and pointy ears.

Some people see these spirits as your typical "devil -pointed ears, forked tongue" kind of creature. These demons are given license through personal or generational sin involving, witchcraft, false religion, freemasonry, horoscopes, fortune-telling and so forth.

I have seen the prince of death and he looks like an emaciated black being. Thin and evil. I have seen the prince of lust. He is attractive, almost feminine in appearance and is dressed lavishly in many different colored silks. When I see this demon, I know that the person I am ministering to is bound by lust.

These are just a few, but you should be able to identify for yourself what you are coming against.

Jezebel spirit: I see the Jezebel spirit as a witch who is haggard and aggressive. When ministering to someone and I see this, I know that counseling as well as deliverance will be needed. I have found this particular demon to be quite aggressive – like with any demon, the person in question will need to deal with personal sin before they can break free.

Princes:

> *Ephesians 2:2 In which in time past you walked according to the course of this world, according to the* ***prince*** *of the authority of the air, the spirit that now works in the children of disobedience*

These demons coordinate and arrange entire structures to help them fulfill their purpose.

This is where you will find your territorial spirits. You will have princes with varied influences.

To name a few of them: family generational princes, territorial princes, and princes who are in control of specific archetypes.

What separates them from the other categories, is that they build the structure in which the other demons can fulfill their purpose.

Territorial demons: The princes are very human in appearance and can even be "good looking" at times. These are the demons placed over an area such as the prince of Persia mentioned in the Word. Yes, there is a prince of America, Mexico, Africa, and every other country, state, and province of the earth. They are given license through the sin and the words of man.

I have seen the prince of America as a half-bull and half-man. Having the face of a man, but the horns of a bull. We have seen the prince of Mexico as looking like a type of Indian chief, with a full feather headdress on.

Wickedness in high places: There are seven main categories of princes that rule the systems of this world. I teach on them in *The Strategies of War*.

Here I will mention the three main leaders of the demonic realm. The first being Lucifer who is in charge of the religious system. The second is Apollyon who is in charge of the world and the attack on us directly, and Pharaoh, who is in charge of the world system and referred to as "The God of This World."

Lucifer: Usually attractive looking – do not assume the enemy is unattractive! He was after all, the son of the morning.

> *Isaiah 14:12 How you are fallen from heaven, O* ***Lucifer****, son of the morning! How you are cut down to the ground, you who weakened the nations!*

Apollyon: I usually see him as half-human and half-reptilian in the spirit. Note that demons are disembodied spirits – how you see them might differ from the way the Lord shows them to me.

> *Revelation 9:11 And they had as king over them the angel of the bottomless pit, whose name in Hebrew is Abaddon, but in Greek he has the name* ***Apollyon.***

Pharaoh: I usually see him as a pharaoh of old, sitting on a huge throne surrounded by the banks of the world.

> *2 Corinthians 4:4 In whom the* ***god of this world*** *hath blinded the minds of them which believe not, lest the light of the glorious gospel of Christ, who is the image of God, should shine unto them.*

See also: Attacked, Hunger, War

DESERT

A season of being set apart. Negatively, it speaks of being spiritually dry.

The desert or wilderness speaks of a place that is barren and without life. Depending on where you are right now in your spiritual walk, this could have two different meanings.

Positive: A season of ministry training
Negative: You walk in disfavor

POSITIVE
Being called to the desert, or going through a time of wilderness, is actually quite positive. It is during these times that you will grow in your relationship with the Lord. Even though you seem so cut off from others, you will draw closer to the Lord.

Consider how John the Baptist became so strong:

> *Luke 1:80 So the child grew and became strong in spirit, and was in the* ***deserts*** *till the day of his manifestation to Israel.*

Jesus also withdrew often to the wilderness to be alone with the Father. It was the only peace and quiet that He had! If the Lord has called you aside and into obscurity, then it is a call to grow and receive everything you can from Him.

> *Luke 5:16 So He Himself often withdrew into the* ***wilderness*** *and prayed.*

To see a wilderness being transformed into a land that flourishes speaks of the Lord's favor and of blessing in everything that you do.

> *Isaiah 41:18 I will open rivers in desolate heights, and fountains in the midst of the valleys; I will make the* ***wilderness*** *a pool of water, and* ***the dry land*** *springs of water.*

NEGATIVE
The wilderness also speaks of being barren and desolate. Nothing can grow there. It speaks of being cursed in Scriptures.

If you see a fruitful land turning into a wilderness, this speaks of a curse that is bringing destruction and theft into your life.

> *Isaiah 64:10 Your holy cities are a **wilderness**, Zion is a **wilderness**, Jerusalem a desolation.*

See also: Cave

DIAMONDS

Diamonds speak of favor and to receive one speaks of receiving an undeserved gift. It is also a picture of wealth and royalty.

Positive: Your potential for excellence
Negative: Someone whose spirit has been crushed through bad leadership

CHARACTER SPECIFIC SYMBOL

Because diamonds hold a particular meaning for most cultures, you need to identify what they mean to you in your dreams. Often diamonds speak of marriage. Other times they speak of having renown and favor.

UNIVERSAL SYMBOL

The diamond is very hard and when used in the passage below means literally "set in stone."

> *Jeremiah 17:1 The sin of Judah is written with a pen of iron; with the point of a **diamond** it is engraved on the tablet of their heart, and on the horns of your altars.*

Receiving a diamond or precious stone speaks of receiving a gift and favor from the Lord. It also speaks of the work we do for the Lord:

> *1 Corinthians 3:12 Now if anyone builds on this foundation with gold, silver, precious stones, wood, hay, straw,*

This passage speaks of the things we build on the foundation that we have received, which is Jesus Christ. When we do things with faith, hope, and love, and in obedience to the Lord, then we are building with gold, silver, and precious stones.

However if you walk in bitterness, strife or vainglory, or other things of the flesh, then you are building wood, hay and stubble, which the Scriptures say will be burned up.

This is a test of the heart. It does not only speak of the work you do for the Lord, but the motivation and the heart you do it with.

Diamond in the rough: Speaks of someone with tremendous potential, but who will require much pressure to bring that potential out.

NEGATIVE
As a ministry trainer, I have often seen one of my disciples as a "diamond in the rough." Through this process the Lord told me how for a diamond to be beautiful it needs to be cut on the flaw. However, if a diamond cutter is not skilled or if the diamond is not properly situated, a chisel on that diamond will shatter it instead of making it shine.

The Lord told me that if I did not chisel correctly, I stood the chance of bringing damage to His people. In addition to that, He said that you also do not chisel coal, but only diamonds – that I was to be discerning if someone was ready for that kind of pressure.

To see a diamond that is crushed or still covered with coal speaks of someone that was handled incorrectly or is not ready for the pressure needed to bring the treasure out of them.

See also: Jewelry

DISEASE

Disease is never a positive picture. It speaks of sin and contamination. It also speaks of being under a curse as this Scripture indicates:

> *Deuteronomy 28:60 Moreover He will bring back on you all the **diseases** of Egypt, of which you were afraid, and they shall cling to you.*

Speaking of sin and the flesh:

> *Leviticus 13:46 All the days wherein the **plague** shall be in him he shall be defiled; he is **unclean**: he shall dwell alone; without the camp shall his habitation be].*

To dream of being diseased, or to see it in the spirit, speaks of the stain of the flesh. This is a warning that you are walking in the flesh and that you have received a spiritual contamination. As a result, a curse is prevalent in your life right now.

Doctor/Physician

A process of healing and restoration to be experienced through another person.

So often when we come to the Lord with hurts in our hearts, we want to hide away and have Him heal them quietly. More often than not though, He will use others to bring healing. He will use "spiritual doctors" to come and reach in.

Consider this: If you were able to receive this kind of healing on your own, then you would be healed already. It stands to reason that if you are still struggling with hurts or conflicts that you need someone from the outside to help.

> *Matthew 9:12 On hearing this, Jesus said, 'It is not the healthy who need a* ***doctor****, but the sick. (NIV)*

Character Specific and Universal Symbols

POSITIVE

If you dream of going to the doctor or being treated for something, this is an indication that there is some "fixing" that the Lord wants to do in your life. This fixing, is something that He wants to do through someone else, so if you have been led to a ministry or to a specific person, it is likely that this is the person that God wants to use.

If you dream of a successful surgery, then the Lord is saying that He is going to complete the work that He has begun. If you are a doctor or dream of a specific doctor that you know, you would need to determine what they mean to you in real life. If they are someone that you rely heavily on, they could very well represent the work of the Holy Spirit in your life.

NEGATIVE

If you have a fear of doctors or have had a bad experience in the past, dreaming of them would also be negative. It would speak of the enemy trying to bring a spirit of fear into your life.

If you dream of having surgery you did not need or of a surgery going bad, then this also speaks of the work of the enemy to try and "dig up" things in your life that are just not there. It is like the passage above – only the sick need a doctor!

So if you dream of being healthy and attacked by doctors or being pushed into surgery you do not need, then it means that the enemy is trying to trick you into digging up things in your life that do not need to be dealt with right now.

On the other hand, if you dream that you need surgery and that a doctor is trying to reach out to you, but you keep rejecting him, this is negative. It means that you refuse to look at the deeper issues that God wants to deal with inside of you. You are trying to avoid painful things in the hope that they will just go away. In situations like this, it is time to submit to the Lord and the person He is using to finally bring healing and change in this area of your life.

Universal Symbol

POSITIVE AND NEGATIVE
As ministers, the Lord often uses us as spiritual doctors. We are there to comfort and to bring healing to broken hearts. When my husband Craig prays for physical or emotional healing for someone, he encourages them to relax and not to try so hard to believe.

He shares the illustration of them being on the operating table and to just trust "the doctor" to do the right job. In the spirit, we will also see a wound that represents a hurt. It is for us to follow up with healing and counsel.

See also: Bruise, Wound

Dog

If negative a dog speaks of attack coming from the world. It can also speak about a spirit of fear. If positive, it can represent trust and loyalty.

Character Specific Symbol

If you dream about your pet dog, then look up *Pet* for a better understanding. If you are afraid of dogs, then they would represent fear in your life.

If you love dogs, then they would speak of joy or a blessing in your dreams.

Universal Symbol

Wolves and dogs have the same meaning in Scripture.

They do not have a positive connotation in Scripture at all. They speak of something that is evil. They also speak of demonic attack. The kind of attack that comes at you from all sides. It also spoke of someone that was lowly or held a low level position.

If you see dogs attacking anyone in a vision, it speaks of the enemy seeking to devour and destroy:

> *Psalms 22:16 For **dogs** have surrounded Me; the congregation of the wicked has enclosed Me. They pierced My hands and My feet.*

See also: Pet

Donkey

The donkey is passive and a picture of humility. Because they are used for cargo, to have many speaks of wealth and so refers to financial blessing.

Negatively though, a donkey is a picture of stubbornness.

Character Specific Symbol

POSITIVE
Do you have any personal experiences with donkeys in your life? If so perhaps it speaks of a pet or something that is special to you.

However, for most cultures I would have to say that a donkey speaks of a beast of burden. In some cultures, it can even have the same meaning as a cargo vehicle.

NEGATIVE
The first impression that comes to most people when thinking of a donkey is stubbornness. I would have to say that in your dream, it is likely that this is the first interpretation you should look at. Are you being stubborn at the moment or struggling with pressing forward?

If so, then perhaps you are being as stubborn as a donkey!

Universal Symbol

POSITIVE
There are many positive pictures for the donkey in scripture. Jesus seated himself on a donkey instead of a grand horse. He was making a point. He was not there to exalt Himself, but chose the way of humility instead.

He was presenting a picture of meekness. A war horse is a powerful animal that could bring fear into the heart of the enemy. The sight of a donkey does not bring fear! This is why Jesus chose such a lowly animal. He was saying, "You have nothing to be afraid of. In my humility, I am here to lead you, not to hurt you."

> *John 12:15 Fear not, daughter of Zion; behold, your King is coming, sitting on a **donkey's** colt...*

Financial blessing: Because the donkey was used as a beast of burden to have many of them was a sign of wealth. They were a lot like camels in the scripture and share a similar interpretation.

NEGATIVE
Balaam was so blind to the angel that the Lord had to speak through a donkey! This lines up with the negative interpretation for dreams. When you get to the place where you are so stubborn, God even has to use a donkey to speak to you.

To see a donkey in a negative sense means that you are stubborn and deaf to the voice of God.

> *2 Peter 2:16 but he was rebuked for his iniquity: a **dumb** donkey speaking with a man's voice restrained the madness of the prophet.*

See also: Camel, Horse

DOOR

A new direction in your life, or one that has passed. A gate, path, door or fence opening all speak of either a new direction in your life or one that has passed.

I often see a door or gate in the spirit when I am releasing someone into something new in their lives.

A door often speaks of a new plan that the Lord has for them. Perhaps someone has been trusting the Lord for a new job or hoping to move house. If I see an open door before them, it means that the way is clear before them. If I see a closed door, it either means that we need to pray and open the door, or that something is blocking them. The same refers to a path or to a gate.

I might see a blockage in the road that needs removing, or the Lord could be saying "Not now, I have put this blockage here for a reason". Once again, it takes a bit of discernment and a look at the person's current condition. Let's look at a few typical scenarios here:

POSITIVE
I see a door, gate or a new path in the spirit most often when I am releasing an individual into their ministry or releasing them into something new. When I have imparted gifts or confirmed a calling in a person's life, then the Lord often shows me a new door that he has for them. This door refers to a new plan, with a new set of circumstances.

This often also involves closing off the doors to the past. At this point the Holy Spirit requires that they commit entirely to this new plan and allow Him to "burn their bridges" of the past and close all past doors.

Referring to a new direction for ministry:

> *1 Corinthians 16:9 because a great **door** for effective work has opened to me, and there are many who oppose me. (NIV)*
>
> *2 Corinthians 2:12 Now when I went to Troas to preach the gospel of Christ and found that the Lord had opened a **door** for me, (NIV)*

If you see a closed door, then the Lord means for you to open it in the spirit:

> *Revelation 3:8 I know your deeds. See, I have placed before you an open **door** that no one can shut. I know that you have little strength, yet you have kept my word and have not denied my name. (NIV)*

NEGATIVE
Most negative doors I see in the spirit refer to an open door to the demonic realm. When I see an open door and darkness behind it, or a demon coming out of it, I know that a person has an "open door" in their lives.

In other words, they have given the enemy license to mess in their lives because of personal sin, generational sin or sin by association. I do not close this door on the person's behalf.

It is vital to remember that you cannot forgive sins that are unto death. In other words, if the person in question opened the door, then it is up to them to repent and shut it.

In a nutshell apply:

> *James 4:7 Therefore submit to God. Resist the devil and he will flee from you.*

Submit to the Lord, confess your sin, and then close that door and tell satan to leave!

Speaking of walking a life of sin (thus giving the enemy license in your life)

> *Proverbs 4:14 Do not enter the path of the wicked, and do not walk in the way of evil.*

In reference to giving license to the enemy:

> *Ephesians 4:26 Be angry, and do not sin: do not let the sun go down on your wrath, 27 nor give place to the devil.*

See also: Gate, Road

DOVE

A depiction of the Holy Spirit. A symbol of peace and promise.

POSITIVE
The Holy Spirit is often represented as a dove in Scripture. Noah also used the dove when seeing if there was dry land yet. So if you see a dove, it speaks both of the Holy Spirit and also of a promise that the Lord is about to fulfill in your life.

Because of its timid nature, a dove also speaks of peace. It is unsettled easily. If you get a vision of a dove flying away in a meeting then it means that the Holy Spirit has left.

The dove was chased away. This often happens when the leadership does not obey His prompting or tries to take things into their own hands.

> *John 1:32 And John bore witness, saying, I saw the Spirit descending from heaven like a **dove**, and He remained upon Him.*

See also: Birds

DRESS

Your image to the world representing who you are and your position.

POSITIVE
You will find the reference to the word "garments" often in Scripture. Depending on what the person wore, that would indicate their station in life, their class distinction, and also what kind of person they were.

A bride wore a dress that was white and without spot. This spoke of a union and being pure and innocent. To wear a dress that is purple and has a rich fabric represents wealth and affluence.

To receive a blue dress is a picture of being given a ministry. If you dream that you are given a new dress to put on, it means that the Lord is about to bring a change in your life.

I often see the Lord giving someone new clothes in the spirit. The clothes that they had in the past perhaps fulfilled a function, but they are old and must be changed.

> *Zechariah 3:3 Now Joshua was clothed with filthy* ***garments****, and was standing before the Angel.*

NEGATIVE
To dream or see a vision of a dress that is moth-eaten and torn is quite negative. It speaks about the stain of flesh and having been involved in the world.

Perhaps when you started out, your intentions were pure, but over time you got discouraged and started to do things your own way. It is time to put those rags aside and to take on the new garments that the Lord has for you.

> *James 5:2 Your riches are corrupted, and your garments are moth eaten.*

See also: Clothing, Purple

DRAGON

A picture of high level demonic attack.

CHARACTER SPECIFIC SYMBOL

NEGATIVE
Because dragons are mythological in nature, if you keep dreaming of dragons, it could mean that you have been getting into writings of this nature.

Universal Symbol

NEGATIVE

The devil is mentioned as a dragon in Scripture, so if you see a vision of a dragon, this speaks of high level demonic attack.

> *Revelation 12:9 So the great **dragon** was cast out, that serpent of old, called the Devil and Satan, who deceives the whole world; he was cast to the earth, and his angels were cast out with him.*

There was a time when the Lord was having me birth something new for our ministry. In the spirit, I saw myself as pregnant, travailing with labor pains. In front of me, stood a dragon, ready to try and take the baby the moment I birthed it.

It was a warning to continue the travail, but also to do spiritual warfare. Yes, the new direction was a fight and the promises that came to pass after that time were not handed to us easily! We have to push forward and fight for each one, in faith!

NOTE: If you always have visions of dragons and other such folklore, then I would say that you have opened up your heart to teachings and fables that are not of the Lord. You have contaminated your spirit and given the enemy a hold of your life.

See also: Alien, Alligator, Demons

SYMBOLS STARTING IN E

SYMBOLS STARTING IN E

EAGLE

A picture of the Holy Spirit and His ability to protect us and do warfare on our behalf.

Positive: Powerful work of the Holy Spirit
Negative: Destructive work of the enemy

CHARACTER SPECIFIC AND UNIVERSAL SYMBOLS

POSITIVE
There are so many positive connotations for the eagle, that you might have many of your own in addition to this book.

My favorite is a personal revelation the Holy Spirit gave me concerning hiding in the shadow of His wings.

I saw myself standing alone, facing the many attacks and pressures that I am used to facing daily. Then I saw a huge eagle come and stand behind me and extend its wings. As it stood behind me, I was covered by its shadow.

When I stood alone, I looked very small when others looked at me. But when that eagle was behind me, the size of His very shadow made them stop dead in their tracks!

Alone, I was helpless, but as I stood in His shadow, they saw His magnificence, and so I was protected!

> *Psalms 63:7 Because You have been my help, therefore in the* ***shadow of Your wings*** *I will rejoice.*

Here is another passage that describes the Lord as an eagle:

> *Deuteronomy 32:11 As an* ***eagle*** *stirs up its nest, hovers over its young, spreading out its wings, taking them up, carrying them on its wings:*

NEGATIVE
In a negative light, an eagle can also speak of destruction. The eagle is a bird of prey, and it tears that prey apart with its powerful beak and claws.

Here is a passage that indicates that an eagle in a vision or external dream, can indicate destruction and an attack from the enemy:

> *Habakkuk 1:8 ... their cavalry comes from afar; they fly as the eagle that hastens to eat.*

See also: Birds, Dove

EARRINGS

A picture of blessing with regards to natural and external things. External beauty and the image you present to the world.

Positive: Favor of the Lord
Negative: Taking on the image of the world

CHARACTER SPECIFIC SYMBOL

POSITIVE

To dream of putting on earrings has a positive picture if you are a woman and the emotion in the dream is positive.

Earrings speak of external appearances and the "face" you approach the world with. It is the way people see you, and in a positive context it would mean that the Lord is blessing and is exalting you in the eyes of the world - that He is giving you a gift.

NEGATIVE

It would not be a positive picture if you were a man and you were putting on earrings in an internal dream. This would mean that you are wearing things that are meant for a woman, and that there is something wrong in the way you are approaching life.

UNIVERSAL SYMBOL

In Scripture, earrings are a representation of what you belong to or ally yourself with. A love slave would have his ear pierced to show that he belonged to his master. In the same way, if you have a vision or dream of being pierced, you need to determine what you are "signing a contract" with! (Exodus 21:6)

POSITIVE

Earrings and jewels (in a positive light) were given to a bride or an engaged person.

In the passage below, the Lord describes how He clothed Israel with beauty and gave her jewels to wear to accentuate that beauty.

So to see jewelry in a vision or external dream could indicate a new gift of blessing from the Lord; not a desire being met, but rather a desire that He will meet. It also means that He is showing His "ownership" of you – a beautiful promise that He is in covenant with you and that you will lack nothing.

> *Ezekiel 16:12 And I put a jewel in your nose,* ***earrings*** *in your ears, and a beautiful crown on your head.*

NEGATIVE

Putting on earrings to draw attention to yourself in a negative way, indicates a harlot and one who is using her charms in a lewd manner.

It is dressing up to impress, or trying to get attention.

> *Hosea 2:13 ... She decked herself with her **earrings** and jewelry, and went after her lovers; but Me she forgot, says the Lord.*

In addition to that, the type of earrings in your vision or prophetic dream could indicate that you are allowing yourself to be influenced by the world. Is the body piercing in your dream worldly or associated with a particular worldly archetype? You are blending things of God with things of the world and the light you shine as a believer, is being diminished.

See also: Diamond, Precious Stones, Jewelry, Ruby

EARS

To have understanding. Also speaks of your ability to hear the voice of God.

Positive: The sign that you understand the Lord correctly
Negative:

- Stubbornness
- Unwillingness to listen to the truth

POSITIVE
Ears speak of receiving into your spirit, the truth of the Lord. To hear with your ears in Scripture means to have understanding.

Luke speaks of the ability to understand in this passage:

> *Luke 9:44 Let these words sink down into your **ears**, for the Son of Man is about to be betrayed into the hands of men.*

NEGATIVE
Deaf ears: To see blocked ears or ears that cannot hear means that the person in question has no understanding of the truth.

Often in Scripture you will read how the Lord said, "Having ears, they did not hear..." speaking of the people's inability to understand His instructions and parables.

That exact meaning is clarified here:

> *Acts 7:51 You stiff-necked and uncircumcised in heart and **ears**! You always resist the Holy Spirit; as your fathers did, so do you.*

See also: Ear Plugs

EAR PLUGS

A deliberate refusal to receive external influences.

POSITIVE
The one time that a dream or vision of ear plugs would be positive is when you are deliberately ignoring the voice of the enemy. For example, if you dreamed of someone that represents the flesh in your dreams and you put in ear plugs, it would be positive. It would mean that you are refusing to listen to the flesh and that you are choosing to hear the voice of God!

NEGATIVE
More often than not though to dream of having blocked ears or putting in ear plugs is a picture of refusing to listen to the truth.

> *Matthew 13:15 For the hearts of this people have grown dull. Their* ***ears are hard of hearing****, ...*

It speaks of knowing the truth, but deliberately refusing to do it. If you function in intercession you might see the ears of God's people being blocked up. This means that they have shut their ears from the truth or they have allowed the enemy to block their ears.

Jesus said that He came to open the ears of the deaf and this refers to both natural and spiritual deafness. There are those that are deaf because they have listened to the lies of the enemy and then there are those that are deaf because they refuse to listen. The truth, being too uncomfortable is put aside in favor of what is more palatable.

See also: Ears

EARTHQUAKE

Refers to a dramatic change of events in your life. It is also a picture of revival coming to the Church.

Negatively, it speaks of the destructive work of the enemy.

Positive: Things being removed that are not of God
Negative: Destructive work of the enemy

CHARACTER SPECIFIC SYMBOL

POSITIVE
I have often interpreted dreams where people have been in an earthquake. Often the interpretation has been that a shaking is coming in their lives to remove things that are not of the Lord.

I have often seen this occurring when someone is about to enter into a new realm of ministry.

In a positive context, an earthquake means that a shaking and a dramatic change is about to occur in the life of that person. My favorite scripture to illustrate this is:

> *Hebrews 12:27 Now this, yet once more, indicates the removal of those things that are being* ***shaken****, as of things that are made, that the things which cannot be* ***shaken*** *may* ***remain***

NEGATIVE
An earthquake can also speak of the destruction of the enemy; that he is attempting to destroy their lives and to remove their feet from under them.

In such a case, I would counsel that this person run to the solid rock which is Jesus Christ, to ensure that their footing remains sure, throughout this attack.

Universal Symbol

POSITIVE
An earthquake in vision and in a prophetic dream speaks of the power of God.

When I have seen an earthquake in vision, it has symbolized the might and power of God. It has symbolized the shaking that occurs as He works in the life of one to bring change.

I have seen earthquakes in the context of revival. In this case, the Lord has said that before He would pour out His spirit on a group, that first there are some people or things that will need to be "shaken" out of their lives.

This shaking brings freedom, as demonstrated in this passage:

> *Acts 16:26 Suddenly there was a great* ***earthquake****, so that the foundations of the prison were shaken; and immediately all the doors were opened and everyone's chains were loosed.*

NEGATIVE
If the earthquake in your vision is negative, it means that the change of events in your life right now are not of the Lord, but rather the enemy who is trying to discourage you. He is trying to "shake you" and manipulate your circumstances to have his way in your life. I suggest the *Strategies of War* book to help you practically.

Please Note: If you see an earthquake in the spirit or in a dream, it does not mean that an actual earthquake is going to strike that area. If you have such a dream and wake up in fear, you can rest assured that this was not of the Lord.

See also: Shaking, Storm

EAST

In Scripture the east is often spoke of as the direction from which the Son of Man came.

Positive: The direction of blessing
Negative: Direction of the destructive work of the enemy

POSITIVE
It speaks of the direction of the Lord and the direction of blessing.

Here is a scripture to consider:

> *Matthew 24:27 For as the lightning comes from the **east** and flashes to the west, so also will the coming of the Son of Man be.*

NEGATIVE
There was a negative element that also came from the east, and that was a terrible wind that dried up all blessing and provision.

While it was the direction of the Son of Man, it is also the direction from which a wind of destruction comes from. You would need to discern the spirit on the vision to clarify whether the interpretation is positive or negative.

> *Jeremiah 18:17 I will scatter them as with an **east** wind before the enemy; I will show them the back and not the face in the day of their calamity.*

EGGS

A conceived promise or curse that is about to manifest in your life.

CHARACTER SPECIFIC AND UNIVERSAL SYMBOLS

POSITIVE
If the eggs are positive in the dream or vision, then the Lord is giving you a promise. He is encouraging you to press on because you will soon see the blessing that He has promised you. Sometimes when you pray to the Lord for something, you can become discouraged as you wait.

If you have a dream of eggs in a nest waiting to be hatched the Lord is saying to you, "Hang in there! The promise is coming soon!" It is also a call to protect the promises that God has given to you and not to give up.

This is a great picture of how the Lord gathers the wealth of nations in His hand.

> *Isaiah 10:14 My hand has found like a nest the riches of the people, and as one gathers **eggs** that are left, I have gathered all the earth; and there was no one who moved his wing, nor opened his mouth with even a peep.*

NEGATIVE

The eggs from an unclean animal or rotten eggs speak of sin that leads to a curse.

> *Isaiah 59:4 No one calls for justice; no one pleads his case with integrity. They rely on empty arguments and speak lies; they conceive trouble and give birth to evil.*
> *5 They hatch the **eggs** of vipers and spin a spider's web. Whoever eats their **eggs** will die, and when one is broken, an adder is hatched. (NIV)*

So to dream of eggs of a snake or of another unpleasant animal speaks about a curse that is about to come into your life. This is a warning dream. This curse has come in through sin and you need to identify if this is a personal sin in your own life or if you are associating with others that have an open door to the enemy in their lives.

To have "all your eggs in one basket" is character specific and speaks of putting all your hopes in one thing. You are so focused in this single direction that you are not allowing the Lord to show you other avenues of blessing that He has in store for you.

See also: Birds, Quail

ELEPHANT

The requirement for great faith or hard work

CHARACTER SPECIFIC SYMBOL

Because the elephant is not in the Scriptures, I can only give you some personal experiences that we have had in the spirit when seeing them.

An elephant is pregnant for 3 full years. So if I am praying for something and see an elephant I know what God is telling me, "This is a big one! It is going to take a lot of time and effort to birth this in the spirit."

When ministering inner healing, my husband will often see a baby elephant chained to a stake in the ground. The interpretation is, that to control an elephant, you chain it as a baby and then as it grows up chained, when it is grown up and powerful, it stays in place. You can remove the chain and the elephant will not try to run away. It will still think it is bound.

This is such a perfect illustration of how it is when we have hurts and insecurities from the past that God has healed. As a child, we could not move, but now we are no longer bound! The restriction is only in our minds. It is time to break free in faith!

See also: Animals

ELEVATOR

A promotion and change in your circumstances/position.

Positive: Promotion
Negative:

- Demotion
- Failure to achieve your goal

CHARACTER SPECIFIC AND UNIVERSAL SYMBOLS

POSITIVE

In both dreams and visions if you dream of going up an elevator or escalator, it means a promotion in your natural or spiritual life. If you are in your workplace in your dream and you go up an elevator, then it means that the Lord wants to raise you up in the sight of man. He wants you to go "up a level" in your skills and position.

> *Luke 1:52 He has put down the mighty from their thrones, and* ***exalted the lowly.***

In a ministry context, the Lord is telling you that it is time to rise up higher now. Let me give you a word of caution though. Have you heard the phrase, "The door to the elevator begins in the basement?" This is very true of a ministry call.

Before the Lord can promote you, it is often accompanied with a sense of demotion or humility first. If this is happening to you, then do not be discouraged, because promotion will soon be on its way!

To dream of being taken by elevator to a new floor speaks again of entering into a new and better season in your life. Depending on what the room is like, will be an indication of what kind of season it will be.

NEGATIVE

If you dream of going down a level, this could have a two-fold meaning. It could mean that the Lord is taking you through a process of humbling or it could mean that you have opened the door through sin and are being brought low because of it.

> *Deuteronomy 28:43 The alien who is among you shall* ***rise higher*** *and higher above you, and you shall* ***come down*** *lower and lower.*

To be stuck in an elevator that is not moving speaks of being stuck on a plateau in your spiritual life at the moment. If you feel smothered or frustrated in your dream, it would be an indication of what you are feeling at that time.

To dream of being in an elevator that is falling speaks of an attack and the enemy is trying to "derail" your spiritual life. This is a warning dream and a call to spiritual warfare. Although the enemy might want to steal God's blessing and position from you, the Lord will be there to help you overcome.

See also: Ladder, Basement

EMERALD

New life and a gift you never had before

UNIVERSAL SYMBOL

Strong's Concordance 5306 nophek {no'-fek} from an unused root meaning to glisten;

The beauty described about the emerald in Scripture is not just its color, but its property to glisten. It is also known as a "glowing stone."

> *Revelation 4:3 And He who sat there was like a jasper and a sardius stone in appearance; and there was a rainbow around the throne, in appearance like an emerald*

The emerald is a beautiful illustration of the new life we have in Christ. Its comparison to light and the rainbow in this passage solidifies this picture. Emeralds speak of a gift of great value – something new that you did not have before.

If the emerald is in a weapon or ministry tool, then the Lord is saying that this ministry function is going to be something completely new to you. It will involve walking in love and reflecting Christ. Just as the face of Moses shone when coming from the presence of God, so also will yours glisten with the presence of Jesus Christ as you step out in boldness.

See also: Diamond, Precious Stones, Ruby

EYES

Eyes are referred to in many cultures as the window to your soul. They show what is really going on inside of you. They are also a picture of the things you allow into your spirit.

UNIVERSAL SYMBOL

POSITIVE

If the eye is good it is positive and means that you walk in the light of the Lord. It means that you can see the truth and that you also walk in knowledge.

However, if the eye is bad, it speaks of darkness and of shutting the Lord out of your life.

> *Matthew 6:22 The lamp of the body is the* ***eye****. If therefore your eye is good, your whole body will be full of light.*

An eye that is full of life speaks of being open to the Lord and also being open and transparent to others.

NEGATIVE
If you dream of an eye that is damaged, it means that you are not seeing things correctly in the spirit, or that your judgment is incorrect.

> *Matthew 6:23 But if your* ***eye*** *is bad, your whole body will be full of darkness. If therefore the light that is in you is darkness, how great is that darkness!*

If you have a vision of wearing colored glasses, it means that you perceive things incorrectly. The Lord is trying to show you one thing, but you are seeing them incorrectly, because of your own ideas.

Putting your hand over your eyes speaks of trying to avoid the realities that are around you. By "playing blind" you do not take away the problems, but only make them worse.

To be blind: Jesus said to the Pharisees that if only they would admit that they were blind, He could take away their sin and set them free. However, because they refused to look at the truth, their sin remained!

> *John 9:41 Jesus said to them, if you were* ***blind****, you would have no sin; but now you say, we see. Therefore, your sin remains.*

Being blind is never a good picture and speaks of being deceived and not open to the things of the Lord.

> *2 Corinthians 4:4 Whose minds the god of this age has* ***blinded****, who do not believe, lest the light of the gospel of the glory of Christ, who is the image of God, should shine on them.*

See also: Blind, Face, Glasses

Symbols Starting in F

Symbols Starting in F

Face

The direction of your intent. The direction that you are taking in life. To set your face as a flint, means to have a conviction in your intended direction.

POSITIVE
To be face-to-face with a person speaks of being open and transparent with them, just as Moses was with the Lord.

> *Exodus 33:11 So the Lord spoke to Moses* ***face to face****, as a man speaks to his friend. And he would return to the camp, but his servant Joshua the son of Nun, a young man, did not depart from the tabernacle.*

To fall upon your face means to give honor to, or to bow down in reverence to someone.

An open face expresses transparency. If you have a vision of the Lord or an angel, you will see that their face is open. They have nothing to hide.

NEGATIVE
This interpretation will change according to your gender. If you are a woman and dream you have a beard and the face of a man, this is certainly negative!

Hidden face: To set your face towards something specific, speaks of making up your mind and following through. To hide your face speaks of shame and embarrassment.

To have a vision where the person or angel's face is hidden denotes an angel of light or someone that has something to hide. To hide your face also denotes embarrassment.

Determine in your vision or prophetic dream if the person in question is hiding their face because they are being deceptive, lack conviction, or are feeling embarrassed. The context and other symbols should narrow that down for you.

See also: Beard, Eyes , Face Mask

Face Mask

Conforming to what others want.

Positive: To be tactful
Negative: A false representation of who you really are

Character Specific Symbol

POSITIVE
Wearing a mask is most often negative, but it could be that you are perhaps just a bit "too real" and keep bringing offense to others. The Lord told me once that I had to meet people where they were at, before I could lead them to truth. The reality is that many people were just not prepared for the "real me" and I had to use some tact until they were.

So to wear a mask that is positive means that you need to show people a part of yourself that they can relate to. From there, you can lead them to the real you.

NEGATIVE
As I said though, a mask is mostly negative. It speaks of being deceptive and not making your true intentions known.

In counseling, there is a principle called "performance orientation." This refers to people who learned, early in life, to be what others wanted them to be, to be loved and accepted. As they now try to approach the Lord, they do not know which mask to wear. We take them through a process of inner healing and letting go of those masks, so that they can break free.

I take the prophets through this healing process in my book *Prophetic Boot Camp*.

See also: Face

Family

Generations linked to you through relationship or blood.

Positive: Those you share the same spiritual DNA with
Negative: The origination of generational curses

Character Specific Symbol

POSITIVE AND NEGATIVE
The first thing to keep in mind when dreaming of anyone that you know is that they are a type or shadow of your own life. They are not literally the person themselves! With this in mind, when you think about the family member you dreamed about, what are the first words that come to your mind? This will be the best indication of what they represent in your own life.

Here are some fairly common interpretations for specific family members. Keep in mind that these illustrations are general and they may not all apply to you. Identify which ones suit you best.

Father: Often a picture of Father God (See *Father* for more on this)

Mother: Often a picture of the Church (See *Mother* for more on this)

Spouse: Can be a picture of the Lord Jesus or of your own recreated spirit in Christ (See *Wife* and *Husband* for more)

Older sibling: Can be a picture of the Holy Spirit, depending on your relationship with them.

Children: What was going on in your life when you had this child? Depending on the circumstances, they could represent different aspects of your ministry. They can also be a picture of your faith, hope and love. (See *Child* for more info)

Cousin: Determine your relationship with that cousin. Do they represent your intellect or strong will?

Grandparents: Can represent generational curses (if negative) or spiritual DNA that has been passed down (can be positive or negative). If your grandparents raised you, then they would have the same interpretations as *Mother* and *Father.*

Spiritual children/disciples: Often represents different aspects of your ministry. If I dream of the leaders of our South African ministry team, I know the Lord is talking to me about the work in South Africa. If I dream of one of my prophetic disciples, I know the Lord is speaking to me about the prophetic training division in our ministry. What is the first thought that comes to you when you think about your spiritual child/disciple?

Your whole family: This is a lovely picture of the Church as a whole. We are known as the family of Christ, so if you dream of all your family being in one place from both sides of your generations, then the Lord is speaking to you of His Church.

Universal Symbol

POSITIVE AND NEGATIVE
If you see someone in a vision, then it relates to them literally. The circumstances in the vision will help you determine what should be done.

See also: Ancestor, Father, Mother, Siblings

Father

A picture of masculinity, strength and authority. Often a picture of God the Father.

Positive: The image of God the Father
Negative: A symbol of fear or generational curses

Character Specific Symbol

Assess your relationship with your father before deciding on what he represents in your dream.

If you have a negative relationship, he might speak of the enemy in your life. He might speak of your failures, weaknesses, pain, hurt or conflict.

More often than not, I have found that a father figure represents God the Father in an internal or internal prophetic dream.

Universal Symbol

POSITIVE
A father is the perfect picture of masculinity and authority.

Seeing a person's father could be positive. He could represent the kind of image they will become.

You might see a father figure to speak healing with regards to any broken relationship. The Lord might be leading you to speak forth a restoration into the lives of those involved.

Here is a passage that speaks positively about taking on the father's image:

> *Luke 2:49 And He said to them, "Why did you seek Me? Did you not know that I must be about My **Father's** business?"*

NEGATIVE
It is common for me to see a person's father when I pray for them.

Sometimes it means that there is a generational curse coming from their father.

If this is the case, I often see an umbilical cord or chains coming from their father to them. This also applies to a mother figure.

Seeing a person's father could also indicate past hurts he inflicted or any bondage or control coming from him.

Once again, the same principle can apply to *Mother*.

Speaking of generational bondage from the line of the father:

> *1 Kings 15:3 And he walked in all the sins of his **father**, which he had done before him; his heart was not loyal to the Lord his God, as was the heart of his **father** David.*

See also: Ancestor, Family, Mother, Siblings

FEET

Your feet speak of your Christian walk with the Lord. Depending on the circumstances surrounding your dream or vision, the interpretation will vary.

UNIVERSAL SYMBOL

POSITIVE
If you dream that you receive new shoes, it indicates that the Lord is going to do something new in your Christian walk.

Perhaps you have been going through a difficult time. This indicates that the Lord is preparing the way so that things will get easier for you.

Perhaps the shoes you see are shoes that belonged to someone you admired.

The dream indicates that you are going in the same direction as that person, or that you have received everything from them.

Speaking of dominion: If you have a vision of your enemies being put under your feet, it means that the Lord has given you the victory! This is a picture of winning the battle.

> *Ephesians 1:22 And He put all things under His **feet**, and gave Him to be head over all things to the church.*

Speaking of a flourishing ministry: Feet that are strong and beautiful are a reflection of your walk with the Lord. It means that you are secure in your calling and in your position as a believer. Press forward and continue shining brightly for the Lord!

> *Ephesians 6:15 and having shod your **feet** with the preparation of the gospel of peace*

NEGATIVE
Hurt feet: Hurt or torn up feet indicates that you have taken some damage in your Christian walk. Have you experienced some rejection and hurt lately? You need to take time for healing and to get back on track again.

To dream of being under someone else's feet means that what they represent, has dominion over you right now. It is time to break free!

Shoes: If you dream that your shoes are torn, it means that you have become discouraged in your Christian walk.

If you are a man wearing high-heeled shoes, it means that you are trying to do something that God never called you to do. So no wonder you feel so uncomfortable!

If you are a woman trying to wear a man's shoe, this means the same thing. You are trying to do a task or accomplish something that was not for you to do.

If you dream or have a vision of trying to wear shoes that are too big for you, it means that you are about to be thrown into the deep end!

You are about to face tasks and responsibilities that perhaps you feel ill-equipped to handle.

See also: Ankle, Shoes

FIELD

An opportunity that is going to require effort on your part.

Positive: Untapped blessing that requires you to walk in obedience to enter into
Negative: Lost or stolen opportunities

A field, particularly one that is fertile, speaks of possibilities and opportunities that await you. However, it also indicates that some action is needed on your part.

A field does not product fruit by itself. It requires someone to work it.

POSITIVE
A fertile field: Seeing a vision of a fertile field speaks of a new opportunity the Lord is putting before you. It is for you then to work and to sow the seeds in this direction.

This can relate to either business or ministry. The Lord will bring the rain and cause the seeds to grow, but unless you plant, you will not see any fruit.

Just because you see a field in the spirit, it does not mean that you will automatically walk in blessing. God is showing you, that He will give the opportunity, but now you must work and make the most of it.

> *Psalms 107:37 And sow **fields** and plant vineyards, that they may yield a fruitful harvest.*

A field with a harvest: If you see a field that is full of wheat and ready to be harvested, the Lord is telling you that ministry opportunities are awaiting you.

It is for you to step forward in faith now. The Lord will back you up with the anointing, but He is waiting for you to get moving and to do something first.

NEGATIVE
Weeds: Often as I have been in intercession for the ministry, I have seen a field that is mixed with weeds and with good seeds as well.

When I see this I know that the Lord is saying that there are some people in the ministry who have come to bring death and destruction.

In a situation like this I pray that the Lord will separate the tares from the wheat. In every case, not long afterwards, the Lord exposes those who have come to bring division.

If you cover a minister in intercession this is something you might see often.

> *Matthew 13:38 The **field** is the world, the good seeds are the sons of the kingdom, but the tares are the sons of the wicked one];*

Dry ground: To see a field with dry ground speaks of the lack of anointing in your life. It needs the rivers of living water that only the Holy Spirit can bring.

> *Isaiah 44:3 For I will pour water on him who is thirsty, and floods on the **dry ground**; I will pour My Spirit on your descendants, and My blessing on your offspring;*

See also: Branch, Desert, Trees, Seed, Plants

FINGER

The work of God or the work of the enemy depending on the circumstances and context of the dream.

Positive: A show of the power of God
Negative: Accusation

POSITIVE
To have a finger "put on" something means to have something exposed or pointed out in your life. (as in the case of the writing on the wall in the days of Daniel)

This can be positive, especially if the Lord is trying to expose things in your life that He would like to deal with or bring healing to.

> *Luke 11:20 But if I cast out demons with the **finger** of God, surely the kingdom of God has come upon you.*

A single finger also speaks of the work of God and His power in your life.

NEGATIVE
If the dream is negative, then the finger you are seeing there is the work of the enemy.

A finger is also a good picture of accusation. (To have fingers pointed at you) Certainly this is a work of the enemy, because he is the accuser of the brethren.

See also: Arm, Hand

FINGERNAIL

A representation of the condition of your spiritual health.

Positive: Your spirit is in good health
Negative: There is a deficiency in your spiritual life right now

Just as the condition of your finger nails are a reflection of your physical state of health, they represent the same in your dream.

It is proven that if you get ill, as your fingernails grow out they will have a mark on them from the time your immune system took that beating!

POSITIVE
Healthy, strong nails speak of good health and an indication that you have successfully recovered from whatever deficiency you had in your spirit.

To dream of lovely nails that are well cared for means that you have been taking care of your spirit and investing into it.

To dream of manicured nails (a woman) is a picture of you nurturing your relationship with the Lord and as a result, maturing spiritually.

To dream that your nail bed is healed and restored is a picture of a spiritual healing that the Lord is about to do in your life.

NEGATIVE
Fingernails that are torn and not doing well means that something is making you spiritually sick right now. You need to get back to walking in the spirit and to make yourself healthy again.

Have you given the enemy a foothold through bitterness recently? Have you done something that you know is directly against the Word of God?

Yellowing and torn nail beds mean the same thing. It means that you need to invest once again into your spirit instead of thinking so much on natural things, just as Colossians 3:1 tells us. It could also be that you have allowed external influences to have an impact in your spirit and you are now reaping the fruit of that.

Just like it takes a while for your nails to show signs of sickness in the natural, so also if you dream of broken nails, it refers to an influence that has been around for a while and has been steadily increasing.

A picture of the spiritual condition of someone who has been cursed because of sin:

> *Daniel 4:33 That very hour the word was fulfilled concerning Nebuchadnezzar; he was driven from men and ate grass like oxen; his body was wet with the dew of heaven till his hair had grown like eagles' feathers and his **nails** like birds' claws.*

See also: Hand

FIRE

This symbol can take on many forms. It can be a picture of passion, cleansing or even destruction. The interpretation will depend on the context of the dream or vision.

Positive: The anointing of God to refine the gold in you
Negative: The destructive work of the enemy meant to bring you pain

CHARACTER SPECIFIC SYMBOL

POSITIVE
Fire in a dream can speak of a purging and a cleansing. It speaks of burning the old to make way for the new.

Depending on the context of the dream, it could mean that the old or the past is being burned, so that the new can come to pass.

This may also represent a death of a vision with regards to your ministry, personal death to the flesh with regards to your own spiritual condition, or sacrifice with regards to the price of the calling on your life.

Fire is also a picture of the passion you have for life and for the Lord.

I see fire as being positive more often than it being negative in a dream.

NEGATIVE
Fire can also speak of destruction and of fear. If you have a fear of fire, then this would represent fear to you in an internal dream.

If you had bad experiences with fire as a child, then fire would not mean a good thing to you. However, if you dreamed that you overcame a fire in your dream, this would represent a healing from those past memories.

UNIVERSAL SYMBOL

POSITIVE
Fire has many interpretations in Scripture. Some of the most common are: anointing, Holy Spirit, purging, glory of God, death and change.

Fire is used to make a clay vessel set in its shape. It is also used to refine gold.

Fire in visions is often positive, and speaks of the work of the Holy Spirit in the life of a person or ministry. It speaks of being made pure, holy and purged of all dross and sin in our lives.

Here is my favorite passage referring to our calling being refined as gold:

> *1 Peter 1:7 that the genuineness of your faith, being much more precious than gold that perishes, though it is tested by **fire**, may be found to praise, honor, and glory at the revelation of Jesus Christ:*

Time and time again we will be called to stand in the fire, so that we might be purified and made as gold for the Lord.

Often the Lord has said to me personally, "Do you want all I have for you? Then stand in the fire. For as long as you stand in the fire, I will continue to use you, for your works and your flesh will bow to my will alone."

It will cost you to stand in the fire, but it will also change you - forever.

I have also seen the Holy Spirit as a pillar of fire many times as I have been in prayer. You can find many references in the Word as to the Lord being like fire. Here are just a few:

> *Deuteronomy 4:24 For the Lord your God is a consuming **fire**, a jealous God.*

Here is a good picture of the Holy Spirit:

> *Exodus 13:21 And the Lord went before them by day in a pillar of cloud to lead the way, and by night in a pillar of **fire** to give them light, so as to go by day and night.*

NEGATIVE
Fire in a negative sense speaks of destruction. The Word says that our tongues are set on fire by hell, meaning that evil and negative words destroy. (James 3:6)

The Scripture also refers to the fiery darts of the enemy. These bring pain, destruction and a curse into our lives.

If you see this in a vision, then you need to stand against those negative words and curses in the name of Jesus!

> *Ephesians 6:16 above all, taking the shield of faith with which you will be able to quench all the **fiery** darts of the wicked one.*

See also: Altar, Arrow, Darts, Death, Earthquake

FISH

A picture of provision for your needs. Fishing refers to your job or business. If your business is "ministry" then it speaks of the work of the ministry.

Catching fish with either a rod or net is also a picture of the evangelistic ministry.

Positive:

- Provision for your daily needs
- Success in ministry

Negative:

- Loss of provision
- Failure to follow through in ministry

Character Specific Symbol

POSITIVE
Fish speak of provision and providing your needs. In the old days, fishing was one of the main sources of hunting and gathering food.

Today it lines up with the saying, "Give a man a fish and he will eat for a day. Teach him to fish and he will eat for a lifetime."

If you dream of fishing, it could have two interpretations. If you personally enjoy fishing as a sport, it could speak of something you enjoy and a recreation.

However, if you do not have any fishing memories, then it speaks of working and providing the things you need.

NEGATIVE
If you dream of a shark or of a fish that is deadly, this speaks of something quite negative. It speaks of attack, or of reaping something negative for your hard work.

Perhaps you are working in an area where you should not be. Or perhaps you put all your effort into something that you thought would be a blessing, but it is not going well.

Dreaming of a shark or a deadly fish would confirm the trouble you are in, and a good idea would be to get out of the situation.

To dream of fish dying indicates two things. If it relates to your finances, it is speaking of your finances dying. This is an attack from the enemy and likely caused by a curse.

Universal Symbol

POSITIVE
Keep in mind that the interpretation for dreams is going to vary from the interpretation for a vision or an internal prophetic dream.

Evangelism: The fish has varied meanings in Scripture, but the most outstanding is the picture of evangelism. Consider this famous passage:

> *Matthew 4:19 Then He said to them, Follow Me, and I will make you* ***fishers*** *of men.*

So if you dream or have a vision that you are fishing, then it is an indication of an evangelistic ministry. The evangelist has two functions:

The first is to see him as a man with a fishing rod, who catches one fish at a time. This speaks of the one-on-one ministry that the evangelist does.

Then he can be likened to the fisherman who casts out the net. This speaks of the mass and public ministry of the evangelist. We see Jesus fulfilling both these functions in His ministry.

Provision: To have a vision or dream of receiving a fish speaks of having your basic needs met by the Lord. In each instance in the Word, you will see that the provision was supernatural, although some work was involved.

This indicates that if you will only obey the Lord in the direction that He has given you, He will move on your behalf and meet your needs miraculously.

> *Luke 9:16 Then He took the five loaves and the two* ***fish****, and looking up to heaven, He blessed and broke them, and gave them to the disciples to set before the multitude.*

NEGATIVE

Of course rotten fish would indicate a curse regarding your daily needs. The enemy is stealing, killing and destroying!

To dream of fishing for dead fish is also negative – you are either trying to evangelize in the wrong area, or those you are trying to reach need the anointing for you to revive them – not just a good speech!

If you dream of fish dying after being caught, it could also speak of the need for ministry follow up for those that are recently born again.

See also: Whale

FLAG/BANNER

The distinguishing mark of a group of people. The Scripture refers to a flag as a banner and each tribe and family of Israel had one. Each had their own ensign, which was distinct and identified them by tribe. A flag then is a symbol of what makes you unique in your particular nationality and social groups.

> *Numbers 2:2 Every man of the children of Israel shall pitch by* ***his own standard****, with the* ***ensign of their father's*** *house: far off about the tabernacle of the congregation shall they pitch.*

CHARACTER SPECIFIC AND UNIVERSAL SYMBOLS

POSITIVE

To dream of the flag of a specific country refers to that nation in particular. To dream of being given a new flag that you do not recognize means that the Lord wants to establish you with unique characteristics.

If you have an apostolic calling, then such a dream would mean that the Lord wants you to become a "father" that has a distinguishing mark that will separate you from others. To receive a flag belonging to someone else means that the Lord is calling you to take on the characteristics and calling of that group.

The Word also tells us that the Lord is our banner. He is not only our distinguishing mark, but he covers us as part of His family. Being under a flag not only means taking on the principles that the flag stands for, but it also speaks of protection from the people that represent it.

So if you see yourself taking hold of a flag or banner that you know represents the Lord, it means that you walk in His favor.

> *Isaiah 49:22 Thus says the Lord God: Behold, I will lift My hand in an oath to the nations, and set up* ***My standard*** *for the peoples; they shall bring your sons in their arms, and your daughters shall be carried on their shoulders.*

To see a flag of a specific nation is a call to intercession for that nation. Pray as the Holy Spirit leads you.

NEGATIVE
If a flag is being imposed on you, it means that you are coming under pressure to conform to that particular group (whether national or something representing a ministry). If you see a banner being destroyed it speaks of compromise and no longer sticking to the principles which distinguished that particular group.

On the other hand, if you have been seeking the Lord about getting rid of old characteristics in your life and you then dream of a flag/banner being destroyed it means that God has answered your prayer and taken these old things from you.

See also: City

FLEAS

An irritation or inconvenience.

Positive: Your big problem is smaller than you realize
Negative: An attack that is no more than an irritation

POSITIVE
Depending on your dream or vision a flea could be positive or negative. In a positive sense, the Lord is saying that the thing you are struggling with right now is small!

Although it might feel so big to you, you can relax. This is a small thing that you can easily overcome.

NEGATIVE
Negatively a swarm of fleas speaks of an attack from the enemy to irritate you and to take your eyes of the direction God has given to you. He is trying to distract you, but there is no real harm in his attack.

The answer is simple. Rise up and push forward. Ignore the attack and do what God has called you to do!

> *1 Samuel 24:14 After whom has the king of Israel come out? Whom do you pursue? A dead dog? A **flea**.*

See also: Flies, Insects

FLIES

The work of the enemy bringing contamination and irritation.

CHARACTER SPECIFIC SYMBOL

NEGATIVE
Flies are loathsome creatures and never have a positive connotation in a dream or a vision.

In a dream they speak of irritations in your life. They also speak of having a contamination in your life.

In visions they speak of the works of the enemy that bring destruction.

In the description for *Beelzebub*, you will read that he was called 'The Lord of the Flies.'

To have a vision of being swarmed by flies speaks of an open door that the enemy is using in your life to overwhelm you.

Because of the unclean nature of flies, this open door has come in through sin. Look for contact with the New Age cult or with sexual immorality.

> *Exodus 8:24 And the Lord did so. Thick swarms of **flies** came into the house of Pharaoh, into his servants' houses, and into all the land of Egypt. The land was corrupted because of the swarms of **flies**.*

See also: Insects

FLOOD

Circumstances that are beyond your control.

Positive: Unstoppable blessing
Negative: A force of destruction

Character Specific Symbol

POSITIVE
Even though being overwhelmed with a flood seems negative at first, it might be that you are being brought to a place of letting go of your control.

If you dream that you keep fighting a flood or trying to keep afloat, it is a picture of your inner struggles. You are trying in your own works to keep pressing forward. It is time to let go of your striving and to let God have control.

A flood washing away something that is a burden to you, means that a circumstance is coming in your life that might seem difficult to face at first. However, the purpose of that circumstance is to take away the things that are weighing you down, so you do not need to be afraid.

NEGATIVE
If you dream of a flood destroying your home, this is negative. It means that the enemy is sending circumstances to try and destroy you.

Universal Symbol

POSITIVE
If the flood you see in your vision is positive, then it is speaking of the blessing of the Lord. It speaks of favor, provision and the Lord answering your prayers.

> *Isaiah 44:3 For I will pour water on him who is thirsty, and **floods** on the dry ground; I will pour My Spirit on your descendants, and My blessing on your offspring;*

NEGATIVE
The work of the enemy is pictured as a flood in Scriptures. This speaks of fear, theft and destruction.

> *Isaiah 59:19 So shall they fear the name of the Lord from the west, and His glory from the rising of the sun; when the enemy comes in like a **flood**, the Spirit of the Lord will lift up a standard against him.*

See also: Ark, Drowning, Water

Flowers

Flowers speak of beauty and promise. Their life is not long though, so they speak of a blessing that does not endure for very long, but is wonderful while it does.

Positive: A sweet promise that is about to come to pass
Negative: A stolen blessing

POSITIVE
They also represent the promise of fruit and reproduction. A flower in bud is a good picture of the birth of a vision.

> *Psalms 103:15 As for man, his days are like grass; as a **flower** of the field, so he flourishes.*

Often in the spirit we have seen the work we have done as seeds that are flowering. Just like flowers give a wonderful harvest but die quickly, so also does it require you to keep sowing seeds.

The minute you stop sowing, the flower that you once enjoyed died and there is nothing more to enjoy.

A bud: A bud speaks of something of promise that is only just starting out. Although it will lead to much fruit in the future, it is still tender and needs to be taken care of.

> *Isaiah 27:6 Those who come He shall cause to take root in Jacob; Israel shall blossom and **bud**, and fill the face of the world with fruit.*

If you are praying for someone, you might see them as a bud. This indicates that they have a lot of potential, but are still growing.

They need to be nurtured and encouraged. To reject or to strongly correct a person like this could mean crushing them.

NEGATIVE

Dried flowers represent an old season. The season for that beauty and promise is now passed and it is time to move on. To dream of hanging on to dry flowers means you are clinging to the promises of the past, when the Lord has something new for you.

Flowers that are wilting is a warning from the Lord that either the enemy is stealing the life out of your promises, or that it is time to start sowing more seeds again. Have you been investing faith, hope and love into the spiritual realm?

See also: Bud, Rose

FOG/MIST

A transitional situation where the future is being hidden from you for a season.

Positive: A time to wait on the Lord
Negative: The enemy blocking your view, so you cannot see God's promises

CHARACTER SPECIFIC AND UNIVERSAL SYMBOLS

POSITIVE

Although you might feel frustrated to see mist in your dreams or visions, the mist is there to protect you. As humans we have the terrible habit of running ahead of the Lord. At times the Lord will hide His plans from you as He puts you in the right position. This prevents you from running ahead of God and doing your own thing.

So to dream that a mist has come up and you have to rest or wait is a good dream. It means that now is a season to wait on the Lord and to allow Him to finish what He has begun in you before heading forward again.

Just like mist is there for a moment, this situation will not be forever, but will end soon.

NEGATIVE
If the mist is negative in your dream, then it is sent from the enemy to try and hide the promises of God in your life. This is not a major attack though, because just as mist evaporates in the sight of the sun, so also will this problem leave you.

The problem just looks impossible, but it is made up of shadows – it has no substance. It is just a trick of the enemy to try and pretend that he has the upper hand, when in reality he is already defeated and will soon have to ease up on the attack that you have been facing.

When I see mist in the spirit and it is not of the Lord, I tell it to leave so that we can see God's plan more clearly.

> *Job 6:17 When it is warm, they cease to flow; when it is hot, they vanish from their place.*

See also: Curtain, Lamp

Food

What you need to survive both spiritually and physically.

Positive: Sustenance for your soul and spirit

POSITIVE
To dream or have a vision of being fed speaks of the Lord providing your needs. This may speak of a spiritual or physical need. Consider Elijah after he felt weak in the desert who was fed by an angel.

> *1 Kings 19:6 Then he looked, and there by his head was a* ***cake*** *baked on coals, and a jar of water. So he* ***ate and drank****, and lay down again. 7 And the angel of the Lord came back the second time, and touched him, and said, "Arise and eat, because the journey is too great for you.*

This is a beautiful picture of the grace and provision of the Lord. When you come to those places in your life where you feel alone and weary, He will come and sustain you.

To dream of being fed means that the Lord is going to revive you again. He is going to restore the strength to you that the enemy has stolen and He is going to make you fit for the rest of your journey.

After Elijah had eaten this food, the scripture says that he continued on 40 days and nights without any food again! It does not take a lot to revive your spirit. Simply some time in His presence and you can keep going.

It does not take a lot for the Lord to move His hand on your behalf. Just one move and all of your needs can be taken care of.

NEGATIVE
Naturally rotten food speaks of not taking advantage of the blessing that God has for you. It also speaks of a curse of theft prevalent in your life.

In the days of receiving manna, if the children of Israel gathered too much or did not eat what they gathered, it went rotten. In the same way, the opportunities and blessings God gives you are for now. Take hold of them.

Lack of food or starvation speaks of not feeding your spirit or of not walking in the blessing of the Lord. The Word promises us that God will provide all our needs. To not have these needs met means that the enemy is stealing from you (or the person you are praying for when you see the vision).

See also: Bake, Boil, Bread, Cake, Fruit, Kitchen, Meat, Milk

FOUNDATION

Dreams: A picture of the things you have based your life on. A good representation of the archetypes that you follow.

Visions: A picture of a doctrinal belief system.

Positive: Plans of the future are secure
Negative: The inability to build for the future

CHARACTER SPECIFIC SYMBOL

If you dream of the foundation of an old house you stayed in, in the past, it represents everything you were and everything that was built into you at that time.

Old foundation: Perhaps you will dream of an old house where the foundation is still standing. It would mean that whatever was built into you at that time still remains. You would need to discern if what was built into you back then was positive or negative!

You could dream of a church building or foundation. It would then represent your spiritual foundation. It is a picture of the things that have been built into you spiritually through the years.

Once again it could be positive or negative depending on the context of your dream. If the foundation or building is cracked, it could mean that there is a flaw in what has been built into you.

If you dream of the foundation or building being destroyed, it could mean that the Lord is smashing all of the old templates that have been built into you over the years.

A new foundation: A new building and foundation being erected could speak of something new that the Lord is going to build into you - spiritually speaking.

Perhaps He is leading you to receive from a new ministry or to head out into something new. Dreaming of a new building and foundation would then confirm that it is indeed the Lord leading you in this direction.

Foundation being laid: In the Word, Christ is our foundation! If you see a new foundation being laid in a vision, this speaks of a new work beginning.

It means that the Lord is about to begin building a new pattern or plan into the life, ministry or church you were praying for at the time.

Keep in mind that you will always receive a vision according to what frame of spirit you were in at the time.

Breaking foundations: I have often seen the Lord give someone a long staff in the spirit, to break up a foundation. This is an apostolic function, and I often see it when we are confirming an apostolic call in a person.

In the old days they would use a rod to smash the foundation so that they might start again. If you see a similar vision, or external dream, then it speaks of smashing and removing the old incorrect pattern of the system, so that the new can be put in its place.

A foundation refers to the foundation of God's house:

> *Zechariah 8:9 ... Who spoke in the day the **foundation** was laid for the house of the Lord of hosts, that the temple might be built.*

It also refers to what we build our lives upon:

> *Luke 6:48 He is like a man building a house, who dug deep and laid the **foundation** on the rock. And when the flood arose, the stream beat vehemently against that house, and could not shake it, for it was founded on the rock.*

Referring to those things that we establish for the Lord through ministry:

> *1 Corinthians 3:10 According to the grace of God which was given to me, as a wise master builder I have laid the **foundation**, and another builds on it. But let each one take heed how he builds on it.*

NEGATIVE
Cracked foundation: A broken foundation or building speaks of something that was not properly built or something that has been broken down.

If you get this kind of vision for a person or ministry, then it would mean that what they have built their spiritual life or ministry on is not solid, and that it has flaws.

I often see the status quo church system like this. It has walls and a building that may look firm, but with a broken and weak foundation.

It is like when someone has fed things into their spirit that were not the correct pattern or of God:

> *Luke 6:49 But he who heard and did nothing is like a man who built a house on the earth without a* ***foundation****, against which the stream beat vehemently; and immediately it fell. And the ruin of that house was great.*

Having a wrong foundation means that you cannot build for the future. You must be prepared today for the plan God wants you to fulfill tomorrow. Without a solid foundation, this is impossible.

See also: Babel, Buildings, Church, House

FOUNTAIN

A fountain is a picture of the things that come out of your spirit. You release what is inside of your spirit through words or actions. Depending on what comes out is a picture of what is really in your heart.

Positive: The blessing you are to others around you
Negative: The darkness of your heart as it hinders others

POSITIVE
A fountain that is clean and pure means that you are full of the life of Christ. You are a blessing to God's people and the Lord can use you to minister.

> *Proverbs 18:4 The words of the mouth are deep waters, but the* ***fountain*** *of wisdom is a rushing stream. (NIV)*

If you have a dream or vision of drinking from a clean fountain, it is a picture that wherever you are receiving your ministry from at the moment is where God wants you to be. You are receiving life and good teaching.

NEGATIVE
On the other side though, if the water is dirty, then the Lord is warning you that the teaching and impartation you are receiving is contaminated.

If the fountain is dirty or bitter, it is a picture that there is something wrong in your life. Your spirit is contaminated with bitterness, and bad teaching and spiritual impartations.

If you tend to travel around just receiving from anyone, it is quite possible that you have received a curse along the way.

If you still hold bitterness in your heart towards anyone, this is contaminating your spirit! Not only is it holding you back from entering into an intimate relationship with the Lord, but it will contaminate others you try to minister to.

Dreaming or seeing a vision of a dirty foundation is a warning to you. You need to deal with the things that are contaminating your spirit.

See also: River, Water

FOXES

Positively they speak of people God is calling you to train and send out. Negatively they speak of a spirit of destruction prevalent in your life.

Positive: Counter Insurgence warfare
Negative: A surprise attack from the enemy

POSITIVE
The best illustration for the fox is the story when Samson took foxes in pairs and set their tails alight.

It talks about setting God's people on fire and sending them out to do His work.

This exact vision is what the Lord gave us at the beginning of our ministry. The Lord said that He would bring us couples that he would train and send out again, to destroy the works of the enemy.

> *Judges 15:4 Then Samson went and caught three hundred **foxes**; and he took torches, turned the foxes tail to tail, and put a torch between each pair of tails.*

NEGATIVE
Foxes in a negative light are a picture of the destruction of the enemy. Foxes are scavengers, and they are a good picture of how the enemy comes to steal, kill and destroy. This attack is not seen openly. It is a "sneak" attack from the enemy from a direction you least expected it to come from.

> *Song of Songs 2:15 Catch us the **foxes**, the little **foxes** that spoil the vines, for our vines have tender grapes.*

See Also: Animals, Dog

FROGS

A picture of an unclean spirit.

Frogs are never seen in a positive light in Scripture. They were a sacred animal to the Ancient Egyptians. They represented fertility and the life cycle.

By the Lord bringing a plague of frogs on them, He showed them that He was indeed the author of all life; that He was God over all creation.

They are also a picture of unclean spirits. To see a frog is an indication of a demonic bondage in your life - something that is unclean and not of God.

> *Revelation 16:13 And I saw three unclean spirits like* ***frogs*** *coming out of the mouth of the dragon, out of the mouth of the beast, and out of the mouth of the false prophet.*

This unclean spirit is usually related to sexual things. If you dream or have a vision of frogs after associating with someone, then the Lord is warning you to be careful to guard yourself from something that is unclean. If you feel that your dream is indicating a generational curse, the frog is giving you an idea of the kind of bondage you are looking at. Look at sexual sin.

See also: Animals

FRUIT

Ripe fruit is a picture of maturity.

Positive: Spiritual maturity that is seen without needed to be boasted of
Negative: The proof of the sin you have kept hidden in your heart

Fruit also speaks of prosperity and nourishment. It is a lovely picture of partaking of the blessings of the Lord.

In addition, it is a picture of the fruition of the things that you have worked so hard at. This fruit can be both good or bad, depending on the work.

POSITIVE
Spiritual maturity:

> *Galatians 5:22 But the* ***fruit*** *of the Spirit is love, joy, peace, longsuffering, kindness, goodness, faithfulness,*

Seeing tasty fruit speaks of spiritual maturity and the final stage of a good season.

Reward of your hard work: Seeing fruit on a tree is a picture of your reward for all your labor. As you have worked hard and pushed through the winter and storms, you are now at a place where you are ready to reap the fruit of all your work.

Seeing whole fruit is an indication that you have reached your destination and completed your task.

I have often seen fruit on trees where the Lord has told me to enjoy the fruits of my labor.

> *Proverbs 31:31 Give her of the **fruit** of her hands, and let her own works praise her in the gates.*

The condition of your spirit: What you put into your spirit will always bear fruit. If that fruit is good, it is a reflection of walking in the spirit and doing things God's way.

What comes out of your mouth is what you have put in.

> *Proverbs 12:14 A man will be satisfied with good by the **fruit** of his mouth, and the recompense of a man's hands will be rendered to him.*

Your disciples and children:

> *Psalms 127:3 Behold, children are a heritage from the Lord, the **fruit** of the womb is a reward.*

If ever you want to know what is inside a person, simply take a look at their kids and disciples. What they try to hide, those that received from them will not.

Our children and disciples are a picture of the "fruit that remains" that John speaks about in John 15:16.

NEGATIVE

Rotten fruit speaks of a curse in your life. Even though you worked hard, now when it comes to reaping, it seems as though everything is stolen from you.

This is a very good picture of a spirit of theft manifesting in your life. There is good news though! You can overcome this work of the enemy, and the Lord will restore to you all that the locust has stolen.

> *Luke 6:44 For every tree is known by its own **fruit**. For men do not gather figs from thorns, nor do they gather grapes from a bramble bush.*

If you see a picture of rotten fruit with regards to others, it means that there is a contamination in their spirits and to be wary of receiving from them.

See also: Apple, Basket, Bud, Trees, Vine

SYMBOLS STARTING IN G

Symbols Starting in G

Garage

A season of waiting on God regarding the future of your ministry

Positive: A season of rest
Negative: Spiritual clutter

Character Specific Symbol

POSITIVE

Because vehicles are stored in a garage, it represents seasons of rest and needing to take time to "repair" your spirit before the next journey. There are times in ministry when we need to "take time out" to be built up again.

It could also be that the Lord wants to give you an upgrade! So if in your dream, a mechanic is doing work on your vehicle, it means that the Lord is making changes to your ministry. Take advantage of this time to rest and fill up in preparation for what lies ahead.

NEGATIVE

The truth is that although a garage should be used just for vehicles, it often becomes a place of clutter. The same holds true for our spiritual lives. When the Lord wants to "do work on us" He more often than not finds a lot of junk that has to be cleaned out first. Before He can even begin His work, He has to take you through a cleansing process.

A cluttered garage speaks of God needing to "clean house" before He can even begin working on your ministry.

NOTE: If the garage you dream about is related to fearful events of the past, realize that these hurts are surfacing in your life and you need healing and deliverance.

See also: Attic, Basement, Buildings, Bedroom, House

Gate

A new season that is either spiritual or relating to business.

Positive: An invitation to enter into a new journey
Negative:

- Restriction
- Obstacles the enemy tries to put in your way

Spiritual:

> *Isaiah 45:1 ... And loose the armor of kings, to open before him the* ***double doors****, to that the* ***gates*** *will not be shut:*

Business:

> *Proverbs 31:23 Her husband is known in the* ***gates****, when he sits among the elders of the land.*

POSITIVE

To see a new gate in a dream or vision is a picture of a new season in your life. Depending on the kind of gate, you will have a clearer picture on the kind of season that the Lord is taking you into.

It represents the start of something new, but also the end of something as well. To go through a gate means to leave the old behind. (Much like the picture of a door) With a gate though, the picture speaks more of not just a single opportunity but a change in your life as a whole.

I see gates often in the spirit and will share a bit of my own experience to help you identify what God is showing you.

Golden gate: I often see the gates as golden in my visions and they are a picture of a new season in my ministry. A clear ministry road. Usually the gate or road ahead is bigger or quite different to the one before.

Gold is a picture of the deity of God and a good picture of ministry. This speaks of a new focus and season in ministry. The birth of a new ministry vision.

Silver gate: Silver is a picture of our redemption in Christ as well as a good symbol for money. A silver gate represents a new season in your business and work place.

Double door gate: I have seen this often relating to couples. How each are going through the same gate, but each have their own aspect to add to the vision that God is giving them.

Garden gate: This speaks of a season of joy and rest. I have seen the Lord lead someone through a garden gate into a garden to tend. This speaks of a season of training but in a secure and pleasant environment.

Desert gate: There are times that I have seen the Lord lead someone to a gate where there is a desert or wilderness on the other side. When this happens, I know that he is leading this person into a season of ministry training.

Jesus Himself was led to the wilderness before his ministry took off and this is valid for us still today.

NEGATIVE
Gate of the city: When the gate is from the enemy to lock us in, then it is not positive. However as in the case with Samson, he simply picked the city gate up and carried it up the hill!

In the same way if you see a gate that is locking you in, it is for you to stand in the name of the Lord Jesus and to come against it! The enemy is trying to hold you back from God's promise!

See also: Door, Road

GIFTS

An undeserved blessing that you did not ask of for yourself.

Positive: The Lord delights in giving you an undeserved blessing
Negative: A temptation forced on you by satan that you unwittingly receive

Gifts or presents are a universal picture for something good - or at least something that is intended for good. They are a picture of undeserved blessing.

I have often seen a vision of many beautifully wrapped gifts coming from heaven. Or on other occasions I have seen the Lord Jesus wanting to give gifts to His people.

In each case it is a picture of undeserved blessing. We do not deserve the grace or blessing of the Lord, but He gives it to us as a gift. That is why even salvation is called a gift. It is not deserved.

Below is one of my favorite Scriptures in the Word, as it describes the nature of the Lord beautifully:

> *James 1:17 Every good gift and every perfect* ***gift*** *is from above, and comes down from the Father of lights, with whom there is no variation or shadow of turning.*

If you see yourself receiving a gift in a dream or vision, it means that the Lord desires to give you something special.

This speaks of either a desire you have, or a surprise that He has for you. This is not something you have earned or something that is a need. It might refer to a spiritual gift or to a natural one.

Your part is to reach out in faith to receive this gift. As you do this, it will be manifest in your life.

Remember, the Lord always responds to faith. He is the giver of blessing, but it is for you to reach out by faith to receive it.

> *Matthew 7:11 If you then, being evil, know how to give good **gifts** to your children, how much more will your Father who is in heaven give good things to those who ask Him!*

NEGATIVE
The enemy delights in giving us "gifts" we did not ask for either! Spurgeon shares an illustration of how the devil drops off his children at our doorstep, hoping we will take them inside and adopt them. Children called guilt and fear. His conclusion is, "These are no children of mine! I am not taking in the devil's children!" This is the kind of "gift" the enemy gives. He lures you, through temptation, to open the door and then traps you with fear, guilt and anger.

To see a gift in a negative light means that you felt compelled to receive something that you did not really want. However, you opened that door!

The kind of "gift" the enemy gives is to lure you through temptation to your flesh and then to ensnare you afterwards when you fall for the trap. It only takes a moment to put your sin under the blood! You do not need to hold on to those curses. You can throw them out!

See also: Chest, Pearls, Treasure

GLASSES

Your view of life both in the spirit and in the natural.

Positive: To be clear on the things of God
Negative: To be fooled into believing something that is a lie

POSITIVE
To dream or have a vision that you get glasses and that they clarify your vision means that the Lord is going to give you the ability to see things that could not be seen before. It also means that your natural weakness and restrictions will be removed as He has given you a strength.

Apostle Paul said that the Lord's strength was only made perfect in his weakness. (2 Cor 12:9) This is much like putting a pair of glasses on that makes your sight better.

NEGATIVE
If you dream that you are wearing dark glasses or that your vision is impaired in any way, it means that you are not seeing the truth as it really is.

You are trying to view the reality of your life or of the Word through "rose colored glasses." In other words, you cannot distinguish the truth from the lie. There is confusion in your perspective of life and also of the Word.

You are being fooled into believing an untruth. What you feel and what your reality is, are two different things.

The Lord wants us to look at him without a veil or anything that would obstruct our view. Consider this passage:

> *2 Corinthians 3:18 But we all, with* ***unveiled*** *face, beholding as in a mirror the glory of the Lord, are being transformed into the same image from glory to glory, just as by the Spirit of the Lord.*

See also: Blind, Eyes, Mirror

GOAT

Positive:

- To stand apart
- A blend of business and ministry

Negative: Rebellion

CHARACTER SPECIFIC SYMBOL

Now if you are a goat farmer, dreaming of your goats can speak of responsibilities and your ministry. Personally knowing a goat farmer, it is uncanny how often the Lord uses dreams of goats to speak about her ministry!

UNIVERSAL SYMBOL

Goats and sheep were herded together in the Old Testament. So for Jesus to talk about "separating the sheep from the goats" spoke of the Lord making a differentiation between those who were His own and those that belonged to the enemy. They might act the same, but to the Father, each one is distinct and He can spot His sheep from a mile!

POSITIVE

Finances: The goat was used for meat, milk and trade in the O.T. So to dream positively of goats speaks of working in both business and ministry. You are not exactly shepherding sheep, but taking care of goats – perhaps your ministry is indeed business. Seek the Lord for further confirmation.

The scapegoat: It seems that goats get a bad rap in Scripture. The goat was used in a ceremony as the "scapegoat" which meant sending a goat into the wilderness, carrying on it the sins of all the people. So to be a "scapegoat" means taking on the blame for others.

As a leader, the Lord has had me carry the blame for my team more than once! Jesus was certainly the ultimate scapegoat. Perhaps the Lord is calling you to love someone enough to take the blame for them. True love covers all sin!

NEGATIVE

Jesus refers to goats as being cursed. They speak of those that choose to rebel against the Lord and do things their own way.

> *Matthew 25:32 All the nations will be gathered before Him, and He will separate them one from another, as a shepherd divides his sheep from the goats*

So to see an "evil goat" speaks of rebellion against the Lord.

Witchcraft: Keep in mind that goats are often used in witchcraft practices. If you are in a culture that still practices animal sacrifice, then seeing such a goat speaks of witchcraft present in your midst.

See also: Demons, Sheep, Shepherd

GOLD

The anointing, the nature of God, your faith being tried as gold, the blessing of the Lord, having been made pure, favor and royalty (child of the King).

Gold has a positive interpretation more often than a negative one. It speaks of the divine nature of the Lord.

Positive: The manifest presence of the Holy Spirit
Negative: The counterfeit of the Holy Spirit

CHARACTER SPECIFIC SYMBOL

Gold can have various meanings. Gold by nature is rare, costly and precious.

You could dream of being given a golden ring. This would have a good connotation, speaking of favor and authority.

Gold is also tried in the fire, and it could speak of having faced many trials and come forth from it as gold.

Gold also speaks of blessing, and so if you see this color in a dream it speaks of the blessing of the Lord and also the nature of the Lord.

A golden car speaks of a ministry that will be blessed. Golden clothing could speak of being clothed in the anointing and in His glory.

In the Old Testament you will see references to the Lord adorning His chosen one with gold and with precious stones.

Solomon was surrounded by gold and much of the temple he built was overlaid with it.

Gold represents the divine nature of God.

It represents His blessing and also our faith, being as pure as gold.

Golden light: I sometimes see a golden light shining through a new door someone is about to enter, spiritually speaking. I have seen golden oil to represent healing.

I have also seen it many times when the Lord Jesus has emphasized His place as King of Kings. His crown will be gold, as is the throne He sits upon.

Representing authority and favor

> *Psalms 21:3 For You meet him with the blessings of goodness; you set a crown of pure* ***gold*** *upon his head.*

Gold ministry symbols: When the Lord gives us a vision of a person's ministry, we often see it as a golden instrument. In the case of a ministry of psalmody, we would see a golden harp. For the prophetic ministry, we see a golden key and for the pastoral ministry we see a golden shepherd's staff.

Gold speaks of the divine nature of the Lord and when you look at the tabernacle in the Old Testament it was wood overlaid with gold. Representing humanity (the wood) being covered by the Lord (the gold).

Gold also speaks of spiritual authority. Gold speaks of royalty and when a person is given Gold (speaking of the divine nature of the Lord) it means that the Lord has delegated some of His authority to them. This is especially applicable to the fivefold ministry which is why the symbols we see in the spirit that represent the fivefold ministry are all gold.

Consider the following Scriptures:

Representing the holiness of the Lord:

> *Exodus 39:30 Then they made the plate of the holy crown of pure* ***gold****, and wrote on it an inscription like the engraving of a signet: HOLINESS TO THE LORD*

Speaking of purification:

> *1 Peter 1:7 That the genuineness of your faith, being much more precious than* ***gold*** *that perishes, though it is tested by fire, may be found to praise, honor, and glory at the revelation of Jesus Christ:*

Speaking of spiritual royalty:

> *Psalms 45:13 The royal daughter is all glorious within the palace; her clothing is woven with gold.*

NEGATIVE

Gold can also speak of greed and of desiring material things. It can speak of external beauty instead of internal beauty. When the gold is corroded or tarnished it is referring to the taint of sin in your life.

In other words, there are issues and parts of your flesh that need to be put in the fire and brought to repentance before the Lord can take you to the next level in your spiritual life.

If the gold is fake (i.e fools gold), then it speaks of deception and falsehood.

Peter said to make sure that we adorn what is on the inside and not only concentrate on externals. (1 Peter 3:3)

Speaking of greed:

> *James 5:3 Your **gold** and silver are corroded, and their corrosion will be a witness against you and will eat your flesh like fire. You have heaped up treasure in the last days.*

Gold idol: Idols of gold were used for worship. The Lord showed me such a golden calf in vision once. He told me that His people were compromising with the world, and that by allowing the world into their worship, they were in fact worshipping it as an idol.

The idol spoke of their own works and of the ways of the world:

> *Psalms 115:4 Their **idols** are silver and **gold**, the work of men's hands.*

See also: Altar, Colors, Death, Earrings, Fire, Jewelry, Tabernacle

GRAPES

A picture of prosperity and abundance.

Positive: The proof of God's promised prosperity
Negative: Bitterness is stealing God's blessing from you

POSITIVE

Grapes were always used in scripture as a picture of God's prosperity. When the spies went into the Promised Land, they brought back a huge bunch of grapes to show the fertility of the land and its treasures. (Num 13:24)

Grapes are only as good as the soil they are grown in. If the soil is good, then the fruit will be good as well.

To dream of ripe grapes means that your spiritual life is in order and that the fruit of your spirit is good.

It also means that your feet are planted in the right place now and that the Lord is going to bless you in this land that He has given you. This can speak of your ministry or of your business and financial land.

NEGATIVE

On the other hand, sour grapes have a number of meanings. Firstly, it means that what is coming out of you is not pleasant.

It means that the land that you are in right now (be it spiritual or natural) is not right and it is producing sour grapes.

> *Jeremiah 31:30 But every one shall die for his own iniquity; every man who eats the sour **grapes**, his teeth shall be set on edge.*

Although you were expecting prosperity or blessing, you are getting quite the opposite.

This is a warning dream or vision and the Lord is telling you that where you are right now in your spiritual life is not in a good place. There is contamination present through sin.

> *Deuteronomy 32:32 For their vine is of the vine of Sodom and of the fields of Gomorrah; their **grapes** are **grapes** of gall, their clusters are bitter:*

See also: Fruit, Vine, Wine

GRASS

Grass is a temporary beauty that speaks of joy and a season of fruitfulness. Grass is also a picture of provision and blessing in your work.

Positive: Provision for the purpose of further investment
Negative: Old seasons

POSITIVE
Grass is the food for cattle, and good grass speaks of nourishment. To dream of green grass indicates that the Lord is going to bless the work of your hands.

> *Deuteronomy 11:15 And I will send **grass** in your fields for your livestock, that you may eat and be filled.*

Grass also speaks of being multiplied. Once again the Lord is promising to take the works of your hands or the things you have invested into and to cause them to grow and multiply.

> *Job 5:25 You shall also know that your descendants shall be many, and your offspring like the **grass** of the earth.*

NEGATIVE
Withered grass is a good picture of a season in your life that has now past. It is time to move on.

> *Isaiah 40:6 The voice said, Cry out! And he said, what shall I cry? All flesh is **grass**, and all its loveliness is like the flower of the field.*

To see land without grass is an indication that you are trying to do things without the help of the Lord. You can work and invest all of your time into many projects, even ministry, but without the help of the Lord, your works will yield emptiness.

> *James 1:11 For no sooner has the sun risen with a burning heat than it withers the **grass**; its flower falls, and its beautiful appearance perishes. So the rich man also will fade away in his pursuits.*

See also: Field, Flowers

GRAVE/TOMB

Graves and tombs share an interpretation. They both represent memorials of seasons past.

Positive:

- Seasons put in the past for good.
- A call to bury the flesh, to prepare for resurrection

Negative:

- Negative elements that are having an influence on your life
- A time of lament
- A season of sorrow and of "letting go"

CHARACTER SPECIFIC SYMBOL

POSITIVE
If the grave you dream of is one you are familiar with, then the Lord is saying that it time to let that person and era in your life go. If you dream of walking away from a gravesite that you know personally, it means you are finally putting the past behind you. (The past that the person buried there represents)

NEGATIVE
If you keep dreaming of graves, zombies, death and rotting corpses, then there is something that is influencing your spirit negatively. Either you are filling your mind with movies and media that are contaminating it, or you are receiving from someone who is. If you keep having such nightmares and demonic attack, the enemy is gaining access in your life. Either a generational curse is prevalent or you have opened the door yourself by getting involved in the occult.

UNIVERSAL SYMBOL

POSITIVE
A gravesite or gravestone: Although you might think a grave or gravestone to be negative, it could also speak of something being completed in your life. As with all things, there comes a time when you complete the task set before you and the season passes. Determine who the grave is for. Is it someone that represents a season in your life? If the dream or vision is positive, the Lord is

saying, "Well done my faithful servant! You have finished running this race. It is time now to let this season go and to begin another."

> *Job 5:26 You shall come to the grave at a full age, as a sheaf of grain ripens in its season*

Resurrection: If you dream of someone coming out of a grave and they represent something positive in your life, this is speaking of a resurrection of a vision. The Lord is saying that the thing you thought was lost to you, will be returned to you in a greater measure than ever before.

> *Ezekiel 37:12 Therefore prophesy and say to them, "Thus says the Lord God: 'Behold, O My people, I will open your graves and cause you to come up from your graves, and bring you into the land of Israel.*

Tomb: Certainly to have a vision or dream of the tomb of Christ is expressing the truth of His resurrection. The Lord is calling you to spiritual resurrection and to be made alive as Christ was made alive. The same spirit that rose Christ from the dead is in you. Rise up and take hold of His resurrection power!

NEGATIVE
Not everything is ready to be brought to death! If you keep dreaming of graves of people that represent something good in you, you need to take this as a warning dream. The enemy keeps stealing your blessings and destroying the good in you. This is a warning dream and you need to determine what it is that keeps bringing your blessings and promises to death.

Tomb: To dream or have a vision of a tomb that is dark and contains a lot of death indicates that you are dwelling on the past and reveling in the flesh. It is time to move beyond your loss and what you feel and to take hold of the power available in Christ.

Here is a beautiful passage that stands as our reminder:

> *Mark 16: 5 And entering the tomb, they saw a young man clothed in a long white robe sitting on the right side; and they were alarmed.*
>
> *6 But he said to them, "Do not be alarmed. You seek Jesus of Nazareth, who was crucified. He is risen! He is not here.*

See also: Bury, Coffin, Death, Tombstone

GRAY

To wax old.

Positive:

- To enter into maturity (gray hair)
- To gain wisdom

Negative:

- Contamination of what is pure
- Stolen strength and vigor (premature aging)

Universal Symbol

POSITIVE
A prophet knows only black and white, with no shades of gray. However, those called to be pastors learn the art of gray. Not everything is "cut and dry" when it comes to counseling. While the Word remains our constant in any conflict, not every hurt heart is "black and white." In fact, it is the shades of gray that bring the most hurt.

I remember the Lord challenging me on this exact thing. When I needed to be a pastor, I had to let go of a lot of my "black and white" thinking to counsel effectively. When it came to hurts of the past, how people perceive events and how they truly were, are not often the same. It takes wisdom and knowledge of the Word to bring balance. If the Lord is saying that it is time to entertain "shades of gray" in your life and ministry, He is saying that you need to think outside of your hard lines and boundaries you have clung to for so many years.

NEGATIVE
When white becomes gray or you dream of a cloth that is stained, this speaks of sin that is prevalent in your life.

Gray also speaks of a contamination. When something unclean is added to white, it is discolored. It is not obvious sin that everyone can see, but rather an underlying sin that is hidden.

While gray hair can speak of wisdom and maturity, to dream of your hair suddenly turning white or gray means that you are losing your strength and that you need to take time to recoup!

> *Hosea 7:9 Aliens have devoured his strength, But, he does not know it; Yes, gray hairs are here and there on him, yet he does not know it.*

See also: Colors, Hair, Silver, White

Green

An exciting new season of growth.

Positive:

- New life
- Wealth
- Abundance

Negative: Immaturity

POSITIVE
Green can speak of nourishment and of things that feed and edify you. It can also speak of peace and provision. It speaks of something that is new and birthed afresh. I have often seen a new seedling coming out of the ground and it is green and fresh.

When I have seen this I know that the Lord is saying that the person I am ministering to is about to grow and although they are just starting out, that something new is being birthed in them that is going to bear much fruit!

Green can also speak of provision of your needs, just like green speaks of food and nourishment, it can also speak of financial provision.

Speaking of peace and provision:

> *Psalms 23:2 He makes me to lie down in **green** pastures; He leads me beside the still waters.*

Speaking of the favor of the Lord:

> *Jeremiah 17:8 For he shall be like a tree planted by the waters, which spreads out its roots by the river, and will not fear when heat comes; but its leaf will be **green**, and will not be anxious in the year of drought, nor will cease from yielding fruit.*

NEGATIVE
Green can be negative in that it speaks of immaturity. Green grass is often spoken of in Scriptures as being weak and not having firm roots. Grass can be plucked up and destroyed by a strong wind. It fades away easily and so it speaks of those things that are not secure and wither away easily.

In a natural sense, green can also speak of greed (referring to money).

Speaking of immaturity: A green fruit has not reached maturity – it is unripe! The same is said in many cultures. To say someone is "green" means that they lack maturity and experience in a certain area.

> *Job 15:32 It will be accomplished before his time, and his branch will not be **green**.*

See also: Flowers, Grass

Symbols Starting in H

SYMBOLS STARTING IN H

HAIL

A destructive force whether from the Holy Spirit or the enemy.

Positive: God fighting on your behalf

Negative:

- A sign of judgment
- A spirit of destruction in play

UNIVERSAL SYMBOL

POSITIVE
Hail was one of the plagues of Egypt where God was humbling the Egyptians because of what they did to Israel. If you dream or see a vision of hail that you feel is positive, then it indicates that God is moving on your behalf. Not only is He fighting on your behalf, but He is humbling those that are standing against you. You need not defend yourself. Rest in His finished work.

> *Exodus 9:23 And Moses stretched out his rod toward heaven; and the Lord sent thunder and hail, and fire darted to the ground. And the Lord rained hail on the land of Egypt.*

NEGATIVE
Hail in a dream or vision is more often negative than it is positive. It speaks of judgment and also destruction in your life. The destruction is directly related to your "daily bread" and finances you need to survive. It is an attack against your daily needs, and the promises God has given to you. It is an onslaught against the things that have taken you time to build in your ministry and life.

Determine if this onslaught is due to walking in disobedience to the Lord, or if the enemy has gained an inroad and is wreaking havoc in your circumstances.

> *Ezekiel 13:13 Therefore thus says the Lord God: "I will cause a stormy wind to break forth in My fury; and there shall be a flooding rain in My anger, and great hailstones in fury to consume it.*

See also: Rain, Storm

HAIR

The image we present to the world.

It is amazing how much a person's looks change simply by changing their hair. It is also a biblical picture of covering (in an authoritative sense).

Positive: You know who you are in Christ
Negative: A problem with your spiritual covering

Character Specific Symbol

POSITIVE
To dream that you are changing your hair is an indication that you are going through a change in your personal image.

How you feel about this change in your dream will tell you if you are in conflict about this change or if you feel ready for it.

To dream of having beautiful hair that you enjoy having means that you are feeling confident in who you are.

NEGATIVE
To dream that your hair is damaged, ruined or destroyed is a picture of a conflict you are going through.

It could be that you are feeling insecure about your image at the moment. It could also be an indication of some insecurity that is coming up inside of you.

Perhaps there are circumstances in your life that are bringing up old conflicts from the past, or situations where you are at a point of weakness and you feel vulnerable.

To dream of going grey means that you are pushing too hard and wearing yourself out. It is time to take a break!

Universal Symbol

POSITIVE
A woman's hair is a picture of her covering. This speaks firstly of her husband, and then of any other spiritual covering that she is under.

If you have a vision or prophetic dream of your hair growing, it speaks of the blessing you will walk in as you come under the covering of your husband or spiritual authority.

> *1 Corinthians 11:15 But if a woman has long **hair**, it is a glory to her; for her **hair** is given to her for a covering.*

Changing your hair color (and you feel good about it in the dream) means that you are about to go through a "face lift" in your ministry. The Lord is about to change your perspective and the way you fulfill your ministry vision.

NEGATIVE
Hair in general: If you have a vision or prophetic dream of hair specifically it is likely to refer to your spiritual covering. If the hair is strong, then this is a promise and the Lord telling you to rest securely under your covering.

As a man: It was shameful for a man to have long hair in the Bible. He was seen as rejecting his masculinity. The same stigma remains even into today's society.

To have a prophetic dream or vision of having long hair, is an indication that you are failing to rise up as the head of your home.

> *1 Corinthians 11:14 Does not even nature itself teach you that if a man has long* ***hair****, it is a dishonor to him?*

As hair is also a picture of spiritual covering, if you as a man dream that you lose your hair, it is a picture of not being under authority.

As a woman: Your hair falling out could have a two-fold meaning. The first could be that you are struggling with insecurity relating to your femininity and self image. The second is that you are not being spiritually covered at present. You need to decide if you are not under covering, or if your authority has not been following the Lord as they should.

See also: Baldness, Gray

HAND

In an internal dream, your hand is the picture of your strength and abilities. In a prophetic dream or a vision, it is a picture of the blessing and the deliverance of the Lord.

Positive: God's power to deliver
Negative: The enemy's intent to steal

CHARACTER SPECIFIC SYMBOL

POSITIVE

To have a strong hand indicates that you are capable and strong in your abilities.

To dream of having a woman's hand if you are a man might indicate that you have artistic abilities. In a negative sense though, it might be indicating that you are weak in some areas where you should be strong.

To dream of someone else's hand could indicate that there are other strengths that someone else can add to you. You do not need to do everything alone.

NEGATIVE

To dream of having your hand cut off, indicates that you are losing or will lose a strength or ability.

To dream of someone else harming your hands or tying them up, speaks of being restricted and being forced to do things someone else's way.

To have a hand interfere in your dream means that someone else is trying to push their own will on you.

Universal Symbol

POSITIVE
The hand is a picture of the blessing and deliverance of the Lord. The hand of the Lord moves on our behalf to fight for us and to provide for us.

> *Psalms 144:7 Stretch out Your **hand** from above; rescue me and deliver me out of great waters, from the **hand** of foreigners.*

Right hand: The right hand specifically speaks of a place of honor and power. It speaks of an appointed position rather than a physical location.

So it does not literally mean to "sit at the physical right hand" as referring to Jesus being seated at the right hand of the Father. Rather it refers to a position of power and authority.

> *Psalms 89:13 You have a mighty arm; strong is Your **hand**, and high is Your right **hand**.*

NEGATIVE
A black hand in the spirit speaks of the work of the enemy. Just as a hand speaks of the blessing of the Lord in your life, so a black hand shows that the enemy seeks to steal from you.

I remember once seeing a black hand holding a bag of gold coins in the spirit. Each time I saw it, I knew that the Lord was telling me that the enemy had a hold on our finances.

After a struggle, the Lord exposed the enemy and we could close the door he had gained access through. From that time onwards our finances were released!

See also: Arm, Finger

Harp

When I have seen a harp in the spirit, it has usually represented psalmody. I have seen angels playing harps in the spirit as well (worship angels).

Mainly though it represents music, and the gift of being able to play music and be inspired musically by the Lord.

Positive:

- The anointing to worship
- The ability to sing and write prophetic songs
- The anointing to decree through music

Negative: The counterfeit of the enemy

There are many other "spiritual instruments" you may see in the spirit. In the message "Prophetic Praise and Worship" in our prophetic courses, I share a bit on instruments I have seen and heard in the spirit during praise and worship.

If you see the Lord giving someone a harp or stringed instrument, then it means that He desires to give them a spiritual gift. This gift involves flowing in psalmody and releasing decrees through praise and worship. It is not simply the call to worship, but the call to release God's will through the agency of worship.

This also refers to writing songs and being able to prophesy in song.

Others have been known to see a guitar or similar instrument. The point of the vision is not the instrument itself, but what it represents - which is Christ-inspired music!

Speaking of praise:

> *Psalms 33:2 Praise the Lord with the harp; make melody to Him with an instrument of ten strings.*

Speaking of prophetic song:

> *Psalms 49:4 I will incline my ear to a proverb; I will disclose my dark saying on the* ***harp****.*

NEGATIVE

Keep in mind that satan was the original worship leader and continues to declare his message through the music industry of today. To see a black harp or a harp in a negative sense is referring to his counterfeit spirit. It means that the person you are praying for is being influenced by the spirit of the world instead of the spirit of God.

See also: Instruments, Music,

HARVEST

Reaping the financial and spiritual fruits of your hard labor.

Positive: The kind of blessing that requires action on your part to bring it to pass
Negative: Much investment with little return (sign of a curse)

POSITIVE

A harvest does not appear overnight. It is something that only comes to pass after you have worked hard and then allowed the Lord to do His part as well.

You sow the seeds and fertilizer and it is the Lord that brings the rain. If you work God's way, then you can expect a great harvest.

Although the sign of a harvest is positive proof of a great reward, it speaks again of hard work. To reap the harvest is heavy labor, but it is enjoyable labor.

In most cultures, this is a time of celebration and joy. So a harvest represents working hard but enjoying that work that will complete the reward that the Lord has given to you!

> *Mark 4:29 But when the grain ripens, immediately he puts in the sickle, because the **harvest** has come.*

If you seek the Lord and He is putting a sickle in your hand, then He is saying that the harvest is ready!

In ministry, a harvest is also a picture of reaching the lost for the Lord and bringing them into the Kingdom.

> *John 4:35 Do you not say, there are still four months and then comes the **harvest**? Behold, I say to you, lift up your eyes and look at the fields, for they are already white for **harvest**.*

NEGATIVE
When weeds are in your harvest, it means that you did not work according to God's plan or that the enemy got in somewhere to bring division. (Matt 13:30)

If the harvest is poor or weak, this is also an indication of the attack of the enemy and a spirit of destruction.

See also: Plants, Seed

HAT

Protection or a representation of status

Positive: Protection and position given from the authority above you
Negative: Representing the wrong image

CHARACTER SPECIFIC SYMBOL

POSITIVE
Change of image and status: To wear a hat that represents someone of greater financial status is the Lord confirming the change He is bringing about in your life. A hat is very much part of our image in both status and personality.

If you are overly serious and you dream of wearing a funny hat, the Lord is telling you to let out your fun side. A top hat? It's time to get serious!

NEGATIVE
Fool/Joker: Not every change is good. I had a vision once of someone wearing the hat of a fool. They were the kind of person that was always hiding behind a fake smile and trying to be the "funny guy" so that people would accept them.

The Lord wanted him to put this away and to allow his true nature to come out. He was called to a leadership position which meant growing up and not being the brunt of everyone's jokes any longer.

Universal Symbol

POSITIVE
Paul often spoke of women "covering their head" in scripture. I am not going to tackle that doctrine, but will rather shift gears to say that seeing a vision or having a dream of a specific hat can well speak of your spiritual covering. What kind of hat is in your dream? A crown or is it a veil?

Spiritual position: Head gear was always used as a representation of status in the Word. A crown spoke of royalty and the High Priest wore a turban that let everyone know his spiritual status.

> *Exodus 29:6-7 You shall put the turban on his head, and put the holy crown on the turban. And you shall take the anointing oil, pour it on his head, and anoint him.*

NEGATIVE
If you dream of being attacked by people with specific hats or turbans, this clearly speaks of spiritual attack where the enemy has been given license. Those attacking you are doing so under his authority. Determine the headgear to see what kind of attack it is.

You need to determine what the hat you see represents. Is it a hat that you can find in Scripture? If not, then consider what the hat means to you personally. Does it speak of position, wealth, loss, image or a change in character? Then determine if the change is positive or negative.

See also: Crown, Hair, Head, Veil

Head

The head speaks of a position of authority. In the Scriptures the husband is the head of the wife, just as Christ is the head of the Church. (1 Cor 11:3)

Positive: Those in authority over you
Negative: Lack of spiritual covering

POSITIVE
To dream or have a vision of receiving a crown or having your head lifted is a good picture. It speaks of being given authority and a promotion.

Because the head is also a picture of Christ and His body, in a vision or prophetic dream, it represents the leadership in the body of Christ.

When the Lord first called us to train the fivefold ministry, He told us that we needed to start with the head of His body. (Speaking of the leadership).

NEGATIVE
To dream or have a vision of losing your head speaks of losing your position and your authority.

To dream of a bride having something wrong with her head or to have a vision of something similar, then the Lord is showing you that there is something wrong with His church.

Their relationship with Him is not where it should be and His leaders are not passing along the correct message. This would be a call to intercession.

See also: Hair, Hat, Skull

HEART

Your heart symbolizes your feelings and emotions.

Positive: The open expression of your feelings
Negative: Flawed expression of emotion, due to hurts of the past

POSITIVE
If you dream of a heart being healed, then this is a good dream, showing you that the Lord has healed a hurt from the past.

A heart can also speak of love in your dreams. A broken heart speaks of lost love.

If you dream of a heart that has been broken or damaged, then it is referring to a hurt that you have experienced. This may relate directly to rejection or to a relationship that went bad.

The heart of the body of Christ speaks of those who are called of the Lord to love His church and to teach it to love Him as well.

NEGATIVE
Bleeding heart: To dream of or see a heart that is bleeding, broken or wounded speaks of emotional pain.

I often see this when ministering to someone with hurts from the past. It refers to past hurts that have not been healed, and affect the person in the present.

> *Psalms 147:3 He healeth the broken in* ***heart****, and bindeth up their wounds. (KJV)*

Stony heart: We have also seen a heart surrounded by stone or ice in the spirit. This indicates a person that has closed off their feelings and refuses to open their hearts to others.

Unfortunately, this prevents them from opening their hearts to the Lord as well, so that they can hear His voice.

> *Matthew 13:15 For the **hearts** of these people are **hardened**, and their ears cannot hear, and they have closed their eyes so their eyes cannot see,*

See also: Blood, Chest, Ice, Stone

HELL

Hell is never a positive picture, and represents torment and the work of the enemy.

If you keep having dreams and visions of hell, I recommend that you are cautious. It could be that you have opened up your heart to an influence that is not of the Lord and have allowed deception into your life.

Always keep in mind that we serve a God of faith, hope and love. If you keep having dreams or visions of hell that leave you confused, guilty or full of fear, then they are not of the Lord.

Consult the chapter on Nightmares, Deception and Demonic Dreams in *The Way of Dreams and Visions* book.

See also: Fire, Prison

HONEY

Honey speaks of the sweetness of the Lord, richness, abundance, prosperity and luxury.

Positive: The Lord meeting the desires of your heart
Negative: Hankering after what God can give you, instead of seeking Him

The Lord spoke many promises of giving honey. It was considered a food of luxury and wealth. If you were wealthy in those days, you ate honey! It was a delicacy and something to be sought after.

POSITIVE
I have often seen honey in the spirit. I remember one time the Lord saying to me, "Open your mouth wide and I will fill it."

Then as I did it, I saw Him fill it with this rich, thick honey that poured into my throat.

As I drank it in, He told me that I was to consume His word this way, that He was going to fill me with his anointing and with his goodness.

The Lord's nature and presence is often likened to honey. It is a picture of His sweetness and beauty. Honey has some wonderful meanings if you take a look in the Word.

Honey is also a picture of knowledge and wisdom (Prov 24:14).

Speaking of blessing and prosperity:

> *Numbers 13:27 Then they told him, and said: We went to the land where you sent us. It truly flows with milk and **honey**, and this is its fruit.*

Speaking of the Lord's nature:

> *Song of Songs 4:11 Your lips, O my spouse, drip as the **honeycomb**; **honey** and milk are under your tongue; and the fragrance of your garments is like the fragrance of Lebanon.*

NEGATIVE

In the book of revelation, a prophet was made to eat a scroll that tasted of honey but was bitter in the stomach. (Rev 10:10)

The Lord told me once that this represented the world, that those who sought after the world and did not know Him chased after everything they thought was fun and exciting.

They sought things that tasted sweet in the mouth (satisfied the flesh). While they were tasting of the world and going to all the clubs, bars and places of sin, they tasted honey in their mouths.

Every time they sinned, it tasted good to them for that moment. But when they went home, then that same honey was bitter in their hearts.

The sin and the offer of the world tasted like honey for but a moment, but left behind a bitterness, emptiness and void deep within.

This is why they kept looking for that taste of honey. They tasted the false, but we have the real honey to give them that never runs dry or makes you bitter. It is Jesus Christ, whose touch is rich and sweet!

It is the same in the Church for those that continue to hanker after the sweetness of the manifest presence of the Lord, but not after His person. They want the gifts and the experiences in the realm of the spirit, but fail to seek His face.

See also: Milk

HORNS

A symbol of strength to either lift up or tear down.

Positive: A representation of strength and authority
Negative: A forceful attack designed to push you backwards

CHARACTER SPECIFIC SYMBOL

I think for most to dream of the horns of a demon or the devil is negative and representative of the occult. The horn of a unicorn represents fantasy or folklore while the horns of an animal represents strength and our ability to defend ourselves.

UNIVERSAL SYMBOL

POSITIVE
A horn was often used to contain wine and oil in the Old Testament. So it was a vessel of blessing. The ram's horn was used in battle to announce the victory given by the Lord!

To have the "horn of the Lord" defend you speaks of the Lord using His strength against the enemy on your behalf. Oil in a horn represents not only the blessing of the Lord, but His strength and authority. The Lord did more than just "anoint" David with oil, but gave him the authority to rule.

> *Psalms 92:10 But my horn You have exalted like a wild ox; I have been anointed with fresh oil.*

NEGATIVE
Israel's enemies were often portrayed as animals with strong horns that charged and tore everyone up. To see horns against you speaks of an aggressive attack from the enemy. This kind of attack is where his full strength is thrown at you from without. This speaks of external spiritual warfare. Do not be discouraged though, because the Lord is well able to give you the victory!

> *Daniel 8:7 And I saw him confronting the ram; he was moved with rage against him, attacked the ram, and broke his two horns. ...*

See also: Bull

HORSE

Horses are a picture of strength. The kind of strength and ability that the Lord determines to give you to "get the job done." Depending on the kind of horse you dream about, will give you an indication of what kind of ability and strength the Lord is going to add to you.

Positive: The strength to accomplish the task God has given to you
Negative: The power someone else is using to oppose you

Character Specific Symbol

POSITIVE
If you always desired to have a horse or do horse riding, then this animal would speak of your hidden desires. If you work with horses, then they would represent your work.

NEGATIVE
If you have a fear of horses, it is a symbol for fear in your dreams. Also if you had a negative experience with horses as a child, it would symbolize hurts or fears from the past that are surfacing in your life again.

A young horse (colt) also speaks of immaturity.

Universal Symbol

POSITIVE
The kind of horse will determine the kind of strength and external ability the Lord wants to give you. I had a vision one of a very specific horse. When I looked it up, I read that it was native to a specific region in the United States.

It confirmed the work the Lord had already been leading me into. He would give me the strength and ability to minister to and reach a nation that I had not grown up in!

In Old Testament times, the number of horses you owned was an indication of how strong your army was. They are strongly linked to warfare and overcoming the enemy.

To see an army of horses and riders on your side is a picture of the army of the Lord fighting on your behalf. He is adding His strength to your cause!

> *Ezekiel 39:20 You shall be filled at My table with horses and riders, with mighty men and with all the men of war, says the Lord God.*

I have often seen the Lord Jesus in the spirit on a white horse. It is a wonderful picture of both His position as King, and the power that He has. It is a confirmation that the Lord does warfare on our behalf.

> *Revelation 19:11 Now I saw heaven opened, and behold, a white **horse**. And He who sat on him was called Faithful and True, and in righteousness He judges and makes war.*

NEGATIVE
The Lord condemned the Israelites for relying on the strength of horses instead of Him. So in a negative light, horses speak of works and striving outside of the Lord. It speaks about using natural strengths or relying on the abilities of others instead of relying on the Lord first and foremost.

> *Isaiah 31:1 Woe to those who go down to Egypt for help, and rely on **horses**, who trust in chariots because they are many, and in horsemen because they are very strong, but who do not look to the Holy One of Israel, nor seek the Lord*

An army of black horses and riders also speaks of the army of the enemy who is coming against you. The enemy is "pitting his strength" against your own.

See also: Army

HORSESHOE

Many believe in the superstition that the horseshoe brings good luck. This of course has no place in the body of Christ, and if you see a horseshoe when praying for someone, then the Lord is telling you that they have held onto superstitious beliefs.

HOUSE

A house in a dream is a representation of your life.

CHARACTER SPECIFIC SYMBOL

POSITIVE

If you dream that your house is being built onto, it means that the Lord is about to add something to your life.

Perhaps you might dream that your house is going through a renovation which speaks of a total rearrangement that the Lord is about to take you through.

If you dream that you suddenly find a new room in your house that you did not notice before, this speaks of a hidden talent or ability that you have not tapped into yet. The Lord is saying that now is the time to step forward and to pick that talent up and do something with it!

If you dream that you are moving out of an old house and into a new, the message is clear. The Lord wants you to leave your past life behind and to press on now towards the new direction that He has for you.

NEGATIVE

Whatever emotion you feel in the dream concerning the house you are in, indicates either the emotional condition you are in right now or something you faced in the past.

If you dream that snakes or something evil enters your house, it means that the enemy has been given license in your life and that you are under attack.

To dream that your house is under attack is a picture of spiritual attack in your life. Identify the other symbols in your dream to determine the source of that attack.

House from past: If you dream of a house from your childhood, the Lord is exposing hurts and experiences from the past that are still a hindrance to you right now.

House destroyed: To dream of your house being destroyed or broken down indicates how you feel right now. You feel like your world is falling apart and that everything is going wrong. Do not be discouraged! The Lord is well able to put the pieces back together and build something new and amazing!

Universal Symbol

POSITIVE
The Lord has often shown me the ministry that I am building as a house. Often He said that I should build all the rooms at once, while at other times, He will tell me to concentrate on one room (one aspect) of the ministry.

It is also the work of the apostle. Apostle Paul said that he would never build on another's foundation. (Rom 15:20)

NEGATIVE
If you have a vision that a house's foundation is broken, this speaks of a doctrinal foundation that is amiss. It means that the teaching they have received was not sound and because of that it is having a bad effect on their spiritual lives.

Building a house on your own and striving and struggling speaks of doing things in your own works instead of letting God step in.

Speaking of building something without the Lord, be it a ministry, a church or even your personal spiritual life and calling:

> *Psalms 127:1 Unless the Lord builds the **house**, they labor in vain who build it; unless the Lord guards the city, the watchman stays awake in vain.*

See also: Attic, Basement, Buildings, Foundation, Kitchen, Garage

Hurricane/Tornado

Tumultuous circumstances designed to either test or destroy you.

Positive: A rapid change of circumstances
Negative: The destructive work of the enemy

Character Specific Symbol

POSITIVE
To dream of being swept up into a hurricane where you feel good indicates a change that is about to take place in your life, that although might seem dramatic, will result in something good.

NEGATIVE
If you experience a lot of fear and anxiety in your dream, then it is a representation of how you feel right now in your life. You are fighting circumstances that seem to have a mind of their own. You are not in control of your circumstances – they control you!

Universal Symbol

POSITIVE
Do not assume that because you have a vision of a hurricane that it is literal or something to be afraid of. If you are praying for a region and see a hurricane, pray further for clarity. Is the Lord leading you to pray against a natural disaster that is about to come into that region?

More likely than not the hurricane represents a dramatic and sudden change about to take place. If you feel positive in the vision, realize that the Lord is coming as a mighty rushing wind to reveal Himself to His people. However, before that change can take place, a change of circumstances and mindsets needs to occur.

NEGATIVE
If the hurricane feels very negative in your vision or external dream, then it represents a spirit of destruction from the enemy. He intends to destroy what has been established and built by the Lord through the years.

See also: Storm, Wind

Husband

Just as in the interpretation for a wife, your husband will represent a different part of yourself in light of your real life relationship with him.

In most cases though, your husband will represent your recreated spirit in Christ or your relationship with Jesus.

POSITIVE
You might dream that your husband takes you to a specific place or that you and he have a disagreement.

The first would mean that your spirit is going to lead you in a different direction. The second interpretation would mean that you have conflict in your spirit!

You might have a dream where you and your husband are trying to make love, but keep being interrupted. You might wake feeling frustrated and confused, wondering how this could relate to the Lord!

The interpretation of this dream would be that the enemy has been sending many interruptions that are preventing you from spending intimate time with the Lord Jesus.

NEGATIVE
If your husband is a negative figure in your life, then it is not likely that he would speak of your spirit or the Lord.

He would then speak of sin, pride, the flesh, fear, insecurity or any other emotion that they trigger off in real life. It is likely that you will dream of him often, so in context of your internal dreams, identify what he might represent.

Ex-Husband: In most cases an ex-husband would not have a good connotation in your dreams. He represents your flesh. Paul tells us in Romans 7 that just as a woman is released from one husband and allowed to marry another, so also have we been released from the law and the flesh, so that we can be married to Christ by faith.

Universal Symbol

POSITIVE
Jesus is our Groom. He is loving and yearns for us. Many times I have seen the Groom desiring to take the Bride to the wedding chambers.

This speaks of His love for us, and His desire to woo us into receiving all He has for us, to become intimate with Him.

Christ as our Husband

> *Ephesians 5:23 For the **husband** is head of the wife, as also Christ is head of the church; and He is the Savior of the body.*

NEGATIVE
In personal ministry it would be common to see a husband or wife in the spirit, depending on the circumstance.

The person might be divorced, in which case the Lord might be telling you to break the ties between the ex-spouse and them. (See *Branch* for more on this).

See also: Branch, Bride, Man, Wife, Woman

Symbols Starting in I

Symbols Starting in I

Ice

In any culture ice represents the same thing: cold, hard and unmoving.

I see this more often when praying for people who have closed their hearts off to others. I see ice around their hearts.

There are many common expressions in English that we use. If someone is cold and unapproachable we say that they are an "Ice Queen".

So if you dream of being surrounded by ice, perhaps this is a picture of how you have closed your heart off to others and become distant. It is time to open up and let the Lord in to bring healing and change.

In this passage below, the presence of an iced river is a sad picture. It is something that should bring life, but because of the ice it brings death and emptiness instead.

> *Job 6:15 My brothers have dealt deceitfully like a brook, like the streams of the brooks that pass away;*
> *16 Which are dark because of the* ***ice****, and into which the snow vanishes.*

A road covered in ice is a warning from the Lord that the enemy is trying to make your road hard to navigate. He cannot prevent you from taking that road, but he wants to cause you to "go off the rails" so to speak.

See also: Heart

Idol

The object of your worship. Things that have the place of honor in your life.

NEGATIVE

I think we can both agree that there is no place for a positive interpretation for an idol in our lives. The only time an idol would be positive is if you saw it being broken down.

An idol in a dream or a vision is a representation of something that is taking your time, affection and worship.

As we know the Word is clear on not having any idols before the Lord. The Lord alone should have this place in your life.

If you have a vision of an idol while praying for a ministry or church, then the Lord is saying that they are putting other things before Him.

People: Often people that are close to you can become an idol in your life. You begin to seek their affection and their direction for your life more than the Lord's. Although the Lord will always use man to speak to you, at the end of the day, it is God that you should worship.

Unfortunately, in a church age of "super leaders" there are many that turn the attention away from the Lord and onto them and "their gifts." It was unacceptable for the Children of Israel and it is still unacceptable in the Church.

Golden calf: To see a golden calf in the spirit speaks of heresy and doctrine that is not of God. This doctrine likely originated from a cultural belief, on which a biblical principle was added. The Israelites were following the archetype of the Egyptians and tried to "add" the worship of their God, using the practices of the world. There was no place for it then and certainly no place for it in the church today.

The work of your hands: Often the things you have accomplished and done with your own works becomes more important than what the Lord wants you to do. Often when these things take priority in your life, the Lord will ask you to sacrifice them just like He asked Abraham to sacrifice Isaac.

> *Acts 7:41 And they made a calf in those days, offered sacrifices to the* ***idol****, and rejoiced in the works of their own hands.*

See also: Altar

INSECTS

In a prophetic dream or a vision where the connotation is negative, various insects can speak of:

- *Destruction, an attack from the enemy.*
- *Negative words spoken against you.*
- *Things that are an annoyance.*
- *Things that bring fear.*
- *A spirit of destruction (as in the ointment that was spoiled).*
- *The presence of satan himself, displayed as the lord of the flies.*

CHARACTER SPECIFIC SYMBOL

POSITIVE

It is important to remember that insects can mean different things to different people. Apply the principles in the *Way of Dreams and Visions* book for all internal dreams, and ask yourself this question:

What does this insect mean to ME (or to the person who had the dream)?

It is very seldom that insects would be positive. However you might dream that you are crushing insects. Or perhaps you are overcoming them in a dream, where you are the main character.

This would be positive! It would mean that you are overcoming something negative in your life.

A lady bug is an insect that pollinates fruit and is a good picture of something that is being used of God to assist you in bringing fruitfulness in your life.

I shared an illustration in the *Way of Dreams and Visions* book of a lady who had a fear of spiders. She had a dream where she was crushing them. Spiders represented fear in her dreams. By dreaming that she was crushing them, it spoke of how she was overcoming fear in her life!

So ask yourself, "How do I feel about this insect in real life? Does it bring fear? Is it just an annoyance? Is it a pet? Does it provide a benefit? (like a bee that provides honey)."

You decide and apply it then to your internal dream.

NEGATIVE
Once again, what does the insect mean to you? If you dream of having insects swarming you, this is not likely a good dream!

It could speak of things annoying you that are overpowering you in real life. It might speak of fears that are assailing you, or problems that are getting to be too much.

I grew up having some horrible experiences with cockroaches. To this day they give me the creeps even more than spiders! Although they clearly speak of the work of the enemy in visions, in my case dreaming of a cockroach would likely speak of my inner fears or things that I would rather avoid.

Do you see how important it is to identify the symbols in an internal dream?

Universal Symbol

POSITIVE
There are some positive references to insects in Scripture. For example locusts were something that the Israelites were allowed to eat. (Leviticus 11:22)

There is another passage that speaks of how Samson was given honey from some bees that had made their home in the carcass of a lion. (Judges 14:8)

Then again let us not forget the plague:

> *Exodus 10:14 And the **locusts** went up over all the land of Egypt and rested on all the territory of Egypt. They were very severe; previously there had been no such **locusts** as they, nor shall there be such after them.*

So my conclusion is this: If your vision or prophetic dream has a positive connotation, then the insects would speak of something that provides sustenance.

It speaks of spiritual food, or the Lord providing for your basic needs.

However, the Lord also sent a plague of insects on Egypt to deliver His people. So in this case, seeing a plague of insects in a positive light could speak of the Lord sending judgment on the system of the world to bring blessing to His people.

NEGATIVE
In general, insects are unclean in scripture and speak of the work of the enemy. I often see insects in the spirit when praying for healing. When I see them I know that I am dealing with a spirit of infirmity.

Bees: David spoke about a swarm of bees that stung like thorns.

Then the enemy of the Israelites was referred to as a swarm of bees. (Deut 1:44) This speaks of an attack that comes at you from all sides – this is usually a physical attack.

Flies: Flies specifically always have a negative connotation. They are often tied in with satan himself, being known as the Beelzebub, lord of the flies.

On a personal note, in the spirit when I have seen Beelzebub, the lord of the flies, the vision has often represented things that relate to the New Age cult.

When I have given personal ministry and seen this demon, after questioning the person it turns out they had some New Age involvement.

I do not encourage you to get hung up on demons, but if you do come across this in personal ministry, you know what it is and how to deal with it.

Remember, the enemy *cannot* attack you, unless he has been given license through sin. The book the Prophetic Warrior is a powerful resource to understanding this better.

> *Leviticus 11:43 You shall not make yourselves abominable with any **creeping thing that creeps**; nor shall you make yourselves unclean with them, lest you be defiled by them.*

Cockroaches: These are loathsome creatures that scurry in the dark and feed in dirt. If you see cockroaches in the spirit, then you know that the enemy has gained license to your life. Because of their nature they are a good representation of small sins that have crept into your life.

The good news is, that just as they are easy to squash in the natural, so can you easily take authority over any work of the enemy in the spirit.

Scorpion: Again this speaks of demonic attack that is meant to poison and discourage you. I often see scorpions when praying for pain in the body.

Revelation 9:10 They had tails like ***scorpions****, and there were stings in their tails. Their power was to hurt men five months*

See also: Ant, Beelzebub, Bees, Caterpillar, Fleas, Flies, Locusts, Wasp/Hornet

INCENSE

The burning of incense in the Old Testament had a two-fold function. The first was to cover over the smell of the animal sacrifice that continued daily at the temple. The second was to offer it up as a form of praise and prayer.

Positive: The beauty of worship
Negative: Praying your own burden instead of the Lord's will

POSITIVE
In the book of revelation, the prayers of the saints are likened to the burning of incense.

Psalms 141:2 Let my prayer be set before You as ***incense****, the lifting up of my hands as the evening sacrifice.*

To dream or have a vision of burning incense is an indication that the Lord is calling you to the secret place to intercede on behalf of His people.

Just as incense covered over the smell of the slain animals, so also does the sweet smell of our praise and prayer cover our sin and the things that are rotten in our lives.

When you pray and give God license in your life and in the lives of others, you are covering a "multitude of sins" with true love and worship.

NEGATIVE
The Lord warned strongly against offering "strange incense" or to offer it to false gods.

This is a picture of praying in the flesh and against the will of God. To burn incense to someone else other than the Lord is a picture of putting your trust and hope in things that are not of Him.

Exodus 30:9 You shall not offer strange ***incense*** *on it, or a burnt offering, or a grain offering; nor shall you pour a drink offering on it.*

See also: Altar, Perfume, Smelling

INHERITANCE

To enter into the fruit of another person's labor.

Character Specific Symbol

POSITIVE

When dreaming of receiving an inheritance, it is important to identify what the person in your dream means to you. Depending on whether you view them positively or negatively, it will change your interpretation.

To receive an inheritance speaks of receiving the fruits of another person's labor. It means that you get the best of what they have.

Perhaps you desired a spiritual gift or ability in this person. Dreaming of receiving an inheritance from them would indicate that the Lord is going to grant you this desire.

It is important to note that the inheritance has a requirement. It means to be close to that person. This is especially true of a spiritual son or daughter. If you dream that your spiritual parent gives you an inheritance, it means that you will receive from them all the things that God gave them.

Through Christ, we share in His inheritance. Through Him all that belongs to God, now belongs to us as well! To dream that you are surprised with an inheritance is a reminder from the Lord of the inheritance you have in Him!

> *Colossians 1:12 Giving thanks to the Father who has qualified us to be partakers of the* ***inheritance*** *of the saints in the light.*

NEGATIVE

If you dream of receiving an inheritance from a family member that has died, it could well be that your dream is indicating that you have inherited a family generational curse.

> *Micah 2:2 They covet fields and take them by violence, also houses, and seize them. So they oppress a man and his house, a man and his* ***inheritance****.*

See also: Gift

Instruments (Musical)

I have already given a lot of detail on musical instruments, so here is a summary of some musical instruments that you might dream about.

Character Specific Symbol

If you are a music teacher, then these instruments would represent your work and personal passions. If you are looking for a scriptural understanding of these symbols, consider my offerings below and see what sits right in your spirit.

Universal Symbol

Drums: A celebration of joy. Similar to the "clapping of hands" in scripture. (Psalms 47:1)

Guitar: To be musically inspired. Similar to the harp in scripture (2 Kings 3:15)

Flute: A call to praise and celebration (Matt 11:17)

Trumpet: A call to spiritual warfare. The sound is intended to bring the fear of the Lord. It is a good picture of prophetic warfare. (Exodus 20:18)

Stringed instruments: Invitation to worship. Stringed instruments mostly accompanied a singer. (Isaiah 38:20)

See also: Band, Harp, Music

Iron

Iron is a picture of strength or oppression, depending on the context of your dream or vision.

Positive: Pressure through circumstances, from the Lord, to shape you
Negative: Pressure through circumstances, from the enemy, to break you

Hot iron: Being seared with a hot iron, in a dream or vision, is similar to the process of "branding" used in cattle. It means to be marked and for that marking to be "set in stone."

> *1 Timothy 4:2 speaking lies in hypocrisy, having their own conscience seared with a hot **iron**.*

Rod of iron: To rule with a "rod of iron" speaks of leadership that is strict and strong, not allowing for any deviation to the rules.

> *Revelation 2:27 He shall rule them with a rod of **iron**; they shall be dashed to pieces like the potter's vessels - as I also have received from My Father.*

POSITIVE

There is a wonderful illustration in Scripture of our common saying "iron sharpens iron". (Prov 27:17)

It is true today also and a good picture of those the Lord has put in your life to bring pressure to your weaknesses.

If you are in a situation where someone is putting pressure on you or you are in continual conflict with them, then dreaming or having a vision of iron being sharpened is a good thing!

It means that the Lord is using this circumstance to change and shape you into a better vessel.

Note that if you are called to the fivefold ministry training, the Lord will very often use those closest to you to bring about the deaths and training needed for your call.

A rod of iron in a positive light speaks of God's hand of strength overcoming the enemy on our behalf.

> *Psalms 2:9 You shall break them with a rod of **iron**; You shall dash them to pieces like a potter's vessel...*

NEGATIVE
The oppression of the enemy is also depicted in Scriptures. The Israelites feared the "chariots of iron" of their enemies. To dream or have visions of iron weapons being thrown at you, speaks of the enemy attacking you through circumstances. The pressure he bears on you means to break you, not to shape you.

> *Job 20:24 He will flee from the **iron** weapon; a bronze bow will pierce him through.*

See also: Bars, Bronze/Brass, Testing

ISLAND

The picture of an island is pretty self-explanatory. It speaks of being separated and cut off from others. Depending on the context of the dream or vision, you will have an accurate interpretation.

Positive: A season of isolation and intimacy with the Lord
Negative: To escape and remove your emotions from others

POSITIVE
If the dream or vision is positive, then it is an indication that the Lord is leading you to be separated to Him for a season.

Perhaps He desires to give you more of His anointing or train you in a certain area.

I have experienced this many times during my various ministry trainings.

Often the Lord will call me aside for a season to just receive from Him.

The Apostle goes through this many times, and we have named it the "Mountain Experience". I give clear teaching on this in the Moses Mandate.

Marriage island: I preach about the importance of having an "island" for you and your spouse. A place where you escape to simply "be." If I had to dream of an island, then I know the Lord is telling me that I need to invest more into my marriage!

NEGATIVE
When it is not the Lord doing the separating, but you, then this is definitely negative. It means that you have cut yourself off from others and the Lord.

In this condition, no one can help you or be there for you - not even the Lord Himself. It will mean having to trust Him and to let go of your independence and insecurity.

This certainly is a good picture of the spirit of independence and will destroy any chances of you working as part of a team.

In addition to that, dreaming of being stuck on an island is an indication that you are trying to escape the pressures and hide away from the things you know you need to do.

See also: Mountain

Symbols Starting in J

SYMBOLS STARTING IN J

JAR/JUG

Your ability to contain what God requires you to.

Positive:

- Your potential for anointing and success
- What is within your power to give out to others

Negative: Limitation

UNIVERSAL SYMBOL

POSITIVE

To dream or have a vision of a jar being filled with wine or oil is positive. The Lord desires to fill you up with His anointing and He has found you worthy. If you see the Lord giving you a bigger jar, then He is saying that you have been tested and are worthy to contain more of His anointing.

To see a jar pouring out oil, water or wine is a picture of the spiritual potential you already have – all you need to do now is pour it out. It is never the jar that is consumed, but its contents. Without anything within, the jar is useless! The Lord wants you to pour out what you have, before He gives you any more.

NEGATIVE

Often it is our mindsets that restrict the fire of God in our lives. This illustration of Gideon is perfect. They hid lamps of fire within jars. For the fire to shine though, the jars had to be smashed. In the same way, dreaming or having a vision of a jar being smashed is the Lord pointing out your limitations. For your "light to shine bright", the way you think and who you are needs to change!

> *Judges 7:20 Then the three companies blew the trumpets and broke the pitchers - they held the torches in their left hands and the trumpets in their right hands for blowing - and they cried, "The sword of the Lord and of Gideon!"*

See also: Clay, Cup, Oil, Water, Wine

JAW

Anyone who had a broken jaw will tell you how difficult it is to speak! Your jaw is a picture of your ability to communicate.

It is also a good picture of your strengths, your communication strengths and the wisdom to choose the correct direction.

When a nation was going in a wrong direction, the Lord said that He would put a bridle on their jaw to lead them to a place He wanted to take them.

Positive: Your strengths lie in your ability to communicate
Negative:

- Pain inflicted on others through hurtful words
- A failure in your ability to communicate

Universal Symbol

Samson used the jawbone of a donkey to defeat his enemies. (Judges 15:16) What an unlikely weapon! To see this when praying for someone means that the Lord is calling you to fight back in your current circumstances, but not in a way that you would anticipate.

He is saying that you need to use what you have available to you right now to overcome! You might not have a sword or great weapons in the spirit, so use what you do have to overcome your current situation! Stop waiting to have "everything in line" before you overcome the attack you are facing right now.

Jaw/Tongue: Because the jaw is so closely linked to communication and strength, to see a broken jaw speaks of a struggle or inability to communicate what is really on your heart.

A jaw of steel is an indication that the way you communicate is hurtful to others.

> *Proverbs 30:14 There is a generation, whose teeth are as swords, and their **jaw** teeth as knives, to devour the poor from off the earth, and the needy from among men*

See also: Bridle, Teeth, Tongue

Jesus

The author and finisher of our faith. Our redeemer, lover of our souls and the source of all blessing.

Character Specific Symbol

In your dreams, someone that is close to you will be symbolic of Jesus. This is often your spouse or someone else that you feel close to.

In my dreams, my husband represents the Lord. So when I dream of my husband taking me somewhere or of us interacting, I know that the Lord is speaking about our relationship and what His plans are.

Decide for yourself who you feel could represent the Lord Jesus in your dreams.

Universal Symbol

To have a face-to-face relationship with Jesus is available to every believer. I discuss this in some detail in the *Way of Dreams and Visions* book.

I also give a description there of how I see the Lord Jesus. What I will cover here are some of the experiences I have had in personal ministry.

NEGATIVE
I have often seen a picture of the Lord Jesus as is seen in the many religious artistic portrayals. When I see this in the spirit I know that the person I am praying for is bound by legalism.

If you know the Lord Jesus personally, you would see that the characteristic image that is painted of Him, particularly the Catholic images, are not what He looks like at all. Rather these are a religious and false image of what He is.

It is important to remember that the Lord Jesus is accepting and loving. If you feel fear or guilt in His presence, then I would caution you to reject that experience or revelation as deception.

If ever you have a visitation that you think is Jesus, keep in mind that He always has an open face. Do not readily accept any impartation or direction from such a visitation where the face is hidden.

See also: Angels, Demons

Jewelry

All over the world, jewelry has the same appeal. It speaks of beauty, wealth, blessing and favor.

It also represents the image you portray to the world.

Positive: Blessings bestowed on you as a gift – unmerited favor
Negative: Treasure that is often overlooked

Character Specific Symbol

POSITIVE
Knowledge is also considered a jewel in Scripture.

> *Proverbs 20:15 There is gold and a multitude of rubies, but the lips of knowledge are a precious* ***jewel****.*

NEGATIVE
In a negative light however, a jewel in a pig's nose is not a positive picture!

> *Proverbs 11:22 As a jewel of gold in a swine's snout, so is a fair woman which is without discretion. (KJV)*

I have covered various pieces of jewelry and jewel stones under their own headings.

Universal Symbol

I have often seen various jewels in the spirit. Once I saw a person working a field, and in it were various jewels of great value.

The Lord told them, that as they just continue with the work that He had for them, that they would discover many things of great value along the way.

This spoke of natural as well as spiritual blessings.

I have also seen someone walking along a road and discovering different jewels at specific places along the way.

The Lord said that the treasures that they are looking for would be found as they continue on the road that He had for them.

See also: Crown, Diamonds, Earrings, Gold, Necklace, Ring, Ruby

Symbols Starting in K

SYMBOLS STARTING IN K

KEY

A key speaks of license, authority and calling. Every believer has been given a key to salvation.

Positive: The authority to bring about change in the earth
Negative: The authority given to the enemy to wreak havoc

UNIVERSAL SYMBOL

POSITIVE
When you became born again, you were given the name of Jesus to use against the enemy. You were given the license to loose and to bind.

I often see keys in the spirit.

We see a golden key when releasing a person into prophetic training, and a large jewel encrusted key when releasing someone into the apostolic.

We see a brass key when releasing someone into the teaching ministry. Either way the key represents your authority. Some are given prophetic, apostolic and teaching authority depending on their calling.

When you see a closed door or gate in the spirit, the Lord will be saying to you, "Take the key (authority) I have given you and open this door!"

This is especially relevant in the prophetic ministry, where the prophet builds up, tears down, opens doors of blessing and cursing, restricts and looses on behalf of others.

Referring to the authority to loose and to bind:

> *Matthew 16:19 And I will give you the **keys** of the kingdom of heaven, and whatever you bind on earth will be bound in heaven, and whatever you loose on earth will be loosed in heaven.*

Referring to Jesus and His authority and kingship:

> *Isaiah 22:22 The **key** of the house of David I will lay on his shoulder; so he shall open, and no one shall shut; and he shall shut, and no one shall open.*

NEGATIVE
Because a key speaks of authority, it can also be put into the wrong hands. A key can be given to the enemy to wreak havoc in our lives. When we sin, we "open the door" to the enemy. We give away our keys!

That is why Jesus had to go to hell after He died – to get the keys of death and hell back for us. This was the authority that Adam had handed satan in the garden of Gethsemane.

Taking back that authority is as simple as repenting of your sin and reminding the enemy who beat him at his game over 2000 years ago!

See also: Door

KING

A representation of a specific realm of authority and leadership.

Positive: A position of authority limited to a specific realm
Negative: Attack from a high level demonic power

POSITIVE
A king is someone who is placed over a specific kingdom. His leadership is limited to that kingdom. The Lord Jesus is our King and High Priest over the Kingdom of Heaven, of which we are a part.

Because of this, we rule and reign with Him in this life.

To dream of being made a king is positive and it means that the Lord is calling you to rise up in the position that you have in Christ.

To dream or see a picture of a specific king represents not only the person, but the kingdom that he is over. So if you saw the King of England for example, then what is being referred to here is the entire nation and not the king himself. A king is defined by his kingdom.

> *James 2:5 Listen, my beloved brethren: Has God not chosen the poor of this world to be rich in faith and **heirs of the kingdom** which He promised to those who love Him?*

NEGATIVE
To dream or have a vision that you lose your position as a king means that you are not walking in the authority that Christ has given to you.

To see a vision of Jesus as a king is a reminder that He should be Lord of your life. However, if you dream that he loses His kingship, it means that he is not being given his rightful place.

Keep in mind that satan has his own kingdoms and to see a demonic king means you are coming against a prince of darkness – a high level demon.

See also: Demons, Throne

Kiss

A kiss speaks of intimacy and vulnerability. It also speaks of opening your heart to others.

Positive: A show of true affection
Negative: Deceit

Character Specific Symbol

POSITIVE
If you dream of kissing or embracing someone, you need to identify your relationship with the person.

Are they someone you care about? If so, then depending on what they represent, will show you what you are embracing.

If you are kissing an unknown male figure in your dream, this is an indication that you are embracing your intellectual side. Kissing a strange woman could speak of embracing your more artistic or prophetic side.

Either way, kissing a person means that you are accepting whatever that person represents in your life.

NEGATIVE
Of course if the person you are kissing is not a good symbol the interpretation would be negative.

Kissing someone from your past could speak of embracing things from your past, which would be better left behind.

Embracing someone that is a picture of the flesh means that you have been neglecting the things of the Lord and started receiving the things of the world and the flesh instead.

Universal Symbol

POSITIVE
A kiss in the Scriptures was both a greeting and a sign of respect. It was not always as intimate as we perceive it today.

To have a vision of the Lord giving you a kiss is a lovely picture of the Lord showing you His affection. He is confirming that you are special to Him and one of His children.

Peter told the early church to greet one another with a kiss, to show their agape love for one another.

> *1 Peter 5:14 Greet one another with a **kiss** of love. Peace to you all who are in Christ Jesus. Amen.*

So in conclusion a kiss, in a non-sexual context, speaks of love and of the unity we have in Christ.

NEGATIVE
Judas' kiss is of course the perfect picture of betrayal, by those who say they care, but in the end turn on you.

> *Proverbs 27:6 Faithful are the wounds of a friend, but the* ***kisses*** *of an enemy are deceitful.*

In this context the kiss speaks of words that seem innocent but actually carry poison and will lead to your destruction. This is also a very good picture of how the enemy works to bring deception in the life of a believer.

See also: Adultery, Arousal, Bed, Incest, Wedding

KITCHEN

The heart of the home.

Positive: The creation place of family and archetype
Negative: The creation place of false doctrine

CHARACTER SPECIFIC SYMBOL

The kitchen is very much the heart of the home and the atmosphere there affects everything else. It is the place where memories are made and where the dynamics of what makes a family, is born. It is the birthplace of family traditions and archetype. Determine from the other symbols in your dream if this is a positive or negative thing.

UNIVERSAL SYMBOL

POSITIVE
I have often related the cooking of food to the work of the pastor teacher. To "cook up" and "prepare" the Word of God in a way that we can receive it. So for the Lord to show me a vision of being busy in a kitchen, the message is clear, "There is a lot of ministry work to do. There are a lot of people to feed spiritually!"

> *Ezekiel 46:24 And he said to me, "These are the kitchens where the ministers of the temple shall boil the sacrifices of the people."*

NEGATIVE
To have food coming out of a dirty kitchen speaks of doctrine or teaching that you have received that is making you spiritually ill.

See also: Bake, Boil, Cooking, Food, House

KNIFE

A knife is an implement used for dividing or cutting. It can be a positive or a negative symbol depending on the context of the dream or vision.

Positive: An instrument of healing, albeit a difficult healing process
Negative: An instrument of hurt

POSITIVE
In the spirit I have often seen the Lord take a knife to a wound that is infested. It is a two-fold picture.

The first is of the Lord applying the cross to our lives to rid us of the things that hinder us. The second is also a picture of healing. Although it starts out as a painful process, it brings healing to things that have been hindering you for a long time.

Just like Joshua applied the knife to the Israelites before they could enter into the Promised Land, so also does the Lord remove things from you that stop you from entering into His blessing.

> *Joshua 5:2 At that time the Lord said to Joshua, "Make flint **knives** for yourself, and circumcise the sons of Israel again the second time."*

NEGATIVE
Because the knife is a weapon used to bring pain, it is also a good picture of the enemy bringing destruction and pain. This is an infliction of emotional pain and an indication that the person needs inner healing.

> *Proverbs 30:14 There is a generation whose teeth are like swords, and whose fangs are like **knives**, to devour the poor from off the earth, and the needy from among men.*

Various knives: Much like the symbol Dagger, if the knife is ceremonial, you need to determine if it is referring to something demonic, or something positive. A kitchen knife can even speak of a teaching ministry, where you have to "cook" spiritual food.

See also: Circumcision, Dagger, Sword

Symbols Starting in L

Symbols Starting in L

Ladder

A ladder speaks of going from one level to another in your life.

Positive: A promotion
Negative: To fail an opportunity for promotion

POSITIVE
If you are going up the ladder, then this speaks of a promotion in the spirit. Going down the ladder means a demotion.

Then we have the lovely picture of the ladder with angels that Jacob dreamed about:

> *Genesis 28:12 Then he dreamed, and behold, a **ladder** was set up on the earth, and its top reached to heaven; and there the angels of God were ascending and descending on it.*

Here the Lord was confirming his covenant with Jacob. It was a clear picture that he had access to all the blessings of heaven, because of the covenant that his father Abraham had made with the Lord.

As believers we tap into this same covenant of blessing, and this ladder to heaven is now open to us as well!

NEGATIVE
Although going down a ladder might seem negative, it could be that the Lord desires to take you through some circumstances, again so that you can receive the full benefit from it.

In the business world "climbing the ladder" is a common term.

If you have been striving in your workplace, then dreaming of climbing a ladder is a representation of what you are facing at the moment. Depending on the context of your dream, it will tell you whether this is a good move on your part or not.

See also: Stairs

Lamb

In both the Old Testament and today, the lamb is an image of innocence and meekness.

Character Specific Symbol

POSITIVE
A lamb could mean different things to you, depending on your lifestyle. For example, if you are in contact with lambs or work on a farm, they would mean something quite different to you, compared to someone that had never handled a lamb before.

If you have some kind of personal memory of a lamb or work with sheep, then they could speak of your responsibilities, or things that are dear to you.

If you have no personal interaction with this animal, then it could speak of something that is innocent or of meekness. It could be that the Lord is asking you to be innocent and meek.

Universal Symbol

POSITIVE
Lambs as Christians: Just as the church is often referred to as "sheep", so does a young lamb represent a new believer in the Lord.

Jesus the Lamb of God: Jesus Himself is called the Lamb of God. In Scripture this is a picture of the covenant Jesus made for us on Calvary. He was the final lamb that was slain on the altar. After Him, burnt sacrifice was no longer necessary.

Slain lamb: To see a vision of a slain lamb is a confirmation of the covenant and that the Lord has completed the work. We can only enter into His blessing by faith, because our works mean nothing.

> *John 1:29 The next day John saw Jesus coming toward him, and said, Behold! The* ***Lamb*** *of God who takes away the sin of the world.*

Being a lamb: To be sent out as a lamb means to walk in innocence. Jesus said to the disciples, that they were being sent out as lambs among wolves, but He also promised later to be with them for all time.

Although you stand in meekness, Jesus in you stands in power. It is for you to have the courage to be vulnerable. Only then can you stand in the strength of the Lord.

NEGATIVE
Flock of lambs: This is a picture of the Church. The pastor is the shepherd and the members are the flock. To see a lamb, speaks of a believer that is still young in the Lord. I have often seen a lamb that is lost and broken and the Lord told me that the vision represented those in the church that have backslidden or been hurt in the system.

I also had a prophetic dream once where I saw small lambs being beaten. The Lord showed me that I was to rise up and protect and free His lambs and His sheep.

They spoke of believers that were still young in Him and were being abused by the leaders over them. My mandate was to raise up the shepherds that would protect the flock and heal the lambs.

Many other times the Lord has shown me a vision of lambs that have been torn apart by wolves. This is a picture of believers who were destroyed by the status quo church.

See also: Sheep, Shepherd

LAMP

A source of revelation. A lamp reveals the road just ahead of you. It speaks of the revelation and direction of the Lord.

Positive: Direction for your next step
Negative: Loss of motivation

POSITIVE

The lamp, although a source of light, does not spread its light very far. It only lights up the road just in front of you.

I have often seen that picture in the spirit. What it means is that the Lord will show you just the next step that you have to take, and that you must trust Him for the rest.

He will show you each step, but just one at a time. He is not going to reveal the entire journey ahead of time to you. So it is for you to walk in faith and let Him reveal His will just one step at a time.

> *Psalms 119:105. Your word is a **lamp** to my feet and a light to my path.*

NEGATIVE

A lamp that has gone out speaks of the passion and love you had for the Lord going out.

If you see a lamp going dim, it means that you are not feeding your spirit with the correct things, and as a result you are not able to hear His voice clearly. You are stumbling around in darkness!

Just one step in the right direction though, and He will be there to ignite your lamp again and give you fresh direction.

> *Matthew 25:3 Those who were foolish took their **lamps** and took no oil with them.*

It is important to feed your spirit all the time with the things of the Lord. If you only take in the things of the world, you starve your spirit. It will become dull, and you will not be able to hear the voice of the Lord clearly.

See also: Candle, Light

LEGS

Your ability to sustain and strengthen yourself through your own will.

POSITIVE
Before the days of airplanes and cars, your best bet was to find yourself a healthy horse or if you could not afford it, your legs just had to do!

Your legs speak of your ability to get yourself from one place to another, your very will to push ahead. As humans we continually strive forward.

This scripture could not have said it any better:

> *Psalms 147:10 He does not delight in the strength of the horse; He takes no pleasure in the **legs** of a man.*

When this ability is submitted to the Lord, we are able to run the race (Heb 12:1) that He has set before us. However, when you leave the Lord out of it, you will find yourself becoming tripped up.

If you dream of your legs being strengthened, it means that the Lord is going to strengthen your ability to get the job done! He has set a race before you and He intends for you to win it, but with His help!

NEGATIVE
Only those that have been through it understand the concept of a "leg-breaking" experience. In training the prophets, we try to familiarize them with it as soon as possible. It is a process where the Lord continually tries to bring a certain area to death in you.

The leg-breaking experience: However, as you continue to push through on your own and try to do things your own way, you end up like these two poor fellows:

> *John 19:32 Then the soldiers came and **broke the legs** of the first and of the other who was crucified with Him.*

You will note that Jesus' legs were not broken. He knew when to yield and He gave up His spirit willingly. If you dream that your legs are being broken, it means that the Lord is going to bring your will to complete death.

The pressure will come from circumstances and the world, just as the Roman soldiers were the ones to break the legs of the thieves.

Lame legs: To be lame means that your will has been taken away from you. You have given up on life and you do not try to push forward any longer. This is quite negative and is a very good picture of someone who has fallen into depression.

> *Proverbs 26:7 Like **the legs of the lame** that hang limp is a proverb in the mouth of fools.*

Jesus took time during His ministry to heal the lame and is still doing it today. No matter how weak you feel or how much has been taken from you, the Lord is here to restore you to full strength!

See also: Ankle, Back, Feet

LETTER

An expression of the heart.

Positive:

- Instruction expressed with emotion
- The thoughts and intentions of you or others

Negative: Curses

CHARACTER SPECIFIC SYMBOL

POSITIVE

A love letter from someone you care for is the Lord assuring you of His love. He is making His intentions clear to you and desires to reveal Himself to you.

NEGATIVE

"Sticks and stones can break my bones, but words will never harm me" is a fallacy! Words have the power to destroy our souls and to dream of a negative letter is the Lord revealing the source of your pain. You cannot ignore it forever. It is time to "go there" and receive the healing you need.

UNIVERSAL SYMBOL

POSITIVE

Paul is our best example when it comes to the use of letters in the Word. He sent out his thoughts, feelings and instructions from the Word. To have a vision of the Lord giving you a letter is clear – the Lord is revealing His heart to you and giving you some instruction to follow.

A letter differs from a scroll because of the emotional content. A scroll is a decree whereby a letter contains more than just instructions – but it also contains the heart of the writer! Take a good look at the emotion expressed in this instructional letter from Paul to the Corinthian church.

> *2 Corinthians 7:8-9 For even if I made you sorry with my letter, I do not regret it; though I did regret it. For I perceive that the same epistle made you sorry, though only for a while. Now I rejoice, not that you were made sorry, but that your sorrow led to repentance...*

Determine what kind of letter you are seeing. Is it from a particular group or person? The Lord is saying that their heart is friendly towards you!

NEGATIVE
Because letters contain so much heart, they also contain curses when the thoughts expressed are motivated by the enemy. If you see a negative letter in the spirit, the Lord is exposing the intents of the enemy. He wants to reveal the plans of the enemy to you, so that you can counter them!

> *Nehemiah 6:19 Also they reported his good deeds before me, and reported my words to him. Tobiah sent letters to frighten me.*

See also: Book, Pen, Scroll

LIGHT

Light in the darkness has always been a picture of hope. Light brings life, and in the Scripture the words life, light and love are used interchangeably.

Positive: Hope for the road ahead
Negative: Deception – angel of light

POSITIVE
The picture of the "light at the end of the tunnel" is common to most cultures. It speaks of hope and the end of a hard and difficult journey.

If you dream of this, then the Lord is telling you that soon you will have the breakthrough in your life you have been looking for.

You only need a small amount of light to remove the darkness, and to see a dark room being dispelled by light is a good picture. It means that the Lord is going to displace the darkness with His presence.

Here is one of my favorite passages on the subject:

> *2 Corinthians 4:6 For it is the God who commanded **light** to shine out of darkness, who has shone in our hearts to give the **light** of the knowledge of the glory of God in the face of Jesus Christ.*

When we see a curse in our lives or believe that the enemy is bringing attack, we ask the Lord to expose it just as it says in the Scripture below. Every single time I have asked the Lord to reveal the works of the enemy, He does so miraculously!

> *Ephesians 5:13 But all things that are exposed are made manifest by the **light**, for whatever makes manifest is light.*

NEGATIVE
I have had a lot of experience with people sharing their revelations with me, which were not of the Lord. In the symbol, *Angels* I share a bit more concerning this.

Any revelation or visitation you get where the "being" comes as a bright and powerful light, I advise you to be cautious of.

Anything that veils its face is not of the Lord, and if you are unsure about a revelation, ask the Lord for confirmation through someone else.

I have also found many who see many bright colored lights of different colors. This is also a very common phenomenon amongst those in the New Age cult.

If you are getting visions or dreams like this, it indicates that the enemy has an open door in your life to bring deception.

Look for any ties to false religion, anything in the occult, or even prophetic materials that promote out-of-body, heavenly experiences and strange angelic manifestations.

> *2 Corinthians 11:14 And no wonder! For Satan himself transforms himself into an angel of **light**.*

See also: Angels, Candle

LINEN

Linen was a fabric used for the purpose of ministry – specifically to the offices of priest and king. It speaks of being called and ordained to the work of the ministry to fulfill a specific purpose.

CHARACTER SPECIFIC AND UNIVERSAL SYMBOLS

POSITIVE
To dream of being given something linen to wear indicates that the Lord has called you to the work of the ministry and that you will be trained and prepared for this office. Linen garments or cloth in your hands speaks about the potential for ministry.

For example, if you are given linen to weave and give out, this would mean that the Lord wants you to train and equip His ministers – giving them what they need to fulfill their calling.

> *Leviticus 16:32 And the priest, who is anointed and consecrated to minister as priest in his father's place, shall make atonement, and put on the **linen** clothes, the holy garments;*

Of course David dancing before the Lord in a linen ephod is a good picture of fulfilling a ministry function, which he was doing as he worshipped God. Linen is mentioned in connection with the work of the ministry in most instances in Scripture.

This depended on the color of the linen or how wealthy it was and also on the office of the person wearing it. See *Colors* for more on the specific functions of the linen garment. Simple white linen is a picture of being called to the work of the ministry.

Finely woven and embroidered linen is a picture of a ministry leadership position.

Sheet: Fresh sheets or linens speak of a time of preparation where the Lord is wooing you into a time of intimacy with Him. It is a picture of intimacy and goes well with what I already shared regarding *Bed*.

NEGATIVE
Seeing moldy or dirty linen speaks of a contamination in a specific ministry or minister. It means that the person wearing the garment has hidden sin that is having an influence on those that he is ministering to.

Contaminated linen is also a picture of the works of the flesh. To see linen that is a patchwork and sewn together unevenly speaks of trying to embrace so many different kinds of ministries, that the person has lost their specific purpose.

When a king wore embroidered linen it accentuated his position and uniqueness. Linen that has been pieced together from many other garments indicates someone that does not have a clear conviction of their own calling.

Dirty sheets: This speaks of being defiled and being lured into sin. It means that you are bringing the world with you, into your relationship with the Lord. Consider this passage that speaks about the adulteress who lures someone to her bed.

> *Proverbs 7:16 I have spread my bed with tapestry, Colored coverings of Egyptian* ***linen***

Bloody sheets: If you continually dream or have visions of sheets that are bloody or dirty, there might also be an underlying hurt of the past you need to consider. Did you have a bad sexual experience in the past? It could well be that this experience is hindering you from coming into a relationship with the Lord. It also means that you need to break spiritual links with that person, because there is something remaining from that time that you need to let go of. It is contaminating your spirit and leaving a mark on your soul.

See also: Bed, Blue, Cloak, Colors

LION

The lion symbolizes many different things. Here are a few:

Positive:

- Royalty and strength
- Lord Jesus
- Defender of the righteous

Negative:

- Destruction and theft
- Satan
- Uncleanness

POSITIVE

A lion often speaks of the Lord Jesus. The Scriptures refer to him as the Lion of the tribe of Judah.

In a positive dream or vision, the lion would represent the Lord as your defender, as a king of strength, and of Him being able to care for and protect you.

Referring to Jesus:

> *Revelation 5:5 But one of the elders said to me, "Do not weep. Behold, the* ***Lion*** *of the tribe of Judah, the Root of David, has prevailed to open the scroll and to loose its seven seals."*

NEGATIVE

The enemy is also referred to as a lion, so you will need to discern if the vision is positive or negative.

In a negative context a lion can represent a spirit of destruction that has been given license through a curse in a person's life.

Referring to satan:

> *1 Peter 5:8 Be sober, be vigilant; because your adversary the devil walks about like a roaring* ***lion****, seeking whom he may devour.*

Referring to destruction and theft:

> *Psalms 7:2 Lest they tear me like a* ***lion****, rending me in pieces, while there is none to deliver.*

See also: Bear

Locust

If positive, they are a picture of your basic needs being provided for. Negatively they speak of a spirit of theft.

POSITIVE

The locust was one of the few insects that the Israelites were permitted to eat. So although it is not a common positive symbol, it is possible that they can speak of your basic needs being met.

NEGATIVE

Although the locust was used as a form of food in the Old Testament, it was known more for the theft it brought to God's people. Devouring crops and every green thing, it left only dust behind.

So the locust in particular is a very good picture of a spirit of theft being manifest in your life.

If you have seen the Lord provide, only to see the provision get suddenly eaten up by circumstances or unexpected expenses, then this is a clear indication of a curse in your life.

> *Deuteronomy 28:38 You shall carry much seed out to the field but gather little in, for the **locust** shall consume it.*

To identify where the enemy is getting license, see when these incidents of theft first began.

See also: Fruit, Insects

SYMBOLS STARTING IN M

SYMBOLS STARTING IN M

MAKE-UP

The image that you intentionally present to the world.

Positive: Confidence in who you are
Negative: Too focused on externals

POSITIVE
As a woman, dreaming of wearing beautiful make-up speaks of reflecting the beauty on the outside that you already have on the inside.

Make-up is also clearly a feminine thing and if you are not one to wear make-up and dream that you are, the Lord is trying to tell you that it is time to let out some of your femininity.

If you dream that you are wearing make-up that you do not usually wear, then the Lord is saying that it is time to change the way that you present yourself to the world.

NEGATIVE
Stripped: If you dream that your make-up has been removed, it means that you have lost your self-confidence and have given up trying to present yourself correctly.

It means that you, as a woman are feeling stripped and bare.

Messing up the application: To dream of messing up your make-up while applying it, is an indication of something you are struggling with right now. You keep trying to "get things right" but continue to mess up! This symbolizes your internal struggle – consider what you are going through in your life right now. It is time to come to peace!

As a man: If you are a man and dream you are putting on make-up then clearly the Lord is saying that you are trying to be something that you are not! That your representation of yourself is too feminine.

It could also be a warning dream to say that you have rejected your masculinity and that it is time to embrace it again.

Fussing over make-up: If you dream that you keep trying to apply your make-up correctly but that you cannot - this is negative. If you are getting stressed in the dream and running out of time, the Lord is telling you that you are too worried with externals.

He is saying that you are making too much of a fuss with what people see on the outside and about "getting things right" than simply shining out from the beauty within.

See also: Clothing, Dress, Hair

MAN

As an unknown figure in your dream or vision a man typically represents your masculine (animus) or intellectual side. In ministry it speaks of a teaching orientation.

CHARACTER SPECIFIC SYMBOL

A man you know: It is important to identify what the character in the dream means to you. If this is a man you know well, what do you think he symbolizes in your life?

Spiritual father: If he is a spiritual father to you, then he could speak of the Lord in your dreams.

Friend: If he is a friend from the past, identify what characteristic stands out to you the most about this person.

If he is a close friend that you often rely on when you need help, he can be a picture of the Holy Spirit to you.

Famous: Furthermore, if you dream of an actor or public figure, consider what he stands for. (This also applies to a woman character). It is common to dream of a famous character such as the president, actor or a pastor. What does this actor represent to you? What is their most outstanding characteristic? (Please note that if you are always dreaming of actors and having "movie" dreams this is simply an indication that you are filling your mind too much with what is in the world. You need to do some cleansing and feed things into your spirit that edifies!)

President: Now when you have a dream of such a person, instead of applying the dream directly to them, consider what they would represent. A president could be a representation of the World System or Government System.

A pastor in your dream, depending on your relationship with that pastor, could represent the church system or even the Lord's work in your life.

An unknown man: A familiar but unknown male character in an internal dream often speaks of your masculine side - the animus. This side is left-brained, analytical, and logical.

Spiritually speaking, a man in your dreams often represents a teaching function. Perhaps you might dream that you are embracing this strange man. This would mean that the Lord desires you to embrace your teaching orientation.

Perhaps you dream that a man that you are familiar with in your dream, but do not know in real life dies. This would mean that your analytical nature is being brought to death.

If the Lord has been leading you into a teaching orientation in ministry, you might dream of meeting or marrying a man that you feel comfortable with, but do not know in real life.

This dream would confirm your direction in moving towards a teaching function.

Review the *Woman* symbol for an all-round look at the animus and anima.

Universal Symbol

POSITIVE

If you see a man in vision, you will likely see someone you know, if they are a real person.

If you are in intercession, then you will likely see a person to direct your prayers towards. This person may actually look like you see in vision, or the vision you see may simply be a representation of what they stand for.

Take Paul's experience with the Macedonian that appeared to him in a dream telling him to come to them. Now the person he saw was not an actual person, but he represented the Macedonian people.

When I see demons or angels in the spirit, they are always masculine in gender. Depending on the level of demon, I will see various forms.

In the case of Paul, the Macedonian he saw was a positive vision. Consider what the man in your vision or external dream is wearing:

> *Acts 16:9 And a vision appeared to Paul in the night. A **man** of Macedonia stood and pleaded with him, saying, "Come over to Macedonia and help us.*

NEGATIVE

A vision of a negative man in Scripture would be Goliath. I have often seen a "spiritual Goliath" in vision.

Goliath represents the spirit of fear, and the Lord often leads me in intercession to break his stronghold over the lives of God's people.

Just take a look at what kind of influence Goliath had on God's people:

> *1 Samuel 17:24 And all the **men** of Israel, when they saw the **man**, fled from him and were dreadfully afraid.*

Goliath also represents your own fears that prevent you from rising up and moving forward.

See also: Father, Woman

MEAT

Universally, meat is a picture of food and having your hunger satisfied.

It is also the picture of solid doctrine.

It is also a picture though of gluttony and of the flesh. Once again, determine the context of your dream or vision for an accurate interpretation.

Positive: Spiritual maturity
Negative: Gluttony and disobedience

CHARACTER SPECIFIC SYMBOL

POSITIVE
If you enjoy eating meat, then this would be a picture of enjoyment and of having your desires not only met, but completely filled.

As a Christian though, if you dream of eating meat, then it likely has more of spiritual connotation and speaks of feeding on the Word of God and coming to a mature understanding of doctrine.

NEGATIVE
If you do not like eating meat or have strong feelings against it, then eating it in a dream would be an indication that you are feeding on things that you know you should not be feeding on.

You are violating your conscience. You need to discern in your own life if you have been feeding your spirit on the things of the Lord, or if you have allowed too much of the world into your life.

UNIVERSAL SYMBOL

POSITIVE
Meat is a wonderful picture of the more complex teachings of the Word. I have often seen myself in the spirit preparing meat and food to give out to others.

This is a picture of preparing the Word of God in such a way that it makes it appealing to others.

A good teacher knows how to take the Word and make it interesting to the hearer.

I used this extensively on my teaching on the Pastor Teacher. I shared how the pastor is like a skilled butcher, who takes a whole hindquarter and cuts it into smaller pieces that He can feed to God's people.

> *1 Corinthians 3:2 I have fed you with milk, and not with* ***meat****: for hitherto ye were not able to bear it, neither yet now are ye able. (KJV)*

NEGATIVE
The eating of meat can also speak of gluttony and of fulfilling only the desires of the flesh.

Although the Lord desires us to be blessed, by allowing the root of temporal values to take control, you can turn even the blessings of the Lord into a sin by dealing with them wrongly.

Consider the Israelites when the Lord sent them quails, and they ate so much that they became sick.

> *Psalms 78:18 And they tempted God in their heart by asking **meat** for their lust.*

See also: Boil, Food, Milk, Butcher

Mentor

As with all people in your dreams, your mentor has a specific meaning to you. Ask yourself the following questions:

1. *What did this mentor teach me?*
2. *What is the first thought that comes to mind when I think about this mentor?*
3. *What role has this mentor played in my life?*

Character Specific Symbol

POSITIVE
Very often a mentor will represent the part of your calling and ministry that they are working with. For example, when I was mentoring a disciple into prophetic office, when they dreamed about me, they knew the Lord was talking about their prophetic calling.

For others, I represent the Holy Spirit in their dreams, because I was the one who was always active in their lives, pushing them to excellence.

> *1 Corinthians 4:15 For though you might have ten thousand instructors in Christ, yet you do not have many fathers; for in Christ Jesus I have begotten you through the gospel.*

NEGATIVE
If your mentorship relationship left a negative influence in your life, then they can speak of old habits, a spirit of control, or hurts of the past. In my case, when I dream of a certain mentor of the past, I know the Lord is speaking about my "old man" that is raising its head in my life again.

Universal Symbol

If you are praying and have a vision of a current mentor, it is likely that the Lord is telling you to pray for them. It is also possible that as your relationship continues that the Lord might warn you when the separation is about to take place or if you are preempting that separation in your flesh!

It is not uncommon for me to pray for someone and see a mentor from the past with an umbilical cord linked to them. The message? It is time to break spiritual links with that mentor and to move on.

See also: Man, Umbilical Cord, Woman

Milk

Milk is a basic need for all human survival. It is a picture of the basic need for survival, relating both to the natural and the spiritual life.

Positive: Basic provision
Negative: Spiritual infancy

Character Specific Symbol

POSITIVE

Dreaming of milk refers to your basic need for survival. A baby cannot live without milk. It is the building block of the first stages of life, so it speaks of your basic needs.

If you dream of drinking milk, then it means that you are being strengthened.

If you have been getting into the Word, then this dream is an indication that the Scriptures are making you strong in the Lord.

Milk in the Scriptures is a picture of the first steps to understanding the Word. This could mean that you have finally understood the basics of the Word.

NEGATIVE

Sour milk is never positive, and speaks of opportunities that have gone bad. Although you had an opportunity to rise up or even enter into a promotion, this opportunity has now passed you.

Rotten milk speaks of a season that has passed that you cannot return to.

If you dream of drinking sour milk, it means that you keep trying to revive something that has long gone. Let it go. The Lord has many more opportunities for you.

For an internal prophetic dream, drinking milk could be an indication that you are too immature for the more weighty teachings of the Word.

Perhaps the Lord is taking you back to doctrinal basics so that you can build up from there.

Universal Symbol

POSITIVE

Where meat speaks of the more mature teachings of the Word, milk speaks of the basic understanding of Scriptures; the building blocks of your faith.

> *1 Peter 2:2 as newborn babes, desire the pure milk of the word, that you may grow thereby.*

Although many believe that we must only teach "meat", the milk must come first.

You cannot give a newborn baby meat to eat! They have to start with the milk. If the process is followed through correctly, then the child can progress.

The same applies to your spiritual walk. You might want to eat the meat of the Word, but are still at a level of immaturity where you still need the milk.

This is a nourishing phase and you should not skip it. It will be the foundation for your Christian faith that can be built on later on.

Milk as a blessing: Milk was also a picture of blessing and wealth in Scriptures. It was a lot like meat, in that it did more than just meet your need, but your desires also.

To see the Lord pouring milk over you or giving you milk, means that He wants to grant you the desires of your heart.

> *Jeremiah 32:22 You have given them this land, of which You swore to their fathers to give them - a land flowing with **milk** and honey.*

Breast milk: The Scriptures often speak of breast milk. It is a picture of the blessing and abundance that you currently have.

When the Lord told the Israelites that they would drink the milk from the breast of kings, He was saying that they would get to have all the goodness that the Gentile kings possessed.

To dream or have a vision of feeding off someone who is a picture of blessing to you, means that you will partake of their blessing.

NEGATIVE

Breast milk: In a negative light, the Lord said to the Israelites that others would drink the milk from their breasts. This meant that others would come and take all the blessings they had away from them.

To dream or see a vision of others feeding off you means that they are taking the goodness and blessing from you and you are losing it.

Needing to still be fed on milk is also a picture of being immature and not ready for the more meaty things of the Word.

> *Hebrews 5:13 For everyone who partakes only of* ***milk*** *is unskilled in the word of righteousness, for he is a babe.*

See also: Breast, Baby

MIRROR

A reflection of who you are or want to be.

Positive: The image that you are being conformed to
Negative: Being conformed to the flesh instead of the Spirit

CHARACTER SPECIFIC SYMBOL

POSITIVE
To dream of looking into a mirror and seeing a good reflection is an indication of how the Lord sees you. It might not be how you see yourself, but the Lord looks past the outside and into your heart. If you have been struggling with your self-image, then this dream would mean that the Lord is trying to give you a new picture of yourself.

To receive a new mirror also means that the Lord wants you to look at yourself and your life with new eyes.

To see a mirror suddenly clear up means that the Lord is about to reveal things to you about your life that were hidden to you before.

NEGATIVE
To see a bad reflection of yourself in a mirror could have two meanings. Either you have a bad self-image and this picture is how you see yourself, or it is a picture of your spiritual condition. The Lord sees to the heart and although everything might look good on the outside, on the inside you are full of "dead men's bones." (Matthew 23:27)

UNIVERSAL SYMBOL

POSITIVE
In vision, the Lord put me in front of a mirror, but instead of my own reflection I saw the Lord Jesus as if He was standing just behind me. The Lord told me to continue looking at that reflection and as I did, the Holy Spirit came and began to work on me until I looked just like Jesus. After that experience, this scripture came to life for me.

> *2 Corinthians 3:18 But we all, with unveiled face, beholding as in a* ***mirror*** *the glory of the Lord, are being transformed into the same image from glory to glory, just as by the Spirit of the Lord.*

NEGATIVE
If you see someone looking at a negative reflection, this is a picture of how they see themselves. It is not a true image of how God sees them and they need ministry. This scripture is your guideline.

> *1 Corinthians 13:12 For now we see in a **mirror**, dimly, but then face to face. Now I know in part, but then I shall know just as I also am known.*

This scripture speaks of maturity and coming to know who we really are in Christ. To see ourselves as Christ sees us.

See also: Glasses

MISCARRIAGE

The loss of either a curse or promise.

Positive: To expel a work of the flesh
Negative: To lose a promise

CHARACTER SPECIFIC SYMBOL

If you are prone to miscarriage in your family and life, then dreaming of miscarriage is a representation of your hidden fears. It does not mean that you will miscarry, but rather that your fear is haunting you. Note that a dream of miscarriage can also be a healing dream.

What are you miscarrying? Are you miscarrying the child of someone that represents something negative to you? This dream is positive. It means that you are "expelling" whatever that negative thing is from your life.

UNIVERSAL SYMBOL

POSITIVE
Not all miscarriage dreams and visions are negative! Just as in the natural, the body will miscarry a malformed fetus, so also dreaming or seeing a vision of miscarrying something dark and unclean is good! It means that you are ridding yourself of the curse!

As a man: As a man, you will likely dream of a woman miscarrying the baby. Determine what the woman means to you.

Someone else miscarrying: Again, determine what that person means in your dream or vision. Do they represent your local church fellowship? Do they represent your calling or a specific group of people? From there you need to determine if a curse is being dealt with or if a promise is being stolen!

NEGATIVE
Miscarriage was seen as a sign of a curse in the Word. A fruitful womb was considered a blessing to the Lord. So if you have a dream or vision of miscarriage that is not meant to be, it means that God's promise is dying! Have you been walking in obedience? Has something contaminated your spirit? Now is the time to FIGHT for your promise and to cling to this spiritual baby in your womb.

> *Exodus 23:26 No one shall suffer miscarriage or be barren in your land; I will fulfill the number of your days.*

Stillbirth: A stillborn baby is slightly different in interpretation, because it speaks of a promise that has not reached completion. You stopped running the race, just before you reached the goal!

If the stillborn baby is something that was meant to die, then the Lord saved you from the work of the enemy. Before he could finish his plans against you, the Lord brought them to an end, and they will not see the light.

> *Psalms 58:8 Let them be like a snail which melts away as it goes, like a stillborn child of a woman, that they may not see the sun.*

Abortion: The deliberate destruction of either a promise or curse. For the most part though, dreaming of abortion is negative. It means that you have a hand in destroying God's promise to you.

See also: Baby, Birth, Pregnant

MONEY

Money does not look the same today as it did in the time of the Old Testament. However, the concept of trade and exchange certainly is the same.

For more understanding on what money means in Scripture, look up gold and silver.

Positive: Provision for needs or desires
Negative: Theft or greed

CHARACTER SPECIFIC SYMBOL

POSITIVE
In a positive light, money speaks of provision for your need.

If you are having financial difficulties and dream of receiving large amounts of finances, then it is simply a picture of your desires at the moment.

Often people dream of receiving money, but unfortunately it does not mean that this will happen in reality.

I do believe it is an encouragement from the Lord to say that He desires to meet your need. However, it is going to take more on your part to make that a reality.

This dream was sent to give you hope, but you also need faith and love to bring it to pass.

Dreaming of money is either an indication of your current desire, or a confirmation that the Lord will provide your need.

Universal Symbol

POSITIVE
Although I have seen visions of money, I usually see it as gold coins in the spirit.

Often I will see a treasure chest that is hidden and filled with money. When I see this, I know that the Lord is saying that He has provided our need, but that we must release it through prayer.

If I see the money hidden, it is speaking of a blessing that is not so clear, but that I have to make effort to look for.

If you see money along your road, it means that as you continue along the direction that the Lord has for you, the blessing will come automatically.

NEGATIVE
In prayer, I have often seen a black hand holding onto money. This is a picture of a spirit of theft. The enemy was stealing the blessing that God had for us.

Also in Scripture, the love of money refers to the root of temporal values which can destroy you. It speaks of bribery, corruption, and as I said before, the root of temporal values.

> *1 Timothy 6:10 For the love of **money** is a root of all kinds of evil, for which some have strayed from the faith in their greediness, and pierced themselves through with many sorrows.*

See also: Briefcase, Coins, Gold, Silver

Monkey

Irritation, mischief and a work of the enemy in your life.

More often than not when I see a monkey in the spirit it is representative of a power demon and an attack in your life.

See also: Demons

MOTHER

A picture of a mother speaks of nurturing, healing and restoration. The mother is the one who cares for the child and feeds it. The role of the mother is also to "lay down the law" in the heart of a child. In other words, to give the child a pattern for life.

CHARACTER SPECIFIC SYMBOL

You need to assess your relationship with your mother to discern if she is a positive or a negative picture in your dreams.

If you did not have a good relationship with your mother and she did not know the Lord, she could represent the flesh in your dreams.

She could represent, pride, jealousy, anger - all depending on what your relationship with her was in the natural.

If you have a good relationship with your mother, she could represent the church in your dreams. Your father often representing the Lord, this would then make your mother a representation of the church (the Church being the bride of Christ).

UNIVERSAL SYMBOL

Depending on the person you are seeing in your vision, the vision could relate to an actual person or simply be a representation of a type of person or group.

Read up on *Man* and *Woman* for more details on people in visions.

If you see someone fulfilling a mothering role, then the Lord would be indicating that they are called to nurture and mature His people. This is a pastoral function.

When giving personal ministry I often see a person holding a baby, as a mother. Now this is not always literal. What it could speak of is that they are about to birth a new ministry.

Always share a vision with someone to see if they can witness with it before jumping to any interpretations.

Referring to how a mother is accepting and loving of her child:

> *Proverbs 4:3 When I was my father's son, tender and the only one in the sight of my **mother**.*

NEGATIVE

When giving personal counsel I often see the actual mother of the person I am praying for. When this happens then I know that the Lord wants to deal with an issue that involved their mother.

There might be a generational curse coming from their mother's line that needs to be broken, or negative words she spoke over them.

It might even mean that their mother had caused childhood hurts that need to be addressed. Be sensitive to the Holy Spirit.

Speaking of generational bondage and sin:

> *1 Kings 22:52 He did evil in the sight of the Lord, and walked in the way of his father and in the way of his* ***mother*** *and in the way of Jeroboam the son of Nebat, who had made Israel sin;*

See also: Family, Father, Woman

MOON

A change of season in your life. Because the moon only rises in the evening, it shares the same interpretation as Night.

Negatively the moon and stars were often the object of pagan worship. Even today the stars are used by the world and fortune tellers to try and tell the future. Star signs and seeing any form of zodiac is demonic and represents the spirit of divination

See also: Darkness, Night.

MOTH

A slow devouring process of corruption and theft that is easily overcome

Positive: If the moth is colorful and beautiful, it has the same interpretation as butterfly
Negative:

- Theft
- Love of money

CHARACTER SPECIFIC SYMBOL

POSITIVE

Do you study moths or have a personal fascination with them? If not, then they are likely a universal symbol in your dreams.

NEGATIVE

Most of us has a relative who is terrified of the smallest moth! If you are one of those relatives, then a moth in your dream would speak of a spirit of fear!

Universal Symbol

POSITIVE
To escape or do away with a moth is very positive. It means that what you have belongs to the Lord and that He will protect you from every theft of the enemy. This passage says it beautifully.

> *Matthew 6:20 "Do not lay up for yourselves treasures on earth, where moth and rust destroy and where thieves break in and steal.*

NEGATIVE
This scripture speaks of how those whose security is their money will lose it all in the end. It speaks about the love of money. To see a moth in a vision or prophetic dream indicates firstly that something has been stolen from you. However, the reason it was stolen was the license you gave to the enemy through the love of money.

> *James 5:2 Your riches are corrupted, and your garments are moth-eaten.*

There is good news! It does not take much to destroy a moth, and its theft is slow and steady. If you leave the sin unchecked, then it will do its work over time. However, when you recognize this work of the enemy, you can easily overcome with a simple change of heart!

See also: Butterfly, Insects, Rust, Worm

Mountain

A mountain in any context speaks of a new journey and obtaining new heights. It can also be an obstacle in your way that you need to conquer.

Positive: An opportunity for promotion
Negative: An obstacle from the enemy

Character Specific Symbol

POSITIVE
If you are someone that enjoys mountain climbing, then your dream would speak of your hobbies and interests.

However, for most people, a mountain will speak of a new goal or level for you to attain. It is a promise of a promotion and seeing a new perspective on things.

NEGATIVE
A mountain in a negative light speaks of an obstacle that is preventing you from reaching your personal goals.

It could be that you are struggling to complete a project or go in a certain direction. Dreaming of a mountain in your road is a confirmation of the blockage.

You will need wisdom to discern if this is a mountain you must tackle or one you need to walk around and avoid.

Of course as believers, when the enemy puts a mountain in our way, we have the authority to pluck it up and cast it into the sea!

Universal Symbol

POSITIVE

For both visions and prophetic dreams, the mountain is a very positive picture! It speaks of an opportunity for you to receive a promotion in the realm of the spirit.

However, it is not going to come without effort. Climbing a mountain is hard work and it will require a lot from you.

It will mean leaving some things behind that you have relied on before. It will mean leaving behind everything you were and possessed, so that you can take hold of the new thing.

In *The Moses Mandate* I share how the Moses apostle is called to the mountain top many times. It is here that He will come into that face-to-face relationship with Jesus and also get his mandate.

A mountain in the Scriptures is often a picture of the presence of God. It is an apt image as it comes with a price. It means leaving behind your own ideas and everything that weighs you down, to come into His presence.

Moses had to obey some strict conditions before climbing the mountain into the Lord's presence. However, the journey was worth it, because there he experienced the glory of God!

Have you been asking the Lord to experience Him in a greater way? If so, then seeing a mountain is a call from the Lord to take the first step; to submit to going through the death and letting go of the old, so that you can take on the new.

Just like in real life, it will be a hard climb. However just as Moses discovered, it will be well worth it when you get to experience God in a new and powerful way.

> *Exodus 24:17 The sight of the glory of the Lord was like a consuming fire on the top of the **mountain** in the eyes of the children of Israel.*

NEGATIVE

When praying for someone or for personal needs, I have often seen a mountain in my path.

This is a negative picture and speaks of an obstacle that the enemy has put there.

It is also a good picture of how you feel when you come to the Lord with a big prayer request. It seems to loom over you, making you feel small and insignificant.

However, you can overcome it! If you see a mountain across your path and you feel that it is something that the enemy has put there, then it is something for you to remove in the name of Jesus.

This is a call to spiritual warfare. I suggest that you get your hands on *The Strategies of War* book for some very practical teaching on this subject.

> *Mark 11:23 For assuredly, I say to you, whoever says to this* ***mountain****, be removed and be cast into the sea, and does not doubt in his heart, but believes that those things he says will be done, he will have whatever he says.*

If you are facing a mountain in your life right now, take this passage, memorize and confess it until it is deep in your spirit. Then stand against that mountain and it will give way!

See also: Bridge, Ladder

MOUSE

A bothersome, niggling attack on your daily blessing.

Positive: Your problem is smaller than you realize
Negative: Consistent attack on your daily provision

POSITIVE
If you have a pet mouse that you are fond of, it likely represents a responsibility or something that is important to you. Read more under *Pet* for clarification on this.

NEGATIVE
Mice are completely negative in scripture.

In most cases, if you see mice in a dream or vision, they are referring to a spirit of theft that is nibbling away at your blessing.

Mice also came in plagues and destroyed everything in their path. They were certainly not seen as a blessing. (1 Sam 6:4)

A rat is similar to a mouse but depicts a greater level of theft and destruction. It is also synonymous with disease because of the black plague and speaks of something being unclean.

See also: Pet

MOUTH

If our eyes are the windows to our souls, our mouths are certainly the doorway!

Positive: The potential to bless
Negative: The potential to curse

Out of our mouths come both words of blessing and cursing. The Word is clear that it is not what passes into our mouths that is a problem, but what comes out of them.

> *James 3:10 Out of the same **mouth** proceed blessing and cursing. My brethren, these things ought not to be so.*
> *11 Does a spring send forth fresh water and bitter from the same opening*

What comes out of your mouth, especially when you are under pressure, is a direct representation of what is really inside of you.

Similarly the tongue has the same meaning as the mouth. It refers to the words we speak.

POSITIVE
A mouth is a good picture of the words we speak.

To see a vision of fresh water or oil coming from your mouth is a good picture. It means that you are speaking the words of the Lord and everyone around you will be blessed by it.

NEGATIVE
This Scripture below is a perfect illustration of curses that are spoken over others. These curses can be in a form of simply speaking negatively over someone, or also praying your own will over their lives instead of what the Lord wants you to pray.

This also includes praying against someone's personal will.

> *Revelation 16:13 And I saw three unclean spirits like frogs coming out of the mouth of the dragon, out of the mouth of the beast, and out of the mouth of the false prophet.*

The untrained tongue is poison and evil, according to James:

> *James 3:6 And the tongue is a fire, a world of iniquity. The tongue is so set among our members that it defiles the whole body, and sets on fire the course of nature; and it is set on fire by hell.*

Fire coming from the mouth is a picture of speaking curses and destroying others with the words of your mouth.

See also: Darts, Eyes, Jaw, Teeth

MUMMY

To see someone wrapped up in the clothing of a mummy is an indication that they are "tied up" and in spiritual bondage. This bondage could be a result from the work of the enemy, but also from trying to hide away from something.

Have you ever heard the saying, "To tie yourself up in knots"? This is valid here as well. It means to get yourself so worked up and bound, that you cannot go anywhere.

Either way, this speaks of restriction and unlike the cocoon of a butterfly, this is very negative. In a cocoon something wonderful is happening and it is a season of being hidden so that you can grow.

Being wrapped up as a mummy though speaks of a process of slow death, meant to suffocate your spiritual life.

See also: Cocoon

MUSIC

A resonance in the natural of what is going on in the realm of the spirit.

CHARACTER SPECIFIC SYMBOL

POSITIVE

Music is a powerful force and unique to us as humans. While animals can sing by instinct, humans have the ability to create a variety of melodies. Music is a spiritual act and an expression of what is going on in our spirits.

So if you dream of playing music or of singing then you are simply expressing what is deep down in your spirit. It is likely that you are not aware in reality of what is going on inside of you. Music and singing in your dreams is a reflection of that.

So if you are singing beautifully or playing a musical instrument that you always wanted to, it means that there is a "new song in your spirit." In other words, the Lord is doing something new in your life that is about to manifest outwardly.

If your song is sad, then it is a picture of what is going on in the spirit realm. Either you are dealing with a personal grief or you are sensing the heart of the Lord for His Church.

Musical instruments: Identify the instrument you are playing. Is it familiar to you? If so, what era of your life does it represent? The first instrument I learned to play was the drums and so when I dream of playing the drums, I know the Lord is speaking of my music ministry in general.

I learned much later to play the piano and at that time the Holy Spirit was revealing Himself to me. So when I dream of playing piano, I know that the Holy Spirit is trying to get my attention to walk in His power again.

So what does the instrument mean to you? Is it one you always wanted to play? If so, then it speaks of a desire. Is it one that you struggle to play? In that case it speaks of your insecurities.

NEGATIVE
To struggle to play music or to hear discord is a clear warning. It means that something is wrong in your spiritual life right now. You are experiencing a blockage that is preventing what God is saying in your spirit to come out. There is a block between the realm of the spirit and experiencing God for yourself.

The context of your dream will indicate where that blockage is coming from. It could be that you are trying to use worldly things to walk out your calling. Discord in the spirit also means that what God is saying and what you are doing are not lining up.

Universal Symbol

POSITIVE AND NEGATIVE
I often hear music in the spirit, but this is not common to everyone. Music is vital to ministry and even Elisha called for a harpist to calm his spirit.

I love the picture in the book of Job where he is speaking of the creation of the world and then goes on to say,

> *Job 38:7 When the morning stars* ***sang*** *together, and all the sons of God shouted for joy?*

As God created this very world there was music in the air as the angels sang. As a musician, this inspires me each time I worship. Each time we worship the angels sing along with us. If you flow in the gift of discerning of spirits, you might see worship angels.

Be sensitive to the music you hear in the spirit. If you hear a funeral dirge, then the Lord is talking to you of a spiritual death. I teach it as hearing the "Music in the Music" in the *Prophetic Anointing*.

Musical instruments: If you see a particular instrument in the spirit when praying then it can have a variety of meanings. It could be that the Lord wants you to play that instrument. It could mean you need to give that instrument away or that the Lord wants to give you a spiritual gift.

Harp: There are many different musical instruments in scripture that have a clear meaning. For example, when I see a harp in the spirit, I know that the Lord is talking about an anointing for psalmody.

Sheet music: If I see music sheets, He is talking about songwriting and composing.

Tambourine: A tambourine is often accompanied by dance and I am reminded of Miriam who led the women in song. When I see this then I know the Lord is speaking about music relating specifically to the ministry of the prophet.

Trumpet: A trumpet is a good picture of a decree going into the earth.

A band: A picture of flowing in the spirit as one.

See also: Dancing, Harp, Instruments, Singing

SYMBOLS STARTING IN N

Symbols Starting in N

Naked/Nakedness

Nakedness in both dreams and visions speaks of being vulnerable and exposed.

Positive: Vulnerability
Negative: Shame and prevalent past hurts

Character Specific Symbol

POSITIVE
Perhaps you are someone that is not comfortable with opening up to others. If you dream of being naked and you do not care, it means that you are coming to the place where you are comfortable with being transparent with others.

So if you dream of walking around naked, but it does not bother you, it only means that you are being transparent and that you have nothing to hide. In ministry this is certainly a good thing.

NEGATIVE
If you are naked in your dream and you are uncomfortable with it, then it means that you feel exposed or vulnerable at the moment. You feel that you are overwhelmed and that you cannot handle the situation that you are in.

It can also mean that you are perhaps being a little TOO transparent with people that you should not be sharing absolutely everything with.

Although we need to be open to the Lord and our fellow believers, there are times when we need to keep things to ourselves so that the enemy does not get wind of what God is doing.

Universal Symbol

POSITIVE
In my book, *The Journey of Tamar* there is a chapter where she is stripped of all her old clothing so that she can be clothed again in something new. It was a picture of the process the Lord took me through and one many believers face.

As you have looked to the Lord for blessing or a new ministry, He is going to take you through change. It will mean letting go of the old and allowing Him to strip you first. Only then can He give you the new blessing that He has for you.

If you have desired to enter into a relationship with the Lord and you see yourself (or someone else) naked, the interpretation is clear.

The Lord is saying that before you can progress you need to allow yourself to be naked before Him.

He already knows your sins and your failures, so you do not need to fear. However, unless you let down your guard and allow the Lord into those secret parts of your life, you will never progress.

You never need to feel afraid of being naked before the Lord, because He does not intend to leave you that way. He simply intends to heal your wounds and re-clothe you in royalty!

> *Genesis 2:25 And they were both **naked**, the man and his wife, and were not ashamed.*

NEGATIVE
Nakedness spoke of shame in Scripture, and this is certainly true when you have faced hurts in your life.

If you see yourself (or someone else in personal ministry) naked, dirty and bleeding, it is a picture of the hurts you have endured in the past and that still plague you today.

See also: Bathroom, Shower

NAVEL

Your belly button is proof of your heritage and it is also a place of weakness.

Out of the entire belly this is a vulnerable spot and it points to the middle of you. It is a representation of who you are and where you come from.

Positive: Secure in being vulnerable
Negative: A generational curse

POSITIVE
It speaks of the things that you feel most vulnerable about. In this lovely verse Solomon speaks of the navel of the one he loves.

In it he is revealing the intimacy they have and also her vulnerability.

> *Song of Songs 7:2 Your **navel** is a rounded goblet; it lacks no blended beverage. Your waist is a heap of wheat set about with lilies.*

NEGATIVE
If you dream that your naval or belly button is dirty or damaged in some way, it means that you are struggling with being vulnerable.

It is also an indication of defilement and is very likely referring to a generational curse that the Lord is trying to expose in your life.

See also: Stomach, Umbilical Cord

NECK

A neck holds up and turns the head. It speaks of strength and of direction. Also when a neck is broken, you die instantly so it is also a picture of your life.

Positive: Strong and victorious
Negative: Bearing burdens that are not yours to carry

UNIVERSAL SYMBOL

POSITIVE
To lay down your own neck, means to give your life for someone else. Have you ever heard the saying "putting your neck on the line for someone"? Apostle Paul used the same expression:

> *Romans 16:4 who risked their own **necks** for my life, to whom not only I give thanks, but also all the churches of the Gentiles.*

It means to both give up your life and your strengths for others.

In the Scripture the Lord promises that we will put our foot on the necks of our enemies. This means that we can overcome every work of the enemy in His name.

A strong neck could also be a positive picture of strength.

> *Job 41:22 Strength dwells in his **neck**, and sorrow dances before him.*

NEGATIVE
A yoke on your neck speaks of cares you have been forced to take on. These cares were put on you by others, and they are not of the Lord.

The Scriptures tell us that His yoke is easy and His burden is light!

To be stiff-necked speaks of being stubborn and insisting on doing your own thing, instead of obeying the voice of the Lord.

It also speaks of pride and of arrogance. Consider these passages:

> *Psalms 75:5 Do not lift up your horn on high; do not speak with a stiff **neck**.*

In other words, do not be arrogant and stubborn, thinking you have all the answers!

> *Acts 7:51 You stiff- **necked** and uncircumcised in heart and ears! You always resist the Holy Spirit; as your fathers did, so do you.*

See also: Back, Head

NECKLACE

A necklace speaks of both a position and also a picture of the things you believe.

Positive: To believe and act on the things God has promised
Negative: To be bound with a doctrine that is not of God

CHARACTER SPECIFIC SYMBOL

POSITIVE

Necklace in a positive context speaks of receiving a blessing or an honor, especially if it is gold.

NEGATIVE

If you dream of receiving a necklace that is heavy or black, it means you are in bondage to something.

UNIVERSAL SYMBOL

POSITIVE

The Israelites were told to tie the law of God around their necks, so that they would never forget it. It is a picture of the covenant we are in with the Lord, and a reminder of His promises. (Proverbs 6:21)

If you see the Lord giving you a necklace in the Spirit, He is reminding you of the blessing and position that you have because you are in covenant with Him as a believer.

It is a picture of honor and promotion in the spirit.

> *Genesis 41:42 Then Pharaoh took his signet ring off his hand and put it on Joseph's hand; and he clothed him in garments of fine linen and put a* ***gold chain around his neck****.*

NEGATIVE

Because the necklace is a picture of the law around our necks, a heavy and black necklace speaks of being in bondage.

It means that you have rather believed the words of the enemy and he has bound you and kept you down. He has prevented you from standing in all the blessings that God has for you.

Literal necklace: In the spirit when praying for someone, we have received revelation concerning the actual necklace they are wearing. Sometimes jewelry can be contaminated with something demonic.

On one occasion we prayed for one gentleman who had a lovely gold chain. However, all of the team kept feeling that this object was oppressed.

He shared that he got it from his parents who were into the occult. It turned out that it had been prayed over before being given to him. He had worn it since childhood.

Getting rid of that necklace was the best thing he ever did, and certainly broke the generational curses he was struggling with at the time.

See also: Gold, Jewelry, Ring

NET

If positive, a net represents mass evangelism or connecting with others. To be part of a group.

Negatively it speaks of the snare of the enemy.

Positive: A positive connection to others that share the same spiritual DNA
Negative: Connections that are designed to trap and not support you

CHARACTER SPECIFIC SYMBOL

Depending on the context of your dream, a net could be positive or negative.

Negatively speaking a net represents being bound, restricted and being under bondage.

Positively speaking, it could represent evangelism (in the case of catching fish), prosperity and provision.

UNIVERSAL SYMBOL

POSITIVE
One of our students shared once how the Lord kept showing them a vision of a net over their bed. They searched and searched but could not find the interpretation to this vision.

It did not seem negative, yet still there was no interpretation. Then one day as he browsed the Internet, the Lord led him to AMI Network. All along the Lord was indicating that he was to become part of a network of believers and ministry leaders.

So in this case the net spoke of linking up with other believers around the world.

Seeing a net in a fishing picture speaks of evangelism, the Lord bringing provision and blessing.

Speaking of provision and blessing:

> *John 21:11 Simon Peter went up and dragged the net to land, full of large fish, one hundred and fifty- three; and although there were so many, the **net** was not broken.*

NEGATIVE
In vision I have often seen the enemy using a net to snare and to steal.

Often when we have been trusting the Lord for provision, I have seen the enemy having horded all our provision into his net. I would then speak forth and demand that he let go of that provision!

When giving personal ministry, I have also seen people bound up in nets. Usually the nets speak of negative words and curses spoken over the person.

It could also be because of personal sin and getting involved in things they should not have. And so they have given satan license to bind them and bring a curse into their lives.

Referring to a net laid by those who speak negative words and a curse over someone:

> *Psalms 35:7 For without cause they have hidden their **net** for me in a pit, which they have dug without cause for my life.*

See also: Fish, Trap

NIGHT

Positive: A season of rest
Negative: Hidden works of the enemy

POSITIVE
Although in many ways nighttime speaks of a time when the enemy is most active, it is also a season of rest. It is during the night that God speaks to us in our dreams and where we find our rest, ready to face the next day.

To dream of a sunset means that your hard work is over and it is time to rest in the Lord and to let Him complete what He has begun.

> *Song of Songs 1:13 A bundle of myrrh is my beloved to me, that lies all **night** between my breasts.*

Midnight: Midnight speaks of a time of dramatic transition coming in your life. The Lord killed all the firstborn of Egypt at midnight (Exodus 12:29). It was also at midnight that Boaz saw Ruth at his feet. (Ruth 3:8)

Pillar of fire: Although the Lord led the Children of Israel by a pillar of cloud by day, by night He led with a pillar of fire.

This is a lovely picture of the power of the Lord. It is during those times when we cannot see our own way or do things with our own strength that God comes with His power. If you see a pillar of fire, the Lord is saying that it is time to stop your own striving and to stand back so that He can move in power (Exodus 13:21)!

NEGATIVE

If you dream of night falling and you sense fear or something negative, then the Lord is warning you that the enemy is at work. This season is not of Him.

If you dream of yourself walking in darkness, then the Lord is saying that it is time to get back into His light!

> *1 Thessalonians 5:5 You are all sons of light and sons of the day. We are not of the* ***night*** *nor of darkness.*

See also: Darkness, Day, Light

NOSE

To be led by your emotions.

Positive: To be aware of the inner mechanics of your decisions
Negative: To be led astray by emotion

CHARACTER SPECIFIC SYMBOL

POSITIVE

Because our noses are a vital sense in the natural to warn us of danger and to evoke pleasure, a good smell in a dream is a symbol of joy. Determine the smell. Is it a smell from childhood? Smell evokes emotion! What emotion does the smell in your dream evoke?

NEGATIVE

To "put your nose in the air" or to "look down your nose" at others speaks of being haughty and arrogant. To dream of your nose being broken means that your arrogance is going to lead you into hitting a wall.

> *Proverbs 16:18 Pride goes before destruction, And a haughty spirit before a fall.*

UNIVERSAL SYMBOL

POSITIVE

The Lord is often angry when He sees His people being destroyed. I love this Psalm where it is speaking of God's greatness. Look at this verse where it expresses how God responds to His servant that is under attack from the ungodly:

Psalms 18:8 Smoke went up from His nostrils, and devouring fire from His mouth; Coals were kindled by it.

A positive dream about a nose speaks of that person's emotion. Is the person's nose you are dreaming of a representation of the Lord in your dreams? The Lord is expressing His strong emotion towards you!

NEGATIVE
A strong and negative nose speaks of arrogance and thinking yourself "holier" than others. To have a vision of someone "looking down their nose" speaks of a haughty spirit.

Isaiah 65:5 Who say, 'Keep to yourself, Do not come near me, For I am holier than you! 'These are smoke in My nostrils, a fire that burns all the day.

Bloody nose: A bloody nose speaks of offense that is not being handled correctly. Yes, emotions have been crushed and "wrath" has come out of it, however how you respond in this moment can produce strife or holiness.

Proverbs 30:33 For as the churning of milk produces butter, and wringing the nose produces blood, So the forcing of wrath produces strife.

NUMBERS

I am not fond of people using numbers to find hidden meanings into dreams and visions. I find that instead of sticking to the Word, many try to break numbers down using human logic, myth and tradition.

However, there are some clear numbers mentioned many times in Scripture, that I will share here.

Please be wary of interpreting every little number that you see as a "sign", as this is no different to the pagans who looked for signs in everything except the Word of God!

Ensure that every symbol has its root in the Word and you cannot go wrong!

One: A lovely picture of unity.

The Lord, even though He is a trinity, is also one. The three being one and the one three. This is a perfect unity.

The Word also speaks of the husband and wife no longer being two, but becoming one.

Two: A picture of balance.

There were two cherubim on the mercy seat. When the number 2 is used in the Word, you will see that they were used in context of objects that were strategically placed to balance one another out.

> *Exodus 25:19 Make one cherub at one end, and the other cherub at the other end; you shall make the cherubim at the **two** ends of it of one piece with the mercy seat.*

Even marriage is a testimony of this, of two becoming one. If you dream that one is missing out of the "two" it means that something is out of balance in your life. If you are single, it could also mean that you need or will receive that other "someone" that will complete you.

Three: The number of the Trinity, as well as the number of days Jesus spent in the grave. It is also the number of days that Jonah spent in the belly of the whale.

Jesus also had three disciples (Peter, James and John), who He shared more with than the others.

King David, although he had thirty mighty men, there were three who were considered mightier than all the thirty.

So the number three can mean various things in a vision. It can speak of coming into a relationship with the Lord completely. However, as in a time period, it can also speak of a season of death to the flesh.

> *Matthew 12:40 For as Jonah was **three** days and **three** nights in the belly of the great fish, so will the Son of Man be **three** days and **three** nights in the heart of the earth.*

When speaking of people, it could speak of your inner circle of contacts or your ministry team.

Five: This is the number of man and a reference to the fivefold ministry.

Seven: This is the number of completion. It represents the end of a season in your life. You have completed the task that was set before you and it is now time for you to enter into rest.

There are many references to the number seven in Scriptures.

The Lord created the earth in seven days. The walls of Jericho came down after seven days.

It is what you would call God's number of perfection. It represents a season of rest, fruitfulness and completion.

> *Genesis 2:2 And on the **seventh** day God ended His work which He had done, and He rested on the **seventh** day from all His work which He had done.*

Twelve: It is a good picture of maturity and being ready for the next phase in your life.

This is the number of the twelve tribes of Israel. Jesus also had twelve disciples.

Jesus was 12 when He went to the temple. Only after he had appointed the 12 could their ministry really begin.

> *Luke 6:13 And when it was day, He called His disciples to Himself; and from them He chose **twelve** whom He also named apostles;*

Also only once Israel had his 12 sons, could his heritage be established.

The book of Revelation speaks of trees that will produce twelve different fruits.

The woman with the issue of blood was healed after suffering for 12 full years.

Seeing twelve people could refer to a ministry team that you are either a part of, or that you are in charge of.

Thirty: A picture of redemption. Jesus was sold by Judas for 30 pieces of silver. This was depicted by the prophet Zechariah who bought the potter's land for the same price.

It was the lowest going rate of the day for the price of a slave. It was a picture of redemption as Christ had come to redeem His bride!

This number is a reminder to you that Jesus has already paid the price for your sin. He has redeemed you from your sin and the curse of the law.

He is telling you to put your faith into Him again instead of your own works. Rest in the finished work of Calvary!

> *Matthew 27:9 Then was fulfilled what was spoken by Jeremiah the prophet, saying, And they took the **thirty** pieces of silver, the value of Him who was priced, whom they of the children of Israel priced,*

Three hundred: A good number representing the people that you will work with in ministry.

Samson tied the tails of 300 foxes, which we have always seen as husband and wife teams being trained up and set on fire to do the work of God.

> *Judges 15:4 Then Samson went and caught **three hundred** foxes; and he took torches, turned the foxes tail to tail, and put a torch between each pair of tails.*

The number of Gideon's army and a picture of your ministry involvement. This could speak of the number of leaders that God wants you to work with or simply a picture of those that are a part of your ministry team.

> *Judges 7:7 Then the Lord said to Gideon, By the **three hundred** men who lapped I will save you, and deliver the Midianites into your hand. Let all the other people go, every man to his place.*

Symbols Starting in O

SYMBOLS STARTING IN O

OCEAN

Also referring to the sea.

Positive: The ocean is a picture of mystery and untapped blessing
Negative: Lacking conviction or direction (Being tossed around)

CHARACTER SPECIFIC SYMBOL

POSITIVE

If you have good childhood memories of the ocean, then it would represent pleasure and joy for you. It would speak of just letting go and floating, letting the tides carry you.

If you dream of floating or swimming in the ocean, then the Lord is saying that you can trust in Him and enjoy His presence. You do not need to be afraid, but can just jump in!

If you dream of a large wave that you surf or that you have control of, it speaks of the blessing of the Lord that is coming your way.

NEGATIVE

If you dream of large waves engulfing you, this speaks of circumstances that are overwhelming you. It can also speak of the attack of the enemy that is coming in like a flood.

Also if you have a fear of the ocean, then dreaming of being in the ocean speaks of being surrounded by your fears or having to confront your fear.

Sometimes you might dream of a wave that washes everything away. Although it might seem negative at first, this could be of the Lord. Perhaps it is time for you to start afresh. This is a good picture of a death of a vision.

UNIVERSAL SYMBOL

POSITIVE

A large wave although it can be negative, is also a good picture of the abundance of the Lord. The Word says that if you cast your bread on the waters, that it will return to you.

This is a picture of investing financially and spiritually into the Kingdom of God. As you keep giving out, you will reap the reward!

> *Ecclesiastes 11: Cast your bread upon the* ***waters****, for you will find it after many days.*

The Red Sea situation: If you see the Red Sea in the spirit, then the Lord has led you to face an impossible direction.

You know that you cannot go back where you have come from, but it seems that the Lord is not talking either. You are unsure which way to go. We call this the "Red Sea Situation".

What the Lord is telling you to do is to make the first move. Moses cried out to the Lord about what to do and the Lord said to him, "Why are you crying to me? Speak to the Children of Israel, that they go forward!" (Exodus 14:15)

God was waiting for Moses to do something! He had brought them so far, but now it was their turn. As they took that step though, then God moved once again and parted the waters.

If God has given you a direction and a promise and you see the Red Sea in front of you, you have a choice to make. Once you step out with that decision, God will back you up.

> *Psalms 106:9 He rebuked the **Red Sea** also, and it dried up; so He led them through the depths, as through the wilderness.*

NEGATIVE
To be tossed around in the ocean speaks of not having a firm conviction of your own. It means that you do not have a secure footing in the Word, and you are allowing the enemy to throw you around.

> *James 1:6 But let him ask in faith, with no doubting, for he who doubts is like a wave of the **sea** driven and tossed by the wind.*

The book of Hebrews also tells us that we should not be tossed around by every wind of doctrine.

The meaning is the same. If you dream of being tossed around, you do not have a firm understanding of doctrine, and the Lord is telling you to get your feet grounded!

See also: Drowning, River, Salt, Swimming, Water, Waves

OCTOPUS

A work of the enemy. Specifically, a combination of attacks on your health or finances.

NEGATIVE
We have often seen an octopus in the spirit. Each time it was when we were seeking the Lord regarding physical attack. It is a good picture because it feels as if you are facing so many different attacks, but they all have the same source.

If you see an octopus in the spirit, the Lord is saying that the many attacks you are facing in your life right now come from a single source. You have authority in the name of Jesus to tell the enemy to leave!

> *Leviticus 11:12 Whatever in the water does not have fins or scales—that shall be an abomination to you.*

OIL

Anointing oil: Anointing oil has many interpretations and symbols, most of which are positive, and depending on the context of your dream or vision it could have the following interpretations:

Anointing, healing, cleansing, beautifying, softening, the Holy Spirit, restoration, prosperity (crude oil), placement in ministry office, call to ministry office.

Oil: Fuel

Oil as used for fuel will have a different interpretation. It speaks of your spiritual resources and ability to "let your light shine" before the Lord. A lamp that is full of oil is one that has the potential to run a long race!

In ministry you are always pouring out. To dream or have a vision of your "oil" or "gas" getting low, means that you are running out of resources! It is time to top up again.

> *Exodus 27:20 And you shall command the children of Israel that they bring you pure* ***oil*** *of pressed olives for the light, to cause the lamp to burn continually*

CHARACTER SPECIFIC SYMBOL

Crude oil: Crude oil has a two-fold meaning. It can speak of untapped financial prosperity, or it can speak of being hindered.

POSITIVE
For example, to dream of tapping into an oil well speaks of locating a hidden potential for financial blessing.

NEGATIVE
To dream of being covered with oil, or feeling dirty by it indicates that you are under attack. Have you been in touch with someone recently that is walking in sin? It is possible that you have "partaken of their leaven" and you need to break spiritual links. (Please read the *Stain of Sin: Dealing With Curses* chapter in the *Strategies of War* book)

Universal Symbol

POSITIVE

I see oil many times in vision. A beautiful vision that the Lord gave me once was of having oil poured over my head until my hair glistened.

It not only spoke of Him anointing me for ministry, but also of Him preparing me and making me His beautiful bride. The emotion that came with the vision was one of feeling beautiful and of being in love with the Lord.

You can find a good illustration of this in the book of Esther, where she was prepared for a year before meeting with the king.

As she was prepared, so are we also prepared and made ready to meet our heavenly bridegroom, Jesus!

I often see the Lord anointing people in the spirit. It speaks of being covered in the external anointing.

At times I have seen Him applying oil to specific parts of their body, speaking of healing and restoration of an ailment they had. It also speaks of a purging and a cleansing.

To drink the oil or to consume it, speaks of being cleansed and receiving inner healing.

Speaking of the anointing:

> *Psalms 133:2 It is like the precious **ointment** upon the head, that ran down upon the beard, even Aaron's beard: that went down to the skirts of his garments; (KJV)*

The love of the Lord, as being a picture of oil. The love of the Bride and Groom:

> *Song of Songs 1:3 Because of the fragrance of your good **ointments**, your name is **ointment** poured forth; therefore, the virgins love you.*

Speaking of favor:

> *Ecclesiastes 9:8 Let thy garments be always white; and let thy head lack no **ointment**.*

NEGATIVE

Oil that has been spoiled has a negative connotation. It means that the anointing has been tainted with something that is not of God. It speaks of sin and of the enemy gaining a stronghold in a person's life. It might also speak of an anointing that has become contaminated through something demonic or an impartation you received from someone else.

See also: Anointing, Balm, Lamp, Perfume

OLIVE

Olives in many forms are mentioned in Scripture. They had many uses - from being used for oil to light lamps, to being pickled and eaten.

The most famous olive grove mentioned in the Word is in Gethsemane, which translated means “oil press”. Before an olive tree dies, new branches sprout from its roots.

Positive: Healing and growth
Negative: A separation (cutting off of branch)

UNIVERSAL SYMBOL

POSITIVE
Olive oil: Oil has always been a lovely picture of the anointing. It also speaks of the healing anointing - as olive oil was often used as a source of medication.

Olive crushed: I teach in the *Practical Prophetic Ministry* book about how the prophet goes through a time of testing during his training. I relate it to being “squeezed”.

My question is, "When you get squeezed, what comes out of you?"

The olive oil being squeezed and letting out its oil is a lovely image of this. It means that when pressures come on you to change, what comes out is the anointing.

It is also an indication that the Lord is about to put pressure on you, or perhaps even take you through a phase of ministry training.

Olive tree: The Lord promised the Israelites their own olive trees as a blessing. It is a picture of abundance and the blessing of the Lord.

The olive tree is also a good picture of a reproducing asset. It is not a blessing that comes once, but one that keeps producing further blessing.

> *Psalms 128:3 Your wife shall be like a fruitful vine in the very heart of your house, your children like* ***olive plants*** *all around your table.*

NEGATIVE
Branch being severed: Apostle Paul shares how those who refused to accept Christ were cut off from the olive tree, and a new branch was grafted in (speaking of the Church).

> *Romans 11:17 And if some of the branches were broken off, and you, being a wild* ***olive*** *tree, were grafted in among them, and with them became a partaker of the root and fatness of the* ***olive*** *tree.*

Often in the spirit we have seen the Lord cut a branch off a tree and graft a new one in its place. This has referred to the Lord removing a person from our lives or ministry and putting in someone new.

In a situation where a marriage has ended and you see this, it is an indication that the old marriage partner is being removed and that the Lord will bring a new one, so that they can become one.

To see an olive tree bearing fruit other than olives is a picture of things not being what they seem. While the person pretends to be one thing, on the inside they are something completely different.

> *James 3:12 Can a fig tree, my brethren, bear* ***olives****, or a grapevine bear figs? Thus no spring yields both salt water and fresh...*

See also: Branch, Tree, Oil

OWL

An owl in a positive context is a symbol of wisdom in most cultures. If your dream is positive, then it is likely that the owl is referring to wisdom.

Positive: Wisdom
Negative:

- Superstition
- The work of the enemy

CHARACTER SPECIFIC SYMBOL

POSITIVE
In many cultures the owl is a picture of wisdom. If you are familiar with this image, an owl could very well represent wisdom in your dream.

NEGATIVE
To dream of owls attacking you certainly speaks of demonic attack, but you need to determine where that attack is coming from. Does an "owl" mean something to you personally? Is it a symbol of an organization or group you are involved in?

UNIVERSAL SYMBOL

NEGATIVE
If your dream is prophetic and the owl is attacking you, it speaks of the work of the enemy.

Owls were considered unclean in the Scriptures. They are nocturnal, and inhabited the wilderness and barren lands.

They speak of desolation and barrenness. It is proof that the enemy has done his work and accomplished what he desired.

If you see an owl when praying with someone, it is an indication that the enemy has a stronghold in their lives and they are spiritually barren.

> *Isaiah 34:13 And thorns shall come up in her palaces, nettles and brambles in the fortresses thereof: and it shall be a habitation of dragons, and a court for* ***owls****. (KJV)*

See also: Birds

Symbols Starting in P

SYMBOLS STARTING IN P

PEARLS

Since the beginning of time, pearls have been a picture of beauty and wealth.

Pearls are a lovely picture of a hidden treasure waiting to be found, but also something that is bought at great expense.

Positive:

- Something of great value and beauty that needs to be sought out
- Wisdom

Negative: A show of external beauty

UNIVERSAL SYMBOL

POSITIVE

In Scripture, pearls speak of wealth and an object of trade. Unlike gold though, its value was in its beauty and not the monetary value alone.

Of course the parable of the businessman who sells all he has for the one pearl is a famous one.

> *Matthew 13:46 who, when he had found one **pearl** of great price, went and sold all that he had and bought it.*

A pearl is something that was usually bought at a great price, and if you owned one, it was an object that was precious and of high value.

It is also a picture of the church, as Jesus had used this parable to explain how He would pay all he had, even His life, for the church, which was His precious pearl.

If you see the Lord giving you a pearl, it means that He is giving you a gift that will increase in value and is something precious.

It is something that came at a great price to purchase. It is a lovely picture of the blessing and prosperity that we can walk in, because of the price Jesus paid on the cross.

If you see the pearl still in the oyster, then it means that the Lord is giving you a blessing, but you will need to do something to get it.

NEGATIVE

Pearls before swine: The Scripture below is another famous one. To cast your pearls before swine, means taking those things that you paid such a great price for and giving them to people who do not appreciate it.

This can often happen in ministry, just as Jesus experienced it.

The calling and the mandate God gives someone comes at a great price. It costs you your life and many phases of death to the flesh. Your calling becomes a treasure in your life.

When you give out to people who do not care to receive it, but only seek to condemn, you are handing something precious over to them that they do not deserve.

Reserve your ministry for those who are open to receive, just as Jesus did.

> *Matthew 7:6 Do not give what is holy to the dogs; nor cast your **pearls** before swine, lest they trample them under their feet, and turn and tear you in pieces.*

External beauty: In 1 Timothy 2:9 Paul instructs women to not over emphasize outward beauty, but inward beauty. If the pearls in your dream or vision feel very negative, the Lord is saying that you are putting on a show. You are trying to get everyone to believe you have great wisdom and worth, but you do not have it within to pour out.

See also: Gold, Jewelry

PEN

To express what is in your heart and spirit through writing.

A dream or vision of a computer would have the same meaning as a pen and a book.

Positive: To declare and establish the Word of God for posterity, by writing it down
Negative: Satan's intended plans

CHARACTER SPECIFIC AND UNIVERSAL SYMBOLS

POSITIVE

Even in our modern computer era, writing with pen and paper still holds a certain romance. To express yourself in writing is tantamount to pouring your very soul out.

This is why seeing a pen in a dream or vision is a good picture of expressing yourself in writing. It means to verbalize what is inside of you.

To put into print the treasures that God has given to you over the years and to express the hidden emotions that not everyone gets to see.

We have often seen the Lord given someone a golden pen in the spirit and it is strongly linked to the teaching ministry. It is an indication that the Lord wants them to write and document the things that He has given to them.

Seeing a pen in the spirit indicates one of two things:

1. Express Yourself!

The Lord is saying that it is time to make known the things that you keep hidden within. It is time to show the thoughts, impressions and emotions that perhaps you do not show others.

If you do have a desire to write and go into ministry, then this is vital. In real life, it is easy to hide who you really are. However, if you are to become a successful writer, it means being vulnerable and transparent.

The best writers are those that are able to convey true emotion. To make others feel what they feel. The pen is a powerful tool to unlocking all your thoughts, intents and emotions.

2. Document It!

Since the beginning of time, the Lord has been revealing His pattern and will to His champions. In the passage below David shares with Solomon the pattern for the Temple that the Lord gave to him through the process of writing.

If you see the Lord giving you or someone else a pen in the spirit, it means that the Lord wants them to document the spiritual principles and pattern that He has for His church.

> *1 Chronicles 28:19 All this, said David, the Lord made me understand in writing, by His hand upon me, all the works of these plans.*

It could be that the Lord wants that person to write a book, but not in every case. Often He might want them to write songs, courses, articles, sermons or document a structure.

NEGATIVE
In this scripture it is said that the scribes made the writings of the law false! What started out as something from the Lord, was contaminated with the ideas of man.

> *Jeremiah 8:8 How can you say, We are wise, and the law of the Lord is with us? Look, the false* ***pen*** *of the scribe certainly works falsehood.*

A black pen or a pen in a negative light speaks of the plan that the enemy has and the heresy he has spread in the church.

See also: Contract, Letter, Signature, Scroll

PENIS

The essence of masculinity and the ability to produce blessing.

Positive:

- Confidence in masculinity
- To reproduce yourself in others
- The sexual strength of a man

Negative:

- Insecurity in masculinity
- Broken masculinity
- Inability to pass on the anointing God has given to you

CHARACTER SPECIFIC SYMBOL

POSITIVE
Without a doubt, a penis represents a man's masculinity. It is also an image of strength and the ability to reproduce the good that is within you. To dream favorably of a penis, you need to ask yourself who the penis belongs to and what they represent to you!

As a woman: Have you feared having sex in the past? To have a positive dream about a penis means that you have overcome your fear. You need not fear masculinity or the sexual act!

As a man: To dream or have a vision of your penis being enlarged or healed means that you have gained confidence in yourself as a man.

NEGATIVE
As a woman: Are you a virgin that fears sex? Then dreaming of a penis is likely exposing those fears. Regardless of your views on sex, if you continually have dreams about penises, that make you feel uncomfortable and unclean, then it is possible that you are under attack from a spirit of lust or an unclean spirit.

If you dream that you have a penis, it means that you are trying to be something you are not. You are becoming aggressive and taking on a role that is not yours to fulfill.

NOTE: To be aroused in such dreams is not sin, but a natural reaction God put in us. If you dream of your husband in this way, it means you crave his masculinity. If you dream of other men, it means that you are seeking the strength that masculinity has to offer and you are looking for it in all the wrong places.

As a man: How do you feel about your masculinity? A shriveled penis or the inability to get an erection is a representation of your insecurity regarding your masculinity.

To dream of not being able to ejaculate or produce children is the Lord saying that you are failing to reproduce yourself in others as a leader. Now, if in real life you are having these exact fears or problems, then your dreams are simply reflecting inner fears that you are not willing to express.

It is time to get help! You need counseling and some inner healing! Face your fears and get the victory!

Homosexual dreams: Now is a good time to mention homosexuality. If you have secret fears that you are homosexual and you keep dreaming of other men in this way, then this is a twofold problem. Firstly, your fear is being exposed. Secondly, you have a spirit of lust that you need help with. In addition to this, you also need healing and a fresh understanding of masculinity.

Have you had homosexual encounters in the past that you want to put behind you? These dreams are exposing your guilt that needs to be put under the blood. Find someone you trust to confess your sin to and to pray you through!

Perhaps you are not homosexual and you still keep dreaming of other men that are naked. I can imagine that is freaking you out round about now. Relax! If you consider that the penis is a picture of masculinity, could it be that the Lord is just telling you to embrace your masculinity as you should? Look up the symbol *Man* for more on this.

Universal Symbol

POSITIVE

It is not likely that you are going to see a penis in vision very often. If you did, I would get a little concerned. It might make for some awkward counseling sessions * tongue in cheek * "So, I, uh, see your penis in the spirit..." Yeah – not the simplest ministry time you ever had.

If you do see a penis in the spirit though, then the Lord is really trying to make a point. Either He is calling that person to a "circumcision of the heart" or they have a physical problem!

I often teach how just as Abraham had to be circumcised as a sign of going into covenant with God, so also does He ask us to circumcise our hearts as we have entered into covenant with Him. That means putting aside our flesh and what "we" want in favor of what He wants.

NEGATIVE

The Lord speaks clearly about a man that loses his penis or has his testicles crushed. He is looked on as "broken" and was not fit to serve in the temple. Now to have a vision or dream of this "brokenness" is not the Lord condemning you! Rather He is calling you to get healing!

> *Deuteronomy 23:1 "He who is emasculated by crushing or mutilation shall not enter the assembly of the Lord.*

Now keep in mind that if you are praying for someone for physical healing and you see his penis in the spirit, He is showing you the source of the physical problem. (I know... pretty awkward – but its been known to happen!) The Lord is telling you to pray for healing!

See also: Adultery, Arousal, Bed, Incest, Kiss, Man

PERFUME

Our praise to the Lord, being beautified, being prepared, being honored and being cleansed.

Perfume, oil, myrrh and incense often share the same interpretations.

Positive:

- Our praise to the Lord, being beautified
- A season of preparation
- To be honored
- To go through a cleansing process

Negative:

- To be lured into a trap
- To lose something precious through bitterness (defiled perfume)

Perfume changes your emotions and causes you to be drawn to it. It can be a pleasant experience, or it can speak of being caught in a trap.

Referring to how perfume lifts the emotions:

> *Proverbs 27:9 Ointment and **perfume** delight the heart, and the sweetness of a man's friend gives delight by hearty counsel.*

CHARACTER SPECIFIC SYMBOL

POSITIVE

A bride was prepared with oils and perfume to prepare her for her wedding night. Esther is a good example of this.

This speaks of the bride of Christ being prepared and made ready for her Groom. It speaks of her falling in love with her Groom - which is Jesus Christ.

The Scriptures also speak of our praise being as incense before the Lord, that it is a pleasing smell before Him.

Incense was offered before the Lord twenty-four hours a day under the Old Covenant. Our incense is our praise and worship.

Speaking of the love of bride and groom:

> *Song of Solomon 4:10 How fair is your love, my sister, my spouse! How much better than wine is your love, and the scent of your **perfumes** than all spices!*

As believers we also diffuse the perfume of Christ everywhere we go - or we should anyway!

Because of the indwelling of the Holy Spirit, as we go through this world, we carry that treasure inside of us.

It is just like wearing perfume. Everyone that passes you should be effected by it. I give a good description of this in the *Practical Prophetic Ministry* book when teaching on the ministry of the prophet.

> *2 Corinthians 2:14 Now thanks be to God who always leads us in triumph in Christ, and through us diffuses the **fragrance** of His knowledge in every place. (KJV)*

NEGATIVE
The Scripture also speaks of the perfume of the harlot and adulteress.

It speaks of being captured and seduced into the things of the world, of being deceived into thinking that you are being offered something good, when in fact it is false and full of sin.

Speaking of the harlot (world) that seduces, a love that is false and empty:

> *Proverbs 7:17 I have **perfumed** my bed with myrrh, aloes, and cinnamon.*
> *18 Come, let us take our fill of love until morning; let us delight ourselves with love.*
> *22 Immediately he went after her, as an ox goes to the slaughter, or as a fool to the correction of the stocks,*

See also: Aloes, Honey, Oil, Rose, Smelling

PET

Because pets are different for each person, the interpretation of your dream will change according to your relationship with the animal that you are dreaming about.

Positive:

- Your responsibilities
- Your emotions

Negative:

- Your fears
- Burdens you do not want to bear

They will also not have any meaning in your visions, unless the Lord is showing you the actual animal in a vision for some reason.

If you dream of a pet that you have and care for, then it can speak of your responsibilities.

However, if you do not have any children and your pets have replaced children in your life, then they could represent aspects of your ministry.

My daughter, being a real dog lover always dreams of her pets when the Lord is telling her something about her work. She might dream that she receives a new pet to care for – she knows that she is about to get a new responsibility!

Birth of puppies or kittens: You are about to be the proud parents of a bunch of new jobs. Ones that will take up your time, but will also be rewarding. This goes for the birth of any kind of pet that you are asked to care for. Because they are babies, this means that the responsibility is new and you will have to take care of it from the ground up!

NEGATIVE
If you dream about someone else's pet, or of an animal that you do not like at all, then it speaks of an irritation in your life.

It can even represent something that the enemy is doing in your life to bring you discomfort.

A sick pet means that you have not been taking care of your responsibilities! A neglected pet is clear – you have not been putting the effort into that realm as you should have.

A dying pet? Could it be that the Lord is telling you to let go of some cares that you think cannot live without you? Determine if it is good or bad that the pet is dying in your dream.

See also: Animals, Birds, Cat, Dog, Horse

PHONE LINE

The condition of your ability to communicate with God and others.

Positive: To be given the ability to “hear” what others do not
Negative: A blockage in your spirit, preventing you from hearing

Character Specific and Universal Symbols

POSITIVE AND NEGATIVE
There is nothing more frustrating than a dream where you are trying to call someone and not getting through. This is a picture of your own frustration right now. You are failing to communicate to those around you correctly, no matter how hard you try.

Have you been struggling in your relationship with the Lord? A disconnected line means that there is something that is coming in the way of your relationship with the Lord. The Lord is able to reach out to you, however, you are struggling to reach out to Him.

If in your dream you feel frustrated and are trying hard, it is possible that the Lord is telling you to just rest. He is right by your side and never left you. Although you might feel that your prayers are "not getting through" He is hearing you and has in fact answered before you asked!

To dream of "making the connection" is a confirmation that you have made a breakthrough in the realm of the spirit. If you make that connection with someone specific, identify what they represent and you will know the area where you are finally getting your breakthrough.

Pig

Universally, a pig is associated with filth and something that is unclean.

Positive: Bacon burger anyone?
Negative: An unclean spirit

Character Specific Symbol

POSITIVE
A pig would be positive in your dream if you have a pet pig that you love or if you are a pig farmer!

Pork: If you do not have anything against a good bacon burger, then to dream of eating it means that the Lord doesn't just want to provide for your basic needs, but He wants to provide more than what you just "need to live".

NEGATIVE
If you are Jewish, eating pork could mean one of two things. It could mean that you are going against your personal convictions or it can mean that the Lord is telling you that perhaps it is time to let go of tradition and to stop telling Him what is unclean! To go by the spirit and Word instead of tradition.

UNIVERSAL SYMBOL

POSITIVE
Peter was asked of the Lord to "kill and eat" when a blanket of unclean animals was lowered down to him. (Acts 10) God was saying – do not judge a book by its cover! What I have made clean, is clean!

NEGATIVE
To see a vision of a pig speaks of an unclean spirit.

Pigs were unclean animals in the Word and the Israelites were forbidden to eat them. A humorous illustration using the pig is found in this Scripture:

> *Proverbs 11:22 As a ring of gold in a **swine's** snout, so is a lovely woman who lacks discretion.*

This passage speaks of a woman who does not have good taste or good judgment.

See also: Animals, Meat

PLANTS

There are many plants in the bible and so I have listed them under their separate symbol headings.

A plant in general though speaks of the work of your hands or the work of God in your ministry. Plants are often seasonal and also represent a specific season in your life.

Depending on the condition of your plant will give you a better idea of what this season is about.

POSITIVE
I have often seen a new ministry like a seedling and a sturdy tree as a mature ministry.

A plant that is flourishing and green means that whatever it is you are working on right now - you are going in the right direction! You are flourishing in your work.

To see a dead plant come to life means that the Lord is going to resurrect something in your life that died some time ago.

To plant: To dream or have a vision of planting a seed means that the Lord is giving you a new ministry, but that you will need to "break ground" first. I remember the beginning of 2013 the Lord showed me a field that needed ploughing. That was a tough year of preparation!

For 2014, He showed me the ploughed field and said, "Now it is time to plant." This year, although also really intense, felt more productive. We felt like the work we did remained. This year involved investing into the lives of others and working on relationships. It was a year when we started many new things. "Planting" means to invest a lot into starting something new and not being afraid of rolling up your sleeves and getting your hands dirty! The years that followed showed the fruit of that year of planting.

NEGATIVE
A seasonal plant that dies represents a season that has come to an end in your life.

If the plant you dream of or see in your spirit has died because of lack of water, it means that you are lacking the spirit of God in this area of your life. If it dies because of no fertilizer or no soil, it means that you are lacking the Word of God in your life.

See also: Aloes, Branch, Field, Grass, Olive, Seed, Trees

POISON

The most common interpretation for poison in Scripture is the presence of bitterness and negative words.

Bitterness, fear and guilt are poison in your spirit.

CHARACTER SPECIFIC AND UNIVERSAL SYMBOLS

Contamination: To dream that you are drinking poison is an indication that you are feeding on things that are deadly to you.

Perhaps you have been browsing websites, watching teachings or even reading books that do not have the spirit of Christ on them. These things are poison to your spirit.

This might not be restricted to things of the world. Have other people hurled bitter words at you? Watch your heart! Allowing those words to effect you will be poison to your soul. No need to participate in their bitterness.

Bitterness: Poison is a good picture of bitterness because of how it pollutes not only your own spirit, but how it defiles everyone else around you as well.

> *Hebrews 12:15 looking carefully lest anyone fall short of the grace of God; lest any root of bitterness springing up cause trouble, and by this many become defiled;*

James knew the power of words! Words have power, and words spoken in a curse against someone is like poisoning them and giving the enemy license to attack them.

*James 3:8 But the tongue can no man tame; it is an unruly evil, full of deadly **poison***

Speaking of negative words:

*Psalms 58:3-4 ...speaking lies. Their **poison** is like the poison of a serpent; They are like the deaf cobra that stops its ear*

See also: Bitterness, Jar, Water

POLICE/OFFICER OF THE LAW

A representation of the laws of the land.

Positive:

- Victory and protection
- God is on your side

Negative: Attack by the world's system

CHARACTER SPECIFIC AND UNIVERSAL SYMBOLS

POSITIVE

If you are a police officer, or have a good relationship with one, then dreaming of someone in the police force would be positive. They would speak to you of order and protection. This is especially true if you see the police in a positive light.

NEGATIVE

If you have a fear of the police force or are negative towards them, then they speak of the world's system in your dreams. If you find yourself often fighting police in your dream, it can have a dual meaning and you will need to discern which is correct in the context of your dream.

It could be that you are being attacked by the world system, and you need to rise up and do spiritual warfare. On the other hand, if you tend to be rebellious then the dream indicates that you are rebelling against your circumstances and the system. You are in a wrong spirit and you need to come in order.

1 Peter 2:13 Therefore submit yourselves to every ordinance of man for the Lord's sake, whether to the king as supreme,

See also: Authorities

POLLEN

Potential for growth that is beyond your control.

Positive: God's part in bringing His promises to fruition
Negative: The negative influence of the spirit of the world in your life

UNIVERSAL SYMBOL

POSITIVE
The beauty of pollination is how it is already built into nature. From wind, to rain, and insects, the Lord has set it up that nature reproduces itself... naturally. In the same way, pollen speaks of the Lord doing His part in the reaping process. You sow and work hard, but then the Lord sends His wind and causes pollination to take place. It's time for you to rest and let God do His part.

NEGATIVE
In the same way that the Lord completes His plan, the enemy also has his structures set up in the world to infiltrate and bring fruit that is bitter. Pollen, if seen negatively, speaks of allowing the spirit of the world to enter your heart and to sow seeds of doubt, fear, and guilt.

See also: Bud, Flowers, Seed, Fruit

POTTER'S WHEEL

A season of shaping that the Lord is about to do in your life.

Many times I saw myself as a clay vessel on the potter's wheel. When I dreamed this, I knew that the Lord was going to take me through another season of change.

When the Lord calls you to do His work, you need to become the kind of person to fulfill that work. This requires change!

It requires a season on the potter's wheel, so that the Lord can change you.

Never forget though, that it is the Lord that will change you. He will apply the pressures through your circumstances, your mentors, and spiritual parents.

The purpose is not to destroy you, but to make you into a vessel of honor!

> *2 Timothy 2:20 But in a great house there are not only* ***vessels*** *of gold and silver, but also of wood and clay, some for honor and some for dishonor.*

See also: Clay

Precious Stones

A depiction of your value and status in the eyes of God.

Positive: To be a person of value
Negative: Something is blocking your potential to display your worth

POSITIVE
Precious stones did not stand alone, but were instead set into jewelry or other artifacts of gold. When the Lord gave Moses the pattern for the Ephod of the High Priest, he was told to set 12 stones in it, representing the twelve tribes of Israel.

> *Exodus 28:21 And the* ***stones*** *shall have the names of the sons of Israel, twelve according to their names, like the engravings of a signet, each one with its own name; they shall be according to the twelve tribes.*

I have often seen individuals in a team as gemstones that are tossed together to rub off one another's hard edges.

There have also been times when the Lord has given me a message to tell someone that they are like a precious stone that He will set in His crown.

> *2 Chronicles 3:6 And he decorated the house with* ***precious stones*** *for beauty, and the gold was gold from Parvaim.*

Depending on the kind of stone that you see, would represent something different. An Emerald, because it is green, is a picture of new life. Where a Sapphire, being heavenly in color, represents the Kingdom of God.

For a precious stone to truly shine, it takes chiseling away the flaws and a season of buffing. In our spiritual walk, the Lord will often take us through seasons of refining to remove the things that take away from the beauty He has put into us.

Just like a precious stone has the potential for beauty, so do you. All it takes is some chiseling in the right direction.

NEGATIVE
A tarnished gemstone means that you have let the things that God has wrought in you go to waste. You have not taken care of what he has done to perfect you. Its time to get up again and to shine for the Lord. Throw off the things of the world, your hurts and fears and run the race once again!

See also: Diamond, Emerald, Ruby

PREGNANT

The beginning of something new in your life that is not yet visible, but will be soon enough. We conceive many things in our spirits, but not everything we conceive is a blessing.

Some of them are the blessings that we have asked the Lord for. Others are things that we do not desire, but have conceived because of fear or sin.

Positive: Conception of a new vision and direction for your life
Negative: The conception of a work of the enemy in your life

CHARACTER SPECIFIC SYMBOL

POSITIVE
To dream that you are pregnant means that something new is about to manifest in your life. If you are a man, you might dream that your wife is pregnant instead, and it would mean the same thing to you.

You need to discern if the child you are pregnant with is good or not.

If you dream that you miscarry or that a baby is stillborn, but do not really feel any concern in your dream, then it has a good interpretation.

It means that you conceived something that was not of God, but that He has prevented it from coming to pass.

It is a good sign that you have left the things of the past behind, or perhaps brought your flesh into line.

Pregnancy term: I have often dreamed that I was pregnant. In one dream I was three months pregnant. It was a clear dream. When I woke up, I calculated the time and realized that I had been released into ministry training about three months ago.

The Lord was confirming that He had indeed started that process in me, and that I would carry it to full term.

If you dream of giving birth early or not realizing you were pregnant, it means that the Lord has been doing something in your life behind the scenes, and it will suddenly come to pass.

NEGATIVE
Pregnant with wrong child: If you dream that you are pregnant with the baby of someone from the past that you do not like, this is negative.

It means that you have held onto something from that time of your life, and it has taken root in you.

Perhaps you were involved with a ministry in the past that you do not feel positive about any longer.

Dreaming of being pregnant surrounding those circumstances means you have conceived something spiritually during that time that you have still held onto.

Someone else's baby: If you dream that you are pregnant with someone's baby that is very negative to you, it could mean that you have given the flesh control of your life and conceived something that is not of the Lord.

Evil child: If you dream that the baby you are pregnant with is deformed or evil, it means that you have conceived something during the last months, in your life, that is not of the Lord. Consider the decisions you have made and the people you have been involved with. Is it possible that you have allowed a belief to enter your heart that is contrary to the Word?

> *James 1:15 Then, when desire has* ***conceived****, it gives birth to sin; and sin, when it is full- grown, brings forth death.*

Miscarriage: If you dream that you miscarry, and you feel the pain and the struggle in the dream, then this is not a good picture.

It means that the enemy is trying to steal the blessing that the Lord has given to you.

If you are in ministry training, consider the tests you have faced over the last while. It could be a warning that you are going off track and need to get back again.

Universal Symbol

POSITIVE

The interpretations for visions can be tricky. Your vision can either speak of a spiritual birth that the person is going through, or it could speak of an actual pregnancy!

If you see a baby in the womb, this could speak of the Lord conceiving and birthing something new in that person.

Just as in the case where the Holy Spirit conceived Jesus in Mary's womb, this would be a picture of something good that the Lord has conceived in their spirits.

In a literal sense, it can also mean that this person you are praying with will have an actual baby! You need to use some tact when interpreting such a vision.

I remember receiving prayer once and the person praying saw me holding a baby. I was trying to take a spiritual picture from it, but I discovered shortly afterwards that I was already 5 months pregnant!

The best thing to do is to share the vision you get with the person. If they have desired a child, then perhaps the Lord is confirming to them that this is His will. Perhaps the Lord is even saying that they are pregnant right now.

While praying for a couple desiring to fall pregnant, a fellow minister clearly saw a baby in the womb. It turned out that the woman was indeed pregnant at the time. That word brought both confirmation and hope that this was of the Lord.

Spiritually speaking, when we have faith, we birth the blessings of God in our lives. This can speak of both spiritual and natural blessings.

> *Hebrews 11:11 By faith Sarah herself also received strength to* ***conceive seed****, and she bore a child when she was past the age, because she judged Him faithful who had promised.*

NEGATIVE
My stepmom has been used of the Lord very often to pray for couples to fall pregnant, because of her own travail in this area.

I remember her praying for a lady once who was having medical problems with her pregnancy. The doctors said that it would be a hard birth, and her chances of having any children in the future were near impossible.

She went into prayer and saw something demonic attacking the child in the womb. She stood against this, and against all odds the woman went on to have not just one, but three children afterwards!

To have a vision of someone that is barren is an indication of a curse in that person's life.

See also: Baby, Birth, Child, Miscarriage

Prison

In the symbol Bars, I cover the description of prison bars. The only time a prison would have a positive interpretation is if the enemy was in it. Otherwise, it mostly speaks of being in bondage.

Positive: To restrict the work of the enemy
Negative: To be captive to circumstances

POSITIVE
If you dream of putting someone in prison, then it could speak of getting rid of something that has been hindering you.

If you dream that you put a wild animal in prison, then it is an indication that you have gained control of the enemy in your life.

Prison is not a nice place to be. However, if Joseph had never gone there, he would never have risen up to be second in command over all of Egypt!

This is also a good picture of someone that has a business calling. It might seem to you that you are blocked on all sides, but it could well be from the Lord as part of your preparation.

Just as in the case with Joseph, the Lord could have put you in this tight situation because He knows that it is the only way to also bring about the blessing that He has in store for you.

So if you have a vision of being in a prison, but feel it is of the Lord, then He is confirming that you must learn to press through this phase.

The key is to use this time to your best advantage while you can. Do not give up hope, but continue to trust Him, as the time of rising up will come soon!

> *Genesis 39:22 And the keeper of the* ***prison*** *committed to Joseph's hand all the* ***prisoners*** *who were in the prison; whatever they did there, it was his doing.*

NEGATIVE

To dream of being in prison speaks of being restricted and bound.

You need to decide for yourself if you put yourself in this prison by your actions, or if it is the work of something else.

It could also be an indication of a conflict you are facing at the moment. If you are feeling frustrated and "locked up" in your current workplace or church, then this would be illustrating how you feel at the moment.

In a vision, to see someone or yourself in a dark prison is not positive. It means that the enemy has bound you.

Keep in mind though, that he needs license to do this. Either you have closed your heart off to the Lord, or you have allowed sin in your life.

There is a solution for sin though and you can break free! The Lord desires to set you free.

> *Isaiah 42:7 To open blind eyes, to bring out prisoners from the* ***prison****, those who sit in darkness from the* ***prison*** *house.*

Spiritual imprisonment: When ministering personally to individuals, we have come across something that we call spiritual imprisonment.

It is a situation where that person experienced hurts in their past, and as a result they hid away from the world. Closing off their hearts to everyone and the Lord, they locked themselves away.

Usually when we pray, we see the age of the person at the time they made this choice.

This condition, unfortunately, prevents the person from entering into a personal relationship with the Lord Jesus. It also inhibits personal relationships, especially in marriage.

Often in these situations we also see a demonic stronghold that the person gave license to. In many cases this relates to a hurt from childhood where they allowed themselves to become bitter.

As a result of this bitterness, they allowed the enemy to have a stronghold in their lives. Once they let the bitterness go, as ministers, we can step in and speak healing to this situation.

See also: Bars, Cage, Cave

PUB

A perfect picture of the world's solution to a spiritual need.

POSITIVE
Although it is hard to imagine, a pub in your dream could be positive if relating to evangelism. If you dream that you are in a pub and finding people there, then the Lord is telling you to go into the world and to reach the lost.

The other positive interpretation is if you dream of handing out wine. Wine is often positive in the Word and speaks of the Spirit. To dream that you are pouring out wine for others to drink actually speaks of giving the anointing out to others. Consider the environment of your dream to determine if it is speaking of something worldly or righteous.

NEGATIVE
This is applicable to all sorts of other worldly entertainment centers. The same interpretation applies to night clubs.

If you dream that you are getting drunk in a pub, it means that you are trying to use the things of the world to satisfy a deep need inside of you.

Instead of getting into the presence of the Lord Jesus, you are escaping into the world.

See also: Bars, Wine

PURPLE

A symbol of status, depicting a position of wealth and royalty.

Positive: Royalty and favor
Negative: Hurts of the past

POSITIVE
In Scripture, purple always has a positive connotation. It speaks of royalty, wealth and prosperity. In the Old Testament, only the wealthy could afford purple clothing. So it was worn by kings and those of good repute. If you sold or

imported purple cloth, then you were considered a wealthy merchant. Purple was also used in the tabernacle, representing the deity of the Lord.

Speaking of Royalty:

> *Esther 8:15 So Mordecai went out from the presence of the king in royal apparel of blue and white, with a great crown of gold and a garment of fine linen and **purple**; and the city of Shushan rejoiced and was glad:*

NEGATIVE
Purple, as in the case of blue, can speak of bruising and hurts. See *Blue* or *Bruise* for a full explanation.

See also: Blue, Bruise, Linen, Tabernacle

PURSE

A purse goes hand in hand with the symbol Money.

Positive: A picture of financial provision
Negative: A picture of lack and theft

POSITIVE
A purse or wallet speaks of finances. To dream of having your purse being filled speaks of blessing and financial provision.

If you see a purse filled with money in the spirit, it is speaking of a financial provision. It is for you to release it and speak it forth into the earth.

NEGATIVE
To dream of your wallet being empty, speaks of lack and a curse.

A purse that has holes in it speaks of a curse in your life. Could it be that you have stopped sowing into the work of the Lord?

> *Haggai 1:6 You have sown much, and bring in little; you eat, but do not have enough; you drink, but you are not filled with drink; you clothe yourselves, but no one is warm; and he who earns wages, earns wages to put into a **bag with holes**.*

A hand stealing money out of a bag refers to a spirit of theft.

> *John 12:6 This he said, not that he cared for the poor, but because he was a thief, and had the **money box**; and he used to take what was put in it.*

See also: Money, Gold, Silver

SYMBOLS STARTING IN Q

Symbols Starting in Q

Quail

The Lord provided quails for the Children of Israel in the desert. They speak not only of having your needs provided, but your desires as well.

I cover this in more detail under *Meat*.

See also: Meat

Queen

A position of honor given because of heritage and not personal accomplishment.

Positive: The proof of your position in Christ
Negative: A demonic prince of the air

POSITIVE
As believers, we are all kings and queens in the Lord. It speaks of our position and authority in Christ. It also speaks of the blessing and favor we have with the Lord because of this position.

Of course a lovely illustration of this is Queen Esther, who I often see in the spirit when ministering to a woman.

When I see this then I know that the Lord is saying that this person should see herself as a queen, and to lift up her head and act like a one, instead of groveling like a beggar!

NEGATIVE
To do spiritual warfare and to see a demon that looks like a queen, realize that you are coming against the systems of the world (Acts 19:35).

I remember experiencing this when we were in Switzerland. I kept coming up against a prince in the spirit that looked like a woman. I came to realize later on that I was coming against the prince over that nation, and by making a noise in the spirit with the spiritual warfare we were doing at that time stirred it up. If the Lord has sent you to another country to start a ministry, realize that your spiritual warfare is about to go up a notch.

To break through, you will face the bondages in the hearts of the people that have been nurtured by the prince in that area. Look up my symbol for *Demons* and also invest in the *Prophetic Warrior* and *Strategies of War* books

See also: King

SYMBOLS STARTING IN R

Symbols Starting in R

Race

The journey set before you having a starting and ending point.

Positive: To progress steadily in your spiritual life
Negative:

- To become weary in doing good
- To be competitive

Universal Symbol

POSITIVE
Universally, a race speaks of putting yourself through the strain for the purpose of reaching the prize. It means to give all you have to see what you are made of. There is always a goal to a race - a point you need to reach. So if you dream or have a vision of running a race, it is speaking of the spiritual journey you are on right now.

Are you racing to the finish line? Then this is going to be a quick journey. The race speaks of a direction God has given to you. It might speak of a specific mandate or set of instructions. It can also speak of your journey as a Christian.

> *1 Corinthians 9:24 Do you not know that those who run in a race all run, but one receives the prize? Run in such a way that you may obtain it.*

A sprint: A short journey that will require all your effort.

A marathon: A longer journey that requires you to be diligent and to pace yourself. Keep pushing through!

Hurdle race: There are a couple of "hoops" you will need to jump through to reach your goal.

Passing the baton: You are not running this race alone. You need to fulfill this purpose as a team – each taking your place.

Three-legged race: Stop trying to do things solo. The journey ahead will require you and someone else to be in complete unity to reach your goal.

Sack race: This is a difficult journey and you are "tied up" right now. You are being hindered from running with liberty.

Team sport: To "run the race" as part of a team. God is calling you to find your place so that everyone can move forward. There is no time for you to go solo.

NEGATIVE
I love the passage in Hebrews 12:1 where it speaks of us running a race with a cloud of witnesses. The part I want to draw your attention to is where it says that we must lay aside every weight. To run a race with a weight slows you down. To see this means that there is sin in your life that is hindering you.

Running someone else's race? Stop trying to fulfill their purpose and set your sights to your own. You must do what God has told you to do and not compare yourself to others.

Tripping in your race? You are becoming distracted. Set your sights on the goal again.

Becoming weary? It is time to take a rest. The journey has been long and you need to fill up again in the presence of the Lord, so that you can go on again.

Consider also whether you are running the race with joy or not. Could it be that you are trying so hard to compete with everyone around you? You are so focused on being the best that you have forgotten that love is the greatest motivator of them all.

A note on competition: If you see a vision of running a race or competing in sport, but it is only about winning, the Lord is exposing a spirit of strife and vainglory. You should be happy with second place, if it means your brother is being lifted up.

See also: Exercising, Trophy, Road, Running

RAIN

The culmination of a long season involving tilling the ground, sowing and nurturing the field God has given to you. You have done your work. Now it is time for God to do His.

Positive: A season of rest after an intense season of labor
Negative: Rain in the wrong season – a work of the enemy in your circumstances, to steal your blessing

CHARACTER SPECIFIC SYMBOL

POSITIVE
If you like rain, then it speaks of a change of season for you. It speaks of being washed clean and having the opportunity to start over again.

Rain is a lovely picture in dreams of putting the old behind you and starting afresh.

NEGATIVE
Being caught in rain is seldom enjoyable, and most of the time you try to get out of it.

If this is the case in your dream, then the rain speaks of pressures and conflicts in your life.

Universal Symbol

POSITIVE
In the Word, rain was always a promise of blessing that was on its way. It is very much the finishing touch on all your hard work.

As you have sowed seeds in the natural and spiritual, you can only go so far and then it is up to the Lord to do the rest.

A vision of rain is a confirmation that it is time for you to step back and for God to now do His part to bring about the blessing in your life.

> *Deuteronomy 28:12 The Lord will open to you His good treasure, the heavens, to give the* ***rain*** *to your land in its season, ...*

NEGATIVE
If the rain you see is a dark cloud and a thunderstorm, it speaks of the work of the enemy and the plan he has for you. His intent is to destroy the blessing you have labored so long for.

> *2 Peter 2:17 These are wells without water, clouds carried by a tempest, for whom is reserved the blackness of darkness forever...*

See also: Clouds, Hail, Storm

Rainbow

Confirmation of God's Promise.

Universal Symbol

POSITIVE
A rainbow does not confirm a new promise, but rather confirms one that has already been given. The rainbow was given to Noah as a covenant sign of the promise God had given him. In the same way, to see a rainbow in a vision or prophetic dream is the Lord saying, "My child I have not forgotten my promise to you – in fact I am bringing it to pass even now. Keep standing in faith!"

> *Genesis 9:17 And God said to Noah, "This is the sign of the covenant which I have established between Me and all flesh that is on the earth."*

NEGATIVE
To see a "pot of gold" at the end of a rainbow is not positive. It speaks of having faith in wishful thinking and fantasy instead of in the truth of the Word. To see a leprechaun is also negative, and you are likely seeing something demonic that is related to something occult that has an influence on finances.

It is either a demonic power that person is using to gain wealth or they are wanting the Lord to "do magic" to bring their promise to pass instead of them simply standing in faith and walking in obedience.

See also: Coins, Rain

RAVEN

A work of the enemy to "pick at you" and wear you down. In a positive light, they speak of the Lord turning what the enemy has sought for evil in your life into good.

Positive: God is going to use what seems like the work of the enemy for His own good.
Negative: The work of the enemy to bring strife, irritation and theft.

POSITIVE
What the enemy sought for evil, the Lord will turn around for good! This is just what happened with Elijah as he finds himself at Brook Cherith being fed by the ravens. Ravens in a positive light means that despite your circumstances, the Lord is going to use even these for His good plan in your life!

> *1 Kings 17:6 The **ravens** brought him bread and meat in the morning, and bread and meat in the evening; and he drank from the brook*

A note for the prophets: If the Lord has called you to the prophetic, to have Him call you to Brook Cherith to be fed by the ravens is a sign that your journey to prophetic office has just commenced. Welcome! Prophetic training has begun. *Prophetic Boot Camp*... get it! You will need it!

NEGATIVE
The raven is a black bird of prey and is negative in scripture and most cultures. I often see these in the spirit, and when I do, I know that the enemy is bringing oppression.

They are also a lot like the vulture in that they are unclean animals that will eat on rotting meat. They speak of the enemy bringing irritation and theft in your life.

Just like ravens are chancers and will try to steal food where they can, so the enemy is trying to steal the provision and blessing that God has given to you.

I also see these black birds in the spirit when there is a spirit of strife in someone's life. A very sordid picture is described here in Proverbs.

> *Proverbs 30:17 The eye that mocks his father, And scorns obedience to his mother, The* ***ravens*** *of the valley will pick it out...*

See also: Birds, Owl

RED

A strong announcement of redemption along with the wealth and position of honor we have gained through Christ.

Positive: Wealth, royalty and redemption (The blood of Christ)
Negative: Destruction and danger

CHARACTER SPECIFIC SYMBOL

Before we move on to the interpretation of Red in scripture, lets consider it in our cultures first.

POSITIVE
If your dream is strictly internal, then the color red is a picture of passion and romance. This stands true for most cultures. In some though, it is a color for fertility and virginity even. Determine what the color means to you personally and for your culture. Does your dream make sense now when you interpret it this way?

If your dream is prophetic, then the interpretation under "Visions" will help you out more.

NEGATIVE
Nothing says "danger" quite like the color red. From red stop signs to the traffic light that flashes red to "STOP!" If you feel a sense of urgency in your dream, it could well mean that you need to tread lightly. It is time to stop and take stock of the direction you are going right now.

UNIVERSAL SYMBOL

POSITIVE
Red mantle/cloak: Red is referred to as scarlet in Scripture and it has a positive connotation of wealth and favor. So to have a vision of a red mantle being placed on your shoulder indicates a promotion in your ministry.

Gold, blue, purple and crimson were all woven into the veil in the Holy of Holies. What a beautiful picture of our position in Christ today!

Blue: Our ministry call in the Kingdom of God
Purple: The position we have as kings and queens

Crimson: Our redemption from sin and death
Gold: The anointing of the Spirit that enables us to walk out our call and position in Christ.

> *2 Chronicles 3:14 And he made the veil of blue, purple,* ***crimson****, and fine linen, and wove cherubim into it*

Red implements: Red also speaks of redemption and of being rescued. Depending what is red in your vision will determine its interpretation. Is it a symbol of ministry? Then the Lord is calling you to bring conviction to His people.

Physical healing: When praying for physical healing the Lord has often shown us the organ of the person that has been infected as either black or purple. As we pray we see it go red in the spirit. When we see that, we know that healing has taken place. Consider the following passages:

Speaking of rescue:

> *Joshua 2:18 unless, when we come into the land, you bind this line of* ***scarlet*** *cord in the window through which you let us down, and unless you bring your father, your mother, your brothers, and all your father's household to your own home.*

Speaking of wealth:

> *Proverbs 31:21 She is not afraid of snow for her household, for all her household is clothed with* ***scarlet****.*

NEGATIVE
Red also speaks of blood, sin and destruction. Consider the following verses:

Speaking of sin:

> *Isaiah 1:18 Come now, and let us reason together, says the Lord, though your sins are like* ***scarlet****, they shall be as white as snow; though they are* ***red*** *like* ***crimson****, they shall be as wool.*

Speaking of destruction and danger:

> *Nahum 2:3 The shields of his mighty men are made* ***red****, the valiant men are in* ***scarlet****. The chariots come with flaming torches in the day of his preparation, and the spears are brandished...*

See also: Blood

RING

The symbol of a covenant vow.

Positive:

- Marriage
- Your commitment to the Lord

Negative:

- To be in covenant with someone you should not
- To have broken covenant with God or man

CHARACTER SPECIFIC SYMBOL

POSITIVE

To receive a wedding ring in a dream may speak of your relationship with the Lord. It is a picture of His desire to draw you into a more intimate relationship with Him.

If you dream of your actual wedding ring, it could speak of your marriage at the moment.

If you dream of a wedding ring from a previous marriage, it could speak of your previous marriage.

If you dream of a ring you received as a child, it could speak of memories or circumstances that are being stirred up in you from that era.

NEGATIVE

If you dream that you lose your wedding ring, it could be an indication that something is wrong either with your relationship with the Lord or with your current spouse.

UNIVERSAL SYMBOL

POSITIVE

In Scriptures the ring is a picture of a covenant, authority and favor.

The signet ring: In the time of Esther, the King gave her his signet ring to send out a decree that could not be overruled.

> *Esther 8:2 So the king took off his signet **ring**, which he had taken from Haman, and gave it to Mordecai; and Esther appointed Mordecai over the house of Haman.*

If you have a vision of receiving a ring, then the Lord is saying that He is giving you some of His authority, and for you to use it in the earth.

It is one thing to receive authority and another to walk in it. Perhaps you have not been standing in the authority that He has given you as a believer.

A vision of a ring is a go-ahead from the Lord to rise up and use His Word to speak things into the earth.

If you are in ministry, then this authority relates to ministry. The Lord is telling you to set His people free, using the anointing and authority that He has given to you.

Ring for decoration: Receiving a ring is also a picture of favor. The Lord is confirming that you are special to Him and that you have found favor in His eyes.

> *Luke 15:22 But the father said to his servants, Bring out the best robe and put it on him, and put a* ***ring*** *on his hand and sandals on his feet.*

Wedding ring: A wedding ring is a symbol of a blood covenant. In a dream it speaks of your relationship with the Lord Jesus.

In a prophetic dream or vision it speaks of a relationship that someone is in.

NEGATIVE

A ring is negative is if it is tarnished or you see it being hidden or stolen. This would indicate that you have given up the authority that God has given you.

It could also mean that the enemy has deceived you into thinking that you have no authority. In either case, it is time to rise up!

Wearing a wedding ring you should not? Have you "cheated" on the Lord or on your spouse? The Lord is warning you that you are committing to something that you should not.

See also: Jewelry, Bride, Bridegroom, Wedding

RIVER

A place of rest. It also represents the anointing of the Holy Spirit.

Positive: The Holy Spirit within
Negative: To allow circumstances or the thoughts of others to control you

CHARACTER SPECIFIC SYMBOL

POSITIVE

A river is a lovely place of rest. If you dream of being by a river, it means that the Lord is calling you into a time of rest and just receiving from Him.

You cannot control a river - you can only go with its flow. So let go of trying to figure things out and doing things your own way and let the Holy Spirit carry you.

A river is also a picture of the life we have in Christ. We have within us rivers of living water! I cover this more in my description on *Fountain*.

NEGATIVE
Rapids and a raging river speak of conflict and upheaval in your life.

Perhaps you feel frustrated and out of control at the moment. Your solution is to come into the presence of the Lord and to let Him take control of your life once again.

Your spirit is like a lake that looks so calm, but if you put a stick into it and stir the water, all the mud at the bottom starts to surface and make the water muddy.

This is such a good picture of when you start to press on into the things of God, all the junk that has been inside of you for years starts coming up.

If this has begun to happen to you, it is good news. The Lord is exposing these things to bring healing and to deal with them once and for all.

Universal Symbol

POSITIVE
We have rivers or streams of water inside of us. This is a picture of the Holy Spirit that dwells inside of every believer, and that continues to give us His power and anointing.

> *John 7:38 He who believes in Me, as the Scripture has said, out of his heart will flow* ***rivers*** *of living water.*

A river is a wonderful picture of the anointing.

When we come together as believers, we all combine our little tributaries to make one raging river! It is the first step towards revival.

> *Ezekiel 47:5 Again he measured one thousand, and it was a* ***river*** *that I could not cross; for the water was too deep, water in which one must swim, a* ***river*** *that could not be crossed.*

Waterfall: A waterfall is also a picture of the work of the Holy Spirit. Because of the power that a waterfall carries, it is a lovely picture of His revival power and the external anointing.

While a waterfall is a picture of the revival power of the Holy Spirit, a gentle stream is a lovely picture of the anointing that bubbles out from deep inside our spirits.

NEGATIVE
A river that is dirty or contaminated speaks of someone who has the anointing, but it has been contaminated with something that is not of the Lord. (Either the spirit of the world, or something demonic.)

To have a vision of sand being dumped into a river speaks of adding the works of the flesh contaminating the anointing. Your sin and works are contaminating the pure work of God in your life.

A raging river you cannot control also speaks of being swept away with the crowd – its time to stand in your convictions! It can also speak of being overwhelmed by your circumstances and allowing them to dictate your direction.

See also: Drowning, Fountain, Swimming, Water, Well

ROAD

A picture of your life, as it lies ahead of you.

Positive: The way God has already prepared for you
Negative: A warning of what the enemy has prepared to trip you up

CHARACTER SPECIFIC AND UNIVERSAL SYMBOLS

POSITIVE
Depending on the kind of road you are on, will determine how the next step of your journey is about to unfold.

A garden road represents a season of restful progress. It will be slower, but more enjoyable.

When in prayer: It is important to take into account who and what you are praying for at the time of receiving the vision. If you are praying as a group, then the road is a picture of what you will face together.

If you are praying for yourself, then that road is a picture of your own future.

The best road to see in Scripture is a straight and smooth road. When you are walking in the blessing of the Lord you can expect no hindrances, but an easy walk in life.

> *Proverbs 3:6 In all your ways know, recognize, and acknowledge Him, and He will direct and make straight and plain your paths. (AMP)*

Sometimes you might see treasures along the side of the road. This is a picture of the things you will learn or obtain as you continue in the direction you are already going in.

A highway is a picture of an open road that has been prepared for you. You might see a new road being opened to you. This is very positive! The Lord has gone ahead and prepared your way. The next season is going to have clear direction and a smooth path.

A hiking trail is a positive picture. It means that the Lord is about to take you on a journey of discovery. This is not a fast road! This is a process and you need to allow Him to complete everything in you according to the purpose of this journey.

A wilderness road is a picture of a direction that the Lord has prepared for you. Even though it might seem impossible and that you are surrounded by a wilderness, He is promising that He will make a way through.

> *Isaiah 43:19 Behold, I will do a new thing, now it shall spring forth; shall you not know it? I will even make a* ***road in the wilderness*** *and rivers in the desert.*

NEGATIVE
A dirt road indicates that the time ahead is going to be bumpy. It is also likely that the way has not yet been prepared and there needs to be a season of waiting before taking a step forward. The message is clear – it is not time right now to take this road!

When I see thorns or rocks along a road, I know the enemy has put things in the way of my goal to trip me up.

The reason why the Lord shows this to you is so that you can take authority over the enemy and clear that road!

If you dream that you take a wrong turn on the road, it means that you made a wrong choice somewhere along the line. You cannot try to find the right way from this vantage point. Rather you need to go back to where you missed it and try again.

To see a detour means that you are going off the main direction God has for you for now.

This is not necessarily all negative, as it could speak of a phase of training you need before you can continue in the direction you had.

> *Hosea 2:6 Therefore, behold, I will hedge up your way with thorns, and wall her in, so that she cannot find her* ***paths****.*

See also: Journey, Traveling

Rock

Something that causes you to stumble, or something that causes you to stand secure.

Positive: To be unmoved. Secure in your conviction
Negative: A big hindrance in your life

POSITIVE
A rock that you lean on or hold onto is a lovely picture of your faith in the Lord. It is there to keep you steady and prevent you from falling.

The best image we have for a rock is Jesus Christ. Solid and the foundation of the church, if you build your life on Him, no storm can overcome you!

> *1 Corinthians 10:4 and all drank the same spiritual drink. For they drank of that spiritual* ***Rock*** *that followed them, and that Rock was Christ.*

Standing on a rock speaks of being secure and not being moved by anything that goes on round about you. It means that you are doing things God's way.

NEGATIVE
A rock that causes you to hurt yourself or to stumble is a picture of a hindrance in your life.

Are you trying to go in a certain direction and you feel that you are being blocked? If so, then your dream is a confirmation of this.

I often see stones and rocks along a path when praying for someone. This is negative and speaks of the blockages the enemy has put in your way.

These things are not from the Lord, and you need to stand up in your spiritual authority to overcome them.

See also: Mountain, Stone

ROD

A position of authority. A tool used for correction.

Positive: The confirmation that you are under God's protection
Negative: To be cast down and beaten into submission against your will

UNIVERSAL SYMBOL

POSITIVE
A rod or staff can be compared to the kingly scepter.

It was Aaron's rod that budded, confirming his call as the first High Priest of Israel. It was Moses who also used his staff to perform the many miracles that took place.

When we have released someone into apostolic training, we often see the rod of Moses. This is showing that this person will function in an apostolic capacity.

To see the staff of the enemy being broken is also good. It means that their authority over you and their strength has been taken away.

> *Isaiah 14:5 The Lord has broken the* ***staff*** *of the wicked, the scepter of the rulers.*

Shepherd's staff: The shepherd also carried a staff to direct the sheep or to lift one up that might have fallen. It is a lovely picture of the ministry of the pastor.

NEGATIVE

As an Apostle, Paul had the authority to bring correction to the churches that were in his care. Seeing a rod in this context speaks needing to either bring or receive correction.

> *1 Corinthians 4:21 What do you want? Shall I come to you with a* ***rod****, or in love and a spirit of gentleness?*

That being said, if you feel that you are being "beaten" in your dream and vision and it feels negative, it could well speak of someone else trying to impose their ideas on you, causing you to submit to their will. They are using principles and the guise of it being "moral" or "from the Lord", but they are in fact asserting their own human will over you, causing you to come under their control and not the Lord's

Determine if the "submission" in your vision or dream is positive (as in the case of Apostle Paul) where God is telling you to give up your own ideas, or if it is negative and someone is imposing their will on you.

See also: Staff

ROOF

The finishing process of the work God has given you to do. It also represents your spiritual covering, both in the home and in the Church.

Positive:

- Your spiritual covering.
- Protection

Negative: Limitation

UNIVERSAL SYMBOL

POSITIVE

A roof is a picture of your covering from the work of the enemy. It is the protection of the Lord.

In the church it would also speak of those who are in authority over you. They are there to stand with you, protect you from the attacks of the enemy, and to be a source of blessing.

In the Old Testament, if someone took a stranger into their home, they were responsible for their lives and to protect them. Consider Lot who protected the two angels who he thought were men.

Construction: To see a roof being put in place is a fantastic picture of the Lord putting the "finishing" touches on your ministry. The roof can only be built once the rest of the building is up. You are making fantastic progress and you will soon see the completion of this season in your life and ministry.

NEGATIVE
To see a house without a roof or with a hole in the roof, indicates that the enemy has license to attack you.

Either you are not in submission to your spiritual authority, or your spiritual authority is not covering you correctly. You need to search your own heart to discern if you have stepped out of line.

If you keep "hitting the ceiling" in your dream or vision, then this means that you are being restricted right now. You have reached the limit of your potential and if you are going to grow further both spiritually and naturally, you need a bigger house!

This will require change. It means that either a renovation of your life is required, or you need to be put in a different set of circumstances that will enable you to grow again. This might mean changing jobs, churches, ministries or ministry functions.

See also: House

ROOT

Something that is permanently resident, having the potential for further growth. To be well grounded in a specific area. Also a representation of something that is grounded inside of you.

Positive:

- To be well grounded in the Word
- To have a solid conviction from the Lord

Negative:

- To be bound by a continual influence of the enemy
- To establish your life on a belief that is not of God

CHARACTER SPECIFIC SYMBOL

POSITIVE
A root is something that keeps the plant in place. It derives all its strength and its position from it.

To dream of roots going down is a picture of being solidly planted in a place.

If you dream of roots being plucked up, then it means that things are about to change in your life! You are about to be uprooted and go through a change of circumstances.

To dream of new roots indicates that you have suddenly matured in a particular area and are coming to the place where you can feel secure and comfortable.

To see a tree that is rooted near the water is a good picture of being rooted in the Word.

To see roots running deep into the soil is a promise that the Lord is going to bring you security and blessing.

> *2 Kings 19:30 And the remnant who have escaped of the house of Judah shall again take **root** downward, and bear fruit upward.*

NEGATIVE

Sometimes the roots in our lives are not positive.

When it comes to things such as roots of the flesh or roots to your past that might be negative, then you have to deal with them using the Word.

In the *Crucified Life* I teach in more detail on the roots of the flesh. There are three main roots being lust, bitterness and temporal values. Bitterness is the tap root.

When ministering to people, I have often seen a black root going down the middle of them. This is a picture of a root of bitterness that they have in their lives.

> *Hebrews 12:15 looking carefully lest anyone fall short of the grace of God; lest any **root** of bitterness springing up cause trouble, and by this many become defiled;*

Seeing a root can also speak of a generational curse, referring to your family roots.

Seeing the root of a tree being cut is a picture of something that has not borne any fruit and is useless.

This could be a picture of things you are holding onto and wanting to take off, but they have not. If you see this vision, then the Lord is telling you to let it go. This is a good picture of a death of a vision.

> *Matthew 3:10 And even now the ax is laid to the **root** of the trees. Therefore, every tree which does not bear good fruit is cut down and thrown into the fire.*

See also: Bitterness, Branch, Plants, Seed, Trees

ROPE

An image of strength, unity and the ability to save.

Positive: A picture of strength and security (As in the threefold cord that cannot be broken)
Negative: Rope, like chain, speaks of bondage and restriction.

CHARACTER SPECIFIC SYMBOL

POSITIVE

If you are clinging on to a rope in your dream, then this is speaking of being saved. It means that even though you feel alone right now, help is on the way. Hang in there. This situation is not going to last forever.

NEGATIVE

If you sense a lot of fear in your dream and you are losing your grip on the rope, it means that you are "coming to the end of your rope." You are emotionally overwhelmed right now and it is time to stop and reevaluate your life and circumstances. You need to find peace in Jesus, because He is waiting right there to catch you!

UNIVERSAL SYMBOL

POSITIVE

To dream of being tied to your spouse or to someone you love, speaks of unity with the Lord.

A ship is tied to the dock with a rope, representing security.

A thread: Once when I was going through a hard time, I saw myself clinging to a scarlet thread. The Lord said to me, "Just cling to me Colette, I will not let you go!" It seemed that it took all my faith to cling to that thread. Not only did I get through that storm with the Lord by my side, but I came out of it stronger than ever before.

A threefold cord speaks of strength and unity. It can be very positive if it is tying a couple together in marriage.

I recall a vision when my husband Craig and I were receiving ministry about being married. My dad saw a vision of us tied together with strong ropes that could not be broken.

Because my parents had been divorced, I feared the same thing in my own life. The Lord made me a strong promise that I had nothing to fear. I am glad to say that our marriage is stronger than ever!

With my husband, myself and the Lord, we are a picture of a threefold cord that could not be broken.

> *Ecclesiastes 4:12 Though one may be overpowered by another, two can withstand him. And a threefold* ***cord*** *is not quickly broken.*

NEGATIVE
To dream of having your hands tied is a picture of being restricted and unable to do the things you need to do.

Being tied by rope to something could also indicate that you are being bound by whatever that object or person represents in your dreams.

Being bound by a rope can speak of the work of the enemy to bind you and prevent you from doing what the Lord wants you to do, just like Delilah bound Samson.

> *Judges 15:13 ... And they bound him with two new* ***cords****, and brought him up from the rock.*

A rope attaching you to someone else could speak of a spiritual bond that needs to be broken. In the spirit, you might see a person tied with cords that are in turn attached to various people.

If the people you see are family members, then that rope is a picture of generational bondage.

You can also see this in relation to past mentors or friends that you have not fully let go yet. If you see this vision, then the Lord is telling you to let those people go and to move on.

For more on how to break spiritual links, read the *Prophetic Warrior*.

See also: Cords, Chains, Prison

ROSE

A rose in bloom speaks of maturity and of beauty.

Positive: Maturity
Negative: A season that has past

POSITIVE
If you dream or see a vision of a rose, it means that the Lord desires to bring the beauty and the potential out of you. This is a time of rejoicing and you should look forward to the future.

> *Isaiah 35:1 The wilderness and the wasteland shall be glad for them, and the desert shall rejoice and blossom as the* ***rose****.*

Rose of Sharon: The rose of Sharon mentioned in Scriptures is not the same as a rose as we know it today. Rather it was a very fragrant but less attractive flower.

This is a picture of someone, who although they are plain on the outside, has something of great worth inside of them.

NEGATIVE
A fading flower speaks of a season that has past. It is a good picture of a death of a vision. It is something that once was wonderful, but now has come to its end.

If you dream or see a vision of a fading flower, then the Lord is telling you to let go of the past season and to move on.

It is also an indication that the harvest you enjoyed a while ago is coming to an end, and it is time for you to start sowing again.

> *1 Peter 1:24 Because All flesh is as grass, and all the glory of man as the flower of the grass. The grass withers, and its flower falls away,*

See also: Flowers, Smelling

RUBY

A picture of favor, royalty and passion. To be held as a Ruby means that the Lord intends to bring you into the open and show you off.

Positive: For the Lord to display the beauty He has put within you
Negative: For your potential to be withheld

POSITIVE
Wisdom is said to be worth more than rubies.

> *Proverbs 8:11 For wisdom is better than* ***rubies****, and all the things one may desire cannot be compared with her.*

It is also a gemstone that stands out and can be seen by many. For the Lord to say that you are His "Ruby" means that He does not intend to keep you hidden, but to hold you up for all to see – because you are of great value!

> *Proverbs 31:10 Who can find a virtuous wife? For her worth is far above* ***rubies***

Out of interest, in the spirit when we have seen the crown of David or the sword of David (in relation to the Apostolic Office), we have often seen it set with a Ruby in the hilt.

This is a perfect image for David and also the David Apostle that tends to be more passionate and prophetic in his orientation. (This is simply personal experience in the realm of the spirit. Your experiences may differ)

NEGATIVE
A tarnished or broken Ruby speaks of being held back from showing your true potential. Your worth is either being hindered or it needs to be increased.

Because a Ruby speaks of your ability and potential, could it be that this measure must be increased in your life?

It could be that what you have is not enough, and the Lord desires to increase your value.

See also: Pearls, Jewelry, Emerald, Diamonds

RUST

Corrosion due to neglect.

Positive: The passing of an old season
Negative: Loss and destruction

UNIVERSAL SYMBOL

POSITIVE

When Craig and I married he had a favorite T-Shirt that he wore with pride. It was threadbare and I could see the color of his skin through it. Holey and raggedy, it soon found its demise in an "unfortunate laundry mishap" not long after we got married.

This is a good picture of this symbol! There comes a time when even the best seasons wax old! There comes a time when we must allow nature to take its course and to let go of the things we hankered after in the past. If you dream or see something in the spirit that is rusted from your past, the Lord is saying, "That season has waxed old! It's time to let it go and move onto the new."

> *Isaiah 51:6: for the heavens shall vanish away like smoke, and the earth shall wax old like a garment, and they that dwell therein shall die in like manner: but my salvation shall be for ever, and my righteousness shall not be abolished. (KJV)*

NEGATIVE

If what is rusted is valuable, then the Lord is saying that your blessings are being slowly eaten away because of your neglect. Living by the coast, I know this well! I left a teaspoon on my balcony once and in just a few days a layer of rust had covered it! I had not taken care. I could have avoided that rust. In the same way, rust is avoidable.

As you fight for your promises and maintain your faith, you nurture your blessings. When you give satan license or walk in doubt, it does not take long for rust to take over.

> *Luke 12:33 Sell what you have and give alms; provide yourselves money bags which do not grow old, a treasure in the heavens that does not fail, where no thief approaches nor moth destroys*

See also: Moth

Symbols Starting in S

Symbols Starting in S

Salt

A subtle influence that brings about an immense change, whether positive or negative.

Positive:

- Joy
- Life
- Healing

Negative: Judgment

Universal Symbol

POSITIVE

Salt adds flavor to life, and it is a lovely picture of who we are as believers.

Just like salt can bring out the flavor of something that is tasteless, so are believers meant to be bringing life and light to the world around us.

> *Matthew 5:13 You are the salt of the earth; but if the **salt** loses its flavor, how shall it be seasoned? It is then good for nothing but to be thrown out and trampled underfoot by men.*

> *Colossians 4:6 Let your speech always be with grace, seasoned with **salt**, that you may know how you ought to answer each one.*

Salt was also used to preserve things and has healing abilities. To see the Lord applying salt to you implies that He is bringing healing in your life.

> *2 Kings 2:21 Then he went out to the source of the water, and cast in the **salt** there, and said, Thus says the Lord: I have healed this water; from it there shall be no more death or barrenness.*

NEGATIVE

Here salt speaks of judgment and of being tested. Although salt can bring healing, too much of it can bring harm.

A good picture of this is the Red Sea. It has no life in it because of the high concentration of salt.

The Red Sea itself is a good picture of someone who always takes in all the ministry and teachings that he can, but never pours out. Instead of being a source of life, he becomes stagnant and stale.

> *Mark 9:49 For every one shall be **salted** with fire, and every sacrifice shall be **salted** with **salt**. (KJV)*

Too much salt can ruin a good meal. Just like salt in a good sense can bring about flavor, this influence can also be negative. What is "salting" your life right now? The influence of someone ungodly? The world? Your own hurts? Consider what is being an influence, because it might be subtle, but it is forever changing the "flavor" of your life and who you are right now. This is very similar to the interpretation for *Yeast*.

See also: Ocean, Yeast

SCHOOL

The interpretation for a dream of a school, college and University is twofold:

1. *Gaining knowledge and qualifying in a particular realm of your life.*
2. *The educational system of the world.*

Positive: The proof of your qualification
Negative: The proof of your ignorance

CHARACTER SPECIFIC SYMBOL

POSITIVE
Depending on your personal view of school, you will have a different interpretation. The most universal of course is a place of learning, and it speaks of the knowledge you have attained over the years.

If you dream that you pass a test or go up a grade in school, it means that you have passed a spiritual test and that you are ready to move forward.

It is an indication that you qualified in the task that the Lord gave you to do, and now you are ready to be promoted to a new level.

Of course with that new level will come more testing and learning.

> *Matthew 25:21 His lord said to him, Well done, good and **faithful** servant; you were **faithful** over a few things, I will make you ruler over many things. Enter into the joy of your lord.*

This may speak of spiritual maturity or of a ministry office.

If you dream of going to a school or University, it means that there is some knowledge that you lack and the Lord wants you to receive it.

If you dream of a school you attended in the past and your emotions are intense, then what you are looking at is a good example of a healing or purging dream that relates to that era in your life.

NEGATIVE

If you dream that you have to write the same test repeatedly or repeat a grade, it means that you have not learned the lesson that God needs you to, and so you keep "going around the same mountain" so to speak.

If you keep dreaming of a school you attended in the past, it could mean that there are still hurts from this area that are troubling you.

See also: Buildings, Testing

SCORPION

A spirit of infirmity that is responsible for a lot of pain.

Dreaming or seeing a scorpion in vision means that you are being attacked by a spirit of infirmity.

I suffered once with terrible sciatic pain. No matter what medication I took or how often I went to the chiropractor, it did not let up.

One evening as my husband Craig was praying for me, he saw a scorpion in the spirit on my back. He took authority over it in the name of Jesus and the pain left instantly.

From having to take medication continuously, I was completely set free.

If you are suffering with a particular pain or sickness and no medication seems to work, then you are dealing with more than just a physical problem. You are dealing with a spirit of infirmity.

> *Luke 10:19 Behold, I give you the authority to trample on serpents and **scorpions**, and over all the power of the enemy, and nothing shall by any means hurt you.*

See also: Demons, Insects

SCROLL

The scroll of ancient times is what we would call books in our modern age. It is a picture of the Word of God spoken as a decree.

Positive: A spoken decree

Negative:

- Bondage to the law.
- A decree spoken against you

POSITIVE
I have seen scrolls many times in the spirit. I have seen a messenger angel carrying a scroll. This indicates that he is bringing a message.

Usually when I see this, someone in the group has a word of prophesy.

I have also seen a scroll that has various seals on it. This is a picture of the decree that the Lord has sent for my life. Each seal represented a different phase of the journey that was ahead of me.

The scroll is a wonderful picture of the Word of God that either needs to be spoken into the earth or has already been spoken.

> *Ezekiel 2:9 Now when I looked, there was a hand stretched out to me; and behold,* ***a scroll of a book*** *was in it;*

NEGATIVE
Negatively a scroll can speak of bondage to the law. It says in Romans 3:28 that we are justified by faith and not the works of the law.

In addition to that, if you see a scroll that feels negative in the spirit, it is speaking of a decree that the enemy has sent out against you. I will often see a scroll in the spirit that the Lord will say I need to burn – thus destroying the plans of the enemy! A good example of this is the letter written against the building of the temple in the day of Ezra.

> *Ezra 4:23 Now when the copy of King Artaxerxes'* ***letter*** *was read before Rehum, Shimshai the scribe, and their companions, they went up in haste to Jerusalem against the Jews, and by force of arms made them cease*

The good news? This was eventually overthrown by the original decree made by the king. In the same way – it does not matter what satan intends because even that will be turned around for your good!

See also: Book, Contract, Letter, Pen, Seal (Wax Seal), Signature

SEAL (WAX SEAL AND "EMBLEM")

Secret instructions that are time sensitive. Usually given by the person who has the authority to give that instruction.

Positive:

- A "set in stone" direction from the Lord
- To be set apart

Negative:

- For the enemy to have set a specific plan in motion that involves you

Universal Symbol

POSITIVE

I have often seen scrolls with a wax seal on it in vision. It usually came at a time when I was seeking the Lord regarding our ministry and direction for the future. I mention in the symbol *Scroll* how I can see a scroll with a number of seals on it. When I see this, I see that there are a number of sets of instructions and seasons I need to pass through.

A seal is also something that is "set in stone." In other words, the decree has been established and it has been determined by the Lord! The purpose for God's plan is set and cannot be undone. This passage says it perfectly,

> *Daniel 6:17 Then a stone was brought and laid on the mouth of the den, and the king sealed it with his own signet ring and with the signets of his lords, that the purpose concerning Daniel might not be changed.*

Speaking of how a seal has a set of instructions that are time sensitive:

> *Daniel 12:9 And he said, "Go your way, Daniel, for the words are closed up and sealed till the time of the end.*

A seal also symbolizes someone's authority. So if you see a specific symbol or "seal," the Lord is telling you the level of authority that they have been given. The Word tells us that we are "sealed" for Christ. In other words, we are "set in stone" in the Kingdom.

Again, it speaks of purpose, however in this case, the purpose is confirmed by the person placing the seal over you. Branding can also fall into this category. The Lord set His seal on Paul, and that seal's purpose was reflected in the Corinthian Church. What does your seal look like today? What is God's purpose for your life and are you fulfilling it?

> *1 Corinthians 9:2 If I am not an apostle to others, yet doubtless I am to you. For you are the seal of my apostleship in the Lord.*

NEGATIVE

A seal broken before it's time, speaks of preempting the work of the Lord. The enemy's seal speaks of his purpose for your life. You might also have a "seal" that means that you are fulfilling someone else's purpose instead of your own.

I suggest looking at the symbol "Tattoo" for more on this.

See also: Scroll, Tattoo

Seasons

The phases of work, rest and reward in your life.

Spring: *A season of resurrection.*

Springtime is a season of potential. It heralds the beginning of something new. If you see a vision of spring it means that you will start to see life once again. After winter has left and the snow has melted all the seedlings that had gone through death now start to come to life.

It is the ultimate season of resurrection!

> *Song of Songs 2:11 For lo, the winter is past, the rain is over and gone; 12 The flowers appear on the earth; the time of singing has come, and the voice of the turtledove is heard in our land;*

Summer: A season of work.

Summer brings with it fruitfulness, but also a lot of hard work because the harvest is ripe. That means that now you must put your hand to the plough and bring it in.

In our spiritual lives there are times when we must work and then times when the Lord works. If you see a season of summer in the spirit, it means that now is the time to work. If you have been waiting for direction or the "go ahead" from the Lord, seeing summer in the spirit means that now is the time to give it all you have.

> *Proverbs 10:5 He who gathers in **summer** is a wise son; he who sleeps in harvest is a son who causes shame.*

Autumn/Fall: A season of eating the fruits of your labor.

This is the season of harvest time. It is a season of eating the fruits of your labor. All through summer you have worked and harvested what was reaped during summer. Autumn in many cultures is a time of rejoicing.

The same applies to your spiritual life. If you dream or have a vision of Autumn, the Lord is saying that it is time to enjoy the fruit of your labor.

> *Leviticus 26:5 Your threshing shall last till the time of vintage, and the vintage shall last till the time of sowing; you shall eat your bread to the full, and dwell in your land safely.*

Winter: A season of rest.

Winter is seen mostly as negative in scripture, but it is also a season of rest. If you have been working hard and then dream that winter is coming, then this means that a time of rest is coming.

Winter is when the fields are allowed to rest and the snow begins to fall. Although it is not always pleasant, that snow or rain feeds the soil. You cannot continually live in a season of work. You also need your seasons of Winter to step back and to allow God to do His work in your life.

See also: Harvest, Rain, Fruit

SEED

A promise of something to come.

Positive: The potential to produce greatness
Negative: A small influence that will lead to bigger problems down the line

CHARACTER SPECIFIC SYMBOL

POSITIVE
To dream of planting seeds speaks of investing into something that will later bear fruit. If you dream of receiving a seed, it has the same picture. In both cases however, some work is involved before you can reap the fruit.

So, although it speaks of a promise of a harvest, you need to be diligent to sow!

If the seeds that you are sowing are related to your business or workplace, then they speak of the effort and the time you are putting into your work.

They are seeds that will later reap many benefits for you.

In ministry you also sow seeds that you do not see the fruit of right away.

If you dream that someone gives you a seed, it means that you have received a blessing, anointing or ability from someone, but again it requires action on your part.

They can gladly give you the seed of their success or anointing, but it is for you to take it and walk it out.

NEGATIVE
If you dream that the seeds are shriveled and useless, then it means that the promises you were given have been stolen from you.

This could be a result of failure on your part, or perhaps a curse prevalent in your life.

If you dream that you receive a seed that you feel is negative, then it means that you are accepting something from another person that is not a blessing at all. You do not need to be forced to take it!

UNIVERSAL SYMBOL

POSITIVE
Speaking of spiritual parenting: A seed also speaks of where you originate from. In a spiritual sense it speaks of your spiritual parents.

If you dream of a seed or a seedling that is growing, it could be a picture of the spiritual blessing you have received from your spiritual parents.

If you see that seedling being plucked up and replanted, it may be an indication that the Lord is going to remove you from your current spiritual parents and give you new ones.

> *John 15:16 You did not choose Me, but I chose you and appointed you that you should go and **bear fruit**, and that **your fruit** should remain, that whatever you ask the Father in My name He may give you:*

Speaking of sowing in ministry: The sower sowing the Word is a perfect picture of real ministry. Daily you sow and give out, but1d not every seed survives.

When we started our first Prophetic School I was very active and directly involved with all the students. We had quite a crowd and I did everything I could to care for each one. I would run after each one and work so hard until I was drained.

The Lord showed me a garden with seeds in it. He showed me how some of the seeds flourished, and how others did not grow at all.

He said that as a gardener I would take care of the seeds that were growing, not neglect them and care for the dead seeds instead!

The message was clear. I was spending so much time on students who had no intention of following through, and neglecting those with a real fire for the Lord.

In my efforts to try and make everyone happy, those who had a real heart for God were being neglected. Certainly this is a good lesson for anyone in ministry. It is important that we sow our seeds in good soil for a good harvest.

> *2 Corinthians 9:10 Now may He who supplies **seed** to the sower, and bread for food, supply and multiply the **seed** you have sown and increase the fruits of your righteousness,*

Speaking of faith: The mustard seed has always been a picture of faith. Although it starts out small, it has the potential to grow very large.

If you see your faith as a mustard seed, then you have a long way to go! Although it is an illustration of faith, it does not mean that your faith should just remain as a seed! It has to grow.

If the Lord shows you a mustard seed, then He is telling you that it is time to increase your faith and grow it into a big tree that many can benefit from.

> *Luke 13:19 It is like a mustard **seed**, which a man took and put in his garden; and it grew and became a large tree, and the birds of the air nested in its branches.*

NEGATIVE

This one can appear both positive and negative. At first it might seem that the seed has died, but it is only for the purpose of resurrection.

If you are in ministry you will experience this often. Your visions will be called to death.

> *John 12:24 Most assuredly, I say to you, unless a* ***grain of wheat*** *falls into the ground and dies, it remains alone; but if it dies, it produces much grain.*

To receive a negative seed means that you are accepting something that at first seems insignificant, but will become a big problem down the line. You might be compromising or taking in just one small idea that does not seem to be a big deal now, but beware – this seed has the potential to grow into something you do not anticipate!

See also: Fruit, Harvest, Trees

Shadow/Shade

Positive: To hide under a shadow means to come under the protection of God.
Negative: Something that appears menacing but holds no power over you.

Character Specific and Universal Symbols

POSITIVE
To dream of resting in the shade, away from the sun, means that the Lord is calling you to hide in His presence, away from the pressures of life. He wants to give you a moment of rest so that you can become strong again.

Hiding in the shadow of the Lord also speaks about being given a position of favor with the Lord. (Psalms 17:8)

Resting in the shadow of the Lord is also a call to know Him intimately,

> *Song of Solomon 2:3 As the apple tree among the trees of the wood, so is my beloved among the sons. I sat down under his* ***shadow*** *with great delight, and his fruit was sweet to my taste.*

NEGATIVE
A shadow is something that is not permanent. It is just a transitional season and so, if you dream or see a vision of being in a shadow, it means that struggle will not last for long.

If you are fighting shadows, it means that the enemy has sidetracked you with trickery. He has tried to appear larger than life, but he is just mist! He has no power over you.

See also: Fog

SHEEP

- *Believers in the church.*
- *Innocence and vulnerability.*

POSITIVE
Sheep are most commonly a picture of people, specifically the body of Christ in Scriptures. The sheep always listen to the voice of their shepherd.

I have often seen sheep in the spirit relating to the Body of Christ. Lambs refer to believes who are still young in the Lord.

Sheep that are well fed and look healthy are a representation of a church congregation that is spiritually healthy.

> *John 10:27 My **sheep** hear My voice, and I know them, and they follow Me:*

Sheep are also innocent, and if the Lord is saying that He is sending you out as a sheep, then He is telling you to remain weak and vulnerable. To be innocent and to accept others.

> *Matthew 10:16 Behold, I send you out as **sheep** in the midst of wolves. Therefore, be wise as serpents and harmless as doves.*

The black sheep: To be different and to stand out from the others. The "one" that Jesus leaves the 99 to find. In our ministry we call ourselves the black sheep, because we often did not fit in anywhere else!

If you are called to the work of the ministry, it is quite likely that you are a black sheep that only fits in when you find your own herd of fellow black sheep!

NEGATIVE
To see sheep being torn apart, speaks of what is happening in the church.

Unfortunately, it is a sad situation when leaders do not care for those under them, and instead abuse or neglect them.

> *Jeremiah 50:17 Israel is like scattered **sheep**; the lions have driven him away. First the king of Assyria devoured him; now at last this Nebuchadnezzar king of Babylon has broken his bones.*

All of the fivefold ministry are called to lay their life down for the sheep; not only in investing themselves into others, but in facing the cross daily.

See also: Lamb

SHEPHERD

- *A protector and a leader.*
- *Also representative of the pastoral ministry*

POSITIVE

The shepherd who cares for the sheep is a lovely picture of a leader that has a pastoral heart. The shepherd has a twofold function:

1. To lead the sheep

2. To feed and protect the sheep

It is a position of administration as well as a spiritual gift. In a ministry context, the shepherd is a picture of the pastor.

> *John 10:14 I am the good* ***shepherd****; and I know My sheep, and am known by My own*

It is said that often in the East many shepherds gather to feed their sheep together, forming one huge flock.

When it is time to leave, each shepherd stands and calls to his sheep. The sheep all know the sound of their master. Even though they might be mingled in one huge group, at the sound of his call each sheep will follow its own shepherd.

If sheep do not want to follow a shepherd, then the message is clear, they are not his! The sheep know their shepherd and will follow no matter what you tell them.

> *John 10:4 And when he brings out* ***his own sheep****, he goes before them; and the sheep follow him, for they know his voice.*

NEGATIVE

The shepherd always goes ahead of the sheep. If you see a shepherd beating the sheep from behind, then what you are seeing is the butcher – not a true shepherd!

A shepherd trying to come in the back door is also negative and a picture of a person who has only come to steal life from God's people.

> *John 10:1 Most assuredly, I say to you, he who does not enter the sheepfold by the door, but climbs up some other way, the same is a thief and a robber.*

See also: Lamb, Sheep

SHIELD

- *Protection*
- *A representation of strength and position*

Positive: A place of temporary rest in the middle of battle
Negative: The hiding place of the enemy

POSITIVE
A shield is a perfect picture of the protection that we have in the Lord. In the middle of battle, we can hide behind His shield! It does not mean that you no longer have to face the battle though. You must still fight, but you can do so, knowing that you will be protected.

A shield is also a picture of faith in the Scriptures.

When you trust the Lord and have faith in Him, then He can protect you and do mighty things on your behalf.

> *Proverbs 30:5 Every word of God is pure; He is a* ***shield*** *to those who put their trust in Him*

Our shield of faith prevents us from coming under the attack of the enemy, or any curse. You do not overcome by sending your own arrows. Rather you just put up your shield of faith!

> *Ephesians 6:16 Above all, taking the* ***shield*** *of faith with which you will be able to quench all the fiery darts of the wicked one.*

> *Psalms 3:3 But You, O Lord, are a* ***shield*** *for me, my glory and the One who lifts up my head.*

Ornate shield: Shields are mostly used in warfare, however an ornate sword was a deliberate show of wealth and position. Solomon made two hundred of them and put them in his palace. It represented the protection he received from the Lord as well as a clear display of his wealth and position.

> *1 Kings 10:16 And King Solomon made two hundred large shields of hammered gold; six hundred shekels of gold went into each shield*

Emblem: Shield: Because a shield was very much part of the uniform a soldier wore it is also a representation of your "tribe" or those things you ally yourself to. What is protecting you? If a specific emblem stands out in a vision or dream it is an indication of what you are using to protect yourself.

NEGATIVE
Shields are positive for the most part, but naturally the shield of an enemy would be negative. A black shield standing against you speaks of opposition from the enemy.

For your shield to become tarnished or to rust is also negative. You are not investing into your spiritual life and remaining in the hand of God. You are walking in the flesh and this is causing you to step out of God's protection.

See also: Armor, Arrow, Bow, Darts, Sword

SHIP

A vehicle for your ministry, or a representation of your business.

POSITIVE
Ships are a picture of both training and releasing God's people to do the work. Here is one of my favorite passages on the subject:

> *Isaiah 60:9 Surely the coastlands shall wait for Me; And the* ***ships*** *of Tarshish will come first, To bring your sons from afar, Their silver and their gold with them, To the name of the Lord your God, And to the Holy One of Israel, Because He has glorified you*

I have often seen our ministry as an aircraft carrier, especially relating to training the fivefold ministry.

Just as an aircraft carrier goes out into the waters and from there releases the fighter jets, so also does a training ministry send out those that qualify.

A sailing ship: In the Old Testament most ships were transport and trade ships. One of their primary functions was to carry cargo.

Because of this, a sailing ship often represents your business in a dream. It can also refer to your job or workplace.

Submarine: Because of its nature, this ship speaks of counter insurgence warfare. It speaks of a ministry that is called to go "under the radar" and bring surprise attacks to the enemy. A good ministry would be that of intercession. Prayer warriors who go "undercover" and undermine the work of the enemy through their hidden prayer closets!

NEGATIVE
Of course, if the submarine you see is negative, it speaks of a sneak attack from the enemy. He has remained hidden and has now revealed himself to attack. I teach more on counter insurgence warfare in my book *Prophetic Counter Insurgence*

If you dream of a shipwreck, then the Lord is warning you that trouble is coming to your business and you need to prepare for it. Depending on the context of the dream, some of the other symbols should be able to tell you the source of this trouble and how to avoid it.

A leak or hole in your boat indicates an area where the enemy is gaining access to bring destruction. There is something in your life or business that is sinking your ship!

More detail is given in the symbol *Boat*

See also: Boat, Vehicles

SHOES

- *Your walk with the Lord*
- *Walk of life.*

POSITIVE

To receive new shoes means that you are about to enter into something new in your walk with the Lord.

Depending on what the shoes look like, will give you an indication of the direction.

Feminine high-heels would mean that the Lord is going to bring out your femininity.

Farmers boots indicates a new season of sowing or of taking care of the sheep.

NEGATIVE

To dream of putting on old and broken shoes is negative. It means that you are trying to walk out an old season in your life that has long past. Let it go!

Just like shoes serve a purpose and a season, so also does our walk with the Lord. The Lord takes us through many seasons of learning and growth. The purpose is to keep walking forward and not to look back like Lot's wife.

I had a dream once where I discovered that my favorite new shoes got chewed up by the dog. The Lord was warning me that the enemy was trying to attack the new direction He had given me.

Big shoes: Shoes that are too big or that you should not be wearing are an indication that you are trying to live someone else's life! Each of us walk out our own call in fear and trembling. You cannot walk out someone else's call or fulfill their responsibility

> *Philippians 2:12 Therefore, my beloved, as you have always obeyed, not as in my presence only, but now much more in my absence,* ***work out your own salvation*** *with fear and trembling*

Struggling to walk: To wear shoes that do not fit correctly or that you cannot walk in means that you are uncomfortable in the situation you are in right now. This is not something familiar to you. You need to determine if the Lord intends for you to make this situation familiar or if you need to be walking in different shoes!

See also: Feet, Road

SHOWER

A very private experience where you are pulled aside to deal with what is currently going on in your life.

Positive:

- A cleansing process
- To be surrounded with blessing.

Negative: Using the flesh to overcome sin

CHARACTER SPECIFIC AND UNIVERSAL SYMBOLS

POSITIVE

To dream of taking a shower is very similar to bathing. It refers to a process of cleansing. In a shower you are completely surrounded with the cleansing and blessing of the Lord.

To dream of being showered with milk or something that is positive, means that the Lord will completely surround you with His provision and blessing.

To be showered with gold means that you have found favor in the Lord's eyes, and that He is going to bless you.

To dream of showering in oil speaks of being covered with the Anointing.

Shower – rain: The Scriptures tell us that we will be blessed coming in and going out. That no matter which direction we turn, that He will be there.

To be showered with the Lord's grace means that He will watch every step you take. Not only will He wash the negative influences from you, but He will lead you out again and surround you with His blessing.

When referring to rain, this kind of shower speaks of the cleansing blessing of the Lord. Not only does it wash away the old, but it brings out treasures and good things.

> *Ezekiel 34:26 I will make them and the places all around My hill a blessing; and I will cause **showers** to come down in their season; there shall be **showers** of blessing.*

NEGATIVE

If you dream of a shower that is dirty, it means that you are trying to deal with your sin using the flesh. Although you recognize that there is something wrong in your life, you are trying to fix it yourself.

Only the Holy Spirit can bring real cleansing. You need His living waters!

See also: Basin, Bath, Rain

SIBLINGS

Consider your relationship with your siblings. Here are some ideas to help you to determine what they might mean.

Positive:

- Faith
- Hope
- Love
- The Holy Spirit
- Your mind, emotions or will
- Your spiritual DNA

Negative:

- Hurts of the past
- Accusation
- Pride
- Your flesh

CHARACTER SPECIFIC SYMBOL

It is important that you identify what kind of relationship you have with your sister or brother.

When you think of your sister or brother, what is the first thing that comes to your mind to describe them? What about them stands out the most?

Perhaps your sister is willful. She could speak of your will. Maybe she is insecure, in which case she would speak of insecurity.

Perhaps your brother is highly intellectual, then he would likely speak of your intellect. Maybe your brother was the kind of person that always protected you. In this case he could speak of the Holy Spirit in your dreams.

UNIVERSAL SYMBOL

When I see someone's sibling during ministry, the Lord usually wants to address an issue. Often the Lord indicates that the person needs to break links with their sibling. Other times inner healing needs to take place.

The Lord will give you an inner knowing or impression to go along with the vision. So remain sensitive to the spirit, and you will be able to understand exactly what the Lord wants you to do with the revelation He gave you.

Speaking of the family of Christ:

> *Matthew 12:50 For whoever does the will of My Father in heaven is* ***My brother and sister*** *and mother.*

See also: Ancestor, Family

SIGNATURE

Authority given for any given task or instruction

Positive: To follow through with your conviction
Negative: For someone to purposefully act against you

CHARACTER SPECIFIC SYMBOL

POSITIVE
To "sign on the dotted line" means to make a commitment to whatever the document represents. You are taking responsibility and ownership. This is certainly a sign of maturity and to dream or see a vision of signing a paper means that you are following through on your conviction and putting your full authority behind it.

> *Galatians 6:11 See with what large letters I have written to you with my own hand!*

In the spirit once, as I was in warfare, I saw Pharaoh (the god of this world) and the Lord had me tell him to "sign" the release to let go of the provision that was rightfully ours! Not long after that, we saw the financial promise that God had given us come through.

Signing a contract is the same thing. It means that you are taking personal responsibility for what that contract/decree represents. It is now in your care, and is for you to follow through.

NEGATIVE
I have often seen papers in the spirit with the signature of the enemy on it. It was his intentions and plans for us, all laid out. This is certainly the realm of those in full-time ministry who will do spiritual warfare at the highest level.

Keep in mind that a signature means using your authority, so if the signature you see is from someone specifically, it means that someone is purposefully acting against you!

See also: Book, Contract, Letter, Pen, Seal, Scroll

SILVER

Positive:

- *Redemption*
- *Humanity*
- *Money*

Negative:

- Greed

The price of a slave was 30 pieces of silver. Judas betrayed the Lord for thirty pieces of silver. (Matthew 26:15)

It is a reminder that we have been redeemed by the blood of Christ and as a result are now heirs. It is a reminder that we were bought at a very costly price.

There was a Jewish Ceremony called the Feast of Tabernacles. On the day of the feast at the crowning ceremony the Priest would go down to the Pool of Siloam and would bring out a golden goblet of water. Then he would pour the water out of the golden goblet into some silver goblets.

This was a picture of what Jesus was sent to do. He was the golden goblet and we are the silver ones. Because of Him we now have the rivers of living water. If you see a silver cup being filled, this means that the Lord desires to fill you with His anointing.

A silver sword speaks of warfare – the kind that is done by someone who is evangelistic. It is a rugged tool that sets the captives free.

Silver is also a picture of money and trade. Depending on the context of your dream or vision, silver could either represent greed or financial blessing. The Lord has often shown me various tools of silver for those with a business calling.

The Lord once gave my husband, Craig and I a two edged sword. The one side was gold and the other was silver. The Lord said He was bringing the two aspects of our callings together. The one being a clear ministry call and the other a business call.

See also: Colors, Money

SKELETON

The inner you, whether strong or weak

Positive:

- Having a strong support system
- To be capable of great strength
- To be spiritually healthy
- A call to "put the pieces together"

Negative:

- Death
- To be spiritually emaciated
- Warning of danger

Character Specific Symbol

POSITIVE

To have a "skeleton" in an administrative sense speaks of putting together an ordered framework. Our skeleton is what supports the rest of our bodies. So to dream of a skeleton being broken or established is referring to a structure that needs to be set in place.

NEGATIVE

In most cultures, a skeleton is negative and speaks of death. It might also be speaking of your personal fears, of a shadow looming over your life that you are afraid of.

Universal Symbol

POSITIVE

In Scripture, a skeleton spoke of the capacity for great strength. To have "strong bones" indicates the ability to accomplish great feats. So if you have a prophetic dream or vision, then a skeleton or "strong bones" would speak of both the potential for strength and being spiritually healthy.

To accomplish the work that God has given to you, you need a strong "spiritual skeleton!" In other words, not only do you need to be well structured, but you also need to be capable and have a strong conviction for that structure.

> *Job 40:18-19 His bones are like beams of bronze, His ribs like bars of iron. He is the first of the ways of God.*

NEGATIVE

A weak skeleton speaks of spiritual ill-health. To have weak bones means you do not have a conviction, nor the power to fulfill the purpose that God has given to you.

> *Psalms 38:3 There is no soundness in my flesh Because of Your anger, Nor any health in my bones Because of my sin.*

Bones in a heap: A lack of structure. Spiritual life is needed. The best illustration of this is the "dry bones of Ezekiel" (Ezekiel 37). To bring forth revival, the bones first needed to be brought into a skeleton. Structure is the starting place for the work God has called you to.

Speaking of death: To see a skeleton that indicates decay and death means that a spirit of death is at work. That death might be physical or it be spiritual also.

When praying for someone and you see a being that looks like a skeleton, either you are seeing a spirit of death, or the person you are praying with is spiritually drained. This is especially true if you are seeing an emaciated figure that is so thin, that you can see all their bones.

> *Psalms 141:7 Our bones are scattered at the mouth of the grave, As when one plows and breaks up the earth.*

Spirit of theft: When there is a spirit of theft at work, I will often see an emaciated hand stealing money. I have also seen it like a person that is very thin. One that keeps eating and eating, but is never satisfied.

See also: Back, Death, Skull, Tombstone

SKULL

Our greatest source of strength.

Positive: To be immovable
Negative: To be stubborn

CHARACTER SPECIFIC SYMBOL

POSITIVE
Because our skull is the strongest bone in our body, in a good sense, it speaks of having strong conviction and being unmoved in the face of adversity.

NEGATIVE
Now you can also be "thickheaded" which means to be stubborn and foolish.

Just like in the symbol *Skeleton*, a skull can also speak of death and destruction. It also speaks of warning in many cultures. Determine the emotion of your dream or vision. Did you feel a foreboding in the vision? Then a warning is being given.

A laughing skull speaks of the enemy mocking you and his intent to bring destruction on your life. Spiritual warfare will be essential in the season ahead of you.

A skull and crossbones is a warning that means, "Continue on this path and you will be lead to spiritual death and destruction."

See also: Head, Skeleton, Tombstone

SNAKES

The deceptive work of the enemy. Subtle and undetected until its influence is already in full swing.

Positive: The Lord turning the work of the enemy around for our good
Negative:

- Deception
- Subversive attack
- Deliberate sin
- Subtle words repeated in your ear, until you think the thoughts are your own

POSITIVE
I was hard pressed to find a positive representation of a snake in the Word. However, I did manage to find one of interest.

> *Numbers 21:9 So Moses made a bronze* ***serpent****, and put it on a pole; and so it was, if a serpent had bitten anyone, when he looked at the bronze serpent, he lived*

This symbol of course is used widely in the medical industry (a snake wrapped around a pole). It speaks of the Lord turning everything around for good! Even though the Israelites sinned, He used their very sin to bring them healing.

The serpent on the pole was a representation of what Christ did for us. The serpents in this part of scripture speak of sin. However, Christ became sin for us. Hence the serpent on the pole.

The only time a snake would represent something positive is if it is your trade or you have a pet snake that you care for. If you are a snake removal expert, then it would represent an aspect of your work. Perhaps something that is important to you or representative of your financial income.

NEGATIVE
Snakes never have a positive connotation in dreams and visions. In my personal experience and in looking at the Word, a snake speaks of deception.

The bronze serpent I spoke about previously, while meant for healing turned into an idol that later had to be destroyed by King Hezekiah (2 Kings 18:4)

In personal ministry, I have often seen a serpent wound around the head of a person, speaking lies into their ears. I expose it and tell it to leave.

It also allows me to minister effectively, because then I can encourage the person. I can tell them that the enemy has been lying to them, and that they do not have to listen to his lies any longer!

I have seen various kinds of snakes in the spirit.

I have seen small snakes, which are more of a hindrance than anything serious. They usually come in through association and by reading materials that contain a curse.

Depending on the size of the snake in my dream or vision, it depends on the strength of the demon.

I remember once stumbling on to a website that concentrated on interpreting Scripture into present day experiences. They had taken the Word and had broken it down according to the current events and events of history.

The site seemed innocent enough, even though I did feel a bit of oppression on it.

Soon thereafter everything seemed to go wrong in my life. I felt as if a heavy cloud had come on my head. I found myself getting into conflict with my family, and everything I touched seemed to break!

When I asked for prayer, we saw a serpent attacking me. As I had browsed that site, I had opened my heart to the articles there and actually invited a curse into my life!

I had received a spirit of deception, but as I repented and closed that door, I told the enemy to loose his hold, and the dark cloud around my head lifted immediately!

Cobra/violent snake/viper: Usually when I see a snake like this in the spirit, it speaks of an attack that is not only motivated by deception, but it is also vicious. Vicious words are being spoken against you from someone in deception.

To see a viper, or other such snakes, confirms what Jesus said in this passage.

> *Matthew 12:34 Brood of* ***vipers****! How can you, being evil, speak good things? For out of the abundance of the heart the mouth speaks*

Python: There was another time in our ministry where I kept seeing a python in the spirit. Others associated with us saw the same thing, and although we knew a snake represented deception, we needed clarification.

It was then that we found out that there was actually a "spirit of python" in the Word. When we looked it up, that specific passage referred to divination. It was very apt to what was going on in the ministry at that time, because the enemy had sent many false prophets to bring strife and conflict.

As we came against that spirit, those operating in the spirit of divination suddenly left, and things immediately calmed down again.

It is interesting that God had Moses and Aaron use serpents against Pharaoh's magicians who operated in witchcraft and divination. The message? God is greater than your spirit of divination!

Here is the reference to the "spirit of python" in the Greek and the corresponding passage:

4436 Puthon {poo'-thone}

from Putho (the name of the region where Delphi, the seat of the famous oracle, was located); TDNT - 6:917,*; n m

AV - divination 1; 1

1) in Greek mythology the name of the Pythian serpent or dragon that dwelt in the region of Pytho at the foot of Parnassus in Phocis, and was said to have guarded the oracle at Delphi and been slain by Apollo

2) a spirit of divination

> *Acts 16:16 Now it happened, as we went to prayer, that a certain slave girl possessed with a **spirit of divination** met us, who brought her masters much profit by fortune:*

Lies and deception:

> *Genesis 3:13 And the Lord God said to the woman, What is this you have done? The woman said, **The serpent deceived me**, and I ate.*

See also: Demons

SPEAR

Positive: Your potential to engage the enemy head-on – receiving the victory
Negative: An attack coming from someone you are intimate with

POSITIVE

The spear or javelin was the personal weapon of a soldier. Even King Saul had his own spear that he was identified by.

The spear is a picture of warfare and victory. Not the kind that is sent from afar like an arrow, but one that is "in your face." To have a vision or dream of thrusting a spear means that the Lord is calling you to engage the enemy and the circumstances that have you bound. It is a call to war and victory!

> *Joshua 8:26 For Joshua did not draw back his hand, with which he stretched out the **spear**, until he had utterly destroyed all the inhabitants of Ai.*

To receive a spear in the spirit means that the Lord desires that you "get involved" with His people and to do warfare one-on-one. In other words, helping them overcome their problems through practical help and leadership.

NEGATIVE

In my book on the *David Dynamic*, I share how David was attacked by Saul who tried to kill him with a spear. This is a picture of the status quo Church system. They will try to kill those who have a real fire for the Lord and keep rocking the boat.

If you have a dream or vision of a spear being thrown at you, then you have certainly upset someone in the church, and they are speaking negatively against you.

For those with an apostolic calling, this is a sign that their apostolic training is soon at hand, and it is time for them to move out into it.

> *1 Samuel 18:11 And Saul cast the **spear**, for he said, I will pin David to the wall! But David escaped his presence twice.*

The common saying "a spear in the side" of course comes from what happened to Jesus on the cross. Not only did He have to go through such a painful death, but they had to pierce him in the side as well.

Although it is not a lovely picture, we have come to realize that when you face death to the flesh that often an additional pressure comes afterwards to see if you really are "dead".

This is figuratively speaking of course. Just when you think you have overcome a situation, you are faced with it one last time.

This is really the spear in the side, and if it does not affect you, then you have really overcome. However, if you flinch and react badly, then you did not really deal with the issue God had brought up.

> *John 19:34 But one of the soldiers pierced His side with a* ***spear****, and immediately blood and water came out.*

See also: Armor, Attacked, Dagger, Sword

SPIDERS

A work of the enemy designed to bring about pain, both emotional and physical.

Positive: To be hard at work
Negative:

- *A spirit of fear*
- *Spirit of infirmity*

POSITIVE
If working with spiders is part of your career, then they speak of work. If you see a spider working hard on a web, then this speaks of work that needs to be done. More often than not though, spiders are seen in a negative light.

NEGATIVE
Spiders to most people are not pleasant creatures. If you have a strong fear of spiders, then they would speak of your fears in your dreams.

Generally, though, they speak of the work of the enemy. The good news however, is that they are not a strong attack and refer to something that you can easily overcome.

Even though a spider can be deadly, it can also be easily killed. The Word says that we can trample on serpents and scorpions, and the same is true of spiders!

Spiders speak of the work of the enemy. If you have been getting involved in things that you should not be, then seeing a spider in a vision is an indication that Satan has gained access in your life.

It speaks of the things that the enemy would like to poison you with, bringing you pain and discouragement.

In the spirit we often see spiders as spirits of infirmity. This is a good picture, because even in the natural their bite causes pain and sickness.

Spider's web: A spider's web speaks of a subtle work of the enemy that is not obvious at first. When we were first starting out, the fivefold ministry was really new and we faced a lot of opposition!

Often in the spirit we saw this huge spider weaving a web trying to slow us down. The Lord showed us that this was the result of the words of many other ministries speaking against us.

Through these negative words, they were licensing a curse against us and giving the enemy a chance to slow us down. There is no work of the enemy that is stronger than the work of Calvary though.

We stood against those words in the spirit and the fact that you are reading this today is proof that we did indeed overcome.

> *Isaiah 59:5 They hatch vipers' eggs and weave the* ***spider's*** *web; he who eats of their eggs dies, and from that which is crushed a viper breaks out.*

See also: Insects, Scorpion

STAFF

- *Authority vested in leadership position*
- *Correction*
- *Pastoral ministry (shepherd's staff)*

Positive: Your position of authority
Negative: Loss of leadership

POSITIVE
Depending on the staff that you see in the spirit, you will get a different interpretation.

When you see the shepherd's staff, this refers to either the Great Shepherd (being Jesus), but most often it is a representation of the pastoral ministry.

Shepherd's club: You might see a rod that is short and thick. This is something that the shepherd also used to carry with him, and he would use it against the wolf! This is called a shepherd's club in Scripture.

When I see this, then I know that the Lord is calling this person to a deliverance type of ministry that deals with attacking the kingdom of darkness to protect the people of God.

Shepherd's staff: If I see a shepherd's staff in personal ministry then I know that the Lord has called this person to the pastoral ministry. Here is an example from Scripture:

> *Psalms 23:4 Yea, though I walk through the valley of the shadow of death, I will fear no evil; For You are with me; Your rod and Your* ***staff****, they comfort me*

A rod: You also get a rod in Scripture. It is sometimes a long rod without any shape. When I see this, I know that the Lord is referring to the rod that brings correction.

In the old days before modern technology, they would break an old foundation using a rod. This is an apostolic function and it involves discipline, smashing old mindsets and templates.

Paul speaks of this rod confirming his apostolic authority in this Scripture:

> *1 Corinthians 4:21 What do you want? Shall I come to you with a* ***rod****, or in love and a spirit of gentleness?*

Rod of Moses: To further confirm the rod to be symbolic of the apostolic ministry, Moses carried such a rod that the Lord used to do the many signs and wonders with.

God speaking to Moses

> *Exodus 4:17 And you shall take this* ***rod*** *in your hand, with which you shall do the signs.*

Rod of Aaron: If you see a rod or staff that has budded, you are seeing the rod of Aaron and very likely a call to an apostolic function (Numbers 17:8). This apostolic type works closely with the Moses apostle and while Moses is responsible for getting the pattern, it is Aaron who builds it!

He is indeed a beautiful picture of a pastoral apostolic type.

NEGATIVE
The negative aspect of all of these symbols also holds true. If the rod is negative, it means the correction you are facing is not of the Lord, but motivated by the enemy.

A broken staff? There is something very wrong with your authority and the position you hold right now. The Lord is warning you that your position is about to be taken away. Determine if it is the enemy attacking your position or if God intends to remove it from you, to give you another one.

See also: Rod, Shepherd

STAGE

To be put into the spotlight.

Positive: A call to "step up to the plate"
Negative: To put on a show to get acceptance and recognition

CHARACTER SPECIFIC SYMBOL

POSITIVE

One thing is sure of a stage, when you are up there, you cannot hide! To be called to step up to the stage means to stop hiding the potential God has given to you and to walk it out. You will not be an influence hiding backstage.

If you have a vision and see someone on a stage, it means that God is calling them to a public ministry. A good picture of this is Paul's encounter on Mars' Hill (Acts 17:22). He stepped up for everyone to see him and then shared the gospel.

To set the stage: To "set the stage" speaks of making preparations before you step out with what God has for you. Before you can fulfill your purpose, some things need to be put in place first. You need to work on these preparations before God can open the way for you to fulfill your purpose.

Various stages: If you see a series of levels or platforms, this indicates a progression of success. As God calls us to fulfill the call, we will go through various "stages" of progress. The more we press forward, the more we will succeed.

NEGATIVE

Unfortunately, though the stage is also a place for "putting on a show" for the purpose of self exaltation. To see someone acting on a stage to draw attention to themselves means that they are "showboating." They are so busy trying to be what everyone wants them to be, that they have neglected their true call and personal convictions.

This indicates "performance orientation" and always being swayed by the crowd. The reason? To get the acceptance and recognition through that display, instead of getting that need met in the Lord.

See also: Audience, Crowd

STAIRS

Your progress in the natural and spiritual. It could indicate either a promotion or a demotion.

See also: Elevator, Ladder

STOMACH/BELLY

The center of your spiritual being. The essence of who you are.

Positive: The expression and positive condition of your spirit
Negative:

- Spiritual ill health
- Feeding the flesh

CHARACTER SPECIFIC SYMBOL

POSITIVE
Most cultures ascribe "inner unction" as a "gut feel." It means to have a sense of something spiritual, but expressed in the center of our being.

A healthy stomach and attractive waistline speaks of self-confidence.

NEGATIVE
To feel that you were "hit in the gut" means to be betrayed by someone close to you. A surprise attack that you did not expect.

A stomach that is hurt or wounded, speaks of damage to your soul. It goes beyond just a hurt of the past. Rather, it speaks of a broken spirit that has formed that way through years of continual hurt and sinful responses to that hurt.

To dream of getting a fat waistline (and you feel awkward in the dream), speaks of your insecurity. You do not feel comfortable with who you are as a person. Do not mistake this with being pregnant, which is another interpretation entirely.

UNIVERSAL SYMBOL

POSITIVE
While "getting fat" is a character specific symbol and is more often negative than not, it is different for a universal symbol as being "fat" was a sign of health and the blessing of the Lord.

Being "obese" though spoke of over-indulgence and gluttony.

> *Proverbs 11:25 The liberal soul shall be made fat: and he that watereth shall be watered also himself. (KJV)*

The New Testament tells us that rivers of living water will flow out of our bellies. This speaks of releasing the anointing from within. A healthy stomach speaks of a spirit that is healthy and generous in pouring out the goodness God has given to them.

NEGATIVE
Because the stomach is the organ that craves for food, it is also a picture of spiritual and fleshly gluttony. It means to over indulge and to feed our own need, often at the expense of others.

> *Romans 16:18 For those who are such do not serve our Lord Jesus Christ, but their own belly, and by smooth words and flattering speech deceive the hearts of the simple.*

To feel sick to your stomach means that you have fed something into your spirit that is destroying you. You have contaminated God's blessing with the spirit of the world. This is what this scripture is speaking of here where the Israelites were craving the meat of Egypt. You fed the flesh and as a result you lost your "sharp spiritual edge."

> *Psalms 106:15 And He gave them their request, But sent leanness into their soul.*

See also: Navel, Pregnant, Umbilical Cord

STONE

As a material, it is a solid foundation that cannot be moved. As small stones, it speaks of attacks that are painful, but can be easily overcome.

Positive:

- Immovable faith
- The Church

Negative:

- Accusing words
- Circumstantial hindrances from the enemy

POSITIVE
The Word says that Jesus is the cornerstone of our faith. This is a foundational stone that held the whole foundation and building together. To see a cornerstone refers to your faith in the Lord Jesus,

> *1Peter 2:7 Therefore, to you who believe, He is precious; but to those who are disobedient, the **stone** which the builders rejected has become the chief cornerstone,*

Jesus said that for some He was a rock of offence. Thousands of years later and still so many are stumbling over Him! If you dream or see a vision of a stumbling stone, but it is positive, it is speaking of the presence of the Lord in your life.

Because He is our cornerstone, this also speaks of unmovable faith. No matter what storm comes your way, you will not be moved because you have built your house on the rock!

Bricks: We are also known as living stones of the church of the Lord:

> *Ephesians 2:20 Having been built on the foundation of the apostles and prophets, Jesus Christ Himself being the chief corner stone, 21 in whom the whole building, being fitted together, grows into a holy temple in the Lord,*

The Church is fit together on the foundation of the apostles and prophets, with Jesus being the cornerstone. What a perfect picture of us being the temple of the Holy Spirit!

To see a vision of bricks or stones being used to build a structure speaks of unity and of bringing people together to accomplish the work of God. Not just any work though – one that the Lord intends to remain for years to come.

Each brick might be weak on its own, but cement them together and they are an immovable force!

Stone (the material/tablets): Because of its natural strength stone in scripture could well be related to cement in today's world. To coin a phrase, "To be set in stone."

It speaks of something that is established and immovable. Its intent is to remain for years to come. A good picture in the word is that of the stone tablets that Moses wrote the law on. The Lord was saying, "My law is set in stone! It is immovable and will go from generation to generation!"

Determine in your dream or vision if the stone or cement you see is positive or negative! If it is positive, it is a promise from the Lord. If it is negative, then it means there is something very powerful in your life that needs to be destroyed.

NEGATIVE
To see a stony heart is negative. It speaks of someone who has locked in their emotions and become hard and cold. This is the same as someone who has ice around their heart.

> *Zechariah 7:12 Yes, they made their hearts like **flint**, refusing to hear the law and the words which the Lord of hosts...*

To be hard as stone means to be stubborn and immovable.

Casting stones: Words of accusation being spoken against you. A good example in the Word is where Jesus spoke to the crowd ready to stone the adulteress. He said, "He is without sin, cast the first stone!" (John 8:7)

Stones on your road: To see stones in your path speaks of hindrances from the enemy. He is sending circumstances your way that he intends to use you trip you up. He does not have any license in your life through your own sin, so he is sending circumstances against you to cause you to falter in your walk and give him license.

See also: Arrow, Foundation, Rock

STORM

Circumstances that are intended to change your direction for either good or bad.

Positive: A needed change of direction
Negative:

- A season of tumult and confusion
- A distraction from the enemy to take your eyes off your focus

POSITIVE
Although it might seem that a storm is entirely negative, this is not true. Although a storm is mostly destructive, it makes way for something new to be born as well.

It is only in the storms of life that we learn to take hold of the hand of God. Consider Apostle Paul who faced a terrible storm and even shipwreck while he was a prisoner. As a result of this storm, an entire island of people came to know the Lord (Acts 28)!

The Lord told me once, "I am sending you a storm. Ride the waves"

He showed me that in order to bring about the promises He had given to me, it would require a drastic change of circumstances. He told me that He would not be bringing the promises to me, but that He would take me to the promises! A series of circumstances followed that indeed changed the course of my life forever.

NEGATIVE
Mostly though, storms are negative and speak of the destructive work of the enemy.

He is sending circumstances in your life with the intent to distract you from what God has said. He desires to take your eyes off the goal.

Practically, it will manifest through people and circumstances steering you in every direction but the one you know you must follow. Accusation, financial struggles, attacks on your health...

To dream or have a vision of a storm that you feel is negative means an onslaught of circumstances. Determine the realm of this onslaught. If you are a prophet, you might have a vision of your church facing a storm. Perhaps you will see a particular person in a storm.

This is a lovely promise though:

> *Psalms 107:29 He calms the **storm**, So that its waves are still*

A note about storms: We all face storms in life and it is not the storm that changes us, but how we handle it.

You can choose to throw your hands up in despair, or you could choose to ride the wave and grow stronger through it.

Jesus chose to walk over the waves that were tossing against the ship. It is a beautiful picture of how the Lord expects you to handle the storms.

There are times when you will say "peace be still" and the waves will stop. Other times though, it is simply a matter of walking over it and getting to the other side.

See also: Hail, Shaking, Waves, Wind

SUN

A new season of hope and promise.

Positive: A promise of hope that things are going to be alright
Negative: Hardship in your circumstances that intend to "shrivel up" God's blessing

POSITIVE
The sun speaks mostly of something positive in scriptures. The sun brought life to the fields and it chased away the darkness.

Ours is a God of light and a sunrise speaks of the start of something new. It is a picture of overcoming darkness by adding life.

If you dream of a sunrise, then the Lord is saying that your season of struggles and frustration are over. Your season of rest is over and it is time to get moving again.

> *2 Samuel 23:4 And he shall be like the light of the morning when the **sun** rises, a morning without clouds, like the tender grass springing out of the earth, by clear shining after rain.*

NEGATIVE
A hot sun can be dangerous though and in a negative sense it can speak of the work of the enemy trying to steal the blessing of God from you. When the enemy cannot dissuade you from the direction God has given to you, He will push you beyond what God intends.

Even though sunshine is a picture of the Lord, a hot sun shrivels up His blessing and it is a work of the enemy. If you feel like you have been pushing through hard and then see a vision of the scorching sun, then the Lord is warning you!

He is saying that the enemy is pushing you beyond what God intended and it is time to stop.

> *Mark 4:6 But when the* ***sun*** *was up it was scorched, and because it had no root it withered away.*

It stands to reason that to see someone worshipping the sun speaks of idolatry and false religion. They are worshipping what God can give them instead of the Lord for who He is.

See also: Day, Light, Night

SWAN

Hidden potential that will soon be brought out (Ugly duckling.)

Positive: Grace and beauty.
Negative: Unexpected attack

When we first started training the prophets, the picture of the swan would often come to our minds. Starting out as ugly ducklings, they rose up into something beautiful as they matured.

Swans are creatures of beauty but the person you are praying with, might feel that they are ugly and the outcast. However, they are destined for greatness!

NEGATIVE
The swan is listed as an unclean animal in scripture right alongside the vulture and raven. So to be attacked by a swan speaks of being attacked from a direction that you would never expect it.

Something that you considered good in your life is now a source of attack and discouragement.

See also: Birds, Raven

SWORD

The power and authority you hold in your hand, received from the Lord or used in the flesh.

Positive:

- Your authority in Christ
- The teaching ministry
- A call to spiritual warfare
- The Word of God

Negative:

- Negative words that have been spoken against you
- Doctrine that is destructive

POSITIVE
Generally, the sword is a picture of power. Of course as believers we receive this power by the Word of God.

Below are some variations of how we see swords in the spirit. This might differ for each person.

The sword is an allegorical picture of the Word of God. It is sharp and it divides the truth from the lie.

If you see a sword bringing a division, then the Lord is about to expose the things that are wrong. This of course is carried out a lot by the teacher, who uses the Word to bring the truth and set God's people free.

> *Hebrews 4:12 For the word of God is living and powerful, and sharper than any two- edged* ***sword****, piercing even to the division of soul and spirit, and of joints and marrow, and is a discerner of the thoughts and intents of the heart.*

So it is no surprise that when I am praying for someone regarding their ministry and I see a golden sword, I know that the Lord is calling them to teacher training.

Ceremonial sword: When the Lord is confirming someone's position of authority, I will see a ceremonial sword, indicating position. This kind of sword, even in the natural is not used for warfare, but to denote position. I often see various ceremonial swords when placing someone into a ministry office.

Weapon of warfare: I often see a silver sword which speaks of spiritual warfare. It is a practical and "gritty" sword and I know that the Lord desires for me to rise up and set His people free. Often, as a teacher this will mean preaching the truth.

As a prophet it might mean doing spiritual warfare through intercession. As an evangelist it means doing warfare by preaching the gospel. Are you a pastor? Your flock is under attack. You need to rise up and defend them. An apostle? It is time to do warfare by building the correct pattern!

NEGATIVE
Speaking of using your own strength: To pick up your own sword and try to win the battle without the Lord speaks of doing things in your own effort. In the end you will only perish, because without God's power you cannot overcome.

> *Matthew 26:52 But Jesus said to him, Put your sword in its place, for all who take the sword will perish by the* ***sword****.*

Negative words: The Word says that bitter words are like a sword. If you see swords coming against you in the spirit, then the Lord is showing you that others have spoken negative words against you and licensed the enemy to attack.

> *Psalms 64:3 Who sharpen their tongue like a* ***sword****, and bend their bows to shoot their arrows - bitter words:*

See also: Dagger, Darts

Symbols Starting in T

Symbols Starting in T

Tabernacle

The dwelling place of God.

Positive: The manifestation of the presence of God
Negative: Disobedience

Universal Symbol

POSITIVE

Just as a house in a dream represents our life and desires, the tabernacle of the temple speaks of God's life and desires.

In the Old Testament, a tabernacle was needed as the throne of God. In the New Testament, we are now His tabernacle! He dwells within us. So to see a tabernacle has one of the two meanings:

1. It represents God in you. His desires and plans for you to fulfill in this earth on His behalf.
2. It represents His Church. His desires and plans for the body of Christ as a whole.

Determine what you were praying at the time when you saw the tabernacle. There are many elements that make up the tabernacle – many that I have already covered.

> *Revelation 21:3 And I heard a loud voice from heaven saying, "Behold, the tabernacle of God is with men, and He will dwell with them, and they shall be His people. God Himself will be with them and be their God.*

> *Hebrews 9:11 But Christ came as High Priest of the good things to come, with the greater and more perfect tabernacle not made with hands, that is, not of this creation.*

NEGATIVE

Because the tabernacle was a place of holiness, we should keep this trait of the Father in mind when approaching Him. The high priest could only enter the Holy of Holies once a year – with blood! Priests could not sacrifice if they had not been cleansed. There is no such thing as "adding" to God's plan and desire for your life.

If you see a tabernacle that is being destroyed or missing a piece it means that you are messing with God's perfect plan. He has a set goal and desire for you and for His church. It is for us to be obedient, not tell the potter how to form the clay!

See also: Ark, Blue, Bronze, Gold, Purple, Silver

TABLE

A presentation of either blessing or cursing relating specifically to your needs.

Positive: The Lord is meeting your needs
Negative: The enemy is trying to get you to accept second best

POSITIVE
The Lord laid a table in the wilderness for the Children of Israel, meeting their needs. To see a table laid with food is a promise from God that He is going to meet not only your needs, but your desires as well.

> *Psalms 78:19 Yes, they spoke against God: they said, Can God prepare a **table** in the wilderness?*

The table was also a place of joy and celebration amongst friends and family. It was not a place to be sad. It speaks of blessing and prosperity amongst those that you love the most.

NEGATIVE
To be put at a table that is dirty means two things. Firstly, you are receiving things that are not of God and secondly, the enemy has taken the blessing from you and brought a curse instead!

Just because the enemy puts something in front of you does not mean you need to take it!

> *Isaiah 28:8 For all tables are full of vomit and filth; no place is clean.*

See also: Banquet, Food, Vomiting

TATTOO

To be marked for ownership.

Positive: To be sealed and set aside for the Lord
Negative: To be "marked" for a plan of the enemy

Just as cattle are branded, so also to dream of being "tattooed" in a positive sense means that you belong to the Lord.

> *Ephesians 1:13 And you also were included in Christ when you heard the message of truth, the gospel of your salvation. When you believed, you were **marked** in him with a **seal**, the promised Holy Spirit, (NIV)*

CHARACTER SPECIFIC SYMBOL

POSITIVE
To dream of being "marked" and you feel positive about it, means that the Lord is placing His seal of approval on you and setting you apart for His work.

Depending on the tattoo is an indication of the kind of work He wants you to do.

To dream of having a tattoo removed (one you have in the natural) means that the Lord is going to wash away your past and the consequences of the sins of the past.

NEGATIVE
To dream of getting a worldly tattoo is an indication that you have been "marked" by the world and because of that are being mastered by it.

Universal Symbol

POSITIVE AND NEGATIVE
When praying, if you see a tattoo, it might be literal. We experienced this once when praying with someone. Craig kept seeing an image of the Grimm Reaper. He could not "get" what God was trying to say so he shared the vision. The man lifted his sleeve to reveal a tattoo of the Grimm Reaper!

If the vision you are seeing is a type and shadow, the image itself will give you a feel of what the bondage is that this person is under. This tattoo is a mark of ownership. So if you see something new age, then it is likely that they have gone into something like that.

See also: Seal (Wax Seal)

Tears

An external expression of intense inner emotion whether positive or negative.

Positive:

- The release of desire, fear or joy
- Conviction of sin
- To sense and release the heart of God through action

Negative: The sign of unhealed, hidden hurt

Character Specific Symbol

It is common to sometimes cry in your dreams. When dreams are intense like this, they are simply an indication of a purging that is going on inside of you at the moment.

If your dream relates to people from the past, then this is a healing dream and you do not need to be concerned. In fact, this is a good sign that the Lord is doing something in you right now, and you should just let Him finish the job!

Universal Symbol

POSITIVE
Tears can be a sign of pain, but also of conviction, healing and joy. It is very common for people to cry when we minister to them.

I started to notice this especially when we played music. One by one, people would just begin to weep before the Lord as they felt His presence.

This is a good sign and it means that God is doing a work.

NEGATIVE
If you have a vision of someone crying, then it is an indication of a pain they are still carrying with them.

Sometimes I will see a person crying at a certain age. I know then that they experienced something around that time of their lives that still needs a touch from the Lord.

The Minister's Handbook is a fantastic book to learn how to minister inner healing or also overcome your own hurts from the past.

> *Revelation 21:4 And God will wipe away every* ***tear*** *from their eyes; there shall be no more death, nor sorrow, nor crying. There shall be no more pain, for the former things have passed away.*

See also: Crying, Heart

Teeth

The current condition of the health of your soul.

Positive: The blessing of the Lord
Negative: Bitterness prevalent in your life

POSITIVE
White and healthy teeth speak of the blessing of the Lord and walking in abundance.

> *Genesis 49:12 His eyes are darker than wine, and his* ***teeth*** *whiter than milk.*

It means that the Lord is pleased with you and wants to give you the desires of your heart. Your heart is good before Him and as a result your convictions are strong and your standing in Him is good right now. This is an encouraging dream, especially if you have had doubt about your right standing with God. A dream of having your teeth fixed or getting new ones is the Lord saying, "I am proud of you! You have overcome! My blessing is on you."

NEGATIVE
To dream or have a vision of gnashing teeth speaks of the attack of the enemy. It is a curse of destruction and its intention is to tear you down.

> *Job 16:9 He tears me in His wrath, and hates me; He gnashes at me with His* ***teeth****; my adversary sharpens His gaze on me.*

To dream of your teeth becoming rotten and breaking means that there is something inside of you that is rotten. This "fruit of the flesh" is destroying the blessing that God intends for you.

This is a very good picture of bitterness, and how it destroys you from inside out.

Bleeding and broken gums have a very similar interpretation. You are certainly weak in an area of the flesh that the enemy keeps playing on.

It means that the enemy is stealing your blessing through your own sin! The kind of sin here though are not obvious external ones that everyone can see, but rather ones deep in your heart.

Bitterness, pride and love of money are the first I suggest you take before the Lord.

See also: Jaw, Mouth, Toothbrush

TENT

Tents are very similar to houses, however instead of your personal life, they often represent your ministry life.

Positive: The expansion of your ministry
Negative: Attack on your ministry

POSITIVE
The Word says that we are the temple/house of the Holy Spirit. Seeing a tent speaks about your personal life or about your personal ministry.

The Lord has often shown us a vision where we saw a tent being enlarged. This spoke of an expansion in our ministry.

We have also had dreams where we saw a tent that was tied down, not being able to move. This showed us that the ministry was being hindered and restricted in some way.

Depending on the condition of the tent that you see, the interpretation will vary.

If you see a tent with a tear in it, this would speak of the ministry having been attacked and damaged, and there needs to come healing and restoration.

Speaking of blessing in your ministry and life:

> *Isaiah 54:2 Enlarge the place of your **tent**...*
> *3 For you shall expand to the right and to the left, and your descendants will inherit the nations, and make the desolate cities inhabited.*

A tent can also refer to your personal life, revolving around your work or business. Tent making for example was a trade and symbolizes business, enterprise and work.

See also: Foundation, House

THIEF

The work of the enemy steals every blessing that God has given to you.

POSITIVE
The Word says that the Lord will come as a thief in the night, speaking of his return. (2 Peter 3:10)

NEGATIVE
Mostly though a thief in a dream or vision is very negative, and speaks of a spirit of theft that is prevalent in your life.

Have you been experiencing loss in your life? Perhaps finances have been stolen from you, or even your health or relationships have been stolen.

To see a thief in the spirit is a revelation from the Lord to let you know that the enemy is at work.

Although a vision or dream of a thief can relate to many things such as health and a work position, it more often than not speaks about financial theft.

See also: Demons

THORNS

Words and circumstances that bring offense.

Positive: To gladly take the offense and to allow the Lord to be your defender
Negative:

- People and circumstances that cause you pain
- Irritation sent by the enemy
- Spirit of theft

POSITIVE

A crown of thorns: To have your position mocked and to be ridiculed as Jesus was when they put the crown of thorns on His head. To have a dream or vision of this means that the Lord not only wants you to to embrace these pressures, but to stand tall within them. Jesus gladly took the crown and what was meant as a mockery became His boast as the King of kings. In the same way – take the offense. Do not defend yourself, but allow the Lord to defend you instead.

NEGATIVE

The saying "a thorn in my side" is quite universal, and speaks of things that hurt you.

To dream of thorns pricking you is an indication that there are people in your life that are causing you pain and harm. Keep in mind that the motivator behind this is always the enemy.

A curse and stolen blessing: Thorns speak of a curse in your life that is taking away the goodness that God has given you. It is a good picture of a spirit of theft.

> *Genesis 3:18 Both* ***thorns*** *and thistles it shall bring forth for you, and you shall eat the herb of the field;*

People that hinder you: This speaks of people that stand against you and speak against you. They are a hindrance to what God wants to do in your life.

The work of the enemy: As you allow yourself to get wrapped up in the things of the world and chasing after it instead of God, this steals your spiritual blessings.

> *Matthew 13:22 Now he who received seed among the* ***thorns*** *is he who hears the word, and the cares of this world and the deceitfulness of riches choke the word, and he becomes unfruitful.*

When praying for the ministry we often see thorns in the road. This speaks of hindrances and often of people that have come against us directly. It is also a picture of the enemy trying to steal the blessing that the Lord has in store.

If you see something similar, you can stand against this in the name of Jesus and overcome.

See also: Rock, Stone, Weeds

THRONE

A position of authority and power.

POSITIVE
To sit on a throne means that you are being given a position of authority and power. The Word says that we are seated in heavenly places with Christ! This means that as believers that we rule and reign with Him!

The Throne Room: I have often had visions of the Lord seated on His throne. In these times I know that He is drawing my attention to His authority. In these times He usually has a decree or direction for me.

If the Lord is calling you to the Throne Room, He is inviting you into a relationship with the Father. The first experience I had with the Father, He called me to climb on His lap as a child and to listen to His heartbeat.

Experiencing a relationship with the Father is one of both understanding the power of His authority and the passionate strength of His love for us.

NEGATIVE
To see the enemy on his throne refers to his influence in the earth. In the spirit, if I see a dark throne with the enemy on it, I know that I am coming against the enemy's plans with the work I am doing for God.

When praying once, I saw Pharaoh on his throne. I knew the Lord was telling me that he was in control of the finances of the world, but that He was greater. He showed me how He worked on our behalf to undermine the authority satan had been given in the earth through sin.

See also: Altar, Angels, Demons, Gold

TOMBSTONE

The finality of a season passed.

Positive:

- Confirmation that the old has passed away
- A season of rest

Negative:

- Premature death of something God intended to live
- A symbol of death

Universal Symbol

POSITIVE
When a stone was rolled over the mouth of a tomb, the message was clear, "The death process is over. It is time to allow nature to take its course." This is nothing that you can control. You cannot cause nature to work faster or bring that thing back to life.

The joy in this, is that what God has put to death in you, is over. Sometimes when we go through dealings and "putting our flesh on the cross," we wonder if the work is really over. To see a tomb or gravestone is a confirmation that the work is over. It is time for you to rest for a while. There is nothing more that you can do. It is up to the Lord now.

NEGATIVE
Because of its strong tie to death, a tomb or gravestone can be negative. It means that you let something die inside of you that did not need to. Is there a name on the gravestone? What does that person represent in you? Do they represent your joy or peace? The interpretation is self-explanatory!

A gravesite or gravestone is also a picture of death. Determine if what you are sensing is a spirit of death (an attack against your natural body) or if it is referring to spiritual death.

NOTE: If you keep seeing graves and people keep dying after you see them die in a dream or vision, then you are operating under a spirit of divination and you require deliverance. Refer back to *The Way of Dreams and Visions* for further instruction.

See also: Death, Skeleton, Skull

Tongue

The words we speak

Positive: The call to send out a decree
Negative: Words that are causing strife and hurt

Character Specific Symbol

POSITIVE
Depending on the context of your dream, the tongue speaks of good words that have been spoken. If you have a problem speaking or lack confidence to speak, then this would be an encouragement to you.

Perhaps the dream is also showing that you need to speak out more. Speaking out blessings and positive words will have a profound impact on your life!

One of the main functions of the prophet is to speak God's decrees into the earth. However, all believers have the authority to release things into the earth.

If you have a vision of the Lord touching your tongue, then He is telling you that it is time to speak out His word. As you do this, you give the Lord license to move on the earth.

> *2 Samuel 23:2 The Spirit of the Lord spoke by me, and His word was on my **tongue**.*

NEGATIVE
If you dream of a tongue that is bleeding or has sores on it, it is an indication that there is something wrong with the words that you are speaking.

Do you keep slipping up and saying things that you should not? These words are causing you harm and harming those around you. It is time to change your language and the words coming out of your mouth.

> *1 Peter 3:10 For he who would love life and see good days, let him refrain his **tongue** from evil, and his lips from speaking deceit.*

Universal Symbol

POSITIVE
A call to sanctification.

To have a vision of a hot coal put on your mouth is a call to sanctification and doing things God's way. It means to "tame your tongue" and to speak words that bring life instead of death.

I also like this passage:

> *Psalms 39:3 My heart was hot within me; While I was musing, the fire burned. Then I spoke with my tongue*

To see fire on your tongue in a positive aspect is the Lord saying, "It is time to speak! It is time to send forth my word."

It is also an indication that you need to speak out the things you have a conviction of in your heart.

NEGATIVE
James refers to the tongue as a fire – a world of iniquity! (James 3:6) It has potential to speak blessing, but more often than not speaks things that destroy others.

If you see a tongue that is diseased or spitting poison, then the Lord is saying that there is negative talk in your midst! It is time to rein in your tongues!

If you have a prophetic dream or vision of having a forked tongue, then the Lord is correcting you. He is saying that you need to stop being double-minded and to tell the truth!

A forked tongue speaks of lies and negative words spoken against you. They are deadly, and if they are coming from those that are close to you or over you, they are actually speaking a curse over you.

Although you do not need to get hung up on it, you can simply stand against these words.

The only time you need to really be concerned, is when you have allowed bitterness into your heart and you allow these words to influence you.

> *Isaiah 54:17 No weapon formed against you shall prosper, and every **tongue** which rises against you in judgment you shall condemn.*

See also: Jaw, Mouth, Teeth

TOOTHBRUSH

Maintaining the blessing of the Lord by walking in obedience

CHARACTER SPECIFIC SYMBOL

POSITIVE
Because a toothbrush speaks of "doing the work yourself" it speaks of what you do to maintain what God has given to you.

Now if you were brought up in a home that promoted strict hygiene this can be positive or negative. Were your parents too extreme? Then a toothbrush speaks of working hard in your flesh and going overboard.

For the most part though, it speaks of doing your part to maintaining the blessings God has given to you.

NEGATIVE
Over brushing or a dirty toothbrush speaks of neglecting your blessings. God has done His part – have you done yours? If you are trying to brush with a dirty toothbrush, then the Lord is saying that you are doing your part in the flesh. You are trying so hard to bring things to pass, but you are using the works of the flesh to do it, instead of the fruit of the spirit!

See also: Jaw, Mouth, Teeth

TOWER

A place of strength and protection.

Positive: The Holy Spirit
Negative: The enemy engaging you in spiritual warfare

POSITIVE

The Scriptures tell us that the Lord is a strong tower round about us, and that we can run to Him for help at any time.

This is a wonderful picture of being secure in the Lord! In yourself you might be weak, but when you just run to the Lord, He is the strong tower that protects you.

> *Proverbs 18:10 The name of the Lord is a strong* ***tower****; the righteous run to it and are safe].*

When I was going through a hard time, the Lord gave me a vision of hiding in His tower. Although I needed to face the storms that waited for me in life, He told me to take a moment to rest and recoup for a season.

A tower is not a place you set up camp. It is a place you hide in for seasons in your life. They are needed most when you are facing warfare and need protection. If you keep dreaming of towers or seeing visions of them, then it is clear that you are facing some difficult situations right now and the Lord is saying, "I am here to protect you! Run into my arms and rest for a while until you are strong again."

Watchtower: This speaks of the function of the prophet, who is called of the Lord to "stand on the wall" on behalf of the Body of Christ. It relates specifically to the intercessory function of the prophet.

> *Isaiah 21:8 Then he cried, A lion, my Lord! I stand continually on the* ***watchtower*** *in the daytime; I have sat at my post every night.*

NEGATIVE

Dark towers also speak of the kingdom of darkness. If you see these in the spirit, then it is a call to warfare, to come against the enemy and to take back the land that He has stolen from God's people.

> *Zephaniah 1:16 A day of trumpet and alarm against the fortified cities and against the high* ***towers****.*

In my teaching on *Tearing Down Strongholds* I teach how the enemy sets up towers in the spirit to attack us with weapons of mass destruction. His goal is to get you to sin and give him license.

If you see a tower in the spirit that is negative, it speaks of the work of the enemy that has been established for some time. Each time people gave him license he moved forward with his plans.

See also: Babel, Buildings, Wall

TOY

A symbol of childhood.

Positive: A call to joy
Negative: A sign of immaturity

CHARACTER SPECIFIC SYMBOL

POSITIVE

If you dream of a familiar childhood toy, determine what it means to you. Was it from a particular season in your life? What is the story behind that toy? Whatever its story is, will tell you what it represents.

If the toy is not familiar to you, but you are excited to receive it, it means that the "child in you" is coming out. This is a good thing!

Playing with a toy means the same thing. Time to have fun! Enjoy this season you are in right now, because you do not know how long it will last.

NEGATIVE

If you are clinging to a toy in your dream that you know you must give up, it means that you are clinging to immaturity. You are clinging to the past instead of stepping into the new things that God has for you.

UNIVERSAL SYMBOL

POSITIVE

Because a toy is something that brings joy, if you see the Lord giving you a gift that is a toy, He is saying, "It is time to let your hair down and have some fun. It is time to be a child for a while – allow me to take this load."

The Lord tells us to come to Him as children. To love and laugh freely! May the child in each of us never die or get weighed down with the cares of this life.

> *Luke 18:16 But Jesus called them to Him and said, "Let the little children come to Me, and do not forbid them; for of such is the kingdom of God.*

NEGATIVE

Because only children play with toys (ok, we know that is not really true, but you get the idea!), to see someone clinging to a toy speaks of refusing to grow up and to mature in either the natural or in the spirit.

> *1 Corinthians 13:11 When I was a child, I spoke as a child, I understood as a child, I thought as a child; but when I became a man, I put away childish things.*

See also: Ball, Bear, Child

TRAIN

A group of individuals, all connected and heading in the same direction.

Positive: The local church
Negative: An all out attack from the enemy

POSITIVE
The Lord has often used the illustration of a train engine with many train cars on it as a picture of the local church.

I find this an apt illustration, because you have the fivefold ministry leadership pulling the train ahead, the Lord who has laid the track and the churches that follow. Each one is unique, but all going in the same direction!

NEGATIVE
To be hit by a "steam train" as the saying goes speaks about being taken by surprise. However, when the train in your dream or vision is negative, it speaks about a united attack against you. The enemy is "pulling out the stops" and has accumulated all his resources for this attack.

This attack may be coming from the church or the world system. The solution is to stand your ground and do spiritual warfare, remembering that you do not wrestle against flesh or blood!

I cover a bit more on the train track under *Vehicles*.

See also: Vehicles

TRAP

A work of the enemy to catch you out and make you fall. A snare intended to discourage you from the direction that God has sent you in.

Positive: To ensnare the enemy in his own plan against you
Negative: To fall prey to the wiles of the enemy

POSITIVE
The enemy is not the only one who sets a trap. The Lord can turn the trap of the enemy against him!

The purpose of a trap is to expose a weakness in your enemy. In the scripture below, Apostle Paul is saying that those who are resisting the church will be exposed for what they are – ensnared in their own ways!

> *Romans 11:9 And David says: Let their table become a snare and a **trap**, a stumbling block and a recompense to them.*

NEGATIVE
More often than not though, a trap is negative. The enemy is trying to "catch you out" and make a fool of you. It is how he discredits those who are called to the work of the ministry.

> *1 Timothy 3:7 Moreover he must have a good testimony among those who are outside, lest **he fall into reproach** and the **snare** of the devil.*

This kind of warfare is very subtle and you only feel the sting once you fall into it. The enemy might push you in a direction that you feel is of the Lord and then as suddenly everything falls apart, you realize your mistake!

It is not uncommon for me to pray for someone and see them caught in a trap. Now is not the time to remain there and to allow self-pity to keep you ensnared.

It is time to get up again and to realize that there is nothing you can do that will disappoint your Heavenly Father. Rise up and turn this attack back on the enemy!

See also: Ambush

TREASURE

A financial blessing that will require effort on your part to put it into your hands.

Positive:

- Blessing that requires a great price from you
- Money
- Something of great value (natural or spiritual)

Negative: The love of money

POSITIVE
A note about treasure: Just because treasure is a blessing does not mean it comes easily. Consider this passage:

> *Matthew 13:44 "Again, the kingdom of heaven is like treasure hidden in a field, which a man found and hid; and for joy over it he goes and sells all that he has and buys that field*

This speaks of a blessing that is going to require you to give something up. There will be a price to pay to take hold of it! Just like our salvation is a treasure, we were asked to give up our own life for it.

To dream that you are digging for treasure, means that you are about to embark on an endeavor that is going to lead to blessing and good things.

The Word says that we have treasure in earthen vessels, speaking of the Holy Spirit within us. He is the ultimate treasure, because from Him, we receive every other kind of blessing.

A treasure hidden in a clay pot is a beautiful picture of the power and authority that we possess because of Christ.

> *2 Corinthians 4:7 But we have this* ***treasure*** *in earthen vessels, that the excellence of the power may be of God and not of us.*

Finding hidden treasure speaks of attaining wisdom and knowledge.

> *Colossians 2:3 in whom are hidden all the* ***treasures*** *of wisdom and knowledge*

Treasure also speaks of money. Jesus said that where our treasure is, there is our heart also. This means that wherever you are investing all of your money, it is where your heart really is.

The Word tells us to store our treasure in heaven. This refers to the money we invest into others in the Kingdom of God, as well as the time and works we do in faith, hope and love.

> *Matthew 6:20 But lay up for yourselves* ***treasures*** *in heaven, where neither moth nor rust destroys and where thieves do not break in and steal:*

NEGATIVE
To dream of losing a treasure, means that a spirit of theft is operating in your life.

If you have a vision of losing your treasure you need to determine if it is a work of the enemy or if you failed to pay the price for it. The price for each person is different. For the rich merchant who found the treasure in a field, he sold all he had for that field.

In the case of spiritual blessings, the Lord will have you give up old anointings.

For financial blessings, the Lord will ask you to pay a price that will change your circumstances so that the blessing can get to you!

Treasure that has rusted speaks of investing your finances into things that satisfy the flesh. You do not allow the Lord any control in your finances, but make all the decisions without him.

Treasures of darkness: I have often seen the treasure house of the enemy in the spirit. These are all the treasures that he has stolen from the Kingdom of God and the treasures of the world.

As believers we will plunder the kingdom of darkness!

> *Isaiah 45:3 I will give you the **treasures** of darkness and hidden riches of secret places, that you may know that I, the Lord, who call you by your name, am the God of Israel.*

See also: Money

TREES

A representation of a group of people, ministry or nation.

Positive: To be firmly rooted in the Lord
Negative:

- Generational curses
- To be restricted by archetype
- To be full of pride

If you look at the dream Nebuchadnezzar had, you will see how he and his kingdom were illustrated as a tree in his dream. (Daniel 4:20)

POSITIVE
Trees can represent being rooted and strong. You might dream of a tree that is immovable. This would be a good picture, as it is saying that you cannot be moved. When a tree's roots are deep you cannot pluck it up!

The Lord has often used the tree to illustrate our ministry.

I remember when we first started out and we saw saplings. We were still growing!

Then from time to time we would see this large tree that became immovable. Soon this tree reproduced, and many more trees began to rest under its branches. Furthermore, we would see various nations gathering under the branches.

What the Lord was saying was that the ministry that we had founded would remain and be strong.

He said that as we poured into others, they would also rise up and become immovable, until the whole earth was filled with the glory of God and His people who stood firm!

A lovely illustration of this can be found in this passage:

> *Jeremiah 17:7 Blessed is the man who trusts in the Lord, and whose hope is the Lord.*
> *8 For he shall be like a **tree** planted by the waters, which spreads out its roots by the river, and will not fear when heat comes; but its leaf will be green, and will not be anxious in the year of drought, nor will cease from yielding fruit.*

NEGATIVE
It is common for me to have many dreams where various trees and branches in a dream refer to family generations.

A branch in Scripture was often used to illustrate the various tribes and families in Israel. This is the most common interpretation in dreams.

You might dream that a tree's branches fall off or that some creature is on the tree. You might see a tree whose root has gone rotten.

In each case it would represent your family generations and the curses that have been passed down to you.

Just as in dreams, branches and roots can have negative interpretations in visions.

When I have been in personal ministry and I see a dark root in a person, I know that the Lord wants me to address a root of bitterness they have in their lives.

You can find reference to the root of bitterness in Hebrews 12:15

Divorce: Sometimes when we have prayed with divorced people, we are led to break ties with the previous spouse.

We often see the link with that spouse as a branch grafted into them. As we pray, we remove that branch and heal the wound.

In cases where the divorcee has remarried, we then ask the Lord to graft the "new branch" in where the old one had been.

A tree stump: To see a tree stump tied with a band of iron speaks of having your strengths removed from you and of being humbled. You are full of pride and the Lord has had to "cut you down to size."

Iron band: Ordinarily a tree would grow again if it's roots are still healthy, however the band of iron would prevent that growth.

If you see this picture, then it means that there is something that is hindering your ability to resurrect again.

It is common in ministry to be called to let everything go and to go through a death of a vision. It is even common to be called to let go of your strengths for a season.

However, the Lord will not keep you there! His intention is for you to resurrect again.

See also: Branch, Root

TROPHY

A symbol of having completed the direction God has given to you.

Positive: Success
Negative: Striving in the flesh

UNIVERSAL SYMBOL

POSITIVE

To accomplish the goal that has been set before you and to pass with flying colors! A trophy is a "job well done." So often we run the race, but feel like we are not getting anywhere! To see a trophy or to get a prize means that you followed through to the end and that the Lord is proud of you.

Race: If you dream of running a race and getting a ribbon or crossing the finish line, the meaning is the same. You have pressed forward in everything that God has given to you and you have overcome! A race goes hand-in-hand with the prize, because while the race is the journey God has put you on, the prize is a symbol of having accomplished just that.

> *Philippians 3:14 I press toward the goal for the prize of the upward call of God in Christ Jesus.*

NEGATIVE

If you dream of losing your trophy or it being stolen, it means that you have given something up that you should not have. You stopped running the race! Its time to get back up again. Keep running and reach your goal.

> *Colossians 2:18 Let no one cheat you of your reward, taking delight in false humility and worship of angels, intruding into those things which he has not seen, vainly puffed up by his fleshly mind*

See also: Crown, Exercising, Road

Symbols Starting in U

Symbols Starting in U

Umbilical Cord

To feed off whatever you feel you need to survive either spiritually or emotionally.

Positive: To be nurtured by the Lord
Negative: To take in influences that are not of God

POSITIVE
Assess the spirit in your dream. If it is positive, then the cord could speak of generational blessing.

If you see the cord attached to you and one of your children or someone else, it could mean that you are investing everything you have into them and that you have a spiritual bond.

A baby needs an umbilical cord to survive in the womb. If the person you are praying for is in a spiritual parenting relationship, then this is a confirmation that they are receiving everything from their spiritual parent.

I have also experienced situations where there was a conflict in a relationship between a mother and her young child. Because of circumstances when the child was still a baby, the bond between the mother and child was broken, making things difficult for them both.

When praying for the mother and child together, we saw the Lord establishing that cord again, indicating that He had brought healing to this relationship.

NEGATIVE
What are you "feeding off?" Is it the Lord, or are you simply taking in influences to make you feel better? Not everything you allow to nurture you is positive. You could be feeding off someone because you need their acceptance. However, you are receiving a contamination, because you should only be receiving that kind of influence from the Lord.

If the cord is negative, then it could speak of a generational curse.

It can also be a picture of those that are draining the life from you, by taking everything you have and not giving anything back in return.

I see umbilical cords often when ministering to others. It usually has a negative connotation rather than a positive one. This is because the things we receive from our generations are often negative due to the sinful nature of man.

In the New Testament we are known as the children of Christ. The Scriptures say that the Lord is the vine and we are the branches.

He feeds into us His blessing and anointing. But if you are receiving things that do not originate with Him, then the "spiritual umbilical cord" you are receiving from is not of God and needs to be severed.

See also: Baby, Cords, Navel, Rope, Stomach/Belly

UMBRELLA

A protection against your present attack. This includes your spiritual covering and the hand of the Lord on you right now.

Positive:

- Protection against the enemy
- Security against circumstances that are assailing you
- Your spiritual covering

Negative: A hindrance to the blessing of the Lord

POSITIVE
An umbrella in the natural protects you against the elements. It means that the Lord has you covered! It does not matter what is coming against you right now, because you are protected by Him and your spiritual covering. You have no need to fear.

NEGATIVE
To dream or see a vision of a torn umbrella means that you are under attack and do not have any spiritual covering! You need to determine if the covering you have is failing or if you are not standing under the covering that God put you under.

If the rain is positive and the umbrella is hindering the water from getting to where it needs to go, then this speaks of a spiritual blockage in your life right now. Something is preventing the blessing and anointing of God from getting to you.

Umbrella is very similar to the interpretation for *Roof*.

See also: Roof

UNCLE

CHARACTER SPECIFIC SYMBOL

You cannot make a hard and fast rule concerning family and friends in dreams. You would usually dream of an uncle or an aunt in an internal dream, and then they would be a representation of a part of yourself.

So identify what your uncle means to you in real life. When you think of him, what comes to your mind?

Universal Symbol

It is also common to see an uncle or aunt in personal ministry when dealing with generational curses or past hurts.

At times when I have ministered to someone with regards to an absent father, I might see an uncle in the spirit that filled that role.

Was this uncle a source of abuse or of blessing?

Be sensitive to the spirit and share what you are seeing with the person you are ministering to. The Lord will not give you a revelation without confirming it!

See also: Aunt, Family

Symbols Starting in V

Symbols Starting in V

Vehicles

That which drives your ministry or life's goals forward.

Positive:

- To have the Lord in control
- To be headed in the correct direction
- An expansion of your ministry
- A promotion
- A change in your ministry focus

Negative:

- To feel out of control
- To "break down" indicating a lack in your ministry
- To take the wheel yourself instead of the Lord being in charge

There are many kinds of vehicles in both dreams and visions. I will share the most common here, and perhaps you can relate the vehicle you saw to one of these.

In internal prophetic and external dreams, vehicles most often refer to your ministry.

In a vision a vehicle may speak of an actual vehicle, but once again it usually speaks of a type of ministry or ministry function.

Bicycle or motorbike: A bicycle speaks of a small personal ministry.

I have often dreamed of trading my car for a bicycle or motorbike. This does not necessarily have a bad connotation. It simply means a change of emphasis in ministry.

I will often see this in personal ministry as well. The Lord is telling the person that they will be traveling alone for a while in personal ministry.

Airplane, helicopter or jet: These also refer to a type of ministry. An airplane has many functions. A fighter jet speaks of warfare and is prophetic in nature in that it surveys the land and routes out the enemy.

I have often seen all my team members as a fighter plane, flying in formation, each one having a place, and each one being a powerful tool in the hand of the Lord.

Bus: A bus is a good picture of a group of believers all following the same direction.

If you are driving the bus, then the Lord is saying that you are the leader of this group. If you dream that someone representing the Lord needs to drive the bus, the Lord is saying that you need to hand over the control to Him!

If you are always the passenger, but you should be the leader, then the Lord is saying that it is time to step forward.

I preached a message called, *Getting on the Bus with Pastoral Training* and the entire premise was that if God has called you, then it is time to GET ON THE BUS!

If you dream that you have a ticket and that you have not got on the bus yet, then the Lord is telling you to hurry up and to get moving in your ministry and call.

Train Track: A train is fast moving and needs a track to run on.

I have often seen the Lord putting a track in front of a person to follow. He was saying that He had laid things out very specifically for them, and that they simply had to follow that track!

You might see yourself laying down the track, which would mean that you are blazing a new trail and laying a new foundation. This could represent an apostolic function, of laying a new foundation for others to follow.

Let's take a quick look into the Word to see how various vehicles represent our modern-day equivalent:

A Chariot would be the modern-day equivalent of a car, airplane or fighter plane.

> *Psalms 20:7 Some trust in **chariots**, and some in horses; but we will remember the name of the Lord our God.*

Horses can also represent cars in Scripture:

> *Ezekiel 39:20 You shall be filled at My table with **horses** and riders, with mighty men and with all the men of war," says the Lord God.*

See also: Airplane, Boat, Car, Road, Ship

VEIL

What we use to hide our vulnerability. What our heart conceals.

Positive: The promise of intimacy
Negative:

- Hindrances to your relationship with Jesus
- Inner fears

POSITIVE
A bridal veil is a lovely promise of intimacy. It is the Lord saying that although there are some things that you are hiding, that He loves you anyway. He desires to draw you aside into an intimate relationship with Him, so that He can "strip the veils."

This is not a painful process, but rather a call to healing and a new relationship with Him.

Just as a bride only reveals herself to her husband, so also are there places in your life that only the Lord gets to see. This is positive! If you tend to "let everything hang out" perhaps the Lord is saying that there are just some things that should be reserved for your spouse and for Him.

Be sensitive with what you show everyone. While a veil to the Lord is negative, sometimes we put a veil to hide intimate things from others that should be reserved for those who we have given license to in our lives.

NEGATIVE
When Jesus died, the veil of the temple was torn in two indicating that nothing stood in the way of our relationship with the Father any longer. Anyone could enter into the Holy of Holies!

To have a vision or dream of veils in a negative sense means that there are things that are hindering your relationship with the Lord. Sin, fear and very possibly guilt are preventing you from entering into His presence.

Are you struggling to feel the anointing and sense the Lord's love for you right now? Then there is a veil over your heart that must be stripped. Do not be afraid, but allow the Lord to see past the wall you put up to keep everyone else out.

> *2 Corinthians 3:15-16 But even to this day, when Moses is read, a* ***veil*** *lies on their heart. Nevertheless, when one turns to the Lord, the* ***veil*** *is taken away*

See also: Bride, Clothing, Curtain, Hat, Wall

VINE

The steady growth of what you have invested over the years.

Positive:

- Blessing and prosperity
- Our position in Christ
- Our relation to others in the Lord

Negative: A curse

POSITIVE

A vine speaks of the blessing of the Lord. Whenever the Lord gave a promise in the Word, He would promise to give each man a vine. Its not just any kind of blessing though, it is a blessing that has resulted in your continued obedience over the years. Season by season you have planted and harvested by being obedient. Now it is time for you to eat the fruit of your labor!

He also refers to Himself as the vine and us as the branches. It speaks of the blessing of the Lord, both spiritual blessings and natural blessings! (John 15:5)

The grapes from a vine are a result of each person playing their part. The grapes grow on the branches, not on the main stem. This is a picture of the fruit of the spirit in our lives.

Because the vine is a perfect picture of the church, the branches speak of ministries and our own Christian walk. As each branch feeds of the stem (which is Jesus) we will bear good fruit!

To see a healthy vine speaks of walking in the spirit and producing the fruits of the spirit.

Pruning: Although pruning might seem negative to you, there is no higher compliment of your righteousness in the Lord. The Word says that the Lord only prunes those that He sees fit.

If you are a prophet and you are praying for a person or a church and see a vine being pruned, then it means that change is coming! The Lord is about to take that church through the fire to burn off the dross. It is likely that people will leave. It is likely that pressures are going to come on them.

However, the good news is that this will result in a massive new spurt of growth afterwards. Not only will the members in that ministry grow spiritually, but so will the numbers also.

I cannot tell you how often I have had the Lord warn me of a "pruning" season in our ministry only to see it shoot up to new heights not long after the cutting shears are done!

> *John 15:2 Every branch in Me that does not bear fruit He takes away; and every branch that bears fruit He* ***prunes****, that it may bear more fruit*

Remember: The Lord only prunes those that are already bearing fruit, so that you can grow even more. This is not a punishment, but the highest form of excellence.

NEGATIVE

You can get a vine that does not bear fruit or that is wicked. This refers to a curse that is stealing God's blessing in your spiritual life. Just like blessing comes from continued investing, so does the curse come from something that has been repeated over a period of time.

A vine that does not bear fruit speaks of being lukewarm and disobedient to God's Word. According to Scripture, such a vine would be cast into the fire.

Speaking of Judgment

> *Luke 3:9 And even now the ax is laid to the root of the trees. Therefore, every tree which does not bear good fruit is cut down and thrown into the fire.*

A vine with branches that looks shriveled means that you have been walking in the flesh and so fulfilled the lusts of the flesh. The anointing and the gifts of the spirit will begin to wane.

Walking in love and peace will become more difficult. The good news? It takes just a moment to repent and to tap into The Vine once again. Walking in the spirit takes a moment of decision. Make that choice right now.

See also: Fruit, Grapes, Trees, Wine

VINEGAR

- *Sorrow due to wrong decisions*
- *The consequences of sin*

Vinegar seldom has a positive meaning and speaks of sorrow in the Word. It also speaks of the consequences that you suffer because of the sin that you committed.

> *Proverbs 25:20 Like one who takes away a garment in cold weather, and like **vinegar** on soda, is one who sings songs to a heavy heart.*

> *Jeremiah 31:30 But every one shall die for his own iniquity; every man who eats the **sour grapes**, his teeth shall be set on edge.*

I find it beautiful that the last thing that Jesus did was drink vinegar before saying, “It is finished.” Just another picture of how He took on the consequences of our sins.

Thanks to Jesus, repentance can remove the sting of sorrow and death and bring you to life once again. Do not allow this “vinegar” to bring you to death, but to lead you to life.

See also: Grapes, Teeth

Symbols Starting in W-Z

SYMBOLS STARTING IN W-Z

WALL

There are walls that we build around ourselves for protection. Some are to keep people safe, while others are to keep people out.

Positive: To stand firm against the enemy
Negative: To restrict the access to your heart from others

POSITIVE
If you are building a way to keep the enemy out, this is a good picture. It means that you are solid in the Word and are overcoming the enemy.

If you dream of being able to hide behind a wall to escape trouble, this is also good. It speaks of your security in the Lord and being able to rest in Him.

The Scriptures speak of the angel of the Lord encamping around us. In this context, the wall speaks of protection and security.

I often see the Lord placing a wall of protection around a person, and when I speak blessing this is one of the blessings I like to pray. I see a large wall surrounding the person as a fence, and not allowing anything harmful to come to them.

City Wall: There is also the wall that surrounds a city that the watchman stands on. This wall refers to the position of the prophet who watches out for the children of God. It is also a form of defense and protection against any work of the enemy.

The Lord has often shown me His watchmen upon the walls, watching and speaking out his decrees.

In fact, I put this very concept into action when I founded the Prophetic Network.

I set up a "prayer wall", where prophets from all over the world would take a time to stand on the wall (spiritually speaking) to watch out for attack, and also to cover their fellow members and church in prayer.

A lot of revelation and words of decree continue to come through the prophets that remain vigilant on that wall!

Speaking of the Lord's Protection and Strength

> *Isaiah 25:4 For You have been a strength to the poor, a strength to the needy in his distress, a refuge from the storm, a shade from the heat; for the blast of the terrible ones is as a storm against the **wall**.*

NEGATIVE

We all build figurative walls around ourselves through life. You do this to hide parts of yourself from others. However, when you are trying to come into a relationship with the Lord, this is a hindrance.

If you dream of strong walls being around you, it means that you have closed your heart off to others and no one can reach you.

If you struggle to show love and affection to those close to you, then this is a confirmation of why you are struggling.

A wall can also speak of an obstacle. Many times I have seen someone come up against a wall in their lives or ministry.

At times I have even been released of the Lord to put a wall in someone's path, to prevent them from continuing in the direction they are going in.

This is a prophetic office function though, so I do not encourage anyone to speak such words, unless they are released to do so from the Lord and stand fully in prophetic or apostolic office.

Speaking of putting someone "between two walls":

> *Numbers 22:24 Then the Angel of the Lord stood in a narrow path between the vineyards, with a **wall** on this side and a **wall** on that side.*

Speaking of a wall as an obstacle:

> *Hosea 2:6 Therefore, behold, I will hedge up your way with thorns, and **wall** her in, so that she cannot find her paths.*

See also: City, Foundation, Tent, Tower, Veil

WAR

Conflict and opposition with a purpose to take back ground.

Positive: To take ground for the Lord
Negative: External attack through circumstances

POSITIVE

We are in continual warfare against the enemy to take back the land that he has stolen from God's people.

When God gave the Children of Israel their Promised Land, He did not just hand it to them. He laid it out, but they had to take hold of it.

The same applies today in our spiritual lives. The enemy is always looking for an opportunity to steal back that land that we received through Christ.

He won when Adam fell, but as believers we have more than Adam did. We have the blood of Christ!

When the Lord leads you into something new or gives you a new promise, expect warfare. Although God has laid out your Promised Land, it does not mean that the enemy is going to just roll over and let you have it.

It will mean standing up in spiritual warfare.

If you dream or have a vision of warfare, then the Lord is telling you to stand in your spiritual authority against the enemy.

NEGATIVE
If you keep dreaming of wars and being caught up in wars, it is an indication of your circumstances and spiritual condition right now. You are under attack! Perhaps your attacks are coming from your workplace or even your ministry.

Either way, determine the setting of the war you are fighting in and see where the attack is coming from.

On the other hand, are you fighting a war that is not yours to fight? Then the Lord is telling you that you are stepping beyond what He intends. This is not your battle. Walk away!

To dream of running away from attackers while in war, depicts your condition right now. You feel as if everyone and everything is out to get you. It is time to stop the fight and to stand in your authority.

You need not run and hide. It is time to stand up and fight!

See also: Army, Attacked, Chasing, Fighting

WASP/HORNET

An aggressive attack whether for or against you.

Positive: The Lord fighting aggressively on your behalf
Negative: Physical attack that induces fear

CHARACTER SPECIFIC SYMBOL

POSITIVE
Unless you are studying hornets or have a keen fascination with them, they are not likely to be positive. If they are the source of study, then this is the aspect of your life they represent.

NEGATIVE
Have you been stung by a wasp or hornet? Then it likely represents fear or pain in your dreams.

Universal Symbol

POSITIVE
The Lord sent hornets ahead of the Israelites to clear the way for them. To have a dream or see a vision of your enemy being attacked by hornets indicates that the Lord is fighting on your behalf. All that is left for you to do now is walk with boldness!

> *Joshua 24:12 I sent the hornet before you which drove them out from before you...*

NEGATIVE
Because of the pain that the wasp and hornet inflicts, it represents attack on your body. I will often see a wasp as a spirit of infirmity when praying for someone who is suffering with pain. It is the kind of physical attack that brings a lot of pain and causes the person to fear.

See also: Bees, Insects

Watch/Clock

The progression of time.

Positive: What lies ahead
Negative: Opportunities lost

Character Specific Symbol

POSITIVE
To dream of going back in time or having extra time left on the clock is positive. It means that you still have time to take advantage of the promise in front of you. Work hard and fight for that promise, because time will not wait for you.

You might also see a clock in a vision where the Lord is giving you a very specific time to do something. What is the time on the clock? Is the Lord indicating that something is going to happen at that time, or is He saying, "Time's up!"

Is it dinner time or bedtime? If so, then the Lord is telling you that it is time to rest or it is time to fill up again! A watch cannot change time - it can only give you an accurate account of what timeframe you are in right now.

To see a watch being turned back means that the Lord wants you to go into your past and deal with something back there.

To receive a new watch means that the Lord just set you on a new course. You have a set amount of time to fulfill this purpose in your life. Do so with all joy, because the Lord will be there every step of the way!

NEGATIVE
For a clock to stop means that you have been put on hold right now. You need to determine if your stubbornness or sin has caused this "hold" or if the Lord is arranging circumstances and needs you to wait on Him for a bit.

To have a clock broken means that you are directionless. You are going in so many directions right now, that you are not reaching any of your goals!

Alarm clock going off? It is time to wake up spiritually. Your season of rest is over and you need to step out in faith now. You are not waiting for God – He is waiting for you to get moving!

See also: Bracelet, Race

WATER

The force that brings about the washing in our lives.

Positive:

- Washing by the Word of God
- The anointing

Negative:

- Circumstances beyond your control
- Taking in contamination

POSITIVE
Being washed with water speaks of being cleansed and of putting things behind you. It also speaks of being cleansed from your sin.

Water is a picture of the anointing. John 4:14 Water is also a picture of the Word of God, and how it sets us free from the dirt in our lives.

> *Ephesians 5:26 that He might sanctify and cleanse her with the washing of **water** by the word,*

To water something means to nurture it and to give it life. If you are in ministry, then it means that you should be watering the seeds that have been planted in the hearts of God's people.

This is primarily a teaching function, just as Apollos functioned in.

> *1 Corinthians 3:6 I planted, Apollos **watered**, but God gave the increase.*

NEGATIVE
Water is a powerful force, known to shape rock. If you dream or see a vision of a force of water coming against you, it speaks of how you feel right now. You

feel like you are being carried away by circumstances that are beyond your control.

Dirty Water: Water that is bitter or dirty speaks of a contamination, likely stemming from bitterness.

It speaks of those that really do have a ministry, but unfortunately are in deception. They have allowed some things in their life that are not of the Lord.

To dream of sitting in unclean water speaks of the things you are getting involved in.

Instead of walking in the spirit, by getting involved with these things or feeding on things that are not of God, you are contaminating your spirit.

It could also indicate that the ministry you have been receiving is not pure and directly from the Lord. Some of it is tainted with the flesh and man's ideas.

When I train God's leaders I share how the Lord takes them through training to get rid of their own ideas.

The revelation and the anointing that God gives is pure when it comes from your spirit. However, if your mind is filled with things of the world or your own ideas, you end up tainting that word. Then what comes out is only a part Christ, and the rest is your own ideas!

See also: Anointing, Baptism, Basin, Drowning, Flood, Jar, Ocean, River, Swimming, Wash

WAVES

A sudden swell of circumstantial change both positive or negative.

Positive: An opportunity for promotion
Negative: Circumstances in your life that are in tumult

POSITIVE:
Just because circumstances feel overwhelming does not mean they are negative! Had Peter not braved the waves, he would never had walked on water!

There are times when God will say, "It's time to ride this wave!"

I was complaining about my circumstances and He said to me, "These waves are meant to carry you to my blessing. Stop fighting them and ride your way to promotion!"

The same holds true for you. Do not fight the waves, but ride them! To dream or have a vision of surfing or riding a wave means taking hold of your circumstances and using them as an opportunity to rise up higher than ever before.

NEGATIVE:
Jesus spoke to the winds and the waves and called them to be still.

Seeing a storm and rising waves is an indication that right now everything around you is in turmoil, but the Lord is greater than those waves! And so just like Jesus, you can also say to your circumstances, "Peace be still!"

> *Psalms 89:9 You rule the raging of the sea; when its **waves** rise, You still them.*

See also: Drowning, Storm

WEAPONS

The ability to defend ourselves and inflict damage to the kingdom of Darkness

Positive:

- Our authority in Christ
- A symbol of archetype
- A symbol of position
- Symbol of function
- Our ability to defend ourselves against the enemy
- Our ability to take back the land satan has stolen

Negative:

- Archetype arrayed against you
- Attack
- Words spoken against you
- Circumstances arrayed against you

The Word says that no weapon formed against you will prosper. It also teaches us to put on our own spiritual armor and weaponry.

Weapons, regardless of their form, are a picture of warfare and of our stand against the flesh and the enemy.

Apostle Paul also tells us that the weapons we fight with are not weapons of flesh, but of spirit. Our authority is vested in the Lord, and any action we take should be with our spiritual authority.

> *2 Corinthians 10:4 For the **weapons** of our warfare are not carnal but mighty in God for pulling down strongholds.*

See also: Armor, Arrow, Axe, Bow, Dagger, Darts, Shield, Spear, Sword

WEDDING

A covenant ritual whereby two become one.

Positive: To conform yourself to the purpose of God
Negative: To conform yourself to the purpose of man or the enemy

POSITIVE
The best illustration we have of this is the wedding of Christ to His bride. The wedding ceremony is in fact a covenant ritual act.

> *Ezekiel 16:8 "When I passed by you again and looked upon you, indeed your time was the time of love; so I spread My wing over you and covered your nakedness. Yes, I swore an oath to you* ***and entered into a covenant with you****, and you became Mine," says the Lord God*

In the Old Testament when two people entered into a blood covenant, they would perform various acts.

Firstly they would cut their hands and join blood. Then they would rub ash into the wound so that it would leave a scar. They would also exchange their belts, representing their strengths.

The scar was a public sign of their covenant, much like the wedding ring is. The mixing of blood is symbolic of the sexual act of marriage.

The exchange of belts in marriage is the joining of two lives. Where your strengths become one.

When the blood covenant was over, the two of them had all things in common. Neither considered what they had as their own.

The Bridegroom: When you realize that this is also a picture of our relationship with Jesus it brings you to a new realization of who you are in Christ.

If you dream of being married, the Lord is reminding you that you are in blood covenant with Him!

All He has is yours and all you have is also His. He is asking you to give your life to Him completely and to also take hold of His completely.

Every physical, psychological and spiritual blessing that Jesus has, is available to you through this covenant.

For more on blood covenant, look at the love of David and Jonathan in 1 Sam 18:3

Divorce: When you came to the Lord, you divorced your old life and married into His. If you dream that you are divorcing someone that represents the flesh in your life, this means that you are finally letting go of your old life to be joined to Christ.

Marrying someone you know: Consider the person you are marrying in your dream and determine what they mean to you. Whatever they represent to you is indicative of a covenant you are entering into right now.

If they represent a ministry or church that you feel positive about, then the Lord is giving you the go ahead to commit to that work.

NEGATIVE
What are you marrying in your dream and vision? Is the person in your dream someone you want to enter into a covenant with? If you dream of someone that represents your business, you need to determine if this is a good covenant or not!

Either way, you are conforming yourself to their desires and attributes. When two become one, you cannot tell whose traits are whose any longer! For the wedding to be negative, means that you are making traits your own that are imposed on you by man or the enemy.

To dream that you are getting divorced from someone that represents the Lord in your dreams means that you have separated yourself from the blessing of God.

Israel lost this blessing because they turned their backs on the Lord and followed idols.

See also: Bride, Bridegroom

WEEDS

A work of the enemy to choke the goodness out of life.

Positive: To be a "contamination" in the field of the enemy
Negative: The undercover work of the enemy to steal

POSITIVE
Although we know how negative weeds are, the Lord gave me a different way of looking at them. He said how the enemy was always planting weeds in our lives, but that we needed to do him the same way!

He said that it was time that we as believers "contaminated" his work so that it would be laid waste! To be such an influence in this world that we change people's thinking our way.

NEGATIVE
Weeds are mostly a negative picture because although they steal the life of other plants, they never give anything in return.

In the parable of the tares and the wheat we get a good example of how the enemy tries to steal the fruit of your labor. Matthew 13:25

He will do this by bringing people who come to take all you have, but give only bitterness in return. This is very true if you have ever been in ministry.

There was a time when the Lord said that He would be separating the tares from the wheat in our ministry. During that time, He exposed many who had come to take our time and all our resources, but to return the blessing with cursing and division.

The great thing about this though is that a weed is obvious! It does not bear fruit and although at the beginning it is not clear, it will be exposed soon enough.

If you see a vision of a weed or dream of weeds, the Lord is making you aware of something or someone in your life that is undercutting you and stealing the blessing and the fruit of your labor.

See also: Thorns, Yeast

WELL

Blessing attained through playing your part. Effort is required for this blessing to come to pass!

Positive:

- Hidden potential for anointing and blessing
- Originating sources of blessing for others

Negative: Restricted blessing

POSITIVE
A well requires great effort to finally reach the water. Although you will have it "on tap" it means putting some work into it.

This relates to both spiritual and natural things. If you see a well, then the Lord is calling you to dig it!

A well is a continual source and although takes great effort, is a work that will remain.

> *2 Chronicles 26:10 Also he built towers in the desert.* ***He dug many wells****, for he had much livestock, both in the lowlands and in the plains; he also had farmers and vinedressers in the mountains and in Carmel, for he loved the soil*

I love this scripture because it describes all the great accomplishments of King Uzziah. It is a testament of the things he left behind for the next generation. When God calls you to "build a well" He intends for you to build a source of blessing that will remain for generations to come.

Relating to the anointing: I often use this picture to illustrate how to tap into the anointing. We call it "setting up your windmill". The concept is that to flow in the anointing we have to get rid of the hindrances that are blocking our spirits.

Speak in tongues for an hour or until you get a breakthrough in the spirit where you will experience a "second wind".

By keeping your spirit free of contamination, you end up with a well of living water that is ready to pour out at any time.

NEGATIVE
What are you building right now that you hope to be a blessing to many? A blocked well means that the enemy is trying to hinder your progress.

> *Genesis 26:15 Now the Philistines had stopped up all the **wells** which his father's servants had dug in the days of Abraham his father, and they had filled them with earth*

This scripture speaks of the blessing that Abraham had left Isaac and that the enemy had attacked. He went and dug the earth out and used them again. We have many divisions in our ministry and once the Lord showed me a number of "blocked wells." The message was clear! The enemy had dried up some of the divisions we had begun.

It was time to do some spiritual warfare, housecleaning and put some more effort into the work God had given to us!

See also: Basin, Bath, Fountain, Ocean, River, Water

WHALE

The hand of God to get your attention.

Positive: Overwhelming circumstances sent to get you back on track.
Negative: Overwhelming circumstances that take you off course

CHARACTER SPECIFIC SYMBOL

Do whales have a specific meaning to you? If you fear them, then they could speak of fear. If they are a fascination to you, then they speak of a childhood joy. Certainly for my son, having seen one at SeaWorld, they would forever speak of a childhood delight.

Because of their size and influence in the ocean they will always be tied to an overwhelming circumstance whether positive or negative.

UNIVERSAL SYMBOL

The most profound illustration is the story of Jonah. Running away from God, he is swallowed by a whale, not allowing him to do anything. He is released when he relents and does things God's way.

Although I am sure Jonah did not see it as positive, there are times when the Lord will use circumstances to "stop you dead in your tracks." If you see yourself or someone being swallowed by a whale it means that God is sending overwhelming circumstances to set them back on track.

On the other hand, if you feel the whale is negative, it means that the enemy is sending the overwhelming circumstances to stop them from doing God's work.

See also: Fish, Waves

WHEAT

- *Provision for your desires.*
- *A call to evangelistic ministry*

POSITIVE

Wheat is a very positive picture in scripture and it referred to provision as well as to the evangelistic ministry.

What was a higher class of grain that barley and you had to be a wealthier to afford it.

If you see wheat ready to be harvested, then the Lord is telling you that a season of hard, but joyful work is about to begin.

If you see wheat already cut, then the Lord is saying that He has provided your need and that you do not need to work so hard at it.

> *Psalms 147:14 He makes peace in your borders, And fills you with the finest **wheat***

NEGATIVE

The scriptures say that the wheat was gathered, but the chaff was burned. The chaff are the husks of the wheat and not edible.

If you see the chaff being burned, the Lord is saying that He is going to take you through a season of refining in your life.

The Word also says that unless a grain of wheat falls into the ground and dies, it cannot product a crop.

If you see a seed being dropped into the ground to die, the Lord is saying that He is about to take you through a season of death to the flesh.

This is positive though, because it also means that He is calling you to resurrect with more than you had before.

When you look at it that way, it is easy to let go of the small portion that you have now.

See also: Barley, Bread, Field, Harvest

WHITE

The universal color of peace and purity.

Positive:

- Purity and innocence.
- Righteousness

Negative:

- False humility
- Religious spirit
- Spiritually sick due to personal sin

CHARACTER SPECIFIC SYMBOL

Skin Color: When it comes to skin color, you need to determine how you feel about white people. This will change depending on the way you were brought up and the experiences you have had. When you think of white people in general, what is the first impression that comes to your mind?

Our dreams are strongly based on culture, so when interpreting dreams for someone of a different culture, you must take this into consideration.

White in most cultures also speaks of purity and innocence. To dream of something being made white indicates that something that was unpleasant in your life has now been removed.

UNIVERSAL SYMBOL

POSITIVE

The Bride of Christ is to be made without spot or wrinkle. Again and again the Word speaks of our sins being made white as snow. You cannot hide even a fleck of dirt on a white surface.

It reflects the very nature of Christ. The best part is, that we do not need to cleanse ourselves. The Lord is responsible for making us clean as snow.

In the book of revelation Jesus is seated on a white horse. There is no better way to depict Him. Full of pure love, authority and righteousness. It is because of Him that we can walk in this complete innocence.

There is no better scripture to explain the power of white than Isaiah 1:18 meaning that not a single trace of our sin is left when we are redeemed by His blood!

A white vehicle speaks of your ministry that is in right standing with God. You are fulfilling His purpose.

NEGATIVE
Not everything that is white depicts righteousness, in this case, it speaks of false humility and a religious spirit. The Pharisees obeyed the law and so boasted in their good works. They used religion as a source of personal power.

Although they performed the right acts, they were not in right standing with God.

> *Matthew 23:27 "Woe to you, scribes and Pharisees, hypocrites! For you are like* ***whitewashed*** *tombs which indeed appear beautiful outwardly, but inside are full of dead men's bones and all uncleanness*

Spotted Garment: Anything white that is tainted speaks of not being in right standing with the Lord. Jesus is coming for a Bride without spot or wrinkle. A single spot on a white sheet denotes an attitude or sin that is hindering you right now.

Leprosy: White that is tarnished also speaks of sin and spiritual ill health. Gehazi sinned and ended up being infected with the leprosy Naaman had. When Miriam stood against Moses, she was struck with leprosy. Both of these pictures speak of being spiritually diseased because of personal sin.

To dream or have a vision of having a disease that leaves you white means that the flesh has infected your spirit! It has made you unclean. Just as Miriam repented and God healed her, so also will you break free of this blockage and the curses in your life!

> *2 Kings 5:27 Therefore the leprosy of Naaman shall cling to you and your descendants forever." And he went out from his presence leprous, as* ***white*** *as snow*

See also: Disease, Gray, Colors

WEIGHTS

Restrictions that have the potential to make you stronger because of their nature.

Positive: Obstacles meant to make you stronger
Negative: Obstacles and circumstances meant to discourage you

POSITIVE
It does not mean that because something is uncomfortable that it is not of the Lord. I heard of a long distance runner that would train by tying a large tractor wheel around his waist.

When the time of the race came, he cut the weight loose and ran as he never had! The weight had strengthened him.

Often the Lord will bring an obstacle in your life to strengthen you. This scripture explains it perfectly:

> *1 Corinthians 13:10 But when that which is perfect is come, then that which is in part shall be done away. (KJV)*

NEGATIVE
If the weight is negative, then it is referring to people that are opposing you and your sin that is causing you to become tripped up.

It is a work from the enemy to weigh you down so that you cannot run the race that God has put before you. These are circumstances that are coming against you that are only slowing you down. You find yourself running around putting out fires all of the time.

The enemy is doing what is known in scripture as "the wearing down of the saints."

If you dream or have a vision of a weight that is clearly negative, then the Lord is telling you that it is time to rise up. These weights are not of the Lord, but the enemy. Rise up in your spiritual authority and shake them off.

> *Hebrews 12:1 Therefore we also, since we are surrounded by so great a cloud of witnesses, let us lay aside every* ***weight****, and the sin which so easily ensnares us, and let us run with endurance the race that is set before us,*

See also: Exercising, Running/Race

WIFE

It is very common to dream of your wife. Depending on your relationship with her, the interpretation will change accordingly.

POSITIVE
Most commonly your wife would represent your recreated spirit in Christ.

You might have a dream that your wife is trying to speak to you, but you cannot hear her. This would mean that your spirit is trying to get a message to you, but something is blocking it.

You might dream that your wife is driving your car and leading you on a new or old road. This would mean that you are being led by your spirit to go in a different direction.

You might dream that your wife gives you a gift. This would mean that the Lord has a new spiritual gift for you. Depending on the gift, the interpretation of what that gift is will vary.

Your relationship with your wife could also represent your relationship with the Lord.

You might dream that you are having an affair and your wife finds out and is upset. This would mean that you are allowing the things of the world to seduce you. They are drawing you away from the Lord and what you know is the direction of God for your life.

NEGATIVE
An ex-wife that you divorced on bad terms might refer to your flesh. She might speak of your pride, your failure or your weaknesses.

Ask yourself, "What comes to my mind when I think of my wife or ex-wife?"

The first impression you have of her will likely reflect what part of yourself she represents in an internal dream.

If your wife has a negative connotation for you, dreaming of her driving your car would not be good! This would mean that your flesh is in control of your ministry.

See also: Adultery, Gifts, Car, Husband, Woman

WIND

A move taking place in the realm of the spirit either positive or negative.

Positive: The work of the Holy Spirit
Negative: Circumstances out of your control

POSITIVE
Standing in a cool wind speaks of a time of refreshing. It is also a sign of rain, which is a promise of blessing.

A whirlwind can be positive, speaking of the move of the Holy Spirit in your life.

The Lord is symbolized as both a mighty rushing wind and as a gentle breeze. Each is a description of His nature.

Hurricane/Mighty rushing wind: A hurricane or strong wind speaks of the might and power of the Lord. Not only does it represent the Lord overcoming the enemy on your behalf, but it is also a picture of revival and pouring His spirit out on His people.

> *Jeremiah 30:23 Behold, the* ***whirlwind*** *of the Lord goes forth with fury, a continuing* ***whirlwind****; it will fall violently on the head of the wicked.*

Gentle breeze of Jesus: Early in our ministry we started experiencing the anointing in an unusual way. Each time we ministered, and especially when we played music, people would begin to cry in the presence of the Lord.

This occurred even in a church where people spoke a foreign language and did not understand any of our English songs! The Lord confirmed that this was His gentle breeze.

We discovered that during these times the Lord Jesus would reveal Himself to people in the congregation and would also heal hurts from the past. In each case we would also see the Lord Jesus walking among the people.

We came to nickname this move of God, the gentle breeze of Jesus. This also brought love with it, and it united people and helped them experience the love of the Lord.

We sometimes also call it the love anointing. This is typified by a gentle breeze that brings life and peace everywhere it goes.

The Word says that God is the author of life. It is this breath, this gentle breeze, that brings life and healing to His people.

> *Ezekiel 37:5 Thus says the Lord God to these bones: Surely I will cause* ***breath*** *to enter into you, and you shall live.*

NEGATIVE
Dreaming of a hurricane speaks of circumstances that are out of your control. The enemy is throwing everything he can at you from all directions. It is time to rise up and stand in your authority in Christ.

Tossed about: To be tossed around by the wind means that you do not have a firm conviction or a Word-based foundation of your life.

Violent wind: A wind that tears things apart and brings damage speaks of a spirit of destruction prevalent in your life.

See also: Clouds, Ocean, Storm

WINDOW

Just as a window gives access to either sunshine or a thief to your life, so also does it represent access in your life, to either the Lord or the enemy.

Positive: Opportunity that awaits you
Negative: An entry point for the enemy

POSITIVE
An open window speaks of a promising opportunity.

The window of heaven is a picture of the Lord providing your needs and pouring His blessing out on you.

> *Malachi 3:10 ... "If I will not open for you the windows of heaven And pour out for you such blessing That there will not be room enough to receive it*

NEGATIVE
A thief usually comes through the window so that he cannot be found out. To dream of an open window through which something evil comes, is an indication that satan has some form of license in your life.

Either that license has come as a result of disobedience or you have opened your heart to someone you should not have. Consider your associations. The good news is that this is not a huge problem. Its just a window that can easily be shut.

This is a good picture of how the enemy works. He comes with deception and causes you to give him license to come into your life. This speaks of a small thing though and it is easily rectified.

> *Joel 2:9 They run to and fro in the city, they run on the wall; they climb into the houses, they enter at the **windows** like a thief.*

See also: Door, House, Thief

WINE

The call to experience the joy and delight of the Lord

Positive:

- A representation of the work of the Holy Spirit
- Joy of the Lord
- The effect of the anointing

Negative:

- Indulging in the flesh
- To use the world for joy instead of delighting in the Lord

POSITIVE
To dream of being drunk but it is positive in a dream, then it speaks of letting go of your inhibitions and your cares.

When the anointing comes on a person, it brings joy and a feeling of euphoria. This is why wine is often depicted as the anointing in visions.

The joy of the Lord is our strength, which is why wine is a good picture of it.

> *Song of Solomon 1:4 The king has brought me into his chambers. We will be glad and rejoice in you. We will remember your love more than* ***wine****. Rightly do they love you.*

To see wine in the spirit speaks a lot more than just the anointing though. It speaks specifically of the nature of the anointing to make the heart glad. Wine speaks of the power of the anointing to change the way we feel.

Wine in scriptures is included with other foods that denote favor and luxury. This blessing that the Lord is pouring over you is not just because you need it, but because He simply wants to make you glad!

NEGATIVE
To dream of being drunk means that you have allowed the flesh to gain control of your life.

Watered down wine speaks of the anointing that has waned. It speaks of the works of man trying to create what only God can. You are trying to "stir up joy" using the spirit of the world instead of just letting the anointing do its work.

> *Isaiah 1:22 Your silver has become dross, your* ***wine*** *mixed with water.*

See also: Anointing, Grapes, Pub, Vine

WINGS

To be given a place of protection and escape from the situation you are in right now.

Positive: Escape from your circumstantial pressures
Negative: To run away from pressures you should be facing

POSITIVE
To see the wings of an eagle or to be covered with wings means that the Lord is telling you to run to Him for protection.

Just as a hen gathers her chicks under her wings, so also does the Lord open His arms for you to hide and escape the pressures for a moment.

> *Psalms 36:7 How precious is Your lovingkindness, O God! Therefore, the children of men put their trust under the shadow of Your* ***wings****.*

Your only escape from the pressures of the world is under the shadow of the Lord's wings. It is always safe to run and hide there. No matter what you are facing, if you dream or have a vision of wings, the Lord is inviting you to take a break and to rest in His presence for a while.

If you see an angel in the spirit with wings, then you are seeing a worship angel as these are the only ones who have wings.

NEGATIVE
For something to "take wing" means for it to escape your grasp. This is a perfect illustration:

> *Proverbs 23:5 Will you set your eyes on that which is not? For riches certainly make themselves **wings**; they fly away like an eagle toward heaven.*

For something such as your finances to grow wings speaks of losing the blessing that God has given to you. You need to look at where the enemy is attacking you.

For you to grow wings and take flight has the same meaning as *Flying*. It means that you are trying to escape your present situation.

See also: Flying

WOLF

A devourer of what is good and beneficial. A picture of a spirit of theft.

Positive: To have the upper hand
Negative: Spirit of theft, meant to steal, kill and destroy

POSITIVE
The only time a wolf would be positive is if you have a personal attachment to it. The Lord said that Benjamin would be as a wolf and devour his prey.

This was positive because it meant that instead of being stolen from, he would fully overcome the thief and take the prey for himself! (Genesis 49:27)

If the wolf in your dream or vision is positive, then it means that instead of being stolen from, you will be the victor and will steal back from the thief!

NEGATIVE
For the most part though the wolf is a picture of a spirit of theft. So if you see one it means that the enemy intends to steal the good blessings of God from you. The wolf is also aggressive which shows that the means the enemy will use to steal from you will be aggressive.

If you have suddenly been experiencing loss and things being taken from you in reality, then the Lord is trying to show you what is going on. The enemy is stealing from you and you need to rise up in your authority to overcome.

False prophets are pictured as wolves in sheep's clothing. They appear innocent; however, their intention is to steal the truth from you and to devour your blessings. Instead of giving to you, they intend to steal.

> *Matthew 7:15 Beware of false prophets, who come to you in sheep's clothing, but inwardly they are ravenous* ***wolves****.*

See also: Dog, Sheep

WOMAN

Your more creative and prophetic side. Represents either your artistic nature or your prophetic call (if you should have one).

Positive:

- Your "right brained" functions
- Your ability to hear God's voice and flow in the spirit

Negative:

- To deliberately indulge in sin, knowing it is wrong

CHARACTER SPECIFIC SYMBOL

POSITIVE

You may at times dream of a woman that is familiar in your dreams, but in reality you do not know them.

As I teach in *The Way of Dreams and Visions*, a familiar feminine character in your dreams often represents your animas - your feminine side. This side is artistic, creative, prophetic and totally allegorical.

In a positive dream you might dream that you are embracing this lady. Some men who have shared such dreams with me felt guilty that they were embracing this woman in their dreams.

But the dream was actually positive, because it meant that the Lord was leading them into a more prophetic orientation or He was telling them that they need to tap into their creativity.

This also applies to women. As a woman you might dream that you are befriending this women character in your dream; perhaps even embracing her.

This DOES NOT mean that you have homosexual tendencies! It simply means that you are moving more towards a prophetic orientation.

NEGATIVE

Depending on how you respond to this feminine character in your dream it could mean different things.

If you are ignoring her, it could mean that you have been ignoring your prophetic side and the Lord wants you to get back to it.

Perhaps in your dream she is killed, which could mean that the Lord is bringing the prophetic in you to death, so that you can move on to the masculine, teaching orientation.

You must identify what you sensed in the dream and what witnesses in your spirit.

Universal Symbol

POSITIVE
Depending on the context of your vision, seeing a woman will have a different meaning.

If it is a woman you know, then the vision relates to her. If it is a woman you do not know, then she could represent something.

A pregnant woman refers to something new that is about to be birthed. Depending on the direction of your prayer at the time, the birth could refer to the ministry, church or person you were praying for.

Of course seeing a bride speaks of the Bride of Christ. Depending on how you see her, will give you the full interpretation.

A bride standing in splendor would speak of the plan the Lord has for His church. A bride whose garments are tattered speaks of the church being in a state of disarray and needing mending.

NEGATIVE
A woman dressed in scarlet has a negative connotation according to this Scripture:

> *Revelation 17:4 The **woman** was arrayed in purple and scarlet...*
> *6 I saw the **woman**, drunk with the blood of the saints and with the blood of the martyrs of Jesus. And when I saw her, I marveled with great amazement.*

This speaks of an adulteress and something that is seducing you to turn your back on the things of God. It means you are in adultery!

A woman that is a harlot or that you feel is very negative speaks of deliberately sinning and satisfying your flesh instead of walking in obedience.

> *Proverbs 7:10 And there a **woman** met him, With the attire of a harlot, and a crafty heart.*

Witch: If you see a woman that looks like a witch, it can have a variety of meanings. It can speak of witchcraft specifically, however in my experience, this is how I see the Jezebel spirit. It speaks of an aggressive nature that seeks to dominate and control through manipulation and guilt.

See also: Demons, Wife

WOMB

A season of incubation and growth

Positive: Going through a phase of hidden change

Negative:

- Immaturity
- Something negative that you are taking comfort in
- Escape from the pressures of life

POSITIVE
To dream or have a vision of being in a womb means that the Lord desires to draw you aside for a season of incubation and growth. There are some changes that you need to go through and you need time.

Do not rush it. Allow the Holy Spirit to finish the work that He has begun in you.

NEGATIVE
If you feel that the womb is negative in your dream or vision, then it means that you are immature and not ready to face "the big world." It could also be indicating that you are hiding away from the realities of life.

A baby has to be born eventually! You cannot be overdue or you will die. In the same way, we sometimes become complacent and do not hear the call to step out!

UNIVERSAL SYMBOL

A healthy womb is our inheritance! If you are praying for a woman and see a picture of a womb, it might be speaking of her actual womb!

When my stepmom was trying to fall pregnant she struggled. After a year of trying, there were still no results. And so she and my dad prayed, and the Lord showed him that there was a blockage in one of her fallopian tubes.

He saw the actual womb in the spirit. They prayed and spoke healing. A very short time afterwards, they conceived their son.

See also: Baby, Pregnant, Mother

WORM

A subversive attack from the enemy that destroys the promise of God before it has the chance to reach fruition.

Negative:

- Decay

- Theft
- A curse that is given license through disobedience

CHARACTER SPECIFIC SYMBOL

I cover Caterpillar under its own category, so I am not going to expand on it here. For most people, worm is negative. They can represent your fears, an unclean spirit, or something that is "niggling" you. To "open up a can of worms" means to make a mess that is not easily cleaned up!

UNIVERSAL SYMBOL

NEGATIVE
Worms have two clear connotations in Scripture. The first is that they are a sign of decay. The Word speaks often of the dead being eaten by worms. In other words, to see worms indicates that death is present and that death is following its natural course. Decay has set in and is irreversible.

> *Exodus 16:20 Notwithstanding they did not heed Moses. But some of them left part of it until morning, and it bred worms and stank. And Moses was angry with them.*

The second aspect speaks of the kind of curse that eats up the blessing of the Lord. Just like worms were found in the manna, they speak of disobedience! So although they are a curse of theft and decay, they are present because of disobedience. Yes, they are a destructive force of the enemy, but the enemy gained license through disobedience. Consider Jonah, where a worm was sent to eat up the tree that was giving him shade!

> *Deuteronomy 28:39 You shall plant vineyards and tend them, but you shall neither drink of the wine nor gather the grapes; for the worms shall eat them.*

See also: Caterpillar, Insects, Moth

WOUND

An aggressive "wake up call".

Positive: A cleansing process
Negative:

- Emotional pain
- Attack from others

POSITIVE
A wound will seldom be positive in a dream. However, a wound that heals means that the Lord has performed inner healing in your life.

The Word says that the wound of a friend is good. It refers to correction that leads to blessing.

Often we need others to point out our failures before we see them. The Lord also will lance a wound (spiritually speaking) to bring healing to hurts that were made in your past.

> *Psalms 147:3 He heals the brokenhearted And binds up their* ***wounds***

NEGATIVE
Receiving or having a wound speaks of being hurt. Perhaps you have had conflict with someone or have been betrayed.

If you dream of giving someone else a wound, then it means that you are bringing pain and attacking others. You are trying to get them to "understand" but you are causing more harm than good.

Someone else having a wound in your dream, means that they have been under attack or that there is something wrong with them.

The enemy wounds and causes damage. Wounds also speak of people speaking against you, as well as referring to hurts from the past.

See also: Bruise

YEAST

A subtle force that has the power to contaminate and then transform something from one form to another.

- *Legalism*
- *Sin*

Yeast has the ability to spread quickly and have a lasting effect on the dough it reaches. It can be both positive and negative.

POSITIVE
Like I shared in "weeds" the Lord told me to contaminate the work of the enemy with His righteous leaven! Leaven is mostly negative in Scripture, but I love the idea of using the same tactics against the enemy.

NEGATIVE
Because the work of leaven is so subtle, you do not know it is a problem until the entire lump of dough has been affected.

> *Matthew 16:6 Then Jesus said to them, Take heed and beware of the* ***leaven*** *of the Pharisees and the Sadducees.*

Doctrine: In this case, leaven is seen as legalism, works and false teaching. The more you sit under incorrect teaching, the more it will corrode your true conviction and transform your mind against the correct principles of the Word. You will replace righteousness with works of the flesh.

Sin: In my teaching *The Stain of Sin* in the *Strategies of War* series I teach on how leaven "the sin of others" can bring you under their bondage. When you ally yourself to the sin of others, you are effected by it and will find yourself partaking not only of their sin, but their curses as well.

> *1 Corinthians 5:6-7 Your glorying is not good. Do you not know that a little **leaven** leavens the whole lump? Therefore, purge out the old **leaven**, that you may be a new lump...*

See also: Bake, Bread, Weeds

YELLOW

Ailment and contamination

CHARACTER SPECIFIC SYMBOL

POSITIVE

For many, yellow might be a favorite color or it might remind them of sunshine. Does this color have a specific meaning to you? Is it the color of your favorite flower? If you have a special attachment to yellow, then to see it in an internal dream represents this attachment. If not, I suggest looking at the universal symbol.

NEGATIVE

To be "yellow" speaks of lacking conviction. Yellow has more negative than positive connotations in our culture. What is the first thing you thought of when you saw this color in your dream? If you are unsure, I suggest moving onto the universal symbol.

UNIVERSAL SYMBOL

NEGATIVE

I did not find any positive connotations for this color in the Word. It mostly represented something unclean – the proof of disease. In Revelation is is used to describe sulphur, which is foul smelling.

Yellow in a dream or vision represents something that is unclean. It began as something pure and righteous, but has become contaminated and is now foul.

Yellow should not be confused with the color gold, which is used extensively in the Word.

> *Leviticus 13:36 then the priest shall examine him; and indeed if the scale has spread over the skin, the priest need not seek for yellow hair. He is unclean.*

> *Revelation 9:17 And thus I saw the horses in the vision: those who sat on them had breastplates of fiery red, hyacinth blue, and sulfur yellow; and the heads of the horses were like the heads of lions; and out of their mouths came fire, smoke, and brimstone.*

See also: Colors, Gold

PART 2

ACTION & EMOTION SYMBOLS

PART 2

ACTION AND EMOTION SYMBOLS

ADULTERY

The act of embracing someone to meet a need, or to fulfill a hidden desire

Positive: To embrace something new
Negative: To conform yourself to someone else's desires

It can be a cause for concern if you dream that you are making love to someone that is not your spouse. You need to discern the spirit of the dream to determine if it is positive or negative.

It is common to dream of embracing an unfamiliar man or woman. This could represent a leaning towards a prophetic or teaching ministry. (Look up the symbol for *Man* and *Woman* to get a full understanding on this)

The sexual act is a very intimate one. In fact, in the Word when a couple made love, they were considered married. It meant that they were one. When you dream of having adultery, you need to ask yourself, "What am I becoming one with right now?"

Do you know the person you are committing adultery with in your dream? If so, determine what they could represent in your dream because this dream is exposing a desire or need you have right now. I will speak more of this when talking about *Arousal*

CHARACTER SPECIFIC SYMBOL

POSITIVE
If you dream that you are embracing an unfamiliar man or woman, but it feels "right" in the dream, then it could mean that the Lord is leading you to embrace something new in your life.

NEGATIVE
When you wake up feeling unclean and negative from your dream, then it is likely negative. If you continue having this kind of dream, then the Lord is trying to tell you that you are marrying yourself to something that is not of Him.

Consider this passage:

> *Proverbs 7:21 With her enticing speech she caused him to yield, with her flattering lips she seduced him.*
> *22 Immediately he went after her, as an ox goes to the slaughter, or as a fool to the correction of the stocks,.*

This scripture is a perfect picture of the world. The New Testament tells us that friendship with the world is enmity with God. If you keep having this sort of dream, then it means that you are allowing yourself to partake of the world and things that are not of God.

If you dream that your spouse is having an affair or cheating on you, you need to determine what your spouse represents to you.

If they represent the Lord in your dreams, it could mean that there is something right now that is taking a greater role of importance in your life than the Lord.

If you have a fear that your spouse is having an affair in real life and then you dream it, then your dream is clearly a purging dream. It means that you are simply living out in your dreams, the inner fears you have in reality.

DO NOT: Accuse your spouse of an affair because you had a dream. You will only increase any fears and conflicts you have in your marriage.

A note on personal fears: If you have a fear of being cheated on and then dream of your spouse or fiancé cheating on you, then a fear of the past is being brought up for the purpose of healing.

Have you experienced this exact situation in the past? Have people always let you down and cheated on you? This dream means that this fear is coming up again and you need inner healing.

UNIVERSAL SYMBOL

God is not in the business of revealing someone else's sins. A person's sin is between them and the Lord. However, it can happen as in the case of David where Nathan exposed his affair with Bathsheba for the sake of the people.

If God reveals anything like this to you, it is for you to pray so that this can be exposed God's way.

If engaged in personal ministry, the Lord shows you the person in an adulterous affair of the past, it is for the purpose of healing and forgiveness. I recommend the use of tact in such a situation, followed up with prayer and counsel.

NEGATIVE
As in with dreams, if the vision you see is symbolic, then it means that the person in question is joining themselves to something that is not of the Lord. Either they are walking in the flesh or they are embracing the things of the world.

See also: Arousal, Bed, Bedroom, Penis

ANGER

An intense release of emotion against either a person or circumstance. More often than not, intense anger in a dream that is uncontrollable is usually the sign of a purging dream.

Positive: The awakening of your passions within
Negative: A demonic force that controls you

If you are facing circumstances or people daily that you are upset with and then dream of being angry and striking them, then your dream does not have an interpretation. It is simply a reflection of the pent up emotion that you built up during the day. I classify this as a purging dream in my *Way of Dreams and Visions* book.

CHARACTER SPECIFIC SYMBOL

POSITIVE

Not all dreams of being angry are negative. Anger can in fact be a positive force when used correctly. It gives you the emotional "push" that you need to get things done. So if you are facing a problem in your dream and you suddenly get angry and overcome it, then the Lord is telling you to use this emotional force to overcome.

Anger is not sin! It is what you do with it that will determine that. Here is the perfect passage:

> *Ephesians 4:26 Be ye **angry**, and sin not: let not the sun go down upon your wrath (KJV).*

In other words, use your anger to sort your problems out right now. Rather do that, than allow anger to bubble inside and so turn into sin. If you are someone that is afraid to show anger, then it could well be that the Lord is trying to tell you to allow this anger to come out and to use it correctly!

NEGATIVE

On the other hand, if you have a major problem with uncontrollable anger, the Lord could be indicating that there is something demonic involved that you need to deal with. Anger is a natural human emotion, but as it says in Prov 16:32 it takes a mighty man to rule that anger correctly.

If you have a problem with anger in real life and in your dreams this topic keeps coming up, the Lord is pointing to a deeper problem. You will have additional dreams of this and I recommend looking up *Demons* for more revelation.

Universal Symbol

POSITIVE

The anger of the Lord is a powerful and real thing. Because anger is seen so negatively in today's society we can often forget that the anger of the Lord is one of His most powerful attributes.

I have often sensed the anger of the Lord against those who are destroying His Bride. It reminds me of the scripture:

> *Hebrews 10:30 For we know him who said, 'It is* ***mine to avenge****; I will repay,' and again, 'The Lord will judge his people.'*
> *31 It is a dreadful thing to fall into the hands of the living God. (NIV)*

I have also felt the Lord's anger towards leaders who deliberately take advantage of His people. If you feel this kind of anger in prayer, it is likely that God is calling you to pray. If you stand in prophetic office, then the Lord is calling on you to decree and release His will on the earth. Be sure though that the anger you feel is of the Lord and not your own human anger.

A good guideline to follow would be that if you have no natural anger against the leader or person in question and you have this emotion rise up out of your heart during prayer, then you are sensing the heart of God and you should pray accordingly.

Moses understood this kind of anger directly from God (Deut 4:21) He was strongly corrected for his mistakes towards God's people to the point of not being allowed into the Promised Land. So walk in wisdom and in confirmation with another believer if you feel led to pray in this direction.

NEGATIVE

When praying for someone regarding hurts of the past, I have seen them as a child throwing a tantrum or being angry. When I see this, then I know that the Lord is showing me the time in their life when they allowed bitterness into their hearts.

Regardless of the situation, when we allow anger into our hearts without God in control of it, we give the enemy license. Such was the mistake that Cain made in Genesis 4:5.

If the person who has come to you for prayer has a history of uncontrollable anger, then pray and ask the Lord for the time they allowed that spirit to enter their hearts. It was likely in response to a rejection or hurt. Although the hurt will need healing, the greater damage is the anger and bitterness they allowed into their hearts.

See also: Bitterness, Demons

ANOINT (TO BE ANOINTED)

To be set apart (consecrated) for a specific function or service.

Here is the dictionary definition for the word "Consecration"

Consecration is the solemn dedication to a special purpose or service, usually religious. The word **consecration** literally means "association with the sacred." Persons, places, or things can be **consecrated**, and the term is used in various ways by different groups.

UNIVERSAL SYMBOL

> *Exodus 28:41 So you shall put them on Aaron your brother and on his sons with him. You shall anoint them, consecrate them, and sanctify them, that they may minister to Me as priests.*

POSITIVE
It is not uncommon to have a dream of being anointed or to have anointing oil poured over you. Have you been seeking the Lord concerning your ministry direction? To dream of being anointed or feeling the anointing means that you have been set apart for the work He has called you to.

A dream or vision of being anointed should always confirm the direction God has been sending you. To anoint someone else means that the Lord wants you to help others find their place in the Body. Samuel anointed David after God told him to. You cannot consecrate yourself! The Lord always used someone else to anoint His chosen ones.

In the New Testament, the Holy Spirit is now the one that anoints and although that anointing can come independently of another man, more likely than not the Lord will use one of his servant to consecrate you for the work. I suggest reading *Prophetic Anointing* for more on this subject.

NEGATIVE
If you feel the opposite of the anointing in a dream, and you feel oppression instead, this is a caution. Either you are under demonic attack in your sleep, or you are going into a realm that you are not ready for. You are not going in armed with the anointing of God, but being pushed beyond what God intended, by the enemy.

For many who go to many places to receive the anointing, to dream of being anointed by someone that feels negative, could well mean that you are picking some things up that you should not!

See also: Fire, Oil

ANOINTING

To experience the manifest presence of God

CHARACTER SPECIFIC SYMBOL

POSITIVE

To wake up feeling the anointing is a wonderful experience. In my own experience, they are simply moments where the Lord chooses to remind you of His sweet presence. In these times He is letting you know that experiencing His presence does not depend on you, but on Him alone. This scripture explains it beautifully:

> *Psalms 127:2 It is vain for you to rise up early, to sit up late, to eat the bread of sorrows; for so He gives His beloved sleep.*

If you dream of receiving an impartation of anointing from someone you know, then the Lord is telling you that He desires you to function in the same capacity as this person. It does not necessarily mean that they will give you an impartation – rather that you will receive, from God, the same anointing or spiritual gift that they have.

NEGATIVE

If you wake up feeling oppression, then this is an indication that the enemy has an open door in your life. Look under Demons and Nightmares for more on this.

If you dream that the anointing suddenly leaves, this is a reflection of an inner fear or insecurity you feel right now. It could also be that the Lord is telling you to trust Him even when you do not feel Him.

Just because you do not feel the anointing, does not mean He has left you! Jesus is with you all of the time whether the anointing is present or not. It could well be that the Lord is calling you into a faith walk and telling you not to depend so much on the signs to believe Him.

> *Luke 11:29 And while the crowds were thickly gathered together, He began to say, This is an evil generation. It seeks a sign, and no sign will be given to it except the sign of Jonah the prophet.*

UNIVERSAL SYMBOL

POSITIVE AND NEGATIVE

The anointing is always a wonderful confirmation when you are flowing in ministry. Sometimes though if there is a blockage in the spirit or a lot of opposition, you might not feel the anointing as usual. This does not necessarily mean that the Lord has left or that you are missing it but rather that you need to push through a little longer.

At times like this, ask the Lord for further revelation. Continue speaking in tongues and act on any visions that He might give to you. If you receive no kind of revelation in the spirit, then speak in tongues until you feel a breakthrough.

As you engage in warfare, you will start to feel something change. You might start by feeling oppression at first as the Lord reveals what is blocking you. Once you work through that, you will then sense the anointing.

A note on the external anointing: (I refer to this anointing as it is taught in *The Prophetic Anointing.*) I have found in personal experience that when I am flowing in the external anointing that I do not always feel it tangibly on myself, but I do see the effects of it on the people.

In times like this, it is important to obey what God is telling you to do regardless of how you feel.

See also: Fire, Oil, Water, Well

AROUSAL

To feed your inner needs, desires and hopes.

CHARACTER SPECIFIC SYMBOL

The sexual act is a marriage covenant act. Within marriage it does two things. Firstly, it brings us into unity with our spouse. Secondly it satisfies both physical and emotional needs that are natural to us as human beings.

Now I have spoken of sex in *Wedding*, *Incest*, and *Bed*, but in this symbol I want to talk specifically about sexual desire, intercourse, and the physical and emotional effect that it has on you when you wake up after having had a sex dream. Consider each point and see which applies to you and what the Lord is saying to you at this time.

POSITIVE

Because of the raw hunger that sexual dreams usually display, they can be daunting. However, when your emotions are strong and you even feel aroused in your sleep, realize that an inner need and desire is rising up inside of you.

Is the sexual intercourse with your spouse? This is completely normal and it is quite possible that the Lord is saying, "My child, I am here to meet the deep needs of your heart. Allow me to be there for you."

Here is how I define the difference between a sexual dream that is speaking of me "embracing" a part of myself that the Lord wants me to, and a sexual dream where I am getting a need met that is not of Him. There is a major difference in the sexual desire and emotion in the dream.

If you have a dream without any sexual desire or wake up feeling aroused, then read *Bed* and *Wedding* for more on this, because whatever you are embracing is speaking about a covenant you are entering into.

When the passion is strong in your dream and you wake up feeling that desire, then it is speaking of one or more of these:

1. Meeting an inner need
2. A natural desire from pent up stress
3. A spirit of lust that is attacking you

Natural desire: Now you need to also consider an important fact. Remember when you dreamed you needed to go to the toilet really badly and you woke up feeling like your bladder would burst because you really needed to go? Sometimes sexual dreams are the same.

If you have been under a lot of stress and have either been sexually stirred up, or not had any sex at all, you will live that fantasy out in your dream. You are not sinning! Are you sinning by dreaming of being hungry or needing the toilet? It is a natural bodily function. It is the same with desire. It is a natural bodily function.

Think back on when you have these dreams the most. Do you have them when you are having great sex with your spouse? Then your dreams are only expressing the emotions and thoughts that are foremost in your mind when you go to bed.

If you are having these dreams when you miss your spouse ... perhaps its time you invest into some romance in your relationship?

If you are single – you are expressing your sexual needs in your dreams. Do not sweat it. It will pass soon enough. Personal suggestion? Get married! (I know I am going to get some fire for that comment!)

NEGATIVE

Now if you are having one sexual dream after another and feel "harassed" by them, then you need to consider that you are under attack from a spirit of lust. When did these dreams begin? Did you watch something lustful or meet up with a person that is bound by lust? Visit your pastor for counseling or ask someone you know to stand in agreement with you against this attack.

Now what if you are dreaming of having sex with strangers or even family members you know? Ok, stop for a moment and answer this question: What does this person mean to you? What do they represent.

Now say for example you dream of having sex with your boss. He usually represents your career. The interpretation is simple: You are using your career to meet a deep need inside of you that can never be satisfied. Only the Lord can fill that craving within you.

See also: Adultery, Bed, Incest, Kiss, Man, Penis, Wedding, Woman

ATTACKED

The onslaught of demonic attack or overwhelming circumstances.

A sudden attack or onslaught from someone you know or an unseen force. It is common for believers to dream of being attacked by demons in their sleep. In ministry, if you have the gift of discerning of spirits, the Lord will show you demonic attacks against the person you are ministering to.

CHARACTER SPECIFIC SYMBOL

POSITIVE

If you have been struggling with circumstances beyond your control and then dream that you are attacked, but overcome, then the Lord is telling you that victory is on the way. You might dream that you are being chased or attacked by an unseen force and in the middle of it you turn and face your attacker. This is a fantastic dream and it means that you are finally facing up to your fears.

Often in life we are forced to face situations that are beyond our control. The easiest reaction is to try and run from them. You might dream of being attacked or chased every night. The solution? Turn around and face your fears and this impossible task! With the Lord's help you will surely overcome!

NEGATIVE

If you keep dreaming of being attacked by the military, it is an indicating that you are engaging in spiritual warfare right now. Remember that the enemy is only too happy to stand against you as you start believing God for something. If you dream of being in a warzone or attacked all the time, then sit up and take notice.

The Lord is trying to let you know that the problems that you are facing right now are spiritual in nature just as it says in Ephesians 6:12.

Attack by demons: On a more serious note, if you are being attacked by demons in your sleep, then something is definitely wrong. This is not the Lord trying to get your attention, but rather an indication that the enemy has an inroad into your life.

In the Chapter on *Deception, Nightmares and Demonic Dreams* in *The Way of Dreams and Visions* book, I instruct you how to identify how the enemy gained license. Be sure though that if demons are attacking you in your sleep, you either have a contaminated object in your room, are experiencing a backlash from ministering to someone or opened your heart to a teaching you should not have.

Identify when these dreams began. Deal with the source and tell the enemy to be gone! If you have had these dreams since childhood, then the bondage is generational and you should deal with generational curses.

UNIVERSAL SYMBOL

POSITIVE

The only time that a vision could be positive is if you are the one doing the attacking in the spiritual realm! The sword of God is an offensive weapon and if you see the Lord giving you a sword, then it is for you to attack the work of the enemy.

It reminds me of Samson who attacked the Philistines on many occasions. Sometimes sending foxes into their fields, other times attacking them with the jawbone of a donkey. Sometimes when you are trusting God for something, He might tell you that it is time to attack the enemy and to take back your land!

The Children of Israel did not just walk into the Promised Land. They had to attack the enemy and take it! In the same way, the Lord will often lead you into spiritual warfare to take back what the enemy has stolen from you.

> *Joshua 10:19 But don't stop! Pursue your enemies,* ***attack*** *them from the rear and don't let them reach their cities, for the LORD your God has given them into your hand.' (NIV)*

NEGATIVE

If you have a vision of being attacked from without, this is a clear sign of demonic attack. This could stem from opposition from others or perhaps going into a situation un-led. If you pray and see someone being attacked by something demonic or by another person, it is a call to spiritual warfare.

It is not the will of the Lord for us to suffer or to be defeated by our enemies. Rather He has called us to rule and reign in life. Look for the source of attack and know that you can overcome.

Wolf attacking: It is the wolf that attacks the sheep. This is a picture of an internal attack coming from the Christian leadership that you are currently submitted to. This attack might be coming through words/curses spoken or perhaps a personal disagreement.

If you have a vision of a wolf attacking a person or a specific group, it means that the attack they are experiencing is coming from their leadership.

> *John 10:12 The hired hand is not the shepherd who owns the sheep. So when he sees the* ***wolf*** *coming, he abandons the sheep and runs away. Then the* ***wolf*** *attacks the flock and scatters it. (NIV)*

Past hurts: On a more personal note when praying with someone regarding hurts of the past, you might see them being attacked and this would indicate an incident or emotion that they felt at this time. In this case you would need to minister inner healing and help them overcome. I suggest reading *The Minister's Handbook* for more practical help on this.

See also: Ambush, Chasing, Demons, War, Weapons

BAKE

A process of preparation - mostly related to the teaching ministry.

POSITIVE
To bake bread, means to prepare and make it ready for eating. In context of ministry the Lord could be indicating that you need to prepare for ministry so that you can give out to others.

The process of baking or actually cooking the food indicates that you will need to get involved to train others, or perhaps be trained yourself.

Raw dough would indicate a ministry or a person that is not yet mature.

To bake that dough would mean to prepare and make that person ready.

We saw this once in the spirit, where the Lord showed us dough and told us that we must go and shape and make His people ready!

> *Psalms 104:15 And wine that makes glad the heart of man, oil to make his face shine, and* ***bread*** *which strengthens man's heart.*

Note: To prepare the dough, it needs to pass through the fire.

NEGATIVE
To leave something unbaked in a ministry context speaks of not following through with your ministry or giving up. It means that you have rejected what you need to do.

Consider this passage:

> *Hosea 7:4 They are all adulterers. Like an oven heated by a baker - He ceases stirring the fire after kneading the dough, until it is leavened.*

See also: Bread, Cake, Cooking, Yeast

BITTERNESS

A deep internal anger or an unpleasant taste in the mouth. An indication of retained anger.

POSITIVE
There is seldom a positive connotation for bitterness. God is never bitter towards man, but has often been angry. Anger and bitterness are not the same thing, however, if anger is not dealt with correctly, it can lead to bitterness which will become a deep root of the flesh in your life.

Bitter taste: John shares in the book of Revelation that he is given a book that is sweet to the taste yet bitter in his belly. This speaks of something that seems pleasant and is what you want, but in the end, the reality is not what you expect. (Rev 10:10) Another good scripture along these lines is:

Psalms 106:15 And he gave them their request; but sent leanness into their soul. (KJV)

NEGATIVE
Bitterness is one of the easiest ways to give license to the enemy in your life. It is a person who is bitter that will speak curses and when you allow it to take hold of your heart, it becomes a poison that defiles everyone else around you.

Hebrews 12:15 looking carefully lest anyone fall short of the grace of God; lest any root of ***bitterness*** *springing up cause trouble, and by this many become defiled;*

A bitter root: If you dream or see a vision of a deep black root, this is a good picture of a root of bitterness. It stems from judging others, un-forgiveness in your heart and anger you have allowed to simmer inside for too long.

To dream of being bitter and angry is likely a purging dream and an indication of what is inside of you right now. This is also a warning dream because it is showing you that there is unresolved anger you need to deal with. If you do not deal with it, that anger will become bitterness and be an open door to the enemy to bring you into bondage.

Others bitter towards you: You can be sure that the enemy has no love for you and so to dream or have visions of others being bitter towards you is a picture of spiritual attack. (Psalm 64:3) Responding in the like is not the solution. The Word says that no weapon formed against you will prosper and that every tongue that rises up against you, you shall condemn (Isaiah 54:17)

Personal ministry: When ministering to someone and you see a bitter root in the spirit or sense that they are bitter, you will need to deal with their personal sin before trying to bring healing. Use wisdom and know when to address that sin. In my experience bitterness is one of the greatest open doors to sickness and poverty.

It literally steals away health and blessing.

See also: Anger, Root

BOIL (COOKING)

A slow process of preparation.

Positive: A slow process towards perfection
Negative:

- Seething anger
- Evil about to break out

Character Specific Symbol

POSITIVE

There are some cultures who tend to boil their food more than roast it. If you have a very cultural specific dream, then it is internal and the boiling refers to an archetype. Is the food being boiled a family favorite? Is it foreign to you?

If it is foreign to you, then perhaps the Lord is saying, "Perhaps it is time you try to do things differently, because the "old way" is not working any longer!"

NEGATIVE

We all understand the concept of "reaching your boiling point." Determine the emotion in your dream. To see a kettle boil is a sign that either you or someone else is at a "breaking point."

There is a lot going on under the surface that has now begun to manifest. You have been "going through" for so long now and things have begun to heat up. You are at boiling point and before you erupt, you need some time in the presence of the Lord. It is time to come to peace once again.

Universal Symbol

POSITIVE

It takes time to boil meat until it is tender enough to eat. It is a slow process and one used when Aaron and his sons were consecrated to office. As a type and shadow, this process perfectly conveys the journey they went on to reach this point. Aaron spent many years in slavery before being released and then given such a high position.

For the Lord to bring a "boiling" process to you in a vision or prophetic dream, is an indication that He is preparing a place of perfection for you. It might be taking some time, but it is worth it. Be patient, your time is coming!

> *Leviticus 8:31 And Moses said to Aaron and his sons, "Boil the flesh at the door of the tabernacle of meeting, and eat it there with the bread that is in the basket of consecration offerings, as I commanded, saying, 'Aaron and his sons shall eat it.'"*

NEGATIVE

A boiling pot with a negative feeling speaks of evil that is about to break forth. Determine what you were praying for at the time of having this vision. Were you praying for someone? Were you praying for a specific circumstance?

Then this boiling pot speaks of something that is about to "erupt" that is not of the Lord.

> *Jeremiah 1:13-14 ...And I said, "I see a boiling pot, and it is facing away from the north." Then the Lord said to me: "Out of the north calamity shall break forth On all the inhabitants of the land*

See also: Bake, Cooking, Food, Kitchen

BUILD

To build means to establish something new. Refers to a new vision, ministry or work that God has called you to do.

Positive: Construction to establish God's plan in your life
Negative: An organized attack from the enemy established as a stronghold in your life

To build is pretty self-explanatory. It means to establish something that is new. Depending on the type of building you have in the dream or vision, the interpretation will change.

POSITIVE
When we spend time together in intercession on behalf of Apostolic Movement International we would often see it as a building in the spirit. Sometimes the building was already built or being repaired. Other times we will see new pieces of land and building tools being given to us.

In each instance the Lord was giving us an indication of what He wanted us to do in the ministry. In some cases, it is to complete a direction He has already given us. In others it is to embrace a new building project.

If you dream of building something new, it refers to something that God is doing in your life right now. The job is not finished yet! This is something you have to work at and participate in. You cannot just sit down and wait for God to do all the work. For God to move on your behalf, you must put your hand to the trowel and work and build in the direction that He has given to you.

NEGATIVE
If your dream or vision is negative, it means that you are doing all the work yourself and not letting God into the picture. This is what happened at the tower of babel. They sought to build themselves a tower to make themselves a name and to take care of themselves. They left God out of it entirely.

This is a picture of works and self-effort instead of relying on the Lord Jesus and letting Him be your Savior.

See also: Buildings

BURY

To get rid of contamination or things that hinder you. The precursor to a season of change and renewal.

Positive: Putting the past behind you
Negative: To hide things that you would rather others did not see

POSITIVE
To bury the flesh means to put aside the old man and to be renewed in Christ. I cover this in great detail under *Death* and *Body*.

To dream of burying the dead is actually a good picture. It means that the Lord is taking you through a cleansing process. One that will not happen instantly, but will mean going through a season of "putting away" the things of the past that have died.

Often the Lord takes us through a death to the flesh process that yields immediate results. However, there are often times when we have to walk out our salvation. A time of putting off the old man and taking on the new. Burying the dead is an indication that you are in the process of "putting off the old man."

> *Ezekiel 39:12 For seven months the house of Israel will be **burying** them, in order to cleanse the land*

NEGATIVE
Achan took some of the plunder for himself and buried it, hiding his actions. By doing this he brought himself and the entire nation of Israel under a curse. (Joshua 7)

To dream or have a vision of something being hidden in this way indicates a sin that is being concealed. If you are a prophet, it is not for you to expose that sin yourself, but to pray that the hidden things are revealed.

When the Lord shows me something like this, I stand on this powerful passage:

> *1 Corinthians 4:5 Therefore judge nothing before the time, until the Lord comes, who will both bring to light the **hidden** things of darkness and reveal the counsels of the hearts. Then each one's praise will come from God.*

See also: Coffin, Death, Grave, Tombstone

CHASING/PURSUING

To be pursued by an inner fear

Positive: To pursue earnestly until you overcome

Negative:

- Seeking to escape fear
- To be under spiritual attack
- Inability to face your struggles
- You are currently feeling as if your situation is beyond your control

Character Specific Symbol

POSITIVE
The best way to turn a dream around where you are being chased, is to turn around and to face your pursuer. The most frightening thing about a dream of being chased is the fear of what might happen if you are caught. When you dream of turning and facing your attacker, it means that you are finally willing to face your inner fears. Have you faced difficult circumstances lately? Is there something in your life right now that you would rather not look at?

Facing your attacker after being chased means that you have finally reached a place of readiness to face something where you are uncertain of the outcome.

To pursue someone: If you are in the pursuit of someone or something in your dream and you feel motivated, this is a great dream! It means that you are not giving up, but that you are fighting for your promises and you will indeed reach your goal!

> *Leviticus 26:8 Five of you shall chase a hundred, and a hundred of you shall put ten thousand to flight; your enemies shall fall by the sword before you.*

NEGATIVE
Dreaming of being chased and you feel anxious and fearful has a number of meanings. Who is pursuing you? Is it someone you know? If so, what part of your life do they represent? This will give you a clue as to what you are fearing in your life.

Are you being pursued in a battle or by some kind of militia? This means that you are under spiritual attack right now and that the enemy is trying to trip you up by wearing you down through inner fears and personal struggles. He will bring this attack through fear, condemnation, and bitterness.

> *Lamentations 3:52 My enemies without cause Hunted me down like a bird.*

Often you will have these dreams when you feel like Jeremiah in the passage above. Overwhelmed! You feel as if your circumstances are beyond your control and you cannot overcome. Do not allow the enemy to lie to you. Stand your ground. Now is not the time to run. Now is the time to pick up your sword and fight back!

See also: Army, Running/Race, War

CONCEIVE

The start of something new in your life.

Positive: Confirmation of a work that God has begun in you
Negative: Seeds from the enemy that you have allowed to gain root in your heart.

POSITIVE
To conceive a baby means that something new has started to take place in you. When the Holy Spirit came on Mary, she conceived Jesus.

In the same way when we get into the Word and submit ourselves to the Holy Spirit, righteousness is also conceived in us.

When you believe the Lord for a miracle in your life, it starts off as a conception. It is for you to continue in the Word and Spirit to make sure that baby grows to maturity.

Dreaming of falling pregnant is often a good sign that the Lord is doing something new in your life.

NEGATIVE
Not everything we conceive is positive. Consider this passage:

> *Acts 5:4 While it remained, was it not your own? And after it was sold, was it not in your own control? Why have you* ***conceived*** *this thing in your heart? You have not lied to men but to God.*

This is a picture of conceiving sin in your heart and allowing it to grow. Bitterness and the love of money are the most common.

See also: Baby, Birth, Pregnant

COOKING

The Lord has often given me both dreams and visions where I see myself preparing food and handing it out.

This speaks of not only ministering out to others what I have, but also training and mentoring them. To give them both the teaching and the training they need to rise up.

I give more description of this under the symbol *Bake*

See also: Bake, Bread, Cake

CRYING

A cleansing process through the release of pent up emotions that have been suppressed or unrealized.

Positive: The external release of your true emotions within
Negative: To be controlled by your emotions beyond what God intends

CHARACTER SPECIFIC SYMBOL

POSITIVE
Dreaming of crying is very common and often positive. Even if the dream is sad or makes you weep, the process of crying is a cleansing one and it is likely that you dreamed about actions that you would struggle to do in real life.

More often than not, crying in your dreams is a result of pent up emotion that you have faced over time. This is a purging dream and has no interpretation.

If you have been going through the Word or facing memories from the past, dreaming of those memories and then waking up crying is a good indication that God has done a healing in your heart. Although tears can often be a sign of hurts, they are also a way for us to come to terms with the inner struggles that we have.

Tears are words that cannot be spoken. If you struggle to express yourself with words, tears in your dreams are an external expression of your internal conflict. This alone can bring a release to the very thing you are struggling with.

NEGATIVE
If you dream of people dying or of things from the past that are not resolved, then your crying is a sign of a deeper wound that needs healing. I suggest going to your Pastor for counsel or asking a prophet to help you through the process of inner healing.

If you find yourself crying with no intention, then you are going through a "trigger". Something is happening to you in your present circumstances that is a trigger to events of the past. Although you might not realize it that trigger is digging up unresolved hurts relating to past events.

You can read more about templates and triggers in my book *Prophetic Boot Camp.*

UNIVERSAL SYMBOL

POSITIVE
I often see someone crying at a certain age when ministering inner healing. This tells me the time that the hurts of the past occurred that are having an effect on their present life. It is also common for someone to weep in the presence of the Lord.

This is a manifestation of the following passage:

> *Romans 8:26 Likewise the Spirit also helps in our weaknesses. For we do not know what we should pray for as we ought, but the Spirit Himself makes intercession for us with **groanings** which cannot be uttered.*

When the Lord moves on you, you cannot always find the words. Tears are often the most beautiful response. A beautiful illustration of this is the woman who wept over Jesus' feet. Sometimes it is our tears of joy and thanksgiving that are the best gift we can give the Lord. He does not need our fancy words, just our hearts.

Intercession and ministry: Weeping is very common in intercession when you will feel the heart of the Lord for His people. If you are interceding for someone you might also sense the exact conflict that they are going through. In personal experience I often feel the heart of the Lord weeping for His people.

I sense the intensity of the Lord Jesus interceding at the right hand of the Father for us. I remember attending a meeting once where the worship team was trying so very hard to get the Lord's attention. They were singing hard and playing hard. They were crying out to God again and again to come.

I heard the soft voice of the Lord Jesus say to me, "They are trying so hard to reach me, but they do not know that I never left. I have been here all along." In that moment I sensed the deep crying of his heart and I could only cry. He longed to hold each one so closely, but while they kept pushing and performing they were pushing Him away more than they were running towards him.

If you experience this kind of thing often, then it is likely you have a prophetic calling and the Lord is calling you to bring His Bride into a closer relationship with Him.

> *Isaiah 35:10 And the ransomed of the Lord shall return, and come to Zion with singing, with everlasting joy on their heads. they shall obtain joy and gladness, and **sorrow and sighing** shall flee away.*

NEGATIVE

When trying to address sin in someone I often come across someone who will cry uncontrollably and distract from the point I am trying to make. Crying like this is simply a smokescreen to distract you from the point you are trying to make.

On the other hand, if you are ministering inner healing and you start digging into hurts of the past, tears are a natural response. All the hurt that has been harbored for years will suddenly come to the fore front. Follow through with healing and ministry and the tears will turn to joy.

Uncontrollable crying: If you continue to cry without any control, then I would caution you to look into this. Even if there is hurt, the Lord is able to heal. To cry without reason or control indicates a demonic bondage that is in charge of your emotions. What might have started out natural, has become something that it should not.

This is especially true if the crying takes place at times when it should not – like when the Lord is trying to move and the crying becomes a distraction.

See also: Tears

CURSING/SWEARING

The expression of your inner thoughts

Positive: A purging dream – releasing pent up frustration
Negative: Words you are speaking against someone, or someone is speaking against you

CHARACTER SPECIFIC SYMBOL

POSITIVE
Every good Christian knows that swearing is wrong, so to dream of cussing up a storm can be more than a little intimidating. Have you been under pressure lately? Is there someone that you really felt like telling off? To dream of swearing at them is simply an expression of what is going on within you. You are trying so hard to put on a good exterior, but inside you are angry!

The Word tells us to not let the sun set on our anger. While this dream is simply purging your pent up emotions of the day, it is also indicating that you have some frustrations that you are trying to "push down" that need to come out, be expressed, and handled correctly. I recommend the series *The Crucified Life* for help in this area.

A moral conviction: What if you dream you are swearing, but never cussed in your life? Do you have a strong doctrinal belief system that swearing is a dark sin? Then this interpretation applies to you. Do you remember when the Lord told Peter to rise and eat the unclean animals? (Acts 10) The Lord said in the end, "What I call clean, do not call unclean!"

Dreaming of swearing, in this context, is the Lord saying that there are some doctrines you are holding on to that are blocking His hand. He wants you to go into something new, but your strict "moral code" has become a bondage to you. He wants you to break out of it and get a new conviction on something you thought you were so sure about.

NEGATIVE
Now if you continue to dream of cussing and cursing all night, there is something amiss. Your spirit is contaminated and you need some spiritual purging. I suggest putting away the internet and television for a while and do a little bit of spiritual house cleaning. Could it also be that you are being

influenced spiritually by someone in your life whose life does not match up with the Word?

I highly suggest journaling and seeking the Lord about what is coming out of your spirit right now. Your thoughts are not God's thoughts and its time to get back into the Spirit.

See also: Arrow

DANCING

The unashamed and public expression of joy (which is a fruit of the spirit).

Positive: To lose your inhibitions
Negative: To perform for the sake of recognition

CHARACTER SPECIFIC SYMBOL

POSITIVE

It is common to dream of dancing – especially if you always desired to do so. To dream of dancing is a message from the Lord to tell you to express the joy openly that is in your heart. If you have been feeling restricted and stuck in your emotions, then the Lord is telling you to break out.

A dream like this is often a purging one as you release all the struggles and tension that you have faced. To dream of dancing with joy is a picture of overcoming your difficult situation and escaping to a place where you find joy and peace.

Dancing unashamedly in your dreams is a call to walk in joy! It is a call to choose praise and to express the fruit of joy that is hidden inside of you. As you do this, you will surely walk in the blessing of the Lord, just as David did!

> *2 Samuel 6:14 Then David* ***danced*** *before the Lord with all his might; and David was wearing a linen ephod.*

To dream of being prepared to dance means that the Lord has equipped you spiritually with joy. It speaks of maturity because you are starting to develop joy in your life. Dancing and joy are used together many times in the Scriptures. You cannot feel joy and not want to move about. On the other hand, when you make a choice to praise and worship the Lord, joy is the natural fruit that develops.

Intimate dancing: To dream of dancing with someone you love is a good picture of coming into unity and flowing together as one. You will need to determine what the person in your dream represents. If they represent the Lord Jesus, then the dream means that you are coming into a closer relationship with the Lord and are walking in His footsteps.

NEGATIVE
To dream of struggling to dance or missing the steps is an indication of insecurity and also that your joy is lacking. If you are a dancer in real life, then this would indicate a security that you feel regarding your abilities. It might even speak of inner fears that you have.

If you are not a dancer by profession though, to feel "left out" of a dance or struggling to dance means that you are battling to enter into joy. The enemy is holding you back from praising the Lord and as a result you are experiencing a blockage in your spiritual life.

> *Lamentations 5:15 The joy of our heart has ceased; our **dance** has turned into mourning.*

If you dream of dancing with someone that represents the flesh or another negative picture in your life, it means that you are allowing yourself to "wallow" and take part of that negative thing. In this case it would be a warning dream, because instead of having your need met and finding true joy, you will end up getting the complete opposite.

Universal Symbol

POSITIVE
If I see a vision of someone dancing I know that the Lord wants to give them joy. If they are the kind of person that does not show emotion openly, then the Lord is telling them to break out of their "walls" and to praise Him with abandon. As they do this, they will enter into real joy.

Sometimes it is a call to prophetic dance and to "pick up the tambourine" just as Miriam did.

NEGATIVE
Often because of hurts of the past someone will "clamp down" on their emotions and be afraid to express them openly. In such a case I see them bound up in the spirit unable to dance or praise the Lord. If they are willing to step out and praise Him, then He will also bring healing and set them free emotionally.

Erotic/worldly dancing: If you see a vision of erotic or other worldly dancing this is negative and speaks about trying to find joy in the things of the world instead of looking for them in the Lord. Instead of putting your praise and love into the Lord, you are pouring your affections into the world. Unfortunately, instead of reaping joy, you will reap emptiness and discouragement.

Putting on a show: To dream of always putting on a show with your dancing, indicates that you are trying to perform for others, to gain their acceptance and recognition. You are "dancing to their tune" with the hopes of gaining their approval.

See also: Audience, Harp, Music

DROWNING

To surrender and be completely overcome by your current circumstances.

Positive:

- To get rid of a bad element in your life, once and for all
- To struggle against and overcome overwhelming odds

Negative:

- To surrender to hardships
- To have your passion quenched

CHARACTER SPECIFIC SYMBOL

Did you have a drowning experience as a child? If so, and you keep dreaming of drowning indicates that you need inner healing from that time. There are still some fears in your life that are lurking under the surface.

Think about what is happening in your life right now. What elements seem to be beyond anything you can handle? Now go back to your dream. Were you fighting to breathe, or were you giving up and dying? Determine if this was good and positive.

If you "drowned" and carried on breathing it means: Your circumstances are not as bad as you think right now. You will survive! Stop struggling and give the control to the Lord again.

If you could not breathe and woke up gasping for air: Your circumstances are taking the life out of you. Do not give in. Fight back!

UNIVERSAL SYMBOL

POSITIVE
There are two positive interpretations for dreaming or seeing a vision of drowning:

Your enemies drowning: The Egyptians were drowned – indicating that the Lord will create circumstances that will remove, once and for all, the trying situation you are facing right now. No trace of it will be left in your life. It will be part of your past and will never return!

> *Exodus 15:4 Pharaoh's chariots and his army He has cast into the sea; His chosen captains also are drowned in the Red Sea.*

You drowning: While drowning seems negative at first, perhaps it is time for you to "drown" the old man! You keep struggling against everything that is coming against you, but perhaps it is time to give up and let the Lord carry you. When you stop struggling, you might discover that you can breathe under water! You will discover that what you thought was impossible, is so easy with the Lord.

I had a lot of these dreams when I was going through my prophetic training. The message to me was always the same, "My child, when will you surrender to me? When will you stop trying so hard in your flesh and allow me to carry you to the place that I need you to go?"

If you are called to the prophetic ministry, I highly suggest you get your hands on the *Prophetic Boot Camp* book. You need it to learn how to "drown in style!" Nothing can drown the love the Lord has for you. No circumstance in this world can destroy God's intention for you!

> *Song of Solomon 8:7 Many waters cannot quench love, Nor can the floods drown it.*

NEGATIVE
Because of the nature of drowning, to have a vision or prophetic dream of drowning and it is negative, means that pressures have come at you from all sides and you are giving in to them. You are allowing yourself to be swept away with the tide and so are giving up the fight.

If the "drowning" is negative in your revelation, then realize that God intends you to push through! You need to change the way you are fighting through. You keep trying to push against your circumstances using your limited ability and you are not winning! Change tactics. It is time to stand in His power and anointing. Stand in your authority as a believer instead of paddling away in the flesh.

God intends for you to walk on the water, just as Peter did! Use the right weapons and walk over your circumstances. Walk in faith, not in flesh!

> *Matthew 14:29-30 So He said, "Come." And when Peter had come down out of the boat, he walked on the water to go to Jesus. But when he saw that the wind was boisterous, he was afraid; and beginning to sink he cried out, saying, "Lord, save me!"*

See also: Flood, Ocean, Paralyzed, River

EVANGELIZING

To reach out to a dying world with the Gospel of Jesus Christ.

Positive: The call to be bold in your salvation message
Negative: Insecurity and fears regarding being bold in your witness

Character Specific Symbol

POSITIVE AND NEGATIVE

There is no better way to wake up than to dream that you are evangelizing someone. Dreaming of evangelizing does not always denote an evangelistic calling though, because it is a function that every believer should be carrying out (2 Tim 4:5).

Determine for yourself which point relates to your present circumstances.

You have a love for evangelizing.

If you have a passion for evangelizing, then this dream is simply an indication of what already burns in you. If you evangelize often and then dream you are struggling or failing, then it represents an attack that you are experiencing from the enemy right now.

Have you been feeling insecure or lacking in your ministry lately? Evangelizing in your dreams and failing is a reflection of your fears and insecurities.

God is trying to remind you of your own salvation experience.

If you wake up feeling the anointing and presence of God, the Lord is trying to remind you of why you started this road in the first place. The Gospel message is not just for when you get saved. It is a daily reminder of what God continues to do in our lives.

The Lord wants you to change your ministry orientation.

If you are a pastor and have such a dream, then the Lord wants you to teach more on the Good News. Have you been sidetracked lately on other issues or perhaps getting too deep into doctrine? It could be that the Lord wants you to move more towards flowing in the external anointing and moving into a new realm.

Realize that evangelism involves a closer relationship with the Holy Spirit and flowing in a specific anointing. The Lord is telling you to be open to changing how you function in ministry and to flow in this new anointing. (Especially if it us uncommon to you)

Depending on the context of the dream, if you are comfortable with this anointing, it could be that the Lord is telling you to move on into another ministry function.

You are being called into a relationship with the Holy Spirit.

Has the Lord been changing your ministry orientation lately? I experienced this when the Lord wanted me to move away from a strict teaching orientation and He wanted to draw me into a relationship with the Holy Spirit.

I kept having dreams of evangelizing and fighting demons! The Holy Spirit was beginning to express His nature to me and give me the heart to move into a new relationship with Him.

The external prophetic dream: If you function as an evangelist and you have an external dream about someone being evangelized then the dream indicates that the Lord wants to bring that person to salvation. Your first course of action is to pray and claim them for the Kingdom of God. The Lord will then lead you or someone else to present the Gospel to them.

Universal Symbol

If you are ministering with someone and see them evangelizing, then the interpretation is pretty clear. The Lord wants them to function in an evangelistic capacity right now. This may or may not be their final calling destination.

If you see someone evangelizing and the Lord is taking them out of the situation and putting them on a new road, then the Lord is saying that He wants to move them onto a new ministry function. This might involve leaving behind all they did before.

They will not lose their anointing and gifts, however, for a season they will slow down as the Lord adds new things to them. In time, they will learn to flow in both the new and the old.

I remember praying with someone regarding a demonic bondage they had in their lives. When we prayed about it, I saw them evangelizing. As I asked them about it, it turned out that they had gone out to evangelize unled into a satanic area. As a result, instead of bringing deliverance, they came back under bondage.

When operating in visions and you see someone evangelizing, the picture is literal and not a type or shadow as it would be in an internal dream. In vision you could see yourself evangelizing someone specific. This is a call to prayer and to present the gospel.

See also: Preaching

Exercising

To condition the flesh for a purpose.

Positive: To bring your flesh into subjection to the spirit
Negative: To put your boast in your natural ability

Character Specific Symbol

If you are not fond of exercising, then dreaming of doing a workout would speak of engaging in something that you know will be good for you, but that will be a price. You will feel uncomfortable with whatever the Lord is leading you into, but it will be worth it in the end.

If you are keen about fitness and your routine, then your workout will represent something to you. They can represent your self-image and personal strengths.

Universal Symbol

POSITIVE
To "buffet" the flesh is very positive. It speaks about bringing your body in line according to what God is doing in your spirit. We are made of spirit, soul, and body. Each part needs to be strong. If you dream or have a vision of working a muscle, it means that the Lord intends for you to strengthen a part of yourself that is weak.

I was ministering to someone once and saw them as a body builder with one buff arm and one scrawny arm. The message? They were unbalanced. They were strong in the Spirit and flowed well in the gift of prophecy, but they were weak in the Word. The Lord told them that they needed both to mature.

If you have a vision or prophetic dream of working muscles you did not before, the Lord is saying that He is about to strengthen a part of your character. So He wants to give you something new, but it is going to take some effort on your part. This is not just going to "happen" overnight. You will not wake up one day and just walk in love, be healed, or be prosperous.

Rather, it will be a steady process that will increase over time. Has the Lord been telling you the same thing again and again? You have some spiritual exercise to do!

> *1 Corinthians 9:25 Everyone who competes in the games goes into strict training. They do it to get a crown that will not last; but we do it to get a crown that will last forever. (NIV)*

NEGATIVE
Now I have seen a vision of someone, where their body was super buff and they looked all strong, however on the inside they were weak and empty. This was negative because the Lord was saying that they were putting all their emphasis on externals. They put their boast on how they looked and acted and not on the true condition of their heart.

A note on exercise: While profitable if your workout routine has become a religion and your boast, it would not be surprising for the Lord to speak to you about putting that effort into your spiritual life and having balance! Here is a challenge for you: Look at your physical and spiritual condition. Do they match up in form and fitness? A perfect believer is one whose spirit, soul and body are equally fit!

1 Timothy 4:8 For bodily exercise profits a little, but godliness is profitable for all things, having promise of the life that now is and of that which is to come.

See also: Race, Running, Weights

FALLING

A situation you have no control of. You are being controlled by an external force in your situation.

Positive: To trust your life into God's hands and not your own
Negative: To be tossed around by circumstance

CHARACTER SPECIFIC SYMBOL

POSITIVE
To dream of falling is an indication of your present situation. Do you feel out of control at the moment? Do you feel as if circumstances are pushing you around? To dream of falling, but you are able to navigate your way is a good picture. It means that although some circumstances are out of your control right now, the Lord will give you wisdom to navigate your way through them.

To dream of falling and stopping just before you reach the ground means that the Lord will intervene in your situation. God is still in control of your circumstances!

Free fall: I often teach our prophetic students the importance of free falling! In the Journey of Tamar, I share a part where Tamar is invited by the Holy Spirit to the edge of a cliff and asked to "jump." She does not know what will happen, but as she takes the leap, hurtling to her death, the Holy Spirit comes, as a mighty eagle and lifts her high into the sky. This is a perfect picture for anyone called to the work of the ministry. It is only when you take a leap into a free fall, that you can truly be directed by the hand of God.

To dream of falling under the power: To dream of falling under the power is a message that the Lord wants you to surrender all of your control to Him. Have you been trying hard to increase your faith or walk in the spirit? Such a dream indicates that it is time to just let go and to give God license to do what He wants.

Stop struggling in yourself and against God and put your trust completely in Him right now. He will not let you down!

If you dream of praying for others and they fall under the power, either it is a purging dream (if this is a secret desire) or it is an indication that the Lord wants you to function more in the power gifts. (See *Evangelizing*)

NEGATIVE
To dream of being pushed and falling means that the enemy is behind your circumstances and trying to manipulate you with them. It is time to rise up in Jesus' name and to take that control back.

To dream of falling and not being able to get up is an indication that the enemy is trying to oppress you and steal your strength from you. In yourself you cannot overcome, but you can stand in Jesus' name and rise up!

Dreaming of falling and being hurt is a picture of attack coming from others and your circumstances. The attack is from things that are not under your control. You need the Lord to intervene. It is also a picture of the inner fears and conflicts you are going through right now.

Universal Symbol

POSITIVE
To dream of a building falling is a picture of the Lord tearing down whatever that building is a representation of.

A free fall: In the *Journey of Tamar* I share a chapter where the heroine is led to the edge of a cliff and told to jump off. There is nothing to catch her but the crashing waves below. In the end she leaps into the air and begins to fall. Half way down, the Mighty Eagle comes from below and lifts her up again.

This is a picture of surrendering your will to the Lord. To put your trust into Him completely and letting Him determine your future. To take a leap of faith based on His Word and not your own understanding. Here is a beautiful picture of how the Lord "catches" and takes care of us as an eagle does her young.

> *Deuteronomy 32:11 like an eagle that stirs up its nest and hovers over its young, that spreads its wings to catch them and carries them on its pinions. (NIV)*

NEGATIVE
If you are ministering to someone and see them trip and fall it is a picture of hurts and disappointments that they have faced during their lives. This vision refers also to the mistakes that they made that led them to this point in their lives.

If you see someone falling and you sense the vision is negative, then it means that they are out of control or that the enemy has control of their present circumstances. The Lord promises to put our feet on solid ground!

See also: Bruise, Flying, Rock, Wound

FARTING

A natural, but uncomfortable situation in which you have no control.

Positive: To be normal
Negative: To unconsciously express thoughts that should rather be kept to yourself

CHARACTER SPECIFIC SYMBOL

I wanted to leave this symbol out at first, but we have had so many people write in with the request, that I will share my interpretation. Determine for yourself it is appropriate for your dream.

POSITIVE
Letting out belching and farting sounds is not exactly something we all go around doing. It is done behind closed doors and is private. We all know it exists. We all know it is natural, but still, we hide it from others. So to dream of farting or burping out loud and not be fazed by it is actually positive. It means that you have finally come to the place in your life where you can be "real." You do not care what people think about you because you have come to terms with who you are in the Lord. In other words, "This is me – the good, bad, and the ugly. Like it or go away!"

NEGATIVE
Now if your dream is negative and the farting and belching caused something bad to happen, it means that you are letting just a bit of the "real you" out lately. There are some words and honesty that is best kept for another time. Sure it might be who you are. Sure it might be the truth – but did you need to express it quite so violently? Its time to have your words "seasoned with salt" so that you can touch the hearts of others, without causing so much offense.

See also: Bathroom

FEAR

A powerful force that can either motivate or paralyze you.

Negative: A paralyzing force that brings death.
Positive: A godly reverence and respect that leads to wisdom.

CHARACTER SPECIFIC AND UNIVERSAL SYMBOLS

POSITIVE
Proverbs 1:7 says that the fear of God is the beginning of wisdom. True reverence and respect for God leads to obedience and faith in the Lord – something that is desperately needed in the Church today!

To experience reverential fear in the presence of the Father is a changing experience. This is the kind of fear that brings humility and a realization of how big God is and how small you are. To feel this kind of fear draws you to God and leaves you in awe of His power.

If you experience this kind of fear in a dream or vision, then God is revealing His greatness to you. He wants you to see that although He is a gracious God, that He is also a righteous God. To fear God in this way draws you closer to Him. A fear that makes you hide from His presence is of the enemy.

If you dream that others experience fear, then it is a picture of the might of God – especially if the people in your dream are unbelievers or those living in sin. Consider this passage:

> *Psalms 119:120 My flesh trembles for **fear** of You, and I am **afraid** of Your judgments.*

I love that the Psalmist says "my flesh" trembles. When you are walking in the flesh and not in the spirit, then you should surely fear the hand of God! As blood-bought believers though, Jesus intercedes for us and shields us from that judgment. This does not give us an excuse not to reverence God, but rather a greater reason to be in awe of Him.

NEGATIVE

The kind of fear that paralyzes is certainly not of the Lord, but a spirit sent from the enemy to distract you from what God is really trying to do. Not once did Jesus produce fear when He walked the earth. People ran towards Him and not away. The only ones who feared Him were the demons that He cast out!

You should not feel any fear in the presence of the Lord Jesus at all. He came to save us from the spirit of fear and to give us hope. If ever you have a dream or vision that brings a gripping fear with it, you can discard it as a direct work of the enemy.

> *2 Timothy 1:7 For God has not given us a spirit of **fear**, but of power and of love and of a sound mind.*

If you experience uncontrollable fear, you can be sure it is a spirit of fear sent of satan. Rebuke it and you will feel an immediate release. Fear comes in different forms such as anxiety and worry. If you find yourself worrying about things that are out of your control, this is also a spirit of fear and you do not have to submit to it.

See also: Attacked, Hiding, Running

FIGHTING

To struggle with influences that are pressing against you from all sides.

CHARACTER SPECIFIC SYMBOL

It seems strange that fighting could be positive, but when you are fighting against a weakness or problem in your dreams and overcome, this is a sign of victory.

Fighting a person, you know: First identify what that person means to you. What part of your character do they represent? If they represent something negative in your life it means that you are trying to overcome that weakness and you are overcoming!

Of course if you are losing the fight, it indicates that you are being overcome and giving into this weakness.

Fighting an unknown force: If you are fighting an unknown force it is a reflection of the struggles you are facing in life right now. You are not sure where the attack is coming from and you feel defeated. This is an indication that you are engaged in spiritual warfare right now.

If the dream is positive, it is a picture of struggling with God just as Jacob did in Genesis 32. It is only when you yield to what God is trying to do in your life that you will finally get the victory. Are you struggling with something that God told you to do? Then this dream is a picture of the inner struggle you are going through.

Boxing: If you are a boxer then this dream speaks of your ability to protect yourself. Determine if the Lord is saying to allow Him to defend you or if He is saying that it is time to step forward with your convictions!

> *1 Corinthians 9:26 Therefore I run thus: not with uncertainty. Thus I **fight**: not as one who beats the air. But I discipline my body and bring it into subjection, lest, when I have preached to others, I myself should become disqualified*

This passage speaks of just hitting wildly and not "hitting the mark." It speaks of being undisciplined and unfocused. It is time to stop running around in the flesh and to use the strength that God has given you in the Spirit!

Fighting unknown man or woman: If you are fighting an unknown woman in your dream then it is a picture of a struggle with your creative side. (If you have a prophetic calling, then this is a picture of struggling against your prophetic call.)

If this is an external dream, then the woman is a picture of the prophetic ministry in the Church that is struggling. The context of the dream will shed light on what the struggle is.

Fighting an unknown man means to struggle or oppose your intellectual side. (If you have been led into the teaching ministry then the man represents that.) Could it be that the Lord has led you to develop this side of yourself and it is a weakness? Dreaming of fighting such a man indicates that you are struggling to come to terms with this and get the victory.

Universal Symbol

You will often see fighting in the realm of the spirit. More often than not it is a picture of spiritual warfare. Depending on how the battlefield is arrayed will let you know which side has the victory.

I often see troops going into battle and waging war. The archangel Michael is the leader of the warrior angels and goes to war on our behalf when the word of God is spoken.

I have also seen the Body of Christ as a large warrior going into battle.

If you are ministering to someone and see fighting, it is possible that the person is struggling with something and trying to overcome in themselves.

See also: Army, War

Flying

A desire to escape the pressures of life. Positively, it speaks of being free of the burdens in your life right now.

Positive:

- Seeing things from God's perspective
- Promotion

Negative: Running away from your problems

Character Specific Symbol

POSITIVE

It is common to dream of flying, especially in internal dreams. This represents your inner desires.

Perhaps if you are under stress, you dream that you are flying away. This is simply a picture of your inner desires and how you feel at the moment. You wish that you could escape the pressures you are under.

NEGATIVE

It is also common to dream that you are being attacked and that you are trying to fly away; or that you are trying to fly but struggle to do so.

This is a picture of the attack and conflict you are currently experiencing in your life. It is a good picture of what you are experiencing in real life. You are trying to "take off", but you keep failing to do so.

Perhaps you are working on a new project or going in a new direction, and things are not going according to plan. You need to identify for yourself why you are not "taking off" in these areas.

I suggest that you journal and ask the Lord for direction. *The Way of Dreams and Visions* book gives full instruction on how to journal.

Universal Symbol

POSITIVE

> *Psalms 55:6 So I said, Oh, that I had wings like a dove! I would* ***fly*** *away and be at rest.*

In a vision or a prophetic dream, flying is a picture of escaping from the pressures and attacks of the enemy and into the presence of the Lord. Here you will find the peace that you are looking for.

In *The Journey of Tamar,* I write often about flying with the Mighty Eagle. As a believer the Lord has called you to fly high above your circumstances with the Holy Spirit.

To have a prophetic dream or vision of flying is a picture of flying high above your problems. The Lord is saying that it is time you start looking at things from His perspective, and to take your eyes off the natural things.

NEGATIVE

> *Proverbs 23:5 Will you set your eyes on that which is not? For riches certainly make themselves wings; they* ***fly*** *away like an eagle toward heaven.*

To see something flying away speaks of something that is fleeting and leaving. This is a picture of something in your life that does not have a firm root, or is built on the wrong foundation.

See also: Wings

Hiding

Taking refuge from difficult circumstances. A time of protection and security.

Positive: To find rest in the Lord, who is your strong tower
Negative: To avoid your circumstantial pressures

Character Specific Symbol

POSITIVE

The Word is full of promises about how the Lord is our place of hiding. The Lord knows how hard life is and how we often need a place of refuge to run to. If you dream of finding a place to hide, then the Lord is saying that it is time to run to Him and to escape for a while. It is alright to take a "breather" from the pressures in your life.

If you dream that you are being attacked and that you find a hiding place from your attackers, the Lord is saying that He will soon give you a moment to hide and recoup from the pressures that you have been facing.

> *Psalms 119:114 You are my* ***hiding*** *place and my shield; I hope in Your word.*

NEGATIVE

To dream of hiding out of fear is an indication that you are not ready to face the conflicts in your life right now. If you dream that you keep being found out in your hiding place, this means that no matter how much you try, that problem will keep finding you.

It could be that you are trying to overcome in your own strength instead of hiding in the hand of God. The Lord is gracious and even in the Old Testament He set up cities of refuge for those who had committed a crime. There they would face fair judgment.

To dream of not being allowed to hide could mean that the enemy is attacking you and has an open door in your life to steal your peace.

On the other hand, if you are hiding away at a time when you do not need to, then it means that you are separating yourself from others and are not allowing them to come close. For example, if you dream of hiding at a party or in a situation that is non-threatening, the Lord is trying to point out that you tend to withdraw from relationships instead of "letting people in."

Universal Symbol

POSITIVE

When I have come to the Lord after a difficult day He has often told me to come and "hide in the shadow of His wings." Sometimes we think that we must push forward and face all the storms by ourselves. However, there are times when we must come aside and "rest a while" as He told His disciples.

The Lord is the best place to hide and when you are in His presence, the pressures and attacks will suddenly grow quiet. If you see a hiding place that the Lord is beckoning you to, this is very positive and it is a call to rest. A good example of this is the time that Elijah hid in a cave in the wilderness after being chased by Jezebel. (1 Kings 19:9)

NEGATIVE
Because of hurts of the past, I often see someone at a particular age hiding away from others. This is a good picture of "spiritual imprisonment" as I have explained it before.

When doing intercession, I have often seen demons hiding away where no one can see them. This is a picture of the subversive work of the enemy in our lives. In such a circumstance I demand that they are exposed for what they are.

See also: Attacked, Cave, Flying, Prison

HUNGER

The inner craving, we all have to nurture what God has given to us.

Positive: To care for our blessings
Negative: To feed a need that can never be satisfied

CHARACTER SPECIFIC SYMBOL

Its not uncommon to dream of being hungry only to wake up with a snack attack. Sometimes it is just a natural response to your natural body's needs. For the most part though, to dream of being hungry or of someone else being hungry speaks of an inner need that must be taken care of.

What are you struggling with emotionally right now? Are you craving some affection or tenderness? Are you hungry in your soul for someone to understand you? This dream is bringing to the light emotions you are trying to push down. It is time child of God, to run into the arms of Jesus. He stands there with milk and honey, waiting to meet every hunger of your heart.

UNIVERSAL SYMBOL

POSITIVE
To dream or see a vision of being hungry indicates a need in your spirit and your soul. While thirst tends to lean more towards the lack in your spirit, hunger speaks more of the condition of your soul right now. Your mind, emotions, and will have lack!

So dreaming of hunger and satisfying it is positive! The Lord is saying that not only is He meeting your need, but He will satisfy it. He will heal what was stolen and bring health to your soul once again. To keep seeing visions and dreams of hunger means that you are searching for "more" in your life. You are not satisfied with the level you are at. God is drawing you deeper into your Christian walk.

This hunger is positive and God Himself has given it to you. Ask for bread! Allow Him to satisfy that hunger. Now just because you dream of hunger, does not mean it is automatically fed. Hunger drives you. So push forward! Seek the Lord. Hunger for Him. Search Him out. Do whatever you must to get your hunger met! Do not just sit around and starve, hoping that just “something” will happen!

> *Matthew 5:6 Blessed are those who hunger and thirst for righteousness, For they shall be filled.*

NEGATIVE

Very often hunger is negative. It speaks of a need within that you just cannot get fed. When ministering deliverance, I have often seen a thin demon that can never be satisfied. I see the spirit of theft like this. I also see the Jezebel spirit like this. Emaciated and hungry all of the time. Need! Need! Need! They take and take and are never filled.

If you have a dream or vision of being hungry in this way, the Lord is saying that you have a need that no one in this world can meet! Firstly, the enemy is increasing your appetite to become insatiable and secondly, only the Lord is able to meet it. Stop trying to get others to meet it – you will only feel continually disappointed.

> *Proverbs 30:15-16 The leech has two daughters— Give and Give!*
>
> *There are three things that are never satisfied, Four never say, “Enough!”:*
>
> *The grave, The barren womb, The earth that is not satisfied with water— And the fire never says, “Enough!”*

Cannibal: That “neediness” is what I call “The Cannibal Instinct.” It is when someone comes and sucks the life out of you to meet their own needs. Just like it says here in Proverbs 30:15 – they are like a leech! Did you ever see a cannibal care about their victim? No, they only want their own hunger satisfied. To dream of this kind of hunger is very negative.

You have a spiritual and emotional need that requires repentance, deliverance, and then inner healing. Only Jesus has what you are looking for.

See also: Demons, Thirst

INCEST

Taking on particular characteristics or allowing yourself to be changed by external influences. To have unclean dreams all the time is an indication of an attack from a spirit of lust.

Although dreams of incest can be very disturbing, they are not always negative. Determine what the person in your dream represents in your life. Once you have that, you will see what it is you are embracing.

Negative: You are trying to feed inner needs through whatever this person represents

Character Specific Symbol

POSITIVE
If you dream of being intimate with someone who is a picture of love to you, then it means that you are getting closer to walking in love. Determining what the person means to you will help you identify what your dreams mean. Embracing them means that you are taking on that particular characteristic and you are allowing it to change you.

NEGATIVE
If you have dreams of incest and sex often, then it could be that you are struggling with a spirit of lust or that you are fellowshipping with someone that is. I remember ministering to a lady one evening and then that night having strange dreams of incest that unsettled me.

When I spoke with her more the next day, she shared that incest was rampant in her family. I was simply picking up the spiritual attack that she was facing. In this case, I was being attacked in my sleep by the demonic bondage that she had in her family.

If you suddenly start having unclean dreams out of nowhere, then identify when they began. Did you start having them after being in touch with someone or watching something? If so, that is your open door and you just need to break spiritual links and tell that unclean spirit to leave!

If you have always been plagued by unclean dreams, then there is a spirit of lust at work in your life. Either it is generational or it is something that gained entry through personal sin. If someone comes to stay in my house that has an unclean spirit, I almost always have dreams like this. Sometimes it is a spiritual attack, other times it is the Lord letting me know where I need to step in and minister.

See also: Arousal, Bed, Kiss

Journey

A season of new experiences and gained knowledge. The call of the Lord to "break new ground" in a specific area.

Positive: To start of a new mandate
Negative: A distraction from the enemy

POSITIVE
Going on a journey (especially to places you have not been to before) speaks of the Lord leading you into something completely new. The purpose is to teach you new principles where you will experience things you never have before.

To journey to a place, you already know (and the journey is pleasant) means that the Lord wants to give you some "missing pieces" from that season of your life. Perhaps at the time you had those experiences, you were not ready for them. Dreaming of journeying to a place in your past means going and completing what God began back there.

To be given tickets for a journey means that the Lord is inviting you into something new. It is for you to accept or decline.

NEGATIVE
To dream of journeying back to places from your past that you are not happy with means that you keep leaning on the old instead of taking hold of the new.

There are things in your past that keep pulling you back and they are standing in the way of what God is trying to do in your life right now.

Needing to go on a journey, but being late for the flight or struggling to "get going" means that there is something holding you back in your life right now. There are things that are distracting you from what God wants you to do.

To lose your tickets means the same thing – a distraction from the enemy from the direction God is leading you into.

Perhaps you feel ill equipped for the task at hand? Do you feel that you are unable to do the work God has told you to do? Then dreaming of being late for the flight or not being properly packed is an expression of your fears and insecurity.

See also: Road, Traveling, Baggage/Luggage

LAUGHING

A sign that a season of death and mourning is over and it is time to rejoice.

Positive:

- You won the battle
- Healing process is complete

Negative:

- Disfavor
- Unbelief

POSITIVE
It is common to laugh in your sleep. This is a good example of a purging dream. Sometimes you might dream of something humorous and it is just a reflection of the influences that you have put into your spirit.

If you wake up laughing and sense the Lord, it is an indication that the warfare you have been experiencing is over and you have won the struggle. You can expect to see things improve.

When we minister to someone, it is normal for them to break into laughter when the Lord has done a work. It is an external sign of the healing that they have gone through on the inside. It is a sign that the season of death in their lives is over.

To have a vision of laughter is an indication that the battle has been won and it is time to rejoice in the Lord instead of engaging in spiritual warfare. The Lord won the battle for you and you can rest in the reward.

> *Psalms 126:2 Then our mouth was filled with* ***laughter****, and our tongue with singing. Then they said among the nations, the Lord has done great things for them.*

NEGATIVE
To be laughed at is an indication that you are getting opposition from those around you. It is also a reflection of your own insecurities that are being exposed at the moment.

To have the enemy laugh at you speaks of attack and disfavor.

To "laugh in the face of God" means that you do not believe Him, much like Sarah did in Genesis 18:12.

When ministering inner healing, you might see someone being laughed at as a child, indicating the source of their hurt. This would have led to insecurities and will require counsel and healing.

See also: Dancing

MUTE

To be held back in your conviction and authority.

Positive: To surrender your own ideas and to take on God's ideas
Negative: To be stifled in your spiritual expression

UNIVERSAL SYMBOL

POSITIVE
The Lord had to shut Zacharias up because his doubt stood against what God wanted to do in the life of John the Baptist. If you dream or have a vision of

being made mute, perhaps it is time to sit and listen instead of always spouting off your own opinions!

So often we are full of ideas and advice, that we do not sit long enough to listen. It is time to sit down and shut up! It is time to listen to what God really wants to do, because His ways are higher than yours. Just because you do not understand it, does not mean God is going to let you down. Take a step back. Cut back on all your opinions and unasked for advice. God has this. He is able to get through to you.

He is able to get through to your boss, spouse, spiritual leader, and friends. Let Him be God. Just have faith that he will get the word out when needed.

> *Luke 1:20 But behold, you will be mute and not able to speak until the day these things take place, because you did not believe my words which will be fulfilled in their own time.*

NEGATIVE
If you dream or have a vision of being gagged and forced into silence, it means that the enemy is trying to stifle your conviction and authority.

He is trying to silence you, and then trick you into believing that there is no power in your voice. If you dream that you are trying to scream and nothing comes out, the devil is trying to trick you into thinking that you have no power.

When you wake up, I highly recommend reminding him of how wrong he is! Although these dreams can shake you up, you do not need to just "take it." Yes, perhaps you feel like your words are bouncing off the ceiling right now. Yes, perhaps you feel like no one wants to listen to you!

You do not have to believe these lies. Take authority over these fears and lies. This is just a dirty trick to get you to doubt yourself! Come now, you know what to do... yeah... the devil better get running!

> *Matthew 9:33 And when the demon was cast out, the mute spoke.*

See also: Paralyzed

NIGHTMARES

Although I cover this in a lot of detail in *The Way of Dreams and Visions* book, I will give a short description here. Nightmares when accompanied with intense emotions and demonic oppression are clearly from the enemy sent to unsettle you. However, not all bad dreams are necessarily demonic.

Some signs that indicate that a dream is not of the Lord is to wake up feeling oppression or to be gripped by fear. Any dream that causes you to feel guilty to the point of not moving forward with God is also an attack. If you experience nightmares often, you need to identify what is causing them. Here are just some ways that you can identify the source of your nightmares:

1. Inner conflicts: If you have unresolved sin in your life, they can manifest in your dreams. You will dream that your "greatest fear" comes upon you. If this is happening, then you need to confront these things in the natural and your dreams will stop.

When I was pregnant I had crazy dreams all the time about losing my baby or going into labor too soon. Each time they were simply inner thoughts and fears that I held in my heart. By just submitting to the Lord and giving these fears up, the dreams stopped.

2. Contaminated objects in your room: If the dreams started up suddenly for no reason, see if there was something that you brought into your house recently. Objects can carry spiritual power!

Not everyone is sensitive to this; however, if you are a prophet or function in the gift of discerning of spirits, then you will be very aware of the realm of the spirit. I personally am quite sensitive and will even go so far as to dream about the particular contamination coming from the object or person I was in touch with. So if this has happened to you... it is simply a confirmation that you flow in the gift of discerning of spirits.

3. Spiritual contamination: This is just like the objects. If you have been in touch with someone that has bondage in their lives and you opened your heart to them, you can come under the attack that they are under. This is a full subject on spiritual links that I will not go into here. However, identify when the nightmares began and line it up with who you have been receiving from lately.

4. Generational bondages: If you have experienced nightmares and demonic attack your entire life, then it is likely a generational bondage you are struggling with. These are easy to overcome! Seeing what it is brings you most of the victory. Break those ties and tell the enemy to flee!

See also: Coffin, Death, Demons

PARALYZED

To be forced into submission.

Positive: An encounter with God that will change your direction
Negative: The forceful work of the enemy to take away your will

UNIVERSAL SYMBOL

POSITIVE

King Saul learned a thing or two about standing against the Lord. The Lord brought His power down and had Saul lie at the feet of Samuel. The point? Saul was hunting David down to destroy him! The Lord made the point, "My power is greater than your own! Stop in your tracks, because it is going to lead you in a way you should not go." If you have an experience of the Lord paralyzing you, then He is really trying to make a point.

You are either not taking time to listen to Him or His direction is completely opposite to your desires. If you dream of being paralyzed, but you are not afraid, that is the Lord saying, "I need you to pay attention! Stop in the direction you are going right now and let me show you what you are meant to be doing!"

> *1 Samuel 19:24 And he also stripped off his clothes and prophesied before Samuel in like manner, and lay down naked all that day and all that night. Therefore, they say, "Is Saul also among the prophets?"*

NEGATIVE
If you have a vision or dream of being paralyzed and you know you should not be, it means that the enemy has stolen your will. He is taking away your ability to pick up your sword and fight. He is winning the battle!

Physically cannot move: Now if you dream that you physically cannot move even after waking, realize that this has no interpretation! This is an outright demonic attack and you need someone to pray you through! Did this come out of nowhere? Who did you minister to lately? What have you allowed into your spirit lately? You have picked up a contamination.

Have you always had this since childhood? Then you are looking at a generational curse. Realize that being pinned to your bed in this way is not of the Lord! No, He is not trying to teach you a lesson. Jesus is a gentleman – He does not need to pin His bride to the bed to get His message across!

This is how the enemy operates! You need deliverance. I teach more on this in *The Way of Dreams and Visions* and *Prophetic Warrior*

See also: Drowning, Mute

PRAYING

An expression whereby your spirit touches God.

Positive: To break past hindrances to reach God
Negative: Blockages in your spiritual life

POSITIVE
To dream of praying is the cry of your spirit to touch the Lord. Have you been busy lately? Your dream means that your spirit thirsts for the Lord and is hungry for His presence. It reminds me of

> *Psalms 42:1 As the deer pants for the water brooks, so* ***pants my soul*** *for You, O God.*

Dreaming of praying is also a call to intercession and the Lord drawing you into His presence.

If you dream that someone you are familiar with prays for you then identify what they mean in your dream. Whatever they represent means that you need to focus more on this area of your life and submit it to the Lord. You need to bring this area of your life under God's control.

If you dream of praying for other people it means that the Lord wants you to take what you have and pour it out to others. He wants you to be like a jug that is filled up and poured out. The kind of people you are praying for will determine the area that He is calling you to.

NEGATIVE
Dreaming of praying and you are interrupted or you struggle means that there is something amiss in your spiritual life. Either you are battling to reach the Lord or there is something that you have received into your life that is blocking your spirit.

If you dream that someone else is praying over you that is demonic, it is a warning that the enemy has been attacking you spiritually.

If you dream or see visions of religious prayer and rituals, it means that you are trying to seek the Lord through works instead of through faith. You cannot perform and expect that performance will reach Him. Only faith pleases the Lord. Approach Him as a child – by faith alone and watch your prayer life take off!

Rituals: Seeing pagan rituals speaks of occult influence. Determine where it is coming from. Past generations? Something you dabbled in yourself? People that you are associated with? Seeing such rituals are also likely an indication that there are people praying against you.

They are not being led, but praying their own burdens or being inspired by the enemy.

See also: Anointing

PREACHING

God's instruction for this season in your life.

CHARACTER SPECIFIC SYMBOL

If you dream of preaching behind the pulpit, it means that there is a particular principle or teaching that the Lord wants you to learn right now so that you can teach it to others.

Of course if you always wanted to preach and dream you are preaching to the masses, then this is just a purging dream – it is a reflection of your own desire. It is not necessarily a call to preach.

Preaching always involves applying specific instruction or principles to your life. So if you dream that someone is preaching to you, it means that the Lord wants you to learn a new principle.

If you are preaching something that you are familiar with, then the Lord is saying that He wants you to take this particular principle and apply it afresh to your life. Then He wants you to teach it to others.

The Pulpit: The pulpit itself is a good picture of principles being taught from the perspective of being a leader. If the pulpit in your dream belongs to a specific church or minister, it could be that the Lord wants you to learn principles from this person.

If the dream is negative though, it could mean that you are teaching old principles based on a ministry that was in the flesh. It also would mean that you are functioning in an old anointing and you need to move into something new.

Universal Symbol

If you see someone preaching in a vision, then it means that the Lord is calling them to preach. Unlike dreams, visions are to be taken more literally.

If you see a vision of a Pharisee preaching it means that you are not practicing what you preach! Matthew 23:3

See also: Audience

Running/Race

The pursuit of a specific goal in your natural or spiritual life.

Positive: To take ground
Negative:

- To push forward in your own strength
- To strive with a spirit of strife and vainglory
- To be competitive

POSITIVE
To dream of running a race and you are making progress is a good dream. It indicates that you are making progress in your spiritual walk with God right now.

To reach the end of a race means that you have accomplished your goal and it is time to move on. Dreaming of running an old race means that you are revisiting accomplishments from the past.

To run towards someone that represents the Lord means that you are in pursuit of the Lord and that you will catch Him.

Running with weights can be negative or positive. In a positive sense it means that you are being tested by the Lord right now so that you can become strong. In a negative sense, it means that the enemy is weighing you down so that you cannot mature in the Lord.

NEGATIVE

To dream of running away for no reason indicates that you are trying to avoid certain responsibilities and conflicts in your life right now.

To run in many directions at once means that you lack conviction and are unsure of what you want in life. (1 Cor 9:26)

To run away from someone that represents the Lord in your dreams means that you are trying to run away from God and what He has told you to do. (Jonah 1:10)

If you are running towards someone that represents the Lord, but you keep "missing" Him, it means that you are struggling in your spiritual walk right now.

To run towards danger means that you are headed for trouble. Is there an area of your life where you are always met with failure? Dreaming of running into a wall or trouble means that you are about to make the same mistake again.

To run a race that you are losing is a reflection of your own feeling of failure and inadequacy. To dream or have a vision of someone "cutting in on you" means that you have allowed yourself to become sidetracked and led astray.

> *Galatians 5:7 You were* ***running*** *a good race. Who cut in on you and kept you from obeying the truth? (NIV)*

If you are dreaming or having visions of running without end, then it means that you are trying to walk out your call using works. Not only are you striving in your flesh, but you are also trying to compete with others.

You are running so hard to prove yourself, that you inadvertently keep pushing others aside, needing to take their position in the race. You are desperate to win this race! This desperation brings a spirit of strife. Rather choose to lose the race. Rather sit down and rest a while in the presence of the Lord.

See also: Attacked, Chasing, Exercising, Hiding, Race, Road, Weights

SHAKING

Everything you know is about to be challenged.

Positive: To discover the core of what God has given to you
Negative: To lose everything you have leaned on

Note: If you are in the habit of being forcibly and physically shaken in your sleep or visions, then I would be very cautious. If this shaking is uncontrollable and you cannot stop when you want it to, then it is an indication of a demonic bondage in your life.

If you experience actual shaking and it is uncomfortable or concerns you, you have every right to renounce it in Jesus' name.

POSITIVE
Although dreaming of your house being shaken seems negative at first, it has a good meaning. Although the Lord is challenging everything you have and are, He is doing it to reveal the things that are of Him!

The following passage was my comfort when the Lord was taking me through a "shaking" in my own life,

> *Hebrews 12:27 Now this, Yet once more, indicates the removal of those things that are being* ***shaken****, as of things that are made, that the things which cannot be* ***shaken*** *may remain.*

The passage goes on to say that we are receiving a kingdom which cannot be shaken. This means that God is "shaking" everything off in your life that is not of Him so that which is solid can remain as a new foundation.

To see a vision of an earthquake or shaking means that God is going to test and challenge the work of your hands. The purpose is to see the gold come out!

NEGATIVE
To dream of something good in your life being shaken means that the enemy is trying to "rattle" you. He is trying to test you to see where your weaknesses are. Like Jesus said to Peter, he is trying to "sift you as wheat." (Luke 22:31)

To see a foundation or building being shaken that you know is of God is also negative and a call to spiritual warfare. It means that the enemy is trying to undermine what God has done in your life.

See also: Earthquake

SINGING

Same as Music: A resonance in the natural of what is going on in the realm of the spirit.

Singing is not only a reflection of what is in the spirit, but a passageway to release spiritual power as well. It is a tool to release the power of God that is in your spirit. If you feel led to sing in the spirit, then God wants you to release what He is doing in the spirit. This carries tremendous power, just as Paul and Silas discovered,

> *Acts 16:25 But at midnight Paul and Silas were praying and **singing** hymns to God, and the prisoners were listening to them.*

POSITIVE
If you always wanted to sing and then dream you are singing beautifully, then it is simply a purging dream of your inner desire. Another interpretation is that the Lord is going to give you a deep desire of your heart. It means that something that was once impossible for you, will soon be possible.

NEGATIVE
If you dream that you are trying to sing, but the words get stuck in your throat, it means that you have a spiritual blockage. The enemy is trying to block you from speaking out the things that God has given to you. This is a call to spiritual warfare.

See also: Dancing, Harp, Instruments, Music

SLEEPING

To be unaware of what is going on around you

Positive: To enter into the rest of the Lord
Negative: To purposefully turn a blind eye to what you know to be true

CHARACTER SPECIFIC SYMBOL

POSITIVE
If you are sleeping and then awaken in a dream, it means that something is coming alive in you that was dormant before. The Lord is giving you a new awareness of something specific. Have you been praying for the Lord to "awaken" something in you that you have lost? Dreaming of "waking up" means that He has answered your prayer.

To dream of falling into a restful slumber is a call to rest in the Lord. He wants you to lay aside your cares for a season and to trust that He has everything under control.

NEGATIVE
To dream of sleeping and you cannot wake up, means that you have neglected something and allowed it to become dormant. Either you are not prepared to "get into" that particular area of your life, or the enemy is squashing something in your life.

To dream of being under attack and you cannot wake up means that the enemy is trying to intimidate you and hold you back. You do not have to accept this, but can rise up in Jesus' name!

To dream of being asleep and not waking up means that you are not being diligent spiritually. You are not putting any effort into your spiritual life. (Mark 13:36)

Note: If you physically cannot wake up or feel pinned to your bed, then a demonic bondage is involved. You need deliverance! Get a hold of your pastor for counsel or call our ministry line for instruction on what to do.

Universal Symbol

POSITIVE
To see the Lord, hold someone in His arms so that they can sleep is a call to rest in Him. He is saying that He is in control of their situation.

NEGATIVE
To have a vision of someone sleeping means that they are unaware of the work of the enemy. Their spirit is dull and they are not being diligent. It could also be that the enemy has lulled them into slumber so that he can take advantage of them.

> *Matthew 13:25 But while men **slept**, his enemy came and sowed tares among the wheat and went his way.*

When Craig and I are ministering publically there are times when people fall asleep the moment the anointing comes. Then once the anointing lifts they wake up suddenly. This is a clear sign of demonic bondage. The enemy "puts the person to sleep" so that they are unable to hear the truth or experience the presence of God.

See also: Hiding

Smelling

A telltale sign of what is going on in the realm of the spirit. It can also be a hint towards what is going on in your own spirit.

> *2 Corinthians 2:16 To the one we are the **aroma** of death leading to death, and to the other the **aroma** of life leading to life. And who is sufficient for these things?*

POSITIVE
Identify the smell in your dream and vision. Is it sweet like a rose? This is a lovely indication that the Lord is present in your life. The Lord required Israel to burn incense before Him and the smell of incense speaks of praise.

If you dream of lighting incense or of smelling it, then it is a call to offer up your praise to the Lord.

Identify also if the smell is something familiar to you. Does it remind you of a person or of a time in your life? If so then the Lord is taking you back to that season in your life for a reason. You need to identify if this is a good or bad thing.

The Scripture also says that we should diffuse the fragrance of Christ everywhere we go. So to smell sweet perfume means that you are walking in the spirit and representing Jesus to those around you.

NEGATIVE
The smell of death is negative and speaks often of the work of the enemy. It can also speak about a spiritual death that God is trying to take someone through, but they are not surrendering. Jesus yielding up His spirit and His body did not undergo decay. In the same way, when the Lord calls us to be "crucified with Christ" it should not be a drawn out process, but one we pass through quickly. In other words, there should not be any stink!

If you smell death in your dream and God has been trying to get your attention to something, then He is saying, "Your flesh stinks! Would you please let it go now?!"

Other bad smells such as sulfur or anything rotting means that the enemy is at large. Some of my students smell this when a demon is in the room.

See also: Rose, Perfume

SWIMMING

To be completely carried away.

Positive:

- To lose yourself in the Lord
- To push against the tide

Negative:

- To follow the crowd
- To be carried away by your circumstances
- To fight against the hand of God

Character Specific Symbol

Swimming is part of many a childhood memory! If you are dreaming of swimming in a setting from your past, then it is this era that is coming up in your life right now. Determine the circumstances where you are swimming. For this symbol I am going to emphasize the universal symbol more as it relates to you as a believer.

Universal Symbol

POSITIVE
It is great to "put your toe in the water" but so much better to swim in it! If you dream of swimming in cool water that makes you feel good means that the Lord is drawing you deeper into Him. He is inviting you saying, "Come my child. Experience more of me. Experience my anointing without any boundaries. Lose your control completely in me and allow me to carry you away into something new."

> *Ezekiel 47:5 Again he measured one thousand, and it was a river that I could not cross; for the water was too deep, water in which one must swim, a river that could not be crossed.*

Against the tide: I have often seen myself swimming against the tide in a vision. Determine the spirit in the dream. When I saw this once, the Lord said to me, "I know this feels difficult my child. I know that you are weary, but keep on going, because the open door is just ahead of you!"

When God has told you to do something, the hardest part is going against everyone else's ideas of what they think you should do! Keep swimming against the tide!

On the other hand, I had this vision and the spirit was different. I felt that my hard efforts were difficult and the Lord had to say, "My child let go! You are pushing so hard against your circumstances instead of allowing me to use them to carry you to where you need to go!"

It is essential to determine, "Is what is happening in this revelation positive or negative?"

Breathing under water: Ever dreamed you are holding your breath and then you finally breathe and discover you can breathe under water? The Lord is telling you that although you think you cannot face your situation right now, it is not as bad as you think. You can breathe under water! You can do this. Put aside your fears and jump in... the water is fine!

NEGATIVE
To dream of swimming and you are surrounding by dark and icy waters is very negative. Your circumstances are pressing in on you and are taking you in a direction that you should not follow!

Being carried by the tide: To feel out of control, being carried away by the tide means that you are just "going with the flow" instead of standing in your convictions. What has God told you to do? Have you been obedient?

Swimming hard and wearing yourself out also speaks of trying to experience God, but you are going about it all wrong! You are trying to perform and "do" everything that is correct instead of just resting in faith. You do not need to twist God's arm to experience the river of His anointing. You just need to trust Him. Rest in faith.

> *Psalms 6:6 I am weary with my groaning; All night I make my bed swim; I drench my couch with my tears*

See also: Drowning, Ocean, River, Water

TESTING (EXAMINATIONS)

The proof of your skills

Positive: The determination of your abilities
Negative: Exposure of your insecurities and weaknesses

CHARACTER SPECIFIC SYMBOL

POSITIVE
The subject of "testing" is quite extensive. When does God test and when does the devil test? I talk about this in *Prophetic Boot Camp* as well as in *The Crucified Life* series if you want more on this. For now, I will give you the "bottom line" of what your vision and dream means.

Dreaming of passing a test that you failed at school is very positive. It means that where you were once weak, you are now strong! In the past, you were incapable, but you have since matured and moved past that insecurity in your life.

NEGATIVE
To dream of writing the same test over and over again is indicating a point of insecurity or frustration in your life. You feel inadequate in yourself and feel that you keep "missing it." You are trying so hard and not realizing that the Lord called the weak and foolish to confound the wise. Why not just trust in the Lord more than you trust in yourself?

Does it matter if you pass or fail? Does it matter so much that you get a perfect grade? Who you are is good enough right now. Sure, in time, more testing will come, but perhaps now it is time to rest. Allow the Lord to bring the kind of tests into your life that display your abilities. Do not fall into the trap of trying to "write tests" that were set up by the enemy to cause you to fail!

UNIVERSAL SYMBOL

POSITIVE

Writing a test and passing it is very positive! It means that the Lord has been testing you to show off your newfound strengths and you passed!

Getting positive results for a test you do not remember writing is also good. You might not have known it, but the Lord has been putting you through your paces! Not everything has to be a struggle. Stop trying to figure out how you got the "good grade" and move forward. The Lord has sorted out your current circumstances so that you can move forward.

Passing an exam and moving to a next grade is a picture of spiritual promotion! You overcame what the enemy threw at you and you allowed the testing of the Lord to shape you – congratulations! You passed and He is promoting you. This kind of dream is quite common for those called to one of the fivefold ministry as they go through seasons of change.

A note on God's testing: God always tests to see what endures and the good that comes out of you. He presents you with tests that He expects you to pass!

> *1 Corinthians 3:13-14 each one's work will become clear; for the Day will declare it, because it will be revealed by fire; and the fire will test each one's work, of what sort it is. If anyone's work which he has built on it endures, he will receive a reward.*

NEGATIVE

To dream of rewriting a test you keep failing means that either you are not getting the point that God intends for you, or you are writing the wrong test!

The enemy is testing you and you are falling for it every time. The enemy tempts, rather than tests. What are you facing right now? Is there a particular sin that you keep giving into again and again? Dreaming or having a vision of failing test after test means that the enemy is testing you here and you keep giving in!

It's time to decide if you want to do this God's way or the devil's way. The choice is yours.

> *James 1:13 Let no one say when he is tempted, "I am tempted by God"; for God cannot be tempted by evil, nor does He Himself tempt anyone.*

See also: School

THIRST

A deep, spiritual yearning.

Positive: An uncontrollable search for Christ
Negative: Consumption of spiritual poison that keeps you thirsty

UNIVERSAL SYMBOL

POSITIVE
There is nothing more life changing than thirsting for a touch from God. In a world where we thirst after entertainment and physical gratification, a thirst for Christ is a stark contrast that washes us clean and revolutionizes our spiritual lives. To dream of being thirsty is a call from the Throne Room.

When you thirst for Christ, you release the hand of the Holy Spirit to come upon you and revolutionize your spiritual life. He will top up the streams within until you are dripping with the anointing. This call is one to seek out God. Do not run to your usual "escape" to get your spiritual need met.

Turn all of that inner craving to Jesus. Thirst after Him and you will experience a waterfall of power in your life.

> *John 7:37 On the last day, that great day of the feast, Jesus stood and cried out, saying, "If anyone thirsts, let him come to Me and drink. He who believes in Me, as the Scripture has said, out of his heart will flow rivers of living water."*

NEGATIVE
To dream of thirsting and drinking poison or something rotten means that the Lord has put a thirst in your spirit for Him, but you are feeding it with the world instead. The world cannot satisfy. You might feel good for a moment, but tomorrow you will thirst again! You are like the woman at the well. You keep drawing out of that well and you keep feeling restless. Don't you realize God put this thirst into you so that you might thirst after Him?

Consider the restlessness and "missing piece" in your life right now. Do not ignore it. Do not try to suppress it. This restlessness is of God – it is designed to thrust you into His arms.

See also: Hunger

TRAVELING

A complete rearrangement of your life that cannot be undone.

Positive: Entering your Promised Land
Negative: Forcing something you are not ready for

Universal Symbol

POSITIVE
What is going on in your life right now? Are you about to make a major life decision? Dreaming of traveling or going on an airplane is a message: When you make this decision, nothing will be the same. There will not be any going back.

When the children of Israel left Egypt, there was no returning. The same with you – count the cost and make sure you have heard from the Lord, because your life will never be the same! There is no back door here. Once you walk through, your world changes.

Now if you have been seeking the Lord about this, then this is the answer to your prayers! Your Promised Land awaits – what is holding you back? Make your decision and get moving!

NEGATIVE
Dreaming of missing your flight or travel plans going wrong? You are facing some hindrances to the change the Lord has promised. The enemy is bringing about distraction to move you away from what you know you need to do. Get a conviction and follow through now. Its time to get this journey started. Deal with the distractions and put aside the fears and take a step of faith.

Negative destination: If you dream or see a vision of a negative destination, then the answer is self-explanatory. Whatever decision you are about to make is going to rearrange your life, but not like you hope it will! The change will be negative and permanent, so make your decision well.

See also: Journey, Baggage/Luggage, Road

Vomiting

To violently expel whatever is poisoning your spirit.

Positive: To be delivered of what is destroying you
Negative:

- Over indulgence
- Filthiness

Universal Symbol

POSITIVE
No one likes throwing up! However, it is the natural function of the body to get rid of anything that might poison it. When you get sick, vomiting is your body's way of getting rid of something that might damage it. In the same way, to

dream or have a vision of vomiting means that you are violently purging your spirit of what has been poisoning it.

This is going to be an uncomfortable process, but once it is over, you will be set free.

It is not uncommon for someone to vomit when being delivered of a demon. This is simply a physical response to a spiritual cleansing. Our bodies always respond to the spirit and vomiting is a perfect picture of what just happened deep within.

Jonah being "vomited" out of the whale is also such a perfect picture of this. He was running so hard in the wrong direction. After he was "vomited" out, he was put on track again.

NOTE: If this seems like a positive process, realize that although the Lord is taking you through cleansing, this is going to be uncomfortable! It is going to hurt somewhat and it will not be over in a moment. It is a process that will take some time until you are fully free.

NEGATIVE
Now when you deliberately poison yourself, then vomiting is proof of that. Drinking until you vomit speaks of indulging the flesh against your own conscience and paying the price for that wrong decision.

Returning to vomit: Just like this passage expresses, this means to go back to what made you sick. Instead of taking hold of healing and victory, you are returning back to your old ways again and destroying yourself.

> *Proverbs 26:11 As a dog returns to his own vomit, So a fool repeats his folly.*

Lying in vomit: To "wallow" in vomit means that you might know that what you did was wrong, but instead of allowing the Lord to cleanse you, you are wallowing in self-pity and justifying your actions.

> *Jeremiah 48:26 "Make him drunk, Because he exalted himself against the Lord. Moab shall wallow in his **vomit***

Instead of lying around in your mess, apply the blood of Christ, take ownership of your mistake and rise up!

See also: Belly

WASH

A process of putting aside the things that mar the real you.

Positive: To break free of everything that is hindering you
Negative: To keep dealing with the same sin repeatedly

In the Old Testament the priest had to ceremonially wash very often. This was a type and shadow of what Jesus would do for us on Calvary.

Although the priests had to wash often, we only need to be washed once.

Isaiah 1:18 says that although our sins are as scarlet, that they will be made as white as snow. The process of washing is a picture of dealing with the contamination and sin in our lives.

Jesus offered to wash His disciples feet, not their entire body. He was illustrating that as believers, when we walk in the world, we become contaminated with it.

We end up falling into temptation or picking up things from others that are not of Him. All that we need to do is get into His presence and receive His cleansing once again.

To dream of washing compulsively means that you keep dealing with the same sin again and again. Let it go! The blood of Christ has cleansed you already. Now you must stand in faith and move forward. You cannot stay on the cross – it is time to resurrect and walk in power!

See also: Basin, Bath, Bathroom, Jar, Shower, Water

About the Author

Born in Bulawayo, Zimbabwe and raised in South Africa, Colette had a zeal to serve the Lord from a young age. Coming from a long line of Christian leaders and having grown up as a pastor's kid, she is no stranger to the realities of ministry. Despite having to endure many hardships such as her parent's divorce, rejection, and poverty, she continues to follow after the Lord passionately. Overcoming these obstacles early in her life has built a foundation of compassion and desire to help others gain victory in their lives.

Since then, the Lord has led Colette, with her husband Craig Toach, to establish *Apostolic Movement International,* a ministry to train and minister to Christian leaders all over the world, where they share all the wisdom that the Lord has given them through each and every time they chose to walk through the refining fire in their personal lives, as well as in ministry.

In addition, Colette is a fantastic cook, an amazing mom to not only her 4 natural children, but to her numerous spiritual children all over the world. Colette is also a renowned author, mentor, trainer and a woman that has great taste in shoes! The scripture to "be all things to all men" definitely applies here, and the Lord keeps adding to that list of things each and every day.

How does she do it all? Experience through every book and teaching, the life of an apostle firsthand, and get the insight into how the call of God can make every aspect of your life an incredible adventure.

Read more at www.colette-toach.com

Connect with Colette Toach on Facebook! www.facebook.com/ColetteToach

Check Colette out on Amazon.com at:
www.amazon.com/author/colettetoach

Recommendations by the Author

If you enjoyed this book, we know you will also love the following books.

The Way of Dreams and Visions

By Colette Toach

This book is the key that will open up the door to the realm of the spirit for you. Whether you have just come to know the Lord or have been saved for many years, you will find a treasure map in each page of this book, opening up the things that God is telling you RIGHT NOW!

Understand the secrets in your dreams and come to a place of confidence in the future God has set for you and a peace in knowing that He is in control of your life!

Dreams and Visions Workshop

By Colette Toach

There is a serious need in the Church today for believers to hear from the Lord. We have all seen how we can be lead astray by not knowing where we should go because we did not get direction from the Lord.

Well, I am here to tell you right now that you no longer have to go running to the nearest prophet so that he can get a vision to tell you what to do. That is because right now, the Lord is talking to you!

In this book, Colette Toach will revolutionize everything you have ever thought about vision and dream interpretation.

Perfect for doing with your church or with a home group, this book will not only teach you how to understand the messages the Lord is telling you through your dreams and visions, but it will help you to build up others so that they can hear from the Lord for themselves as well.

STRATEGIES OF WAR

By Colette Toach

Warfare is a very important part of our Christian lives. Whether we know it or not, the enemy is always looking for a way to take down the children of God. Now it is time that you learned how to stop taking the hits and take the fight to him instead.

No more allowing the enemy to have his way. Take back your land and remove him from your life for good.

Your victory is at hand. So, take hold and allow Colette Toach to guide and teach you the strategy to tearing down the kingdom of darkness.

SPIRITUAL DISCERNMENT WORKSHOP

By Colette Toach

The enemy is a liar. This we all know. The enemy comes like a thief in the night to steal, kill, and destroy everything that is good in our lives. Here is the thing though, sometimes a thief will disguise himself like a friend so that he can get the layout of your house before he breaks in.

We are children of God, and there is a power and a treasure that Lord has given to us that threatens the kingdom of darkness. This is why the enemy will do everything he can to take you out.

However, there is something you should know. God gave us the authority and the ability to overthrow what the enemy has intended for evil, and turn it over for good.

In the pages of this book, you will find the tools you need to discern where the enemy is coming from, how he got in, and how to kick him out. Here is your guide to the realm of the spirit, and your battle plan for stopping him in his tracks once and for all!

PROPHETIC WARRIOR

Book 5 of the Prophetic Field Guide Series

By Colette Toach

A true warrior holds no excuses of why he cannot defeat his enemy and so is true with a genuine prophet of God. He is ready to take up the weapons of warfare that God has prepared for Him and to set the captive free and to heal the broken hearted.

The prophet that God has called is ready to step onto the battlefield, gain victory in their own lives, and then share the secrets to obtaining victory to all those around them.

Prophet of God, now is the time to face your own limitations and your own bondages and to see what has been holding you back from walking as the warrior that God has called you to be.

THE JOURNEY OF TAMAR

By Colette Toach

“Ordinary” was never in Tamar's vocabulary. However, when the Mighty Eagle finds her, she is living a life that is stuck in a rut of reality. He called her on the adventure of a lifetime where Tamar will discover that it is time to accept invitation she received from the King at a young age.

Invited on a journey that will challenge the hunger she always had to be something, she will find out that the mettle of a warrior is carved in the heart.

Fall in love with the Prince of Peace that saves her. Be in awe of the Mighty Eagle that carries her high above the clouds. Tremble in the presence of the Mighty King that reveals His glory to her.

Join Tamar on a journey that will shape her from a child into the warrior she was always meant to be. Along the way, you might find out that it is you that has been called on the adventure of a lifetime.

Contact Information

To check out our wide selection of materials, go to: www.ami-bookshop.com

Do you have any questions about any products?

Contact us at: +1 (760) 466 -7679
(9am to 5pm California Time, Weekdays Only)

E-mail Address: admin@ami-bookshop.com

Postal Address:

A.M.I.
5663 Balboa Ave #416
San Diego, CA 92111, USA

Facebook Page: http://www.facebook.com/ApostolicMovementInternational

YouTube Page: https://www.youtube.com/c/ApostolicMovementInternational

Twitter Page: https://twitter.com/apmoveint

Amazon.com Page: www.amazon.com/author/colettetoach

AMI Bookshop – It's not Just Knowledge, It's **Living Knowledge**

INDEX

A

B

C

D

E

F

G

H

I

J

K

L

M

N

O

P

Q

R

S

T

U

V

W

Y

Z

Made in the USA
Middletown, DE
17 June 2025

77093173R00294